Mind the Screen

Mind the Screen

Media Concepts According to Thomas Elsaesser

Edited by Jaap Kooijman, Patricia Pisters and Wanda Strauven

AMSTERDAM UNIVERSITY PRESS

Cover illustration: Screen on Rembrandtplein
Photo: Katinka Schreuder

Cover design: Kok Korpershoek, Amsterdam
Lay-out: JAPES, Amsterdam

ISBN   978 90 8964 025 3
e-ISBN   978 90 4850 646 0
NUR   674

Table of Contents

ACT II   Europe-Hollywood-Europe

ACT III   Archaeology, Avant-Garde, Archive

A Looking Glass for Old and New Screens

Jaap Kooijman, Patricia Pisters and Wanda Strauven

Perhaps one of the longest videos on YouTube, IN A YEAR WITH 13 MOONS, is dedicated to a very classic topic of film studies: auteur cinema. The video documents a 92-minute round table discussion of Rainer Werner Fassbinder's homonymous film at the New York Philoctetes Center for the Multidisciplinary Study of the Imagination on 13 January 2007.[1] One of the panelists is Thomas Elsaesser, whose knowledge of German cinema in general and of Fassbinder in particular is widely respected. Although Elsaesser's performance on this new medium is a contribution to traditional film studies, that does not necessarily mean that Elsaesser considers YouTube and other developments of contemporary screen culture as mere "remediations" of the film screen. On the contrary, besides his ongoing passion for classical Hollywood and (European) auteur cinema, Elsaesser has always kept a sharp eye out for historical, institutional, and technological changes related to audiovisual media. In January 2008, at an Amsterdam conference on the video vortex of the Web 2.0 revolution, he proposed to picture contemporary image culture as a living organism with cell growth and selection (YouTube deletes or censors 20,000 videos daily, while 60,000 new ones are added) which requires a different set of analytical tools than for the study of a single masterpiece.[2] This combination of cinephile passion for the silver screen with its aesthetic and historical implications on the one hand, and mindfulness of new developments in screen culture on the other, has always characterized Elsaesser's academic approach, making him one of the most important first-generation film scholars to have contributed to the establishment of film, television, and media studies within academia.

Twenty years ago, in 1988, the Faculty of Humanities at the University of Amsterdam took the first steps toward the creation of a chair in Film and Television Studies. A committee was established to investigate how the "new media" of film and television could be studied as seriously as the written word from a humanities perspective. Unlike the United States and a few other European countries, Film and Television Studies had never been considered a full-fledged academic discipline in the Netherlands, even though pioneers such as Janus van Domburg, Jan Marie Peters, and Jan Hes had been teaching film since the 1940s, and the department of Theater Studies at the University of Amsterdam had been offering courses in film analysis and film history since the mid-1980s. In 1991, the University of Amsterdam appointed Thomas Elsaesser to the first chair of Film and

Television Studies in the Netherlands. Prior to his Amsterdam appointment, El-saesser had initiated a film studies program at the University of East Anglia in Great Britain. The University of Amsterdam press release at the time empha-sized the uniqueness of the program in taking the audiovisual image as an object of study.[3] Likewise, in his opening speech on 6 November 1991, Elsaesser re-ferred to the traditional study of literature, while at the same time clearly distan-cing from it in terms of aesthetic parameters, institutional influences, and tech-nological conditions that continue to evolve at such a rapid pace in the fields of cinema and television. Whereas video recorders and television sets in the early 1990s were still fairly strange objects at the universities and laserdiscs seemed futuristic, they are now considered as part of media's archaeological past in the classroom with its beamers, DVD players, and WiFi, where fragments from film history and media culture at large can be "Googled" or seen on YouTube and similar websites. The Film and Television Studies program that was established in 1991 with 75 students has grown into the Media Studies department, which currently counts around 1500 students and is one of the biggest departments of the Faculty of Humanities at the University of Amsterdam. Many people have contributed to this development, but Thomas Elsaesser, as a "founding father" of the department, has played a crucial role in the various phases of its program building.

The city of Amsterdam became not only Elsaesser's new home where he both worked and lived, but also a "playing field" for his conceptual thinking, which spans from film historical mapping to new locative media applications. Fasci-nated by the visible and the not-so visible traces of Amsterdam's rich past of movie theaters, traveling exhibitors, and film traders, Elsaesser has invited us to take an interactive walk from the Muntplein to the Rembrandtplein along the apparently insignificant Reguliersbreestraat to discover media-archaeological connections between the porn shop windows and a Toshiba TV screen advertise-ment, between the McDonald's Restaurant (and its Disney placemats) and the rooster of the French Pathé logo, between the pre-cinematic slot machines of a casino and the imposing towers of the Tuschinski Theater; cinema's history seems to be everywhere.[4]

One year after the 9/11 attacks on the World Trade Center in New York City, Elsaesser wrote a memorial piece that once again positions us in the center of Amsterdam, on the Rembrandtplein, to describe "what look[s] like a scene from a Beckett play" and to reflect on the impact the new media have on our notion of (social) "normality." On the square that he crosses every evening on his way home, he encounters two men who have nothing in common except for their "behavior" in this public space: a homeless man and a business man are both gesturing and talking to themselves, the former out of despair, the latter interacting with his hands-free mobile phone.[5] The same Rembrandtplein now has a huge plasma TV screen, forcing us to digest an endless stream of (commercial) images. On the other side of the city, at the WTC's Zuidplein, another enormous screen has recently been installed: CASZuidas (Contemporary Art Screen Zuidas). The "opening hours" of this virtual museum are from 6 a.m. to midnight, offering a daily program of works by local and international film and video artists. The target audience for this screen are the "managers and office workers, students and academics as well as other inhabitants and users of the Zuidas."[6] Elsaesser's knowledge of locative media practices has made him eager to develop a 21st-century high-tech platform for the city of Amsterdam, where old and new screens can be connected and where historical and theoretical research results on media and mobility can be utilized in real time and space. This platform, which Elsaesser would like to create in the near future, could then be used for (cultural) tourism and city marketing/branding purposes, with the intention of showing "a different Amsterdam."[7]

In 2004, upon the occasion of Elsaesser's 60th birthday, a book was published in his honor. *Die Spur durch den Spiegel: Der Film in der Kultur der Moderne*, edited by Malte Hagener, Johann N. Schmidt, and Michael Wedel, contains 33 essays by internationally renowned authors, including Raymond Bellour, David Bordwell, Siegfried Zielinski, and Slavoj Žižek, and pays tribute to Elsaesser's contribution to the field of film studies by focusing on the cinematic and the culture of modernity. *Mind the Screen* is a second tribute, which specifically focuses on Elsaesser's importance in the development of media studies in Amsterdam. The contributors to this book have all worked with Elsaesser in Amsterdam at some point in time: as PhD student, staff member, or colleague. Thus, Amsterdam serves as the nodal point of an international network of the various contributing authors. Furthermore, the book aims to cover the very broad range of media concepts that a prolific author like Elsaesser has been involved in over the years. The contributions are thus not limited to (traditional) film studies, but also address issues involving television studies, new media studies, art and cultural memory, system theory, and telecommunications, as a looking glass for various screens, from the archaeological pre-cinematic screen to the silver screen, from the television set to the digital e-screen. The book is divided into three "acts," which are organized thematically rather than chronologically and mind the gap of medium specificity by making consistent cross-references between the various media. Two more playful "intermezzos" appear between the acts, consisting of scholarly essays. These two contributions transform Elsaesser's legacy into potential films in the form of a screenplay, Catherine Lord's "Scholars, Dreams, and Memory Tapes," which explores the underworld, and a storyboard, "Where Were You When?"[8] by

Bruce Gray, which pinpoints some important geographical coordinates between Amsterdam and New York City.

The first act opens with three M-words that have been of great concern to Elsaesser's development in thinking the media: Melodrama, Memory, and Mind Game. As a preamble to these concerns, Malte Hagener and Marijke de Valck deal with the foundation of all academic work involving audiovisual media, which is the passion for the moving image. They discuss the developments of and transitions in (the concept of) cinephilia. The next two essays, by Warren Buckland and by Sudeep Dasgupta and Wim Staat, revisit the "Tales of Sound and Fury," Elsaesser's early-1970s essay that has been of great importance in the (re)evaluation of popular film genres such as the Hollywood melodrama, which until that point in time had been considered nothing more than mere shallow entertainment. Buckland systematically reconstructs Elsaesser's article, following Rudolf Botha's method of linguistic inquiry, in order to emphasize its significant problem formulation, whereas Dasgupta and Staat investigate the legacy of the article in contemporary film theory. Elsaesser's work on melodrama and trauma is also the point of departure for Tarja Laine, who examines the "spectorial logic of shame" in Ingmar Bergman's SKAMMEN / SHAME (1968), which is one of Bergman's most overlooked films. Inspired by a course she taught with Elsaesser, José van Dijck recounts how their discussion of the interrelation between media and memory gave shape to her concept of "mediated memories." In "Running on Failure," Drehli Robnik analyzes how the notion of "productive pathologies," already present in classical melodrama, is even more significant in the post-classical, post-Fordist cinema since the 1970s up to the mind-game films of the new millennium. Pepita Hesselberth and Laura Schuster offer a close reading of two such mind-game films, MEMENTO (Christopher Nolan, 2000) and CODE 46 (Michael Winterbottom, 2003), by focusing on the motif of a failing memory. Jan Simons closes the first act by connecting the notion of "productive pathologies" to both mind-game cinema and to the crisis paradigm that Elsaesser introduced into media studies.

The second act is dedicated to the correlation between European cinema and Hollywood cinema that Elsaesser has analyzed in great depth and in a variety of ways. Floris Paalman opens this section with a discussion of system theory and cultural ecology, which portrays Hollywood as a predator that "eats Europe's talent, but in order to do so it also has to invest in it." In the next essay, Dominic Pettman looks at Werner Herzog's GRIZZLY MAN (2006) to argue how the German New Wave auteur in this documentary presents the "bear life" of its main character by confessing to the camera in an "autoscopic" way. Michael Wedel in his case study focuses on another important German auteur, Fritz Lang, to discuss how Elsaesser's notions of "historical imaginary" and "place of rupture" can reveal the true essence of Lang's cinema better than the traditional and structuralist auteur theories. In her approach to the Europe-Hollywood connection, Patricia Pisters compares the work of European auteurs Rainer Werner Fassbinder and Paul Verhoeven, by examining their particular fascination with Hollywood and the role played by women throughout history. In "Amsterdamned Global Village," Jaap Kooijman traces Elsaesser's footsteps through the Reguliersbreestraat and continues to explore the cityscape by looking at Dutch films set in Amsterdam, based on Elsaesser's concept of "karaoke Americanism." Senta Siewert analyzes the Turkish-German film GEGEN DIE WAND / HEAD ON (Faith Akin, 2004) by applying Elsaesser's notion of "double occupancy" and focusing in particular on the film's use of pop music. In her discussion of global Hollywood directors, Melis Behlil challenges the traditional distinctions between Hollywood and European cinema, and argues that Hollywood should instead be perceived as a transnational cinematic space. Eleftheria Thanouli enters the postclassical Hollywood cinema debate by applying Elsaesser's five-step "what is different" formula to INSIDE MAN (Spike Lee, 2006). Inspired by Elsaesser's writing on the "Wag-the-Dog" principle in advertising, Charles Forceville closes this act by analyzing how bumpers that mark blocks of commercials on Dutch television have changed over the years, gradually blurring the clear distinction between commercials and television programs.

The third act brings together essays that place more emphasis on the historical dimensions of Elsaesser's work and is structured around the notions of Archaeology, Avant-Garde, and the Archive. Michael Punt offers us a media-archaeological account of the laserdisc, arguing that the origins of cinema go back to the early 18th century when the first modern orreries were designed. In "S/M," Wanda Strauven describes a series of Futurist snapshots by which she aims to rethink film history as a large network outside or beyond the entertainment industry. Richard Rogers deals with surveillance theory with respect to contemporary "data bodies" and consumer technologies such as mobile phones. In the next essay, Mieke Bal draws connections between Elsaesser's important essay on the transformation of the RAF (*Rote Armee Fraktion*) images in the period between the 1970s and 1990s and her own concept of "migratory aesthetics." Frank van Vree also looks at the archival images of terrorism, but his analysis focuses on how "indigestible images," such as those of the Holocaust, are in danger of fading away in the echo chamber of history. Julia Noordegraaf, on the contrary, argues that archival images not so much fade away but actually allow us to gain new perspectives, as she shows with her case study on colonial history in the work of Dutch video artist Fiona Tan. Jennifer Steetskamp continues the discussion on video art by examining the works of Harun Farocki and Johan Grimonprez through the lenses of reenactment, appropriation, and "meta-television." And, concluding this act, Jeroen de Kloet and Jan Teurlings offer a critical account of YouTube and its Chinese variant Tudou by returning to some of the issues raised by Thomas Elsaesser in the late 1990s, when the implications of digital media convergence were only starting to take shape.

In *European Cinema*, Thomas Elsaesser recalls his first personal encounter with the late Johan van der Keuken in 1993, just before the renowned Dutch director was to begin filming his documentary Amsterdam Global Village (1996). Elsaesser tells Van der Keuken that he has been hired by the University of Amsterdam to chair the Film and Television Studies program. Van der Keuken responds by asking: "And what do you know about Dutch cinema?" Taken aback, Elsaesser explains that the university is looking for a broad focus that will approach audiovisual culture from an international perspective. But Elsaesser's response cannot prevent the meeting from turning into a "near-miss collision."[9] The irony of the failed encounter between the filmmaker and the film scholar is not lost, however, as each – in his own way – has succeeded in finding the global in the local and has moved beyond Dutch parochialism into the transnational realm of cinema culture, without dismissing its local significance. It is, therefore, fitting that *Mind the Screen* is being published by Amsterdam University Press, which is also the home of Elsaesser's Film Culture in Transition series. With his work in and about Amsterdam, Elsaesser has shown that Amsterdam is indeed a global village, one of the hubs in a worldwide network of audiovisual culture where old and new media meet in space and time.

Notes

1. <http://www.youtube.com/watch?v=ri_1N3R7T-E>. Last viewed 10 Feb. 2008.
2. For an online summary of Elsaesser's lecture, see Michael Stevenson's blog: <http://mastersofmedia.hum.uva.nl/2008/01/19/video-vortex-thomas-elsaesser-on-constructive-instability>. Last viewed 10 Feb. 2008.
3. "Eerste Nederlandse Leerstoel Film- en Televisiewetenschap wordt geopend," press release, Media Studies archive, University of Amsterdam.
4. Thomas Elsaesser, "Inleiding: Hollywood op straat," *Hollywood op straat: Film en televisie in de hedendaagse mediacultuur*, ed. Thomas Elsaesser (Amsterdam: Vossiuspers AUP, 2000) 15-18.
5. Thomas Elsaesser, "Where Were You When . . . ?"; or, "I Phone, Therefore I Am," *PMLA* 118.1 (Jan. 2003): 120.
6. <http://www.caszuidas.nl/site/main.php?page=about&id=1>. Last viewed 10 Feb. 2008.
7. Freely quoted from an internal report written by Thomas Elsaesser and Wanda Strauven in March 2006, after their first orientation meeting with Waag Society.

8. The source of Bruce Gray's storyboard is Elsaesser's aforementioned essay "Where Were You When . . . ?" written upon the occasion of the first anniversary of the 9/11 attacks.

9. Thomas Elsaesser, *European Cinema: Face to Face with Hollywood* (Amsterdam: Amsterdam University Press, 2005) 193.

ACT I

Melodrama, Memory, Mind Game

Cinephilia in Transition

Malte Hagener and Marijke de Valck

When discussing the concept of cinephilia, the first and perennial question that inevitably comes to mind is what do we actually mean by cinephilia, this rare and elusive feeling of nostalgic attachment to images, stories, and sounds, this strangely elitist relationship to an art form that is still often derided as blatantly commercial. As popular as the term has proven to be, at least since the *Cahiers du cinéma* critics launched it as a battle cry in the 1960s, it seems hard to nail it down to any foolproof definition. The problem of theoretically understanding one's libidinal, emotional, and affective attachment to a medium in its totality has haunted many commentators, from Jean Epstein and Ricciotto Canudo in the 1920s to Paul Willemen and Susan Sontag in the 1980s and 1990s. Yet, arguably no one has returned to the concept as consistently as Thomas Elsaesser, who from his early writings for the *Brighton Film Review* and *Monogram* until today has regularly theorized and written about cinephilia.

Elsaesser came of age as a cinephile during the 1960s, founding and running a film magazine (*Monogram*), writing one of his earliest major articles on Hollywood auteurs while receiving his cinematographic education at London's cinemas.[1] Yet, unlike so many former cinephiles of his generation, while remaining an ardent champion of Minnelli, Preminger, Sirk, Hitchcock, and Lang to this day, he never resorts to any kind of cultural pessimism about the state of film culture in general and the demise of cinephilia in particular. When Elsaesser was confronted at the *Cinephilia, Take Two: Re-Mastering, Re-Purposing, Re-Framing* conference with one hour of "old man's mumble" by Dutch film critic Peter van Bueren who complained about the state of the cinema, lamenting the downward slope that film culture had taken ever since he was young, he exploded, ending his fifteen-minute response with "Look at you, you old bag!"[2] In fact, Elsaesser's cinephilia is alive and kicking precisely because it constantly adapts to the ever changing circumstances of cinema. Or, to quote a famous line from a cinephile film *par excellence*, Luchino Visconti's IL GATTOPARDO / THE LEOPARD (1963), cinephilia is a constantly evolving phenomenon: "*Cambiare tutto, per non cambiare nulla*" / "If we want everything to stay as it is, everything has to change."

But we have still not answered the question of what cinephilia is. Instead of addressing the question head on, maybe it is better to circumvent it for the time being and approach it from a slightly different angle: firstly, by providing a short archaeological sketch of cinephilia in terms of its generational logic, and secondly, by examining the various applications of cinephilia in the past. The under-lying assumption here is that cinephilia has never been just a neutral term to describe an emotional attachment to specific films or to cinema as a medium, but that it has always been an ambivalent critical concept with which people have tried to capture a specific mood of film experience while at the same time aiming to articulate an ontology of cinema. If one includes the French discourse on *photogénie* – promoted by intellectuals such as Louis Delluc, Jean Epstein, and Emile Vuillermoz – as a direct forerunner of the debates on cinephilia (and there are good reasons to do so), the idea has always exceeded and transcended a mere description of a love for cinema, and should instead be considered an attempt to conceptualize the medium on an immanent plane.[3]

Our assumption, then, at this point, will be that cinephilia does not permit any fundamental doubt about the audiovisuality that has become so pervasive and omnipresent in the world we inhabit. Because there is no external position, no place where one can escape the mediated moving images, even our thinking has become cinematic. In this sense, cinephilia might more closely resemble a set of religious belief. Or, as Patricia Pisters has explained: "we now live in a metacine-matic universe that calls for an immanent conception of audiovisuality and in which a new camera consciousness has entered our perception."[4] Cinephilia does not permit an external view to the cinema or a fulcrum from which to gain an overview or complete picture, or an Archimedean viewpoint from which to frame the medium. Cinephilia attempts to describe and conceptualize the totality of cinema as precisely that: a totality. In the sense that cinephilia addresses the boundlessness of the audiovisual universe, it might follow a gaming logic similar to a "certain tendency" of contemporary cinema which Elsaesser has termed "mind-game film" and in which questions of epistemological doubt and ontologi-cal groundlessness are played out.[5] But let us begin by delving into the history of cinephilia because the archaeology of cinephilia is also the genealogy of the uni-verse as meta-cinema.

Three Generations, Three Cinephilias

If there are, as Elsaesser has suggested, at least three generations of cinephiles (roughly divided into three time frames – the 1960s, the 1970s-1980s, and the 1990s until the present), each with their own brand of cinephilia – then he him-self belongs to all three of these generations equally.[6] A generation is a temporal concept which groups people according to their birth year in relation to the larger cultural and historical shifts, although this seemingly simple classification sys-tem has recently been criticised.[7] By including elements of (Foucauldian-inspired) genealogy and by mixing in psychoanalytical and literary concepts (elective affinities, adopted parents, oedipal rejections, etc.), the term "generation" may assume a new meaning and urgency in a world governed by *Ungleichzeitigkeit* (non-synchronicity). Applying it in this sense to cinephilia seems all the more logical since both generation and cinephilia are also complex time-shifting devices, as they elaborate a temporal logic that exceeds a clear-cut linear and chronological order. In this respect, the generational logic with its unexpected returns and repressed inheritances is not only similar to cinephilia, but also resembles the twisted time structure of the melodrama. In his seminal piece "Tales of Sound and Fury: Observations on the Family Melodrama," Elsaesser had already located the central characteristic of the melodramatic tradition in American cinema in its "structural changes from linear externalization of action to a sublimation of dramatic value into more complex forms of symbolization."[8] In this respect, melodrama, generational distinctions, and cinephilia are all conceptual devices allowing the theorization of non-linear temporal structures.

Cinephilia, as Susan Sontag, Paul Willemen, and many others have reminded us, is always already tinged with nostalgia, possible loss, and retroactive temporalities.[9] Of course, for decades, watching films and going to the cinema was founded on the fleeting nature of its experience, each projection irrevocably unique, and each image already irretrievably lost upon its appearance, so that every film screening was a rare and cherished sensation that could not be repeated. Therefore, being a cinephile in the early 1960s in London for Elsaesser meant "being sensitive to one's surroundings when watching a movie, carefully picking the place where to sit, fully alert to the quasi-sacral feeling of nervous anticipation that could descend upon a public space, however squalid, smelly or slipshod, as the velvet curtain rose and the studio logo with its fanfares filled the space."[10] It was this attention to the unique circumstances of the screening as well as the wish to retain the fleeting experience that emerged as one of the hallmarks of the first generation of cinephiles.[11] Other important writers on film such as Antoine de Baecque became ardent cinephiles in the 1960s, as well as, of course, the *Cahiers du cinéma* critics who went on to become directors: François Truffaut, Eric Rohmer, Claude Chabrol and, above all, Jean-Luc Godard and Jacques Rivette. Thus, the first generation of cinephiles was, more than anything else, a topographical movement that gravitated on a global level towards Paris, and on a local level, towards the cinema of choice.

There is a certain overlap with the second generation that came of age in the politicized 1970s, when many began to criticize cinephilia as a bourgeois exercise, which kept people trapped in illusory cinematic worlds and away from the real revolution that was happening out in the streets, which is illustrated rather ambivalently by Bernardo Bertolucci's THE DREAMERS (2003). Here, the protagonists

Matthew, Isabelle, and Theo are portrayed as typical first-generation cinephiles, protesting the closure of the Cinémathèque Française, quizzing one another on their film knowledge, and reenacting memorable scenes from their favorite films, but being otherwise oblivious to the socio-political upheavals taking place just beyond the walls of their Parisian flat. The incestuous love triangle between an American exchange student and French twins ostensibly alludes to the tainted relation between Hollywood and French cinema. Set in 1968, the youngsters, obsessed with cinema, each other, and their sexual awakening are brought back to reality when a stone, perhaps thrown by a demonstrator in a street protest, breaks the window and their idyll to their enclosed semi-fictional world.

In the 1970s, many disillusioned cinephiles began to wonder how people could attach so much value (let alone energy) to films at a time when the cinema was seen as an overpowering capitalist tool as Jean-Louis Baudry and others were so eager to point out. The apparatus theory reacted to a perceived crisis in cinema, which had been historically triggered by the development of new audiovisual technologies and economically reinforced by changing audience habits and demographics. It reacted with a kind of mournful response: in the face of the imminent decline of cinema as a whole, the nostalgic and loving gaze of the cinephile turns into a deeply felt, intense, and theoretically grounded hate-love relationship. The vast majority of film theory in the 1970s, with its paranoid hermeneutics – an epistemological conspiracy theory of the highest order – testifies to a deep feeling of loss and betrayal because the object of their love did not actually deserve their affection. This led to the transfer of the emotion from unconditional admiration to deep levels of mistrust. Given this perspective, the psycho-semiotics of the 1970s became a kind of inverted cinephilia, a disappointed love's labor's lost. The world as we perceive and inhabit it (in the cinema) could no longer be trusted, and there was no easy solution, no position from which to claim a newly found overview.

Despite the negative energy generated by the then contemporary film theory, cinephilia persevered through the 1970s and 1980s, even though it now tended to discard this label. Cinephiles of this generation, such as Australian film critic Adrian Martin or Viennese film critic and director of the Austrian Film Museum Alexander Horwath, found their cherished things and *objets trouvés* on late-night television instead, and began circulating copies of rare videos in the early 1980s. Strange rituals and eccentric characters abounded in this phase. There were rumors about a cinephile who had to rent an extra flat just to store all of his videotapes – storage space became a real issue for the second-generation cinephiles unlike the first generation (who depended on memories, and for whom cinephilia was largely an imaginary collection) and the third generation (files no longer took up physical space as their collections were now largely digital). Indeed, it is the second wave that stands between a supposedly "originary" cinephilia and a (re)new(ed) cinephilia that emerged in the 1990s and has become a full-blown movement ever since the millennium. The proponents of the third wave of cinephilia frequent film festivals, but also watch DVDs, they download rare films from the Internet, and communicate via blogs. This third generation of cinephilia is only now fully emerging as they discover one another among the various IMDb discussion boards, dedicated fan sites where the intricacies of the latest Tarantino, Fincher, and Lynch movies are discussed, or in the *blogosphere*.[12]

Many triple jumps can be formed around these three generational moments, which are never fully independent from one another and exist in a continuum, blending into one another. In fact, these three stages continue to coexist not unlike the classic psychoanalytic phases (oral, anal, and oedipal), even though they seem overcome from the outside. The cinema listings for the first generation was replaced by the TV guide for the second, which has since been replaced by p2p file sharing services – which allows one to search a list of titles for a coveted film one that is finally available. Indeed, to browse the various lists of titles (or drawing up lists of one's own) might be the cinephile moment *par excellence*, even more precious than the encounter with the actual work. Whereas the first generation of cinephilia was marked by local trajectories and one's favorite seat in a specific cinema, the second wave was marked by international trajectories toward specific festivals (Deauville, Rotterdam, Pesaro) and retrospectives, while contemporary cinephilia relies on the dispersed and virtual geography of the link and the directory. Furthermore, each generation boasts its own preferred directors: while the first wave was weaned on Howard Hawks, John Ford, and Alfred Hitchcock, the second was characterized by border-crossers such as Rainer Werner Fassbinder, Bertrand Tavernier, and Peter Bogdanovich; and the third has broken down most of the geographical distinctions, so that David Fincher and Quentin Tarantino are featured right next to Miike Takashi, Tsai Ming-Liang, and Wong Kar-Wai, or Fatih Akin and Lars von Trier next to Apichatpong Weerasethakul and Julio Medem. The first generation started their own film magazines, the second now runs many of the major *cinémathèques* (i.e., Alexander Horwath), while the third generation tends to run websites, digital film festivals, or mailing lists.

The "Post-Classic" State of Cinephilia

Let us now turn to the contemporary shape of cinephilia. Perhaps one can effectively adapt the concept of post-classical cinema to the notion of cinephilia, claiming that the seemingly fundamental break distinguishing a classical from a post-classical cinephilia is perhaps less than clear, as both also share a lot of common ground (as do classical and post-classical Hollywood films). Indeed, Elsaesser, as a theorist of post-classical cinema, has argued for a less mutually exclusive and binary division between the classical and the post-classical:

> [T]he difference between classical and post-classical cannot be established on the basis of a binary opposition such as spectacle vs. narrative, nor, we suspect, any other "either/or" construction of difference. One suggestion was that we may have to look for a definition of the post-classical more along the lines of an excessive classicism, rather than as a rejection or absence of classicism... [T]he post-classical ... [is] a distinct mode: not only of representation and style, but also of production and reception.[13]

At this point we would like to propose a reframing of cinephilia, by defining post-classical cinephilia as "classical-plus," as it still adheres to the typical values of cinephilia with lists of favorite films and auteurs, cherished styles and preferred periods, while, at the same time, it has become something more and something very different in how it uses contemporary technology and recent shifts in media utilization. Like post-classical cinema, post-classical cinephilia is invested with a series of transformations that diversify its manifestations. Post-classical narration moves away from an overwhelming cause-and-effect logic, undermines the linear trajectory, and complicates character development, to enjoy a large degree of freedom in presenting and relating various motives, and to revel in temporal and psychological disorders, whereas post-classical cinephilia also appears to feel freer in its selection of *punctums*. The classical preoccupation with locating the evidence of authorial signatures in the *mise-en-scène* has been expanded in the age of post-classical cinephilia; nowadays a scriptwriter like Charlie Kaufman, a cinematographer like Christopher Doyle, a composer like John Williams, and a genre chameleon like director Michael Winterbottom are all the objects of contemporary cinephile affection as much as any one director with a highly idiosyncratic and recognizable style.

Post-classical cinephilia, in its relation to space and time, resembles the transformations toward the multifaceted practices of post-classical cinema, such as intensified continuity, fast cutting, and non-linear trajectories. Contemporary cinephilia is no longer limited to *cinémathèques* and small art-house theaters where regulars take their preferred seats. Alongside the spatial (local) specificity of the movie-going tradition, new practices emerged that are spatially decentered and that rely on various forms of technological mediation. Contemporary cinephiles watch films not only on the silver screen, but also at home, which used to mean on videotape, but, since the late 1990s, also on DVD and, into the millennium, increasingly via the Internet (as well as on collector formats such as Blu-Ray and

HD-DVD). The public space of the cinema was supplemented by the private space of the home, the fixed schedule of theatrical programming was supplemented by the time-shifting devices of the remote control, the VCR, the rental services, and downloading. While classical cinephilia demanded that one complied with the schedules created by others, post-classical cinephilia allows much more freedom to engage in cinephile activities at one's own pace and leisure. Like post-classical cinema, post-classical cinephilia is more of a hybrid, more diverse, and maybe more self-reflective and self-referential than its classical counterpart.

Arguably, one of the most "classical" of contemporary cinephile practices is the festival visit. This becomes particularly clear when we scrutinize the spatial and temporal characteristics of film viewing at a festival. Unlike the new technologically enabled practices, film festivals revolve around classic theatrical immersion. Festival visitors have to travel to specific sites if they want to see the films. Moreover, they have to adjust to the festival's schedule and go through some (at times great) trouble to see the movie(s) of their choice. The exclusivity of the festival film screening and the effort required to be at a specific place at a specific time in order to see the screening of one's choice is reminiscent of classical cinephilia. However, here too it is a kind of "classical cinephilia plus": similar at the core, but different in its manifestations. Cinephiles who frequent film festivals could go both to the smaller, peripheral festivals and the larger, more popular festivals. They are attracted by the films, but are also lured by the whole festival atmosphere. In fact, festivals often use their specific location as an attraction because they have to compete with each other in terms of the global space economy, as Julian Stringer has convincingly shown.[4]

This means that even if the exhibition format of festivals appears to be similar to the theatrical immersion model of classical cinephilia, it points simultaneously to the influential dynamics of spatial competition, city marketing, festival branding, and urban programming that have also become part of the cinephile experience. The theatrical immersion that takes place at film festivals is much more spectacular than its classical prototype. Black boxes are replaced by open-air screenings in town squares, on beaches, and in forests, while the local settings of the festival are also taken into consideration; exotic locations such as ski resorts (Sundance), war zones (Sarajevo), and remote locations (Midnight Sun) benefit from additional (spatial) appeal. However, not unlike Elsaesser's argument regarding the classical/post-classical cinema divide, the relation between traditional theatrical immersion and festival screenings should not be seen in oppositional terms – a mutually exclusive disjuncture between an exhibition situation in which the attention is exclusively focused on the films vs. one in which the context itself is foregrounded – but rather as a specific historical cultural practice and its aggregation. Post-classical cinephilia wants to have its cake and eat it too – see the film and see it in the context of spectacular surroundings, experience the text as well as its context.

Another typical manifestation of contemporary cinephilia is the video installation that uses fragments culled from cinephile objects of worship. Regardless of whether we are talking about Douglas Gordon's 24 HOUR PSYCHO (1993), Matthias Müller's HOME STORIES (1990), Johan Grimonprez's LOOKING FOR ALFRED (2005), or Harun Farocki's ARBEITER VERLASSEN DIE FABRIK / WORKERS LEAVING THE FACTORY (1995), these works all engage the material of classical cinephilia, which is still charged with libidinous desire and for that reason recognizable and attractive, yet liberated from their immediate context, thus also available (both as material and as cultural signifier) and marketable.[15] It is as if it is only now that we are finally able to make these forays into the shambles of our everyday existence, which Walter Benjamin anticipated in the 1930s for cinema in his Artwork essay. However, we have also come to realize today that the shambles of our everyday existence involves nothing more than fragments of the audiovisual universe of the twentieth century, to which there appears to be no outside. Even a seemingly banal and quotidian activity as leaving a factory is already presented to us in a mediated format, as another film. Although the cinematic installation is typical of post-classical cinephilia, it still manages to take us on a guided tour across the immanent plane of our media universe, demonstrating how much of our identity and past has indeed been shaped by film, television, and media in general.

From this fact we could conclude that any theoretical division between classical and post-classical cinephilia should also be understood as an indication of the weight that historical developments exert, under the influence of which, cinephilia is turned into several historically defined practices. As our opening anecdote demonstrated, some will belong to only one generation, while others – like El-saesser – will belong to many. The former will be quick to judge any change as degeneration, while the latter is capable of embracing change. For example, the latter are able to see technological innovation and new modes of production and reception as opportunities for rejuvenating one's personal cinephile experience. It is precisely because disagreement on what qualifies as cinephilia will continue to rage that cinephilia remains a contested concept, heavily debated in academic discourse, discussed in public debate, and a favored topic for flaming someone online or denouncing face-to-face.

Cinephilia as an Approach

The question that remains to be answered despite this archaeological sketch of cinephilia as both practice and discourse is how to approach the study of cinephilia. Is it enough to focus on its historical practices, to present taxonomies of generations and types of cinephiles? Is it sufficient to merely uncover the discursive maneuvers and (dis)agreements? Or, should we also be endeavoring to get to the heart of the cinephile emotion? As the very word "cinephile" makes unmistakably clear, love is at the heart of cinephilia. But can one ever really theorize love? As Jenna Ng argues: "[Cinephilia] is ultimately a phenomenon that is deeply subjective and personal. It cannot be fully contained in objective theory, and that is its glory."[16] But one aspect has become clear; that there is a thin line between cinephilia as a concept and cinephilia as an individual emotional experience. We believe that one reason why cinephilia has proven to be such an enduring concept – it has survived several decades and periodically manages to reinvent itself – may have to do with the fact that it forms a bridge between the biographical and the theoretical. Many film scholars must consider their own enthusiasm for certain films, directors, or genres as being terribly estranged from the proper way of thinking, talking, and writing about cinema. Ever since the *Cahiers du cinéma* critics began elevating cinema to that of an accepted art form, one has been able to justify one's own emotional attachment to cinema by pointing to established figures whose example one follows. So cinephilia allows one to follow one's libidinal instincts while simultaneously being taken seriously. The concept of cinephilia occupies this middle ground, which allows for the transformation of a personal obsession into a theoretical preoccupation. We are left to wonder whether this might also be the reason for the importance of anecdotes which inhabit the middle ground between the personal (specific) and the abstract (general), which are often held together by a joke or some kind of slippery slope of meaning.

If we consider this work of transference where anecdotes are able to operate on a more abstract level, then cinephilia is indeed characterized by a constant double-movement between the biographical and the theoretical, the singular and the general, the fragment and the whole, the incomplete and the complete, the individual and the collective. At this point we can return to the question of a methodology for studying contemporary cinephilia by asserting that any approach should engage these double-movements while accepting the concept of cinephilia as a centripetal force. In this way we may be able to scrutinize concrete historical forms and periods of cinephilia as practices while also understanding the mystical, illogical, and intangible aspects of cinephila as love.

Elsaesser's thinking on the concept of cinephilia includes a particularly useful view of how the biographical and theoretical (and historical for that matter) can be combined. We have already established that the understanding of cinephilia involves memory, imagination, and the anxiety of possible loss. Like Paul Willemen and Susan Sontag, Elsaesser has hinted at the overtones of necrophilia in cinephilia, connecting one's lived presence with his or her past experiences. Because cinema is comprised of moving images that exist only in the fleeting moment during projection, it is undead by nature. However, it affects the spectator in the present and ultimately comes alive in one's memory. There is an obvious similarity to Deleuze's time-image here, because he envisioned a crystal image as the partitioning of time into memory and past. However, Elsaesser understands that the temporal registers that define the moment of cinephilia also have a significant psychoanalytic dimension, a quintessential strategy that links personal obsessions and theoretical reflection.

Elsaesser not only distinguishes between generations of cinephiles, but also identifies three distinct psychoanalytic temporalities that can be at work in cinephilia at any given moment: 1) the oedipal time of François Truffaut, for example, which adopts André Bazin and Alfred Hitchcock in order to attack "le cinéma de papa," 2) the lover's discourse time as conjugated by Roland Barthes, and 3) the strictly mediated time. Elsaesser's "method" for explaining the ambivalent feelings that troubled cinephilia in the mid-1970s can be characterized as a close reading of the confusing presence of these three temporalities (simultaneously):

> By 1975, cinephilia had been dragged out of its closet, the darkened womb-like auditorium, and revealed itself as a source of disappointment: the magic of the movies, in the cold light of day, had become a manipulation of regressive fantasies and the place of the big male escape from sexual difference... It is not altogether irrelevant to this moment in history that Laura Mulvey's call to forego visual pleasure and dedicate oneself to unpleasure was not heeded.[17]

Occupying the middle ground between the biographical and the theoretical, Elsaesser identifies these "disenchantments" – the doubt, ambivalence, and disappointments that tainted the love for cinema – as significant drives for cinephilia.

Cinephilia has always had a darker side. The gap between what is expected and what will be experienced, the anxiety of being disappointed, seems to be an essential precondition for a cinephile experience. Film lovers have always feared that the latest movie by a favorite auteur will not live up to their expectations. In other words, they tend to prioritize memory and imagination, and define their affectionate "loving" relation with the cinematic subject primarily in the past tense. As Elsaesser has argued, the major advantage of this temporal deferral is that it allows the cinephile to maintain a sense of self in the face of the overwhelming power of the cinematic experience. Instead of simply losing control and letting oneself be carried away by *scopophilic* thrills or perverted fantasies, the mechanism of disenchantment ensures that the cinephile performs an intellectual – or at least individual – act to maintain this bond. If one pursues this line of thinking, one could of course also claim the opposite: that cinephilia is not about love at all, at least not in the sense of a mutual bond of affection, but more like a form of (narcissistic) identity formation that responds to the (subconscious) needs of individuals who happened to have chosen the cinema as their means of distinction. But let us not forget the level of penetration of cinema into our every-day lives, homes, and minds. We live in a cinematic age and are thoroughly accustomed to the cinematic mode of perception. Cinephilia, one could argue, befits our time, as it presents a totality while being smooth and malleable enough to change with the whims and desires of new generations of film lovers.

Coda

Some have questioned whether the idea of loving a medium more or less uncon-ditionally is still fathomable in a time when cinema, although still important cul-turally, is less so as an agenda-setting medium – functioning more like a bill-board in time, which provides advertising space for the latest "content" to be marketed as a DVD, a TV series, a computer game, and/or a toy.[18] Or, as Homer Simpson put it so succinctly (as always) in the recent THE SIMPSONS MOVIE (Da-vid Silverman, 2007): "Why be so stupid and pay for something at the cinema if you can have it for free on television?" Our argument has been that the "movie mutations," as Rosenbaum and Martin have aptly dubbed the transformations that are occurring worldwide in cinephilia today, should not be seen as degenera-tions of an authentic classical cinephile practice, but instead as a "natural" evolu-tion of a cultural practice that is firmly intertwined with historical conditions.[19] Thus, instead of one, there is room for many cinephile generations. In this situa-tion, it is not simply the medium, but also our intimate connection to the meta-universe of moving images that matters.

Therefore, another response would be that cinephilia – and by extension the cinema as a whole – is capable of offering the spectator an experience that has become the norm for contemporary media culture. Thus, even if we are watching a film at home on a large flat screen with a multi-speaker system or on the move on a laptop with headphones, the cinema experience remains as a norm and yardstick, but it is also internalized and fantasized. As we noted earlier, there is no outside to the audiovisual universe, we all inhabit a world that is saturated by the media, its images and stories, its celebrities and formats. However, it is only at the cinema where we can fully comprehend and absorb this fact of life that has been theoretically elaborated, but not yet completely understood. In fact, the re-cent popularity of Deleuze's books on cinema may hint exactly at this juncture since his central premise is that the cinema is immanence.

Deleuze has sometimes been criticized for following the orthodox Parisian ci-nephilia style, especially in what he chooses to write about in his books on cinema. Perhaps, instead of accusing Deleuze of being an old-fashioned cinephile, who has merely taken his cue from the *Cahiers du cinéma* critics and pimped it with pseudo-philosophical jargon, as his detractors would have it, one should see him more as a contemporary cinephile whose work on cinema is, at least in some respects, a blog *avant la lettre*. His cinema works open up a dialogue with the canon of the first wave of cinephilia, but from a position where he was one of the first cinephiles to realize that there is no outside to cinema, no transcendental perspective, that there is only immanence. Instead of sticking to a dogmatic exegesis of holy scripture like the more traditional Deleuzians would, one should view his books on cinema as screening notes and blogger's comments. One can compare Deleuze's books on cinema to a blog and the community of Deleuzian scholars to the blogosphere on at least three levels. Firstly, his texts create an almost endless surface to surf on, a textual plane that might leave some marks, paragraphs and elisions, but is not structured strongly along any hierarchical lines. A typical blog does not have page breaks and dipping here and there, while Deleuze's work creates a similar feeling of a seemingly endless stream of thoughts and observations. Secondly, and related to this, Deleuze's lateral thinking is akin to the web logic of linking and thereby creating your own context at any given moment. Of course, his idea of the rhizome has been applied to Internet logic that favors non-hierarchical and non-linear connections over strong top-down organization. Thirdly, and taking its cue from here, the community of Deleuzian scholars show some similarity to the blogosphere in the way that cross-referencing prevails, thus creating a complex layer of overlapping texts. In these ways, Deleuze, like Elsaesser, and possibly inadvertently, has always *already* been a post-classical cinephile.

Notes

1. See Thomas Elsaesser, "Tales of Sound and Fury: [Observations on] The Family Melodrama," *Monogram* 4 (1972): 2-15; reprinted in *Movies and Methods II*, ed. Bill Nichols (Berkeley / Los Angeles: California University Press, 1985) 166-189. See also Thomas Elsaesser, "Von der Filmwissenschaft zu den Cultural Studies und zurück: Der Fall Großbritannien," *Zeitschrift für Kulturwissenschaft* 2 (2007): 85-106.
2. The conference *Cinephilia, Take Two: Re-mastering, Re-Purposing, Re-Framing* was hosted by the Department of Media Studies (University of Amsterdam) and held in Amsterdam, 16-17 June 2003.
3. For a discussion of the historical use of the term *photogénie* see, for example, Frank Kessler, "Photogénie und Physiognomie," *Geschichten der Physiognomik*, ed. Rüdiger Campe and Manfred Schneider (Freiburg: Rombach, 1996) 515-534.
4. Patricia Pisters, *The Matrix of Visual Culture: Working with Deleuze in Film Theory* (Stanford: Stanford University Press, 2003) 16.

5. See Thomas Elsaesser, "The Mind-Game Film," *Puzzle Films: Complex Storytelling in Contemporary Cinema*, ed. Warren Buckland (Oxford: Blackwell, 2008).

6. Thomas Elsaesser, "Cinephilia or the Uses of Disenchantment," *Cinephilia: Movies, Love and Memory*, ed. Marijke de Valck and Malte Hagener (Amsterdam: Amsterdam University Press, 2005) 27.

7. See Sigrid Weigel, Ohad Parnes, Ulrike Vedder, and Stefan Willer, eds., *Generation. Zur Genealogie des Konzepts – Konzepte von Genealogie* (München: Fink, 2005).

8. Elsaesser, "Tales of Sound and Fury" 178.

9. Susan Sontag, "The Decay of Cinema," *New York Times*, 25 Feb. 1996, final edition, section 6: 60; Paul Willemen, "Through the Glass Darkly: Cinephilia Reconsidered," *Looks and Frictions: Essays in Cultural Studies and Film Theory* (London: BFI, 1994) 223-257.

10. Elsaesser, "Cinephilia or the Uses of Disenchantment" 28.

11. There are, of course, earlier generations of engaged film fans. Among these are the French theorists of *photogénie*, mentioned earlier, and the visitors and organisers of ciné-clubs in the 1910s-1920s. The reason they have been excluded in this generational overview of cinephilia is linked to the emergence of the term cinephilia in the 1960s. The earlier generations are, however, considered important precursors of the "first" cinephile generation.

12. See, for example, <http://dr-mabuses-kaleido-scope.blogspot.com>. Last viewed on 10 June 2007.

13. Thomas Elsaesser and Warren Buckland, *Studying Contemporary American Film: A Guide to Movie Analysis* (London: Arnold, 2002) 61.

14. Julian Stringer, "Global Cities and the International Film Festival Economy," *Cinema and the City: Film and Urban Societies in a Global Context*, ed. Mark Shiel and Tony Fitzmaurice (Oxford: Blackwell, 2001) 134-144.

15. See also Thomas Elsaesser, "Casting Around: Hitchcock's Absence," *Johan Grimonprez: Looking for Alfred – The Hitchcock Castings*, ed. Steven Bode (Ostfildern: Hatje Cantz, 2007) 138-160 and Thomas Elsaesser, ed., *Harun Farocki: Working on the Sight-Lines* (Amsterdam: Amsterdam University Press, 2004).

16. Jenna Ng, "Love in the Time of Transcultural Fusion," *Cinephilia: Movies, Love and Memory* 75.

17. Elsaesser, "Cinephilia or the Uses of Disenchantment" 32.

18. See Thomas Elsaesser, "The Blockbuster: Everything Connects, But Not Everything Goes," *The End of Cinema As We Know It: American Film in the Nineties*, ed. Jon Lewis (New York: New York University Press, 2001) 11-22.

19. Jonathan Rosenbaum and Adrian Martin, eds., *Movie Mutations: The Changing Face of World Cinephilia* (London: BFI, 2003).

Theorizing Melodrama

A Rational Reconstruction of "Tales of Sound and Fury"

Warren Buckland

On one of my many visits to Thomas Elsaesser's home in the center of Amsterdam, I took down from his library shelves the complete run of the two journals he edited between 1968 and 1975 – the *Brighton Film Review* and *Monogram*. As I leafed through the journals I witnessed, issue by issue, the progressive development of an increasingly sophisticated critical discourse on the cinema, as well as the emergence of the journal editor's influence and reputation. Volume 1 no. 1 of the *Brighton Film Review* (4 December 1968) is modestly subtitled "A Fortnightly Guide to the Cinema in Brighton." The film reviews are modest in scope, consisting primarily of auteurist readings of a director's dominant themes and styles. The first issue includes Elsaesser's review of Anthony Mann's BEND OF THE RIVER, Otto Kruger's review of Polanski's KNIFE IN THE WATER, and Elsaesser's review of Michael Powell's TALES OF HOFFMAN – a review which, we are informed at the end, was (bizarrely) published in a shortened version in *Wine Press*.

Of course, as any cinephile knows, Otto Kruger is the name of a character actor who played the stereotypical German in many Hollywood films of the 1940s and 1950s (including Sirk's MAGNIFICENT OBSESSION). Kruger did not change careers and become a film critic. Instead, what happened is that the editor, working single-handedly to try to fill the pages of the first issue of the *Brighton Film Review* by writing most of the reviews himself, occasionally used some pseudonyms. I imagine that the editor also typed up the first issue by himself on – judging from the quality of the typing – an old, portable Underwood or Royal typewriter.

By the time the *Brighton Film Review* became *Monogram* in April 1971, the typing had given way to typesetting, and the agenda had broadened beyond the scope of auteurism and film reviewing. This shift is apparent in "Tales of Sound and Fury: Observations on the Family Melodrama," (or "Tales" for short) which Elsaesser published as the lead essay in *Monogram* no. 4 in 1972.[1] Moreover, this essay not only took *Monogram* to a new level of analysis and sophistication, it influenced a whole generation of film scholars, demonstrating the explanatory power of historically informed criticism and Freudian psychoanalysis in the serious examination of one of the most neglected genres (at that time) in film studies – the Hollywood family melodrama. Just as Robin Wood cited Shakespearean themes in his analysis of Hitchcock's thrillers as a way of conferring legitimacy on what was perceived in the 1960s to be light entertainment films,[2] so Elsaesser cites eighteenth-century forms of European melodrama and Freudian psychoanalysis (and uses a Shakespearean title) to legitimize his study of what appeared to be one of the most frivolous and superficial genres of classical Hollywood cinema.

In this short paper, I aim to rationally reconstruct "Tales of Sound and Fury" to both determine what it is stating and how it states it. In terms of my reasoning strategies, I shall use Rudolf Botha's philosophical study into the conduct of inquiry to analyze the way Elsaesser formulates conceptual and empirical problems and how he solves them.[3] I focus on problem formation because I have been convinced by Botha's (and Larry Laudan's[4]) argument that the rationality of an argument is based on its problem-solving effectiveness. Arguments are important, therefore, to the extent that they provide solutions to conceptual and empirical problems. Botha focuses on problem formation in linguistic inquiry, although his analysis is, of course, applicable to other fields of research as well. I have already used Botha's work to analyze the formation of problems in film theory – most notably in my chapter "Film Semiotics" in Toby Miller and Robert Stam's edited volume *A Companion to Film Theory*, in my review of Francesco Casetti's *Inside the Gaze*, and also in my rational reconstruction of Tom Gunning's "Cinema of Attractions" paper.[5]

Botha lists four activities that are involved in formulating theoretical problems: (a) analyzing the problematic state of affairs; (b) describing the problematic state of affairs; (c) constructing problems; and (d) evaluating problems with regard to being well-formed and significance.[6] This list is based on the distinction between a "problematic state of affairs" and "problems." Whereas the former refers to an aspect of reality a theorist does not understand, a problem formulates what a theorist needs to do to resolve the problematic state of affairs. This includes understanding and gaining insight into the general nature or specific properties of an object that has not been previously examined (or not examined adequately).

In carrying out (a), an analysis, the researcher must know exactly what is problematic, isolate each component of the problematic state of affairs, determine how they are interrelated, and identify the background assumptions informing his or her inquiry, such as the nature conferred upon the object of analysis.

In carrying out (b), a description, the problematic state of affairs must be accurately recorded and formally described. For Botha, this involves three processes: (i) collecting data; (ii) systematizing data; (iii) symbolizing the results.[7] In collecting data, the researcher must determine whether it is the data or the researcher's theory that generates the problematic state of affairs. Systematizing data involves the activities of classifying, correlating, and ordering. These activities enable the researcher to identify common properties among data, put similar data into classes, and determine the relations between the classes. Finally, symbolizing involves representing data in a concise and accurate manner. By carrying out these procedures, the theorist ensures that his or her description is genuine, correct, and comprehensive.

In carrying out (c), the constructing of problems, the researcher employs several different concepts (since a problem is made up of concepts) to solve the problematic state of affairs. Botha identifies four types of concepts involved in the construction of problems (here I have modified his list to fit film studies): phenomenological concepts, which concern factual data and are intuitively known; filmic concepts (which Botha calls grammatical concepts), general background assumptions concerning the nature of individual films; cinematic concepts (which Botha calls general linguistic concepts), which concern background assumptions about the nature of film; and meta-theoretical concepts (which Botha calls meta-scientific concepts), which concern the aims and nature of theoretical inquiry.[8]

In carrying out (d), the evaluation of problems, Botha recognizes that only problems satisfying the criteria of being well-formed and significance are relevant problems worth pursuing. A well-formed problem is one that is solvable – in other words, is based on correct assumptions and is clearly formulated. A significant problem is one that expands our existing knowledge of film. A problem may, therefore, be well-formed, but may not be significant.

Authors do not necessarily formulate and write out their research in the manner made explicit by Botha's systematic and logical steps; these steps are the privilege of the philosopher. This adds indeterminacy to the analysis of any text in terms of Botha's categories. Furthermore, the stage of research I concentrate on here, the formation of problems, is only one stage – albeit one of the most important – in the development of research. Other stages include: giving descriptions of the object of study, giving explanations, making projections, justifying hypotheses, and so on.

A Rational Reconstruction

a. Analyzing the Problematic State of Affairs

The essay has a literary title that alludes to the following lines from *Macbeth*:

> ... it is a tale
> Told by an idiot, full of sound and fury
> Signifying nothing.

The subtitle ("Observations on the Family Melodrama") is less literary and more informative, identifying the main object of investigation – the family melodrama – and hints at Elsaesser's method of investigation – namely, "observation." I shall take Elsaesser's identification of his own research as inductive observation seriously, and examine the status of his inductive arguments.

After the Shakespearean title, the opening paragraph shifts registers and quotes from a Douglas Sirk interview, in which the director is asked about the color scheme in his film WRITTEN ON THE WIND. Sirk replied:

> "Almost throughout the picture I used deep-focus lenses which have the effect of giving a harshness to the objects and a kind of enameled, hard surface to the colors. I wanted this to bring out the inner violence, the energy of the characters which is all inside them and can't break through." (43)

For Elsaesser, this quotation encapsulates "how closely, in this film, style and technique [are] related to theme" (43). The Sirk quotation and Elsaesser's comment on it reveal one set of theoretical background assumptions behind "Tales": a traditional auteur analysis focused – as all auteur analyses do – on a particular director's distinctive visual style and thematic concerns. At first the essay seems to address a very common problem in film criticism – the relationship between style and theme (in Sirk's films). Yet the subtitle phrase "Family Melodrama" suggests that the essay will offer a more in-depth investigation into the themes of a film genre, of which Sirk's films are a mere subclass. The phrase "Family Melodrama" in fact hints at a different set of theoretical background assumptions behind the essay – it echoes Freud's term "family romance," thereby suggesting a Freudian reading of the genre's themes.

In the second paragraph, Elsaesser identifies the problematic state of affairs he addresses and the objectives he aims to pursue:

> My notes want to pursue an elusive subject in two directions: to indicate the development of what one might call the melodramatic imagination across different artistic forms and in different epochs; secondly, Sirk's remark tempts one to look for some structural and stylistic constants in one medium during one particular period (the Hollywood family melodrama between roughly 1940 and 1963) and to speculate on the cultural and psychological context which this form of melodrama so manifestly reflected and helped to articulate. (43)

The problematic state of affairs the essay addresses is generated by a property of the data (the color scheme of WRITTEN ON THE WIND), but is not limited to that data. In other words, the essay promises more than a traditional auteur analysis of one of Sirk's films. In the *Brighton Film Review* and *Monogram*, Elsaesser wrote traditional auteur analyses of directors such as Vincente Minnelli and Nicholas

Ray. But from "Tales" onwards, his theory, methods, and problems became more general. In "Tales," Elsaesser calls his more general problem "an elusive subject," to be pursued in two directions: a general investigation that transcends a single medium, epoch, and country; and a focused, delimited investigation into one type of film in one country during a specific period of time (the Hollywood family melodrama between 1940 and 1963).

The essay's problematic state of affairs to be analyzed is the "melodramatic imagination" perceived from both a general and specific perspective. Elsaesser describes it as elusive, no doubt due to its abstract, conceptual status, and because it has never been studied in any depth before in film studies. What more can be said about the relation between style and theme, or how the characters' interior states of mind are expressed in film style? Elsaesser's primary innovation is to graft the concept of the melodramatic imagination onto this traditional issue in film studies. Rather than abandon the study of style and theme in film, Elsaesser digs deeper: he begins by drawing parallels between the film melodrama and the history of the European novel and drama, in which individual heroes internalize class conflicts and turn them into personal struggles. He also speculates on the influence of Freudian psychoanalysis on the Hollywood film melodrama, although he draws back from proclaiming any direct influence (59).

As we shall see in the next section, Elsaesser's primary source of data derives from canonical literary and dramatic texts from Europe, and half a dozen melodramas from Hollywood. There is a clear bifurcation of the essay's direction (signified in the title's Shakespearean overtones and the first paragraph's quotation of Sirk): historical European high culture vs. contemporary American mass culture. Justifying their juxtaposition is going to be a fundamental rhetorical strategy of "Tales."

b. Describing the Problematic State of Affairs

Elsaesser's general concern is to investigate the genealogy of the "melodramatic imagination" in the novel (especially the eighteenth century sentimental novel), various forms of drama (especially the romantic drama), the ballad, street songs, and the opera in England, France, Germany, and Italy between the late medieval period and the early twentieth century (44-45). Elsaesser argues that the message to be found, in particular, in the eighteenth-century sentimental novel and the romantic drama is that "they record the struggle of a morally and emotionally emancipated bourgeois consciousness against the remnants of feudalism" (45). Moreover, this struggle is represented, not through a general class conflict, but through individual heroes who interiorize the conflict and turn it into a personal struggle. This creates a radical ambiguity in the melodrama between its functioning either as subversive social and political commentary, or as mere escapism (47). But however it functioned, melodrama "served as the literary equivalent of a particular, historically and socially conditioned *mode of experience*" (49).

Elsaesser's specific concern is to identify "some structural and stylistic constants in one medium during one particular period (the Hollywood family melodrama between roughly 1940 and 1963)" (43). These constants serve as the organizing principles behind the data, the underlying traits that confer unity on a series of films within a delimited space and time. This is a question of genre, indicating that Elsaesser is transcending the boundaries of auteur criticism by combining it with its complement, genre criticism. Whereas auteurism privileges what is specific, unique, unusual, inventive, exceptional and challenging in a film or small group of films, genre criticism privileges what is general, standard, ordinary, typical, familiar, conventional, average and accepted in a film or group of films.

One central dimension of film genre criticism deals specifically with the collecting of data to be classified, correlated, ordered, and measured, and then systematized into a genre or universe of genres, without distorting the data. Elsaesser classifies, correlates, and orders what he considers to be the dominant structural and stylistic constants of family melodramas made between 1940 and 1963:

- The characters' central dramatic conflicts – or inexpressible internal contradictions – are not externalized as action (as in the Western and *film noir*), but remain internalized, unreconciled, and sublimated "into décor, color, gesture and composition of frame, which in the best melodramas is perfectly thematized in terms of the characters' emotional and psychological predicaments" (52).
- This perpetual internalization of inexpressible contradictions leads to "a conscious use of style as meaning" (54).
- The perpetual internalization of inexpressible contradictions also leads to masochistic tendencies of self-pity and self-hatred in the characters, usually in the form of alcoholism (65).
- The family melodrama "records the failure of the protagonist to act in a way that could shape the events and influence the emotional environment ...: they emerge as lesser human beings for having become wise and acquiescent to the ways of the world" (55).
- The melodramas of Ray, Sirk, and Minnelli deal with "an intensified symbolism of everyday actions, the heightening of the ordinary gesture and a use of setting and décor so as to reflect the characters' fetishist fixations" (56).
- The plots of melodramas have a distinct rhythm: "A typical situation in American melodramas has the plot build up to an evidently catastrophic collision of

counter-running sentiments, but a string of delays gets the greatest possible effect from the clash when it does come" (60).

- The plot can either be "objective" (with no central hero, but an ensemble of characters) or "subjective" (it emanates from a single consciousness) (63).
- Family melodramas "concentrate on the point of view of the victim" (64).
- "In Minnelli, Sirk, Ray, Cukor and others, alienation is recognized as a basic condition, fate is secularized into the prison of social conformity and psychological neurosis, and the linear trajectory of self-fulfillment so potent in American ideology is twisted into the downward spiral of a self-destructive urge seemingly possessing a whole social class" (64-65).
- Family melodramas have exaggerated, compressed narratives (see below, under "phenomenological concepts").
- Family melodramas manifest irony or pathos: "Irony privileges the spectator vis-à-vis the protagonists" (in other words, irony is created by means of omniscient narration); "Pathos results from non-communication or silence made eloquent ... where highly emotional situations are underplayed to present an ironic discontinuity of feeling or a qualitative difference in intensity, usually visualized in terms of spatial distance and separation" (66).

Elsaesser concludes that characters in Hollywood family melodramas experience the impossible contradictions of the American dream, with the result that these films "record some of the agonies that have accompanied the demise of the 'affirmative culture'" (68).

Elsaesser examines the Hollywood family melodrama both synchronically and diachronically. Synchronically, he constructs a system of structural and stylistic constants that define the genre of the Hollywood family melodrama (although it is unclear whether Elsaesser thinks all of these properties are necessary to define this genre) from the inductive observation of half a dozen films. Diachronically, he constructs a historical argument suggesting that many of these structural and stylistic constants can be traced back to eighteenth-century European melodrama. This historical dimension of his argument offers a plausible explanation for the occurrence of these constants, the historical conditions of their possibility. Elsaesser establishes a causal link between eighteenth-century European melodrama and the Hollywood melodrama, implying that both manifest the melodramatic imagination. He also identifies the agents who establish this causality – script-writers and directors: "any discussion of the melodrama as a specific cinematic mode of expression has to start from its antecedents – the novel and certain types of 'entertainment' drama – from which script-writers and directors have borrowed their models" (43). In addition, he argues that the predominance of Freudian psychoanalysis in post-World War II American culture also influenced the form and themes of the Hollywood family melodrama (58-60; discussed below).

c. Constructing Problems

In constructing problems, which involves solving the problematic state of affairs, Elsaesser briefly comments on the phenomenological dimension of film, and uses a number of filmic concepts, that is, general background assumptions concerning the nature of individual films (especially melodramas, of course). He uses very few cinematic concepts (background assumptions about the nature of film itself), but makes a number of meta-theoretical comments concerning the aims and nature of theoretical inquiry.

In terms of phenomenological concepts, Elsaesser mentions the "raw" experience of the melodramatic film: "when in ordinary language we call something melodramatic, what we often mean is an exaggerated rise-and-fall pattern in human actions and emotional responses, a from-the-sublime-to-the-ridiculous movement, a foreshortening of lived time in favor of intensity – all of which produces a graph of much greater fluctuation, a quicker swing from one extreme to the other than is considered natural, realistic or in conformity with literary standards of verisimilitude" (52). Elsaesser aims to go beyond this experience and explain its occurrence by identifying melodrama's constants, and by arguing that film creates a specific melodramatic experience, because of its compression of long novels into standard feature-length films (especially in the films of Minnelli and Sirk).

In terms of filmic concepts, Elsaesser formulates a number of propositions concerning the nature of silent and sound films (50-52) before examining the nature of the Hollywood family melodrama (listed under (b) above).

In terms of meta-theoretical concepts, we have already discovered under (a) "Analyzing the problematic state of affairs," that Elsaesser pursues his problem – the "elusive subject" of the melodramatic imagination – in two directions: a general investigation and a focused, delimited investigation. He immediately adds a few other meta-theoretical comments: his study is not historical in any strict sense of the term, nor is it exhaustive in its breadth due to the unavailability of the films (back in the pre-video and pre-DVD days of film studies). He therefore delimits his research, by indicating that he will develop a general theoretical argument on the basis of the close viewing of half a dozen films, but especially WRITTEN ON THE WIND. His own understanding of these delimitations is twofold: "it is difficult to see how references to twenty more movies would make the argument any truer. For better or worse, what I want to say should at this stage be taken to be provocative rather than proven" (43). He implies that his argument is driven by the data, and that the data at this stage are sufficient for supporting the truth conditions of his theoretical propositions. But, at the same time, he acknowledges that his theoretical hypotheses (like all hypotheses) are defeasible in nature and alterable upon the discovery of additional data (the viewing of additional films).

The inductive nature of Elsaesser's argument is most clearly expressed in the tentative way he states his hypotheses and conclusions – which, in all inductive arguments, are not logically entailed in the propositions of the argument, but are always open to revision. Elsaesser's tentative stance is expressed in his use of hedges (adverbs and auxiliary verbs that modify the knowledge claims stated in the propositions of the argument). On one single page we find the following hedges (in italics):

> Even if the form *might* act to reinforce attitudes of submission, the actual working-out of the scenes *could* nonetheless present fundamental social evils.

> All of this is to say that there *seems* a radical ambiguity attached to the melodrama.

> [M]elodrama *would appear* to function either subversively or as escapism.

> The persistence of melodrama *might* indicate ... (47).

In sum, the propositions and conclusions of an inductive argument are not meant to be universally true. Instead, they are probable and acceptable according to whether they explain the evidence, and whether they constitute solutions to the problems.

Although based on inductive observation and historical analysis, the essay is also informed by Freudian psychoanalysis. "Tales" is important because of its innovative use, in 1972 (three years before Laura Mulvey's seminal "Visual Pleasure and Narrative Cinema"), of Freudian psychoanalysis to analyze the textual structure and underlying themes of a film genre. But Freud is used in the essay not only as a source to analyze textual structure and deep thematic meanings. He is also cited as a possible cause (along with eighteenth-century European melodrama) of the formation of the Hollywood family melodrama: "More challenging, and difficult to prove, is the speculation that certain stylistic and structural features of the sophisticated melodrama may involve principles of symbolization and coding which Freud conceptualized in his analysis of dreams..." (59). These principles of symbolization include Oedipal narrative conflicts plus the figures of condensation and displacement. Elsaesser uses Freud in an attempt to explain why and how inexpressible internal contradictions become sublimated into setting and décor:

Melodramas often use middle-class American society, its iconography and the family experience ... as their manifest "material," but "displace" it into quite different patterns, juxtaposing stereotyped situations in strange configurations, provoking clashes and ruptures which not only open up new associations but also redistribute the emotional energies which suspense and tensions have accumulated in disturbingly different directions. (59-60)

d. Evaluating Problems with Regard to Being Well-formed and Significance

"Tales" demonstrates that Hollywood family melodramas certainly do not signify nothing, nor do they consist of tales told by an idiot. Elsaesser successfully established melodrama as a significant object of study in film studies, via a dual historical and theoretical analysis. It is via the lenses of history and theory that Elsaesser formulated a well-formed problem: How and why the melodramatic imagination occurs in the structure and style of a specific Hollywood genre, and how and why its *mise en scène* manifests a character's inexpressible internal contradictions. Elsaesser also helped legitimize Freudian psychoanalysis as a theory and method of analysis, mainly by demonstrating that it can account for the unusual textual structure of the Hollywood family melodrama, and generate knowledge on a deeper level than thematic criticism and thus solve problematic states of affairs. Besides formulating a well-formed problem, Elsaesser also formulated a *significant* problem, one that influenced an entire generation of film scholars, ensuring that "Tales" would emerge as a classic reference point for all subsequent studies of film melodrama.

Notes

1. Thomas Elsaesser, "Tales of Sound and Fury: [Observations on] The Family Melodrama," *Monogram* 4 (1972): 2-15. For ease of reference, I shall quote from the version of the essay published in *Home is Where the Heart is: Studies in Melodrama and the Woman's Film*, ed. Christine Gledhill (London: BFI, 1987) 43-69. All references will be cited in the text in parentheses ( ).
2. Robin Wood, *Hitchcock's Films* (London: Zwemmer, 1965) 122.
3. Rudolf Botha, *The Conduct of Linguistic Inquiry: A Systematic Introduction to the Methodology of Generative Grammar* (The Hague: Mouton, 1981).
4. Larry Laudan, *Progress and its Problems: Towards a Theory of Scientific Growth* (Berkeley: University of California Press, 1977).
5. Warren Buckland, "Film Semiotics," *A Companion to Film Theory*, ed. Toby Miller and Robert Stam (Oxford: Blackwell, 1999) 84-104; "The Last Word on Filmic Enuncia-

tion?," *Semiotica* 135.1-4 (2001): 211-26; "A Rational Reconstruction of the 'Cinema of Attractions'," *The Cinema of Attractions Reloaded*, ed. Wanda Strauven (Amsterdam: Amsterdam University Press, 2006) 41-55.

6.   Botha 54.
7.   Botha 66.
8.   Botha 85.

Of Surfaces and Depths

The Afterlives of "Tales of Sound and Fury"

Sudeep Dasgupta and Wim Staat

Introduction

In the previous chapter, Warren Buckland pointed out that Elsaesser's "Tales of Sound and Fury" has become a key text for film scholars who resist the idea that Hollywood melodramas are superficial and not worthy of any in-depth analysis of style and meaning. "Tales of Sound and Fury" has become, in Buckland's words "a classic reference point." The present chapter attempts to prove Buckland right in two ways: in the context of contemporary cultural studies and in Elsaesser's own recent work.

In the first part of this chapter, Wim Staat traces two of Elsaesser's more recent conceptual contributions to the study of Hollywood cinema to "Tales of Sound and Fury." He suggests that Elsaesser's background in comparative literature, in "true" comparatist spirit, can be taken as the cue for a reading of "Tales of Sound and Fury" through a text that in its own right and in its own field has also become a classical point of reference, Eric Auerbach's "Odysseus' Scar." This comparison, as exemplified by Pedro Almodóvar's HABLE CON ELLA / TALK TO HER (2002), shows that Elsaesser's stand on post-classical Hollywood, and his lesser-known poetics of Hollywood *Fehlleistungen* (parapraxis), were prepared by "Tales of Sound and Fury."

In the second part of this essay, Sudeep Dasgupta presents a contemporary version of Hollywood melodrama, Todd Haynes' FAR FROM HEAVEN (2002), as a case in point for the relevance of Elsaesser's article. "Tales of Sound and Fury" has been instrumental in the reconsideration of style in women's genres and for resisting a Europe-versus-Hollywood divide in film studies. This reconsideration has emphasized the importance of a formal analysis of a text's aesthetics. The focus on aesthetics, and in particular the place of formal elements in the production of meaning and experience of a text, is significant given that the problematic turn to audience studies and sociological categories within Media Studies was at the expense of textual analysis.

1. Parapraxis and Parataxis Signifying Nothing

Throughout his career, that began in the late 1960s with a piece on Vincente Minnelli to a very recent article on FORREST GUMP (Robert Zemeckis, 1994), Thomas Elsaesser has taken mainstream films seriously. With a PhD in Comparative Literature (1971) it is not surprising that Elsaesser refers less to sociology or economics than to traditions of literary criticism and art history. Given the relatively short history of film studies, it is also not surprising that film scholars are recruited from elsewhere, from fields like comparative literature, for example, which in part explains the strong foothold that film studies has in the humanities. In Elsaesser's list of publications, however, there is no indication of a trajectory away from comparative literature towards film studies. From his earliest publications on, it appears that he has not written anything that is now considered outside – what has become, partially through Elsaesser's publications – the field of film studies. On the other hand, as much as all of his publications have always belonged to film studies, his comparative literature background has never been explicitly abandoned. In fact, it continues to reveal itself, and not just paradigmatically in general attitudes towards the function of academic criticism, but sometimes also unexpectedly, for example, in his claim that Forrest Gump should not be considered some average white boy, but rather an African-American, who has remained the unacknowledged protagonist in American history. Elsaesser grounds his argument for what is accomplished by Gump's failed recognition, his *Fehlleistung* ("parapraxis" in English), in the fact that we as viewers begin to acknowledge what has been left out in American history, in the clues the film itself gives for Gump's blackness.[1] He points out – and this is where his comparative literature background comes to the fore – that Forrest Gump is preceded in American literature by the controversy concerning the voice of Mark Twain's *Huckleberry Finn*, and by William Faulkner's *Absalom Absalom!*, books that have made their readers identify – often without their knowledge – with a black protagonist.

The first part of Elsaesser's best-known article, "Tales of Sound and Fury: Observations on the Family Melodrama" (1972), is yet another token of comparative literature scholarship. These pages place Hollywood melodrama in European melodramatic traditions reaching back to at least eighteenth-century pre-Revolutionary French novels and nineteenth-century French and English fictional accounts of the modern experiences of industrialization and political upheaval. Moreover, as the comparative literature plot thickens, the article's title is yet another invocation of Faulkner, whose novel *The Sound and the Fury* (1929), in its turn, referred to *Macbeth*'s Tomorrow soliloquy: "Life's but a walking shadow, a poor player / That struts and frets his hour upon the stage / And then is heard no more. It is a tale / Told by an idiot, full of sound and fury / signifying nothing" (Act V, scene v). It makes one wonder what insight the idiot's achievement through failed signification might bring, or has already brought to the field of film studies. For Elsaesser in 1972, obviously it is not Forrest Gump who is telling these tales, it probably is the cinema as such. Paradoxically, while cinema appears to be "signifying nothing," one can still write about its achievement.

Paratactic and Syntactic Styles in Comparative Literature

Within the field of comparative literature, there is a canonical text that resembles "Tales of Sound and Fury" in a number of ways. It has also been much anthologized, has also been paradigmatic in a young field, more specifically, in the English-speaking comparative literature departments, also values style above authorial intention, and also deals with the contradictions inherent in "lowly" popular texts filled with over-determined fragments, full of sound and fury, signifying nothing. This text is "Odysseus' Scar," which forms the opening chapter of Erich Auerbach's *Mimesis: The Representation of Reality in Western Literature*, and sheds an interesting light on Elsaesser's article, precisely because of how it takes the tales of real but shadowed and poor players seriously, giving us, in hindsight, an intriguing clue to what Elsaesser was after.

"Odysseus' Scar" establishes a dichotomy of styles via the close reading of two exemplary texts: Odysseus' homecoming in Homer's *Odyssey* and the story of Abraham in the *Old Testament*. Homeric narrative style, Auerbach claims, does not differentiate between foreground and background. Nothing remains hidden, every element of the story is present in the plot: "Homeric style knows only a foreground, only a uniformly illuminated, uniformly objective present."[2] There are neither shadows in the background nor personal perspectives in Homer's work, through which recounted episodes from the past give depth to the present. For example, it is Odysseus' scar that enables his housekeeper to recognize her master beneath his disguise. However, as soon as the scar is mentioned in the text, a long digression follows involving how he received this scar. Auerbach points out that it would have been easy to present this digression in the form of a personal recollection by Odysseus, so that the story of the boar that caused the scar could be easily integrated into the scene of recognition. However, Auerbach claims, "any such subjectivistic-perspectivistic procedure is entirely foreign to Homeric style" (7). Homeric episodes are always presented in their own fixed time and space, there's no need for any interpretive activity that would put the different episodes into an integrated perspective.

The story of Abraham, on the other hand, does require some interpretative activity: "the decisive points of the narrative alone are emphasized ... time and place are undefined and call for interpretation" (11). The *Bible* is "fraught with background" (12), and it is up to us to relate the experiences of our own lives to what remains unexpressed in the text. Whereas Homer seeks "merely to make us forget our own reality for a few hours" (15), the *Bible* asks us to relate to the suggestion of the "heavy silence" (11) that arises between the father and the son, after the father has been ordered to take his son's life. In later chapters, Auerbach characterizes the style that only recognizes the present, as "paratactic," which is already circumscribed in "Odysseus' Scar" as follows: "a continuous rhythmic procession of phenomena pass by, and never is there a form left fragmentary or half-illuminated, never a lacuna, never a gap, never a glimpse of unplumbed depths" (6-7). By contrast, a style that does differentiate between foreground and background, the style of the functional hierarchy of surface structures and "the depths of the picture", is called "syntactic" (9). It is the style of the organization of the *Old Testament*'s concealed meanings.

These two styles are the "basic types" detailed in *Mimesis* (23). With its depictions of life as "enacted only among the ruling class" (21), Homeric style belongs to antique literature, along with the classical tragedies. The subject matter of Homeric poetry clearly conforms to the prescriptions of a classical elevated style. Even if Odysseus is presented as a beggar in order to prevent his being recognized upon his return, Auerbach insists that, "the poor beggar Odysseus is only masquerading" (18). In clear contrast, the *Bible*'s protagonists are not noblemen in disguise; indeed, "Adam is really cast down, Jacob really a refugee, Joseph really in the pit and then a slave to be sold" (18). It would seem then that Homeric parataxis is the embodiment of classical elevated style and Biblical syntaxis as the epitome of "low" style. However, for Auerbach, the Homeric and Biblical styles are not as divergent as "the rule of the separation of styles" (22) seems to suggest. Indeed, Homer's poetry, with its "leisurely descriptions of everyday happenings" conflicts with the rules of the elevated style to which classical tragedy belongs. And "the two realms of the sublime and the everyday are not only actually unseparated but basically inseparable" in the *Bible* (22-23). Neither Homer nor the *Bible* follow the rule of the separation of styles according to which the realism of daily life characterizes comedy, and heroic elevation characterizes tragedy.[3] What remains distinct, however, despite Auerbach's undoings of his earlier distinctions, is that Homeric parataxis, with all of its events located in the foreground, still appears to be "displaying unmistakable meanings" and that Biblical syntaxis with its unexpressed suggestions can still be characterized by its "need for interpretation" (23).

Freud in the American Home

Elsaesser claims that the post-World War II Hollywood family melodrama is un-mistakably marked by "the fact that in those years America discovered Freud."[4] In the section "Where Freud left his Marx in the American home," Elsaesser analyzes the implications of Freud's popularization. On the one hand, many symptoms or marks appear to require an interpretation that assembles them into the integrated perspective of, for example, the diagnosis of hysteria. The aes-thetics of manifest excess exhibited in symbolically charged props, color-coded studio light plans and costumes, and melodically enhanced exhibitions of affects could then be interpreted as a syntactically organized arrangement of latent con-tent. However, on the other hand, these latent meanings are certainly not unmis-takable, nor are they on display. These are not the marks that Freud left behind in the American home. What does appear to be on display in WRITTEN ON THE WIND (Douglas Sirk, 1956) is Kyle Hadley (Robert Stack) "making unmistakable gestures with an empty Martini bottle in the direction of his wife."[5] What is un-mistakable, Elsaesser suggests, is that the film knows that its 1950s audience, nursed on Freud, takes pleasure in recognizing "an unconsummated relationship ... when two brimful glasses remain untouched on the table."[6] These objects of excess do not signify anything hidden; there is simply nothing being unveiled. The images of excess and their over-determination do not require the interpreta-tion of symptoms in order to diagnose Kyle's sterility as representing the moral bankruptcy of the Hadley dynasty or, by extension, American society at large. First and foremost, excess and over-determination are not signs of latent subver-sion on the part of Sirk or even the melodramatic genre as a whole. What is excessive, first of all, is that the images are, as Laura Mulvey has pointed out, "extraneous to the story."[7] After Kyle is diagnosed with "a correctable weakness" – "believe me, you're not sterile... and there is hope, real hope" – his staggering walk from the drugstore is delayed by the images of a small boy riding a rocking horse in front of the store. Mulvey claims that "the over-determined nature of the image, the vulgar Freudianism [will] register with the audience, which then re-acts with self-conscious laughter and the amusement of 'I See!'"[8] The audience is in on the joke.

Elsaesser, in 2002, reminded us that films with an Oedipal trajectory, inter-pretable, to be sure, by critics and academics, often also carry their Freud on their sleeves. This occurs "when our own theory or methodology suddenly turns up in the film itself, looking us in the face."[9] Elsaesser's prime example here is DIE HARD (John McTiernan, 1988) in which the protagonist John McClane's (Bruce Willis) "vulnerability is graphically shown," unlike classical cinema in which male "Oedipal wounds have remained symbolic, the bodily envelope largely unaffected."[10] McClane's bleeding bare feet are in plain sight; "how can one not think of the name of the mythic hero, and the impediment to which he owed his name: Oedipus, the club footed."[11] DIE HARD is, therefore, considered paradigmatically post-classical, not because it replaces classical cinema (usually chronologically confined to 1917-1960) but rather because it adds to it a "knowingness about itself as self-display."[12] Of course, presenting DIE HARD as a paradigm of post-classical film in Studying Contemporary American Film is a provocation in the context of the prevailing derision of DIE HARD as a mere spectacle. Even more provocative in its anachronism, however, is the notion that Elsaesser is rekindling an argument he developed some thirty years earlier. In retrospect, we should say that the Hollywood family melodrama has always been post-classical.[13]

Depths of the Surface

Thus, we should be more precise about these tales of sound and fury. The Hollywood family melodrama is not so much signifying nothing at all; rather, it is always *also* signifying nothing. To wit, the irresistible interpretation of symptoms into an integrative whole, syntactically belongs to the melodramatic style. Syntactical style, however, does not exclude parataxis: the unmistakable gestures on display always paradoxically signify nothing but uncompromised presences as well. The digression of the images of Kyle Hadley observing a boy on a rocking horse, can surely be explained away by means of an integrative interpretation. Kyle's troubled look accompanied by ominous music as he observes the boy, then, would signify doubts about Kyle's fatherhood which will be confirmed later on in the film. But as Auerbach points out, "the first thought" of the exclusively classical viewer "that this [digression] is a device to increase suspense, is, if not wholly wrong, at least not the essential explanation of this Homeric procedure" (4). Indeed, "the digressions are not meant to keep the reader [viewer] in suspense, but rather to relax the tension" (4), that is, if the viewer is in on the paratactical joke. In other words, the pathos of Kyle Hadley's predicament, his "silence made eloquent," as Elsaesser characterizes it,[14] does request audience participation, but not the kind that is produced by suspense, i.e., the urge to warn the hero of the dangers we are already aware of. Instead, we are asked for an emotional involvement that cannot be anything but ironic vis-à-vis the character's anxiety. Thus we laugh to relax the tension.

Elsaesser's point in describing the melodrama as leaving behind Marx while introducing Freud into the American home seems to be that the theories of class struggle fraying ways of interpretation for Hollywood melodrama are succeeded by Oedipal trajectories. But it is not that the melodrama can no longer be interpreted along the lines of broader social conflicts, although the melodrama does indeed seem to demand less Marxian and more Freudian interpretations. Instead, what Elsaesser appears to pursue is the idea that, on the surface level of the Hollywood melodrama, Freud was already there, and that the intellectual efforts of recognizing the relevance of Freud – or Marx for that matter – are not the critical achievement of academic interpretation. Elsaesser does not so much resist certain interpretive frameworks; in fact, "Tales of Sound and Fury" actually demonstrates their relevance. Instead, Elsaesser was already resisting in 1972 what thirty years later he would describe as "the prevailing notion that attention to surface must mean being intellectually or emotionally 'shallow.'"[15] The corollary to such an investment in the unmistakable gestures on the surface of the film text is a stance in the debate concerning analysis and interpretation in film studies, a discussion of which features prominently in the conclusion of *Studying Contemporary American Film*. Of course, the very fact that post-classical film displays and sometimes even psychoanalytically names its own symptoms "may itself be a form of defence and disavowal,"[16] requiring, as a trumped-up symptom of repressed meanings, yet another round of interpretation. Nevertheless, the digressions in melodrama may also resemble paratactic Homeric poems, which Auerbach claims "conceal nothing ... no teaching and no secret second meaning. Homer can be analyzed ... but he cannot be interpreted" (13). In other words, we should be analyzing these digressions, not interpreting them. Note, however, that Elsaesser's occasional leanings towards the analysis of parataxis in "Tales of Sound and Fury," not unlike Auerbach in "Odysseus' Scar," do not come at the expense of interpretation. There appears to be no "either ... or."

Subversive Escapism

The contemporary melodrama HABLE CON ELLA / TALK TO HER (Pedro Almodóvar, 2002), which is about idly talking (signifying nothing) to comatose patients, is an example of paratactic sound and fury, in this case involving the traditional Spanish love song "Cucurrucucú Paloma" (performed by Caetano Veloso), a song of passion about the reincarnation of a heart-broken lover in the form of a dove. On the one hand, the song is syntactically organized into the film as the recollection of one of the protagonists; on the other hand, all three-and-a-half minutes of the song are found in the film's diegesis, most of it in an actual performance by Veloso. Moreover, its paratactical presence is contrasted with a yet another recollection (a memory within a memory) shown in superimposed, fragmentary images next to the protagonist's face, as illustrations of the verbal rendition of his recollection. The images suggest a screening of the past within the protagonist's mind, a clear example of images being syntactically integrated into a personal perspective. The song, by comparison, is not a sideshow slideshow; it is not in the background, and it literally appears in the same light as the protagonist's actions. The song, or better yet, Veloso's singing, in all of its abundance, is clearly there for us to enjoy. What is "excessive" here – and in this scene it is the equivalent of the pop Freudian symbols found in the Hollywood melodramas of the 1950s – is the filmmaker's campy indulgence of the knowing audience with the "truth" of tear-jerking songs. It is tempting to interpret the memories this song conjures up as being induced by the protagonist's relation to the lyrics, as they are about the possibility of souls reaching out over the boundaries of death, affirming the advice to always "talk to her."

But, in a way, the song is more immediately unmistakable than that, as it also signifies nothing, because it is a digression that slows down the unfolding of the story without creating suspense. It will, however, in Auerbach's words, "court our favor" (15). But then again, is that all it achieves? Is this forgetting of our own reality, this bewitching of the senses (14), all that this concrete example of not-signifying-by-way-of-excess creates? Is forgetting its *Fehlleistung*? For if that was the extent of it, then cinematic melodramas would more resemble the melodramas of the French Restoration "providing escapist entertainment with little social relevance."[17]

What *is* the parapraxis of melodramatic parataxis? The answer to this question may help us to understand what is characteristic about "the persistence of the melodrama," namely the way in which melodrama "has ... taken note of social crises" and displayed "a healthy distrust of intellectualization and abstract social theory."[18] For, if we qualify this distrust of intellectualization and theory as subversive, not so much with respect to societal demands for conformity, but rather vis-à-vis interpretations, be they of Marxist, Freudian, or cultural studies signature, then there will be no more contradiction concerning the significance of melodrama. Although we may have first thought that melodrama functioned "either subversively or as escapism,"[19] we will now see that melodramatic cinema can be both subversive and escapist at the same time. We will be able to recognize it as such, when we take note of Elsaesser's seemingly self-evident description of melodrama "as a particular form of dramatic *mise en scène*, characterized by a dynamic use of spatial and musical categories, as opposed to intellectual or literary ones."[20] When Lucy (Lauren Bacall) "in an oleander-green dress is just about to disappear behind the curtains" in WRITTEN ON THE WIND, just after a funerary black silk ribbon has blown across the concrete pavement, Elsaesser points out the "emotional resonance" of *mise en scène* parallels. He calls it a "non-dramatic sequence," a scene with "no plot significance whatsoever,"[21] a scene filled with, what he in later pages would call: eloquent silence, i.e., pathos. The song in TALK TO HER achieves a similar resonance. But the real parapractical significance of these scenes is that we, as academic critics, have come to realize that in our urge to interpret, we are subverted by these abundant presences of para-taxis. We ourselves are implicated by the melodrama. This is the parapraxis of parataxis in cinematic melodrama: we are always already, even if we may think we are just analyzing and not interpreting yet, too late to pick up on what the melodrama has already achieved.

2. Style as Meaning

The previous section emphasizes a certain mode of analysis in Elsaesser's read-ing of melodrama, which has been characterized as "over-signification." Psycho-analysis literally takes place on the surface level of the film, and Elsaesser avoids the stock practice of plumbing the depths of a text, to salvage meaning through interpretation. Instead, for him, meaning appears on the surface, itself a symp-tom of the popularization of Freudian psychoanalysis in the United States. If the abundance of surface meanings and the redundancy of a depth-hermeneutic is one aspect of his influential reading of melodrama, another aspect of his reading of melodrama can be characterized as the instability of meaning, and the ambiva-lence of the signification of melodrama. Meaning cannot be easily read from the text; rather, *style*, another surface phenomenon that "signifies nothing," becomes the condition of possibility for the destabilization of meaning. Elsaesser argues that directors like Vincente Minnelli and Douglas Sirk "encouraged a conscious use of *style as meaning*, which is a mark of what I consider to be the very condi-tion of a modernist sensibility working in popular culture."[22]

Aesthetic Ambiguities

In "Tales of Sound and Fury," popular melodrama and modernist aesthetics are not mutually exclusive. Indeed, if modernism distrusts realism and the surface meanings in film, then Elsaesser's argument that melodrama is *also* modernist points in a different direction. Surface meanings are not necessarily fixed; in-stead, Elsaesser's emphasis on the materiality of signification in film, from the use of sound and color to *mise-en-scène*, highlights the disruption of any easy reading off the surface of the visual. As he puts it, in describing one such aes-thetic strategy "[T]he *feeling that there is always more to tell than can be said* leads to very consciously elliptical narratives proceeding often by visually condensing the character's motivation into sequences of images which do not seem to advance the plot."[23] By drawing attention to the stylistic rendering of a narrative, he opens up the door to the importance of analyzing the particular formal qualities of the film text, the construction and deployment of images, and the innovative use of sound, that makes the drama *melo*drama. *Melos* as the musical accompaniment to dramatic progression indicates the role of the material (formal) supports of film language that are placed into a relation with the production of meaning through sound and image. He thus argues that "this type of cinema depends *on the way* 'melos' is *given* to drama by means of lighting, montage, visual rhythm, decor, style of acting, music."[24] One would expect that "melos" serves as the faithful handmaiden to drama, such that material elements function to unambiguously signify meaning to the audience. That is, a representationalist logic of realism would determine the way "melos" gives itself to drama (the coincidence of stylistic and thematic content).

What is innovative in Elsaesser's argument is his identifying a modernist sensibility in the use of style, in relation to meaning. That is, "melos" gives itself to drama as enigma, and as an ambiguity where the "what" of the content cannot be easily related to the "how" – that is, the aesthetic mode of the film has a destabilizing agency of its own that clouds the desire to explain away the language of film itself. The ambiguity triggered in the reading of a melodramatic text through stylistic features such as music, and color, produces a perplexed response – "the feeling that there is always more to tell than can be said,"[25] or what Marcia Landy calls the "What happened?"[26] question. Style as meaning thus calls attention to the importance of the formal analysis of melodrama in order to address the ambiguities of meaning. Style as meaning is the *indetermination* of meaning.

In her analysis of Todd Haynes' films, Marcia Landy draws attention to precisely this indetermination of meaning produced by a thwarted and inscrutable relationship between signifier and signified. Unlike Elizabeth Anker's understanding of melodrama as a genre "which employs emotionality to provide an unambiguous distinction between good and evil,"[27] it is precisely the ambiguity of film in its formal qualities that leads Landy to argue that Haynes' films "destabilize normative responses to the world that conventional forms of cinematic representation produce."[28] Even the representation of emotion must pass through an aesthetic that invites speculation rather than clear meaning – as Haynes puts it, "You laugh, but you're not really interested in the story or the ideas or the emotions. It's not helping you identify with the film; in fact, it's keeping you outside of it in ways that provoke ... thought."[29] This sense of alienation and distance from the text as a result of the anti-realist filmic style is seen in its most pronounced fashion in FAR FROM HEAVEN (2002), Haynes' homage to Sirk's ALL THAT HEAVEN ALLOWS (1955). In Haynes' film, what Elsaesser identified as the oddness of the aesthetic, the insistent drawing of the spectator's attention to the artificiality of the filmed situation, the stilted gestures, the use of color, exemplifies his argument about style as meaning. To simply fix the meaning of Haynes' film as a melodrama about the emptiness of marriage (Cathy and Frank), homosexuality (Frank), alcoholism (Frank), and inter-racial desire (Cathy and Raymond) is to ignore the mode in which these issues are represented. The style of the film accompanies, actually *produces* the thematic content, triggering a "why?" response in the spectator. This interrogative position for the spectator is produced by the enigmatic quality of the style and was one mode through which modernism aimed to broaden the political question of social critique.

The cold reflective surfaces of the suburban home, the brilliant shine of Cathy's dresses, the agonizingly slow movement of the camera, and most obviously, the use of artificially brilliant color focus our attention onto the film as a destabilizing and necessary medium through which one must pass before ascribing meaning. The theatricality of the characters' behavior heightens the artifice of the film, and its insistence on drawing our attention to itself as film does little in Elsaesser's terms "to advance the plot." "Style" here needs to be seen as the mode through which the concrete practices of filmmaking underline their presence to destabilize a realist visual epistemology. This focus on style in film studies, which Elsaesser called attention to in melodrama, had the merit of drawing attention to the specificity of the film medium itself, the work it does, and does to us as spectators which, as I shall argue later, was almost lost when film began being characterized in terms of social categories such as "women's genres." By focusing on style and its relation to meaning production, I argue that a clearly political mode of analysis was being offered, which was later diluted when film *as a specific mode of presentation* was sacrificed to another kind of politics based on social categories (identity politics) and reception studies. Landy, in referring to another of Haynes' films, VELVET GOLDMINE (1998), argues that the film is not "about identity politics ... the production of 'positive' images of homosexuality."[30] She goes on to point out that "it is an exploration of vision and the incommensurability of the visible and the expressible so critical to understanding the destabilizing nature of media."[31] Landy brings up two issues which I consider crucial to the value of Elsaesser's reading of style in melodrama as meaning. Firstly, she underlines the specificity of film as a medium and its potential to destabilize meaning and provoke thought. This argument, where the experience of an artwork is a cognitive experience of the uncertainties of knowledge was underlined by Theodor Adorno and avoided what later were to become the modes of interpretation, where an artwork's form was sacrificed to the straightforward theories of referentiality and eventually to "audience readings."[32] Secondly, Landy extrapolates the question of artifice and the materiality of style in Elsaesser's reading of melodrama, by highlighting how the *medium* of film complicates and questions "identity politics." Films, when understood in terms of formal play and experimentation, are not only about who is represented (women, homosexuals, immigrants, etc.) but also about *how* the medium of cinema and its stylistic strategies complicate the process through which we ascribe meaning – that is, it complicates the fixation of images as being "about" a particular category of person. This second point is crucial, in relation to melodrama, because it impinges on how certain forms of feminist media studies were to develop, a point I will elaborate upon below.

Theoretical Implications

By highlighting the importance of style as a modernist dimension of melodrama, a number of conclusions can be drawn about its importance. Firstly, Elsaesser's argument, which centralizes aesthetics in analyzing the social meaning and political importance of melodrama, reverses and disturbs the *spatialization* of film criticism, which has traditionally produced a bifurcated space of Hollywood "classical narrative," on the one hand, and European "art" cinema and its aesthetic of playfulness, on the other. His argument, which entails a modernist sensibility (read the European avant-garde) *within* popular culture (Hollywood), twisted the doubled-space of Europe/America and their respective aesthetics, and provided a useful corrective to the assignation of national cinemas to specific cultural forms. He argues, in his reading of Minnelli, for example, that the existential theme of a character is explored *filmically* by exploring "the philosophical questions of freedom and determination" (which are central to melodrama) by focusing inventively on "the aesthetic problem of how to depict a character who is not constantly externalizing himself into action, without trapping him in an environment of ready-made symbolism."[33] Thus the "melos" refuses to give the drama a "ready-made symbolism," which in turn, gives the film an enigmatic character by forcing the audience to ask what the relationship is between the Hollywood film's style and its thematic content.

Secondly, the implications of Elsaesser's reading of style reformulates an analysis of excess. Here that excess is identified *stylistically* rather than in terms of "over-emotionality," the traditional understanding of "women's films." The style of melodrama skews any referential theory of representation and meaning, producing ambiguities that exceed our attempt to seek a conventional correlation between signifier and signified. In Terry Eagleton's terms, "meaning has leaked from the signifier."[34] It approached the question of "excess," which has traditionally been connected to over-emotionality, in the formal characteristics of the text itself. That is, rather than identifying the modernist, and therefore politically progressive potential of melodrama with the subjective excess of over-emotionality of the characters portrayed, Elsaesser's argument suggests that it is necessary to analyze the excessive, that is, non-conventional and enigmatic character of the *style of the film itself*. Moreover, the value of this reading of stylistic excess is that although it draws attention to the "materiality of the signifier," thus "in the way that 'melos' gives to drama," it does not turn the social importance of melodrama into a purely formalist aesthetic. In other words, the link between aesthetics and meaning remains a very important question for the political significance of melo-drama. Elsaesser's emphasis on style does not become merely a politics of style, a course arguably pursued most enthusiastically by the *Tel Quel* group. Elsaesser's reading, on the contrary, still keeps the question of meaning, interpretation, and referentiality in play. His argument concerning style simply reorients the rela-tionship – rather than choosing between either the signifier (style), which coin-cides with signified (meaning), or a purely formalist aesthetics of "materialism," he maintains the tension by continuing to investigate the nature of the relation-ship between the formalist play on style and the social intelligibility of the narra-tion. The importance of this relationship between style and meaning is that it combines an interest in the marking of aesthetic modernism, with an expansion of this focus to include a genre of cultural production – the Hollywood melodra-ma – which had until then been excluded from serious considerations.

In addition to the materiality of excess and counter-intuitive disruption of geo-graphical delineations of aesthetics and ideology, Elsaesser's reading also pro-vided some pointers for further research, some of which were picked up, while others were not. A third line of inquiry might investigate how the disciplinary developments in visual cultural analysis explored the growing importance of what came to be called "women's genres." Research in the areas of film studies and cultural studies that focused on such genres as melodrama in film, soap opera on television, "women's" magazines, and the like developed along roughly two lines, which were sometimes related. In cinema studies, melodrama became identified with the analysis of female subjectivity, the role of popular cultural forms in the production of sexist stereotypes, and a critique of patriarchy and *ocular-centrism*. Texts could be clearly identified as patriarchal. Style is generally considered as secondary to the meaning of the text. When the analysis of the representation of women focused on the question of style, the result was that the link between style and meaning was usually either unproblematically perceived, or simply ignored. Maria Laplace, for example, opens her otherwise convincing reading of Now VOYAGER in terms of consumerism and the historically specific discursive construction of femininity by stating that for "feminists interested in how cinema constructs female subjectivity and female desire, it is necessary *to move away from purely formal analysis of the internal workings of a film text* to a more historically specific analysis of the relation of text to content."[35] While she is right to relate the film text to its place in a broader historical discursive forma-tion, this desire to move away from formal analysis runs the risk of leaving the text behind. The necessary critique of patriarchy downplayed the possibility that the communication of sexist ideologies of gender might be jammed by the enigmatic quality of the medium doing the communicating.[36] That is, the question of filmic style was reduced to an argument about conventional forms of signification that produce patriarchal ideologies. The "style as meaning" argument, in other words, dissipated into analyses of subject positioning. Hollywood melodrama was identified as ideological and patriarchal, and this aesthetic of manufactured reality was accepted as more or less successful. The specificity of the working of the text, of style as meaning, and its relation to history, is sacrificed in the process. The increased importance of historical analyses of discourses *outside* the text, while crucial to convincing analyses of the politics of popular culture, led to an almost complete eclipse of formal analyses in other fields.

In cultural studies, for example, the move toward ethnographic critique and the interpretation of audience readings, dissipated the materiality of the text and the ambiguities of signification. One text was replaced by another, so that the object of study became the text produced by the audience. As a reaction to the perceived "high cultural" argument that denied women readers "pleasure" and ascribed all power to the patriarchal discourse of the text, cultural studies became an analysis of demographic categories (young women, subcultures, etc.) and their practices of meaning-production. The legitimate importance that was simultaneously placed on spectatorship came at the expense of any engagement with the specificity of style and the possibility that the text in question might call itself into question, that its meaning was not clear, whatever audiences made of it. Feminism in cultural studies gained on the one hand what it lost through the other. By becoming more narrowly focused on audiences and "resistant readings," a thoroughly legitimate analytic reorientation nevertheless unnecessarily ended up limiting itself. In the process of evaporating the text and the complicated relationship between style and meaning, another mode of orienting the political importance of popular culture was lost. Elsaesser's argument of "style as meaning" began pointing towards the relevance of analyzing the link between aesthetics and politics through the exploration of this modernist sensibility in popular culture, which was later erased in the increasingly polemical debates between "high" and "low" culture.

The relationship between the materiality of style and the meaning of the film text, which Elsaesser highlighted by problematizing the relationship between the two, did find its specific disciplinary articulation within the field of art history. At least one tradition of broadly Marxist art history continued to pay close attention to the specific materiality of the art work, and its relation to historical context and political power.[37] Elsaesser's argument about the enigmatic quality of the "melos" in melodrama, and the fact that in some films, the style often avoids "readymade symbolism" and produces images whose concrete materiality destabilizes an easy ascription of meaning, can also be related to Jacques Rancière's approach to art in

general, and film in particular.[38] In his analyses of films like Eisenstein's STAR-
OYE I NOVOYE / THE GENERAL LINE (1929) and Godard's HISTOIRE(S) DU CINÉMA
/ HISTORY(S) OF THE CINEMA (1998), Jacques Rancière takes the pure materiality
of the film image and the non-signifying concreteness of objects in the frame
seriously, however, like Elsaesser with regard to melodrama, he does not sacrifice
this focus on style to the analysis of meaning. His approach to the aesthetics-
politics question very precisely extends what Elsaesser calls a "modernist sensibility," even though Rancière rejects terms like modernism. Rancière, like Elsaesser, resists the temptation to either erase style through a realist argument, or
focus only on style through a formalist aesthetics. His film analyses focus on the
interplay between (film) language, thought and the world, and thus develop in an
interesting direction similar to what Elsaesser noticed, and complicated, in his
reading of style as meaning in melodrama.

Elsaesser's reading of filmic style in melodrama paved the way for film to be
taken seriously *in its materiality* as form. The value of this reading of form resides
in the way in which it is tied to a historical and social analysis. Elsaesser's focus
on form eschewed the temptation of formalism (Clement Greenberg, for example); rather, it linked a close attention to the specificity of film to broader questions of power, subjectivity, and history. Furthermore, by undercutting the division between classical Hollywood narrative cinema and European modernist
film, Elsaesser's essay pointed forward towards the discussion on the viability of
concepts such as national cinema and national identity. "Tales of Sound and
Fury" is a crucial text in Elsaesser's oeuvre not just for the salience of its argument but for the way it foresaw what were to become important developments in
film studies, for the years to come.

Notes

1.   Elsaesser points out that the presentation of what is lacking, i.e., the scandal of Amer-
     ican history, cannot be fictionalized through what would be a counterbalancing act of
     offering us "the good black American"; the only modus available is the *Fehlleistung*,
     for this is only way that we can come close to historical truth: "denn sie [die Fehlleis-
     tung] allein entspricht den historischen Wahrheit" (Thomas Elsaesser, "Geschichte
     (n) und Gedächtnis: Zur Poetik der Fehlleistungen im Mainstreamkino am Beispiel
     von *Forrest Gump*," *Experiment Mainstream? Differenz und Uniformierung im populären
     Kino*, ed. Irmbert Schenk, Christine Rüffert, Karl-Heinz Schmid, and Alfred Tews
     (Berlin: Bertz + Fischer, 2006): 31-42, 41). In "Tales of Sound and Fury" Elsaesser
     mentions Freudian slips, although he refers to them as *Fehlhandlungen*, a term which
     Freud also used, but which lacks the connotation of accomplishment attributable to
     Leistung. Moreover, Elsaesser does not consider Freudian slips specific enough for
     melodrama, which is why there appears to be no "parapractical poetics" in "Tales of

Sound and Fury" (yet). Thomas Elsaesser, "Tales of Sound and Fury: [Observations on] The Family Melodrama." *Monogram* 4 (1972): 2-15; reprinted in *Home is Where the Heart is: Studies in Melodrama and the Woman's Film*, ed. Christine Gledhill (London: BFI, 1987) 43-69.

2.   Erich Auerbach, *Mimesis: The Representation of Reality in Western Literature*, trans. Willard R. Trask (Princeton: Princeton University Press, 1953) 7. Auerback wrote *Mimesis* in Istanbul between May 1942 and April 1945. The book was first published in Bern, Switzerland, in 1946. Further references to page numbers in text.

3.   A.D. Nuttall claims that the distinction between high and low style in *Mimesis* "has an inner tendency to change back into a material rather than formal antithesis" (A.D. Nuttall, "Auerbach's Mimesis," *Essays in Criticism* 54.1 (2004): 62). Nuttall continues: "Auerbach suggests at times that paratactic sentence structure is naturally low, inherently associated with comedy, while syntactic sentences, logically graduated, are naturally high. But Homer's sentences are often surprisingly paratactic. Yet Auerbach sees Homer as the great example of 'heroic elevation'" (62-63). I think Nuttall is right. He is also correct in suggesting that the distinction between high and low style, in the end, is not about form but about content. That is actually the point Auerbach is trying to make, i.e., that the classical rule of high / low style separation, which has yet to emerge, after Homer and the Bible, is fraught with contradiction. Hence, Nuttall is also right when he answers his own question: "so, is Auerbach wrong about Homer? I think not" (65).

4.   Elsaesser, "Tales of Sound and Fury" 58.

5.   Elsaesser, "Tales of Sound and Fury" 65.

6.   Elsaesser, "Tales of Sound and Fury" 65.

7.   Laura Mulvey, *Death 24x a Second: Stillness and the Moving Image* (London: Reaktion, 2006) 150.

8.   Mulvey 150.

9.   Thomas Elsaesser, "Classical / post-classical narrative (DIE HARD)," chapter 2 of Thomas Elsaesser and Warren Buckland, *Studying Contemporary American Film: A Guide to Movie Analysis* (London: Arnold, 2002) 66.

10. Elsaesser, "Classical / post-classical narrative" 70.

11. Elsaesser, "Classical / post-classical narrative" 74.

12. Elsaesser, "Classical / post-classical narrative" 78.

13. In *Studying Contemporary American Film*, Elsaesser writes: "The problem of the classical / postclassical is ... like a crystal: it occupies several dimensions and can be turned in different directions .... [T]he post-classical, quite correctly still contains the term 'classical,' but ... in relation to the classical it is both 'reflexive' and 'excessive,' and therefore can neither be situated conceptually in a linear, progressive, chronological line, nor pictured as a dialectical or directly antagonist relationship." (289) Classical and post-classical, then, qualify ways of reading rather than the films itself, cf. sub-headings like 2.3 "Classical analysis" (43) and 2.6 "Post-classical analysis" (66).

14. Elsaesser, "Tales of Sound and Fury" 66.

15. Elsaesser, "Classical / post-classical narrative" 74.

16. Elsaesser, *Studying Contemporary American Film* 232.

17. Elsaesser, "Tales of Sound and Fury" 46.

18. Elsaesser, "Tales of Sound and Fury" 47.

19. Elsaesser, "Tales of Sound and Fury" 47.

20. Elsaesser, "Tales of Sound and Fury" 51.

21. Elsaesser, "Tales of Sound and Fury" 53.

22. Elsaesser, "Tales of Sound and Fury" 53; emphasis added.

23. Elsaesser, "Tales of Sound and Fury" 53; emphasis added.

24. Elsaesser, "Tales of Sound and Fury" 55; emphasis added.

25. Elsaesser, "Tales of Sound and Fury" 54.

26. Marcia Landy, "'The Dream of the Gesture': The Body of / in Todd Haynes' Films," *Boundary 2* 30.3 (2003): 124.

27. Elizabeth Anker, "Villains, Victims and Heroes: Melodrama, Media and September 11," *Journal of Communication* 55.1 (2005): 24. It is striking that while Anker's definition of melodrama is derived from Elsaesser's essay, she ignores the ambiguity of style that he finds crucial to the filmic specificity of melodrama.

28. Landy 123.

29. Justin Wyatt, "Cinematic / Sexual: An Interview with Todd Haynes," *Film Quarterly* 46.3 (Spring 1993): 7. Quoted in Landy 124.

30. Landy 127.

31. Landy 127.

32. Theodor Adorno, *Aesthetic Theory* (Minneapolis: University of Minnesota Press, 1996).

33. Elsaesser, "Tales of Sound and Fury" 54.

34. Terry Eagleton, *The Ideology of the Aesthetic* (London: Blackwell, 1990) 334.

35. Maria Laplace, "Producing and Consuming the Woman's Film: Discursive Struggle in *Now, Voyager*," *Home is Where the Heart Is* 138; emphasis added.

36. It is precisely this necessary passage from the destabilizing of meaning through style, *before* the ascription of meaning in terms of "representations of women," that Landy has highlighted, and was developed earlier in this essay.

37. See, for example, T.J. Clark's *Farewell to an Idea: Episodes from a History of Modernism* (New Haven / London: Yale University Press, 2001).

38. See, in relation to film, Jacques Rancière, *Film Fables* (London: Berg, 2006). See also his analyses of films in the collection of essays *Chroniques des temps consensuels* (Paris: Seuil, 2006).

Failed Tragedy and Traumatic Love in Ingmar Bergman's SHAME

Tarja Laine

> Sometimes everything seems just like a dream. It's not my dream, but
> somebody else's that I have to participate in. What happens when the one
> who dreamt us wakes up and feels ashamed?
> – Eva (Liv Ullmann)

Shame is painful. Shame is mortifying. Shame is essential. As I have shown else-where, shame is more than an emotion.[1] Shame is a concept that can be placed in a theoretical framework of interlinked concepts, and, by so doing, shame can reveal the inner consistency, social dynamics, and affective bonds within the work of art and between the work of art and its spectator. However, I seem to keep on returning to shame, or perhaps it is shame that keeps on returning to me. As a devotee of shame, I think that it is important to examine the value and necessity of this emotion and thus, as I was told right after having defended my PhD dissertation, it would be a shame indeed if I was done with shame. One such illustration of "shame as necessity" can be found, for instance, in Gilles Deleuze's ethology, where "you do not know beforehand what good or bad you are capable of; you do not know beforehand what a body or a mind can do, in a given encounter, a given arrangement, a given combination."[2] This "ethological condition" of human experience explains why some people are more vulnerable to shame than others. It could also explain why, in conditions of war, some people lose their humanity and others do not.

An exploration of the disintegration of humanity in war, Ingmar Bergman's 1968 film SKAMMEN / SHAME bespeaks this ethological condition and the failure of action related to it, a situation in which the individual cannot help but continue doing something but in ways that contain the inability or unwillingness to take action. The film is, therefore, best approached as a melodrama of "failed tragedy" that, according to Thomas Elsaesser's definition, confronts its characters with a tragic universe, but ultimately denies them any sense of resolution. As a result, a traumatic mode of spectatorship can be found at the heart of failed tragedy, which is rendered palpable in Bergman's films such as TYSTNADEN / SILENCE (1963), PERSONA (1966), and especially VISKNINGAR OCH ROP / CRIES AND WHIS-PERS (1972), where (like in SHAME, as I shall argue) Bergman makes possible "those imperceptible transitions between past and present, inner and outer space, [traumatic] memory, dream and anticipation which also give contemporary post-classical cinema its intellectual energy and emotional urgency."[3] The emotional urgency of failed tragedy is shame, since shame is the association *par excellence* of a (moral) failure with the self that brings about a traumatic configuration of indicative (what is) and conditional (what could have been) for the person in shame. Shame, therefore, also structures the traumatic mode of spectatorship epitomized in the logic of failed tragedy of SHAME.

It is therefore perhaps surprising, and certainly undeserved, that SHAME is one of the least known films in Bergman's oeuvre, a film defined as a masterly vision of war that has "the inevitability of a common dream."[4] Harshly shot in black-and-white by Sven Nykvist and set in Sweden in the clutches of an imaginary (and apparently meaningless) civil war, SHAME depicts Jan (Max von Sydow) and Eva Rosenberg (Liv Ullmann) living a relatively peaceful existence on an island that has so far been saved from the destruction. Jan and Eva's sense of security ends abruptly when their island is invaded. Unable to control or comprehend the situation, Jan undergoes a transformation from a useless, annoying coward to a brutal killer, but without any purpose other than contempt and aggression toward other war victims, thereby epitomizing the prototype of the traumatized male who communicates his symptoms through violence and rage.[5] As James Maxfield observes, "He has been potent to destroy, not to create ... [his] survival leads only to physical and spiritual death."[6]

The film opens with a black frame over which the title sequence appears, played to the pattering of gunfire, deformed voices, and bursts of distorted radio stations. In the first scenes, the husband and wife go through their morning routines, the noises of which all sound exaggerated. In the distance, church bells clang ominously. The phone (which is supposedly out of order) rings repeatedly like a warning bell of the events yet to come, but there is no one on the other end of the line. In a similar scene, Eve's dialogue with Filip (the fisherman, later the leader of the partisans, and even later the boatman for the refugees) is drowned out by rushing water. Throughout the film, sound resists the attractive valence of the visual, often preceding the image and forcing it to abandon its expected context. As a result, there is no singular, stable, privileged point of audition but a traumatic position of displacement, torture, and conflict; a sound that "does not reassure but perplexes."[7] The sound of approaching troops – roaring planes, machine gun fire, explosions – are displaced sounds, at first only aurally present in the scenes. Violence invades through the order of sound, taking on a centrifugal force of its own, while the spectators are forced to stay with Jan and Eva who are clearly powerless to do anything about their lives falling apart.

This becomes an experience that only the state of trauma can explain, an enduring devastating event that overwhelms the individual and disables him or her from coping emotionally with and acting on the traumatic situation. Jan's shock takes on an especially numbing form and results in a trauma that cannot be overcome, which is "so irretrievable in terms of temporality, event and body"[8] that not only is Jan powerless to act, he does not even have the desire to act despite the disastrous nature of the situation. Both Jan and Eva are depicted as victims, groundlessly accused by both sides in the war of collaborating with the enemy. They are shown in scenes of violence and emotional confrontation over which they have no individual control or agency except the "power" to helplessly give in to them. Sound plays an important role here; it effectively denies Jan and Eva the power to act, and, even more importantly, it relates trauma to shame insofar as shame also represents the failure of self with a sensed inability to take control, leading to a devastating situation of hopelessness in the first place and to abusive violence in the second.

The silence that abruptly follows the first battles fails to bring relief to Jan and Eva, and the spectator. The silence, broken only by the sounds of singing birds, remains disturbing, since it epitomizes both Jan and Eva's powerlessness to deal adequately with the situation, as well as their inability to discuss their emotions. Because they cannot translate their trauma into words, they are "forced to look at each other, and to realize that the only honest feeling they have about their relationship is shame."[9] The close-ups of Eva and Jan's blank faces staring individually, without interaction, into nothingness reveals "the fear of the face confronting its own nothingness,"[10] its own shame. The face is the site of shame, and Bergman's shots of the faces expressing shame mirror Eva and Jan's relationship that is now changed forever. However, the fact that their relationship is recognized as such comes a moment too late and, as a result, is transformed into a traumatic mode of love. Their love is traumatic because it signifies a temporality of regret, which is characterized by bad timing, missed opportunities, or dislikes for personal actions, past and present. The traumatic love that exists between Eva and Jan also connects shame to the notion of failed tragedy in the conditional sense of "if-only," as a tension that highlights the inevitability of their present actions.

The Realm of If-Only

In his book *Melodrama and Trauma*, Elsaesser defines the genre of melodrama in terms of the temporality of regret, as a genre of "if-only" that always contains the seeds of a painful and shameful inner torment. It is this state of "if-only' in

SHAME that links shame to trauma, while Eva and Jan's love becomes a traumatic mode of love inasmuch as it exists only in that shameful realm of "what could have been." It is already evident in the beginning of the film that Jan and Eva can barely tolerate each other, with Eva frequently appearing almost disgusted with Jan. Eva escapes this situation by becoming overtly assertive while Jan daydreams and turns to nostalgia. Jan, upon awakening, recalls a dream: "I dreamt we were back in the orchestra again, rehearsing the 4th *Brandenburg Concerto* – the 4th movement. All that is happening now is behind us. We only remembered it as a nightmare." Before the war, Jan and Eva both played violin in the national philharmonic orchestra, which serves as a symbol for the "if-only" realm throughout the film. Later in the film, Jan discusses Pampini (the maker of his violin) with Eva, and as he takes up the bow to play it, he suddenly stops because it sounds too awful: "My hand is completely ruined," he says.

The violin, like a number of other antique articles, serves as the witness of the realm of "if-only" in the past, reminding Jan and Eva of the love that could-have-been theirs in the future. The montage sequence of Jan and Eva's visit to Fredrik Lobelius's shop includes close-ups of antique objects which are further emphasized with the nostalgic sounds of an 18th-century Meissen musical box. This is followed by a reaction shot of the apparently sentimental Jan and Eva escaping into that realm of "if-only." However, it is not only the past, but also the future and even the present that represent various "if-only" realms in the film. Eva's first encounter with Filip by the stream, for instance, evokes the mode of "if-only" in the present because it is concealed from both the spectator and from Jan at the aural level. Like Jan, we do not know the precise nature of Filip and Eva's relationship. Suddenly we see Eva happy, smiling, beautiful, but the sound of rushing water is all we hear. In this scene, Eva is depicted in another, unattainable realm beyond Jan's reach, and, paradoxically, it is this unattainable state that makes Jan, in his own words, feel that he is really in love with Eva again.

The future "if-only" manifests itself in the impossible or insignificant plans – under the existing conditions – that Jan and Eva have: that of learning Italian and rehearsing their music. While eating lunch and drinking Fredrik's wine (a rare luxury), Eva brings up the topic of children as a possible remedy for their failing marriage, after which Jan and Eva end up making love. This is the last serene moment in the film. The harmony ends abruptly with the sound of booming guns and roaring fighter planes spewing fire and annihilation, permanently destroying their plans, hopes, and longings. "It is good that we do not have children," says Eva unhappily afterwards, "We will never have children." The time for self-deception is over. The encroaching evidence of war forces Jan and Eva to finally take stock of their situation and realize that their life together as they once knew it has been nothing but a delusion – and a shameful one at that. Later on in

the film, as they are waiting to be interrogated by some soldiers who have suspected them of treason, Eva asks: "What happens when the one who dreamt us
wakes up and feels ashamed?"

Why shame? Why this emotion and not some other one like grief (over the loss
of love) or anger (about their lack of control over the situation) or guilt (about
being a war survivor)? I think that the answer is best formulated in Silvan Tomkins's definition of shame:

> [S]hame operates only after interest or enjoyment has been activated; it inhabits one,
> or the other, or both. The innate activator of shame is the incomplete reduction of
> interest or joy. Such a barrier might arise because one is suddenly looked at by an-
> other who is strange; or because one wishes to look at, or commune with, another
> person but suddenly cannot because s/he is strange; or one expected him to be famil-
> iar but he suddenly appears unfamiliar; or one started to smile but found one was
> smiling at a stranger.[11]

According to Tomkins's definition, shame is not necessarily related to some vio-
lation of social norms (even though it often is), but to the fact that shame can
appear only when the individual has shown an interest in someone or something, and when that interest has been rejected. This connects shame to love
insofar as interest often involves a desire for connection, which is love reciprocated. Therefore, love always involves the fear that love will not be mutual, and
this contains the potential for shame. The catastrophe in losing one's love is not
necessarily the loss itself but the deeply shameful experience of the rejection of
interest; in other words, the state of "if-only." Jan and Eva's love is shameful because it only exists in this "if-only" realm, which is: in a past that is lost forever, in
the impossible future, and in the self-deceptive present. But Jan and Eva cannot
express their shame in words and thus learn to cope with it, which, again, leads
to a traumatized love. Traumatic love, then, is precisely the shameful and painful
love of "what-would-have-been."[12]

After the calling of the war truce, Eva's love affair with Jacobi (the mayor) adds
yet another dimension to the trauma of love. They kiss passionately in front of
Jan, and even though Eva seems to have entered into the affair solely to obtain
various commodities and presents in exchange, Jan is deeply hurt because her
affair allows Eva to escape from him again to that "if-only" realm where he is
denied entry. When the partisans break Jan's violin and burn down their house,
things once again change dramatically. The realm of "if-only" turns out to be just
an empty state, "the negative power that displaces lost humanistic values" where
"no authentic love is any longer possible" and where "life does not make sense
anymore."[13] Authentic love is no longer possible because it was never there in the
first place. Bergman's film would seem to suggest that traumatic love is the only

kind of love available to us, because it speaks of a more general failure of love, a loss that in Ronald Barthes's *Lover's Discourse* is defined as the only origin of love:

> Similarly, it seems, for the lover's anxiety: it is the fear of a mourning which has already occurred, at the very origin of love, from the moment when I was first "ravished". Someone would have to be able to tell me: "Don't be anxious anymore – you've already lost him/her."[14]

Hence, for Barthes, there is no basis for love other than loss, and that self-deception is therefore built into the very heart of love, becoming "a *sine qua non* of love."[15] However, the instant that Jan recognizes their love as such arrives one moment too late for him to be able to react in a constructive manner; instead, he acquires a taste for violence in the name of survival. First he shoots Jacobi and later murders a child soldier apparently for no reason except to steal his boots. But, in Jan's violent rage for survival, he destroys himself as shame begins to gnaw at him with doubts concerning his humanity.[16] The film's final images of a boat of refugees in a sea of dead bodies in the static, compositional arrangements that are so characteristic for Bergman are among the most despairing in film history, arousing negative emotions that cannot find an outlet through action. These paralytic images are unable to transform emotion into action; instead, they introduce the experience of trauma, suggesting that since loss is the origin of love (and thereby the source of all inhumanity), there is no hope for mankind. Traumatic love contains no seeds of hope, only seeds of torment, except in the guise of self-deception, escapism, and bad faith.

The Spectatorial Logic of Shame

How are we, as spectators, to respond to these images? These are inexplicable images that call for a failed, traumatic mode of spectatorship, firstly because we are involuntarily confronted by them, and secondly because we, like Jan and Eva, are denied a resolution or any sense of relief. It is significant that throughout the film we do not see the acts of violence (they always occur offscreen), only the results, of which the final images of corpses floating on the sea are the most powerful ones. The only exception to this is the scene of Jan shooting Jacobi, but this is filmed from a distance. In this way, the camera denies us both our role as "privileged witnesses" to the action and an outlet for our emotions through catharsis (it is always already too late to act).[17] As a result, our emotions become enduring, bespeaking the traumatic reality of violence. But at the same time, the film denies its own process of creating meaning and its "mastery" over the events it depicts and thus, by so doing, shames its own world (and, accordingly, we are never told the reasons for the war). Geoffrey Nowell-Smith has defined melodrama as a failure of representation, a genre that has a built-in impossibility of a "happy ending."[18] Yet, as Elsaesser points out, melodrama also calls for the "failure of spectatorship" that needs to be defined as traumatic. The definition for the failure of spectatorship is trauma not only because it cannot be articulated, but also because it refuses to connect to memory, resulting in a crisis of experience and confining the spectator to the eternal recalling of the traumatic event.[19]

Furthermore, this failed mode of spectatorship is paradoxically the only successful mode of spectatorship, since it is a solution for what Elsaesser calls the "new economy of experience" where "shortcuts, blackouts and gaps are what saves the self from an otherwise ruinous psychic investment in the multitude of events observed, of human beings encountered, of disasters and injustices witnessed – which no personal memory nor even public history could encompass or contain."[20] In other words, trauma is, oddly enough, a protective mode of spectatorship that does not shatter (as Leo Bersani and Ulysse Dutoit suggest[21]) but "saves" the spectator from the "spectatorial logic of shame"[22] that can be found in SHAME in a transformational sense where the stage is set for the flooding of the spectator by the shame that is rendered elliptical.[23] Trauma saves the spectator from the immediacy of experience, on the one hand, through a process of substitution, which absorbs the shame, and through a process of distancing, on the other. Similarly, traumatic love "saves" the lover from the loss that is the true origin of love, the shameful "if-only" condition. The loss that is at the heart of love thus describes a more general failure of love that is the source of all inhumanity, making the full circle complete for the eternal return of shame. It is no accident that the trauma of love and the shamefulness of war (shameful in its meaninglessness) go hand in hand in SHAME, since the discourse of both love and sovereignty exists only in the form of self-deception, and this is why SHAME remains as topical today as it was when it was made.[24] Shame assumes a numbing form in Bergman's film, resulting in trauma and depression, neither of which can ever be overcome. Eve Kosofsky Sedgwick has argued that (traumatic) shame can have transformative power, that shame can become a source of creative expression and transformational energy.[25] But the failure of love in SHAME means that there is no way out of the enclosing circle of shame, and, as a result, shame loops back upon itself, becoming "the generalized 'foundational' moment of any individual's sense of identity and person-hood, and thus the basis of his/ her life's narrative and source of its ultimate meaning."[26]

In the film's final scenes, the outcomes of this failure of love are either suicide (symbolic) in the case of Filip or starvation in the cases of Jan, Eva, and the rest of the refugees. Leonard Kaplan's notes that, in these scenes, Bergman "shows us a world where guilt and shame ceased to affect human response. He shows us a set of consequences where such emotions no longer motivate [responsible action]."[27] In relation to this, Berenice Fisher views shame "not as a mark of our inadequacy but as a sign of our commitment to *act*, as a mark of the tension between the present and the future, as a touchstone for understanding when we expect to achieve and how."[28] For this reason, SHAME contains the possibility for the circulation of shame as a cinematic experience linked to ethics. The ethical dimension of SHAME is the individual responsibility for the self and for the other, which rests upon a principle other than that of citizenship, the state, or the nation; namely, it depends on "an ontology of being-with-one-another ... an ontology for the world."[29] The Deleuzian ethology introduced at the beginning of this essay also insists that one must take the other into one's world while respecting the other and his or her relation to the world. One must welcome that other regardless of who he or she is and whatever beliefs and values he or she might possess, and even regardless whether he or she hates one or not.[30] When one fails to live up to this ideal of responsibility for the self and for the other, shame eventually sets in.

This is also how shame circulates in SHAME, as the discerned inability to act upon the tension between the present and the future, which is also felt by the spectator "in the flesh" – in the affective operations of the body and the senses whilst one engages with the film. Thus we see that at the heart of Bergman's film there is the hope that shame will be acknowledged in the mode of self-reflection, as a question of moral agency and as a willingness to live up to one's chosen ideals. As Sartre noted, ethics are free acts, which are not ethical if they are not enacted. We can consciously choose to bring others along into our world as we accept loss and the dreadful possibility that our choice will not be reciprocated, the possibility of the shameful "if-only" which lies at the heart of love. Only then can shame gain transformational power that both acknowledges and turns away from the eternally returning trauma in which shame originates. But this requires a certain awareness of shame that the characters in SHAME do not possess, which renders them unable to act on their shame, and leaves them vulnerable to the traumatic mode of love. In other words, Eva and Jan become imprisoned in their own existence, fixed in the mode of self-deception, because they have lost the power to love and to act. The failure of love becomes a failure to be, except in the always-unattainable, shameful realm of "if-only".

The spectators, however, do have the option to become aware of shame by viewing the film not merely as a representation of nihilism, but as an expression of self-assessment that may encourage them to take responsible action in their own lives when necessary.[31] In this sense, SHAME can be seen as a mirror held in front of the spectators, which forces them either to assume the reflected image or to alter it, and thus break the circle of shame, allowing for something new to emerge. This emergence is not framed as a haunting sense of nostalgia (as it was for Jan and Eva), but as a future-oriented acknowledgement that we, too, are vulnerable to traumatic love and thus all too prone to escape either into self-deception or into self-destruction, where shame can then make its eternal return. Furthermore, this acknowledgement opens up an avenue for responsible self-determination that, nevertheless, takes us outside of ourselves. SHAME depicts an egocentric, starving world of individuals concerned only with their own survival and motivated solely by the trauma of love. But this is precisely the process that allows the film to become ethical, since it demands recognition of the shame that is the result of traumatic love. In the end, SHAME appeals to a responsible, loving commitment of the self to the other as the only option to true freedom and humanity, since love (as open totality) assumes the capacity of all individuals to participate in the community of each and every one.

Notes

1. Tarja Laine, *Shame and Desire: Emotion, Intersubjectivity, Cinema* (Brussel: Peter Lang, 2007).
2. Gilles Deleuze, "Ethology: Spinoza and Us," *Incorporations*, ed. Jonathan Crary and Sanford Kwinter (New York: Zone Books, 1992) 625-633.
3. Thomas Elsaesser, "Ingmar Bergman: The Art Cinema," *Sight and Sound* (April 1994): 22-27.
4. Pauline Kael, *Going Steady: Film Writings 1968-1969* (New York: Marion Boyars, 1994).
5. See also Kaja Silverman, *Male Subjectivity at the Margins* (New York: Routledge, 1992).
6. James F. Maxfield, "Bergman's SHAME: A Dream of Punishment," *Literature/Film Quarterly* 12.1 (1984): 34-41.
7. Rick Altman, "Moving Lips: Cinema as Ventriloquism," *Yale French Studies* 60 (1980): 67-79.
8. Thomas Elsaesser, *Melodrama and Trauma: Modes of Cultural Memory in the American Cinema* (London: Routledge, forthcoming).
9. Tom Milne, "Shame," *Time Out Film Guide*, <http://www.timeout.com/film/74447. html>. Last visited 25 April 2007. In this sense, there is an interesting connection between SKAMMEN and Jean-Luc Godard's 1963 film, LE MÉPRIS / CONTEMPT, where it is the emotion of contempt that enacts the traumatic mode of love between the central couple. In an interview, Godard spoke of the "people who look at one another and judge one another, and who are then in turn looked at and judged by cinema..." Jean-Luc Godard, *Godard on Godard*, ed. and trans. Tom Milne (Cambridge, MA: Da Capo, 1986) 201.
10. Gilles Deleuze, *Cinema 1: The Movement-Image*, trans. Hugh Tomlinson and Barbara Habberjam (Minneapolis: University of Minnesota Press, 1986).

11.   Silvan S., Tomkins, *Exploring Affect: The Selected Writings of Silvan S. Tomkins*, ed. E. Virginia Demos (Cambridge: Cambridge University Press, 1995).

12.   See also Elsbeth Probyn, *Blush: Faces of Shame* (Minneapolis: University of Minnesota Press, 2005).

13.   András Bálint Kovács, "Sartre, the Philosophy of Nothingness, and the Modern Melodrama," *Journal of Aesthetics and Art Criticism* 64.1 (Winter 2006): 135-45.

14.   Roland Barthes, *A Lover's Discourse: Fragments*, trans. Richard Howard (New York: Hill and Wang, 2001).

15.   Ronald de Sousa, "Love as Theater," *The Philosophy of (Erotic) Love*, ed. Robert C. Solomon and Kathleen M. Higgins (Lawrence: University of Kansas Press, 1991) 477-491.

16.   This is also what I feel Jean-Luc Nancy means when he writes that the destroyer is always already in the process of destroying himself in the process of destruction. "It isn't a 'strong me' that destroys," he writes, "it is a me that lacks a self." Jean-Luc Nancy, *A Finite Thinking* (Stanford: Stanford University Press, 2003) 84.

17.   On emotions and action tendencies in the cinematic experience, see Ed S. Tan, *Emotion and the Structure of Narrative Film: Film as an Emotion Machine* (Mahwah, NJ: Lawrence Erlbaum Associates, 1996) and Torben Grodal *Moving Pictures: A New Theory of Film Genres, Feelings and Cognition* (New York: Oxford University Press, 1997).

18.   Geoffrey Nowell-Smith, "Minelli and Melodrama," *Home is Where the Heart Is: Studies in Melodrama and the Woman's Film*, ed. Christine Gledhill, (London: BFI, 1987) 70-74; Peter Brooks, *The Melodramatic Imagination* (New Haven: Yale University Press, 1976).

19.   Thomas Elsaesser, "Was wäre, wenn du schon tot bist? Vom 'postmodernen' zum 'post-mortem'-Kino am Beispiel von Christopher Nolans *Memento*," *Zeitsprünge. Wie Filme Geschichte(n) erzählen*, ed. Christine Rüffert, Irmbert Schenk, Karl-Heinz Schmid, and Alfred Tews (Berlin: Bertz, 2004) 115-125.

20.   Elsaesser, *Melodrama and Trauma*.

21.   Leo Bersani and Ulysse Dutoit, *Forms of Being: Cinema, Aesthetics, Subjectivity* (London: BFI, 2004).

22.   The expression comes from Ruth Leys in her book *From Guilt to Shame: Auschwitz and After* (Princeton: Princeton University Press, 2007).

23.   See Eve Kosofsky Sedgwick, *Touching Feeling: Affect, Pedagogy, Performativity* (Durham: Duke University Press, 2003).

24.   See also Jean-Luc Nancy, *Being Singular Plural*, trans. Robert D. Richardson and Anne E. O'Byrne (Stanford: Stanford University Press, 2000).

25.   Sedgwick 63-64.

26.   Elsaesser, *Melodrama and Trauma*.

27.   Leonard V. Kaplan, "SHAME: Bergman on Responsibility and Blame," *Brooklyn Law Review* 68.4 (2003) <http://www.brooklaw.edu/students/journals/blr/blr68iv_kaplan.pdf>. Last visited 19 May 2007.

28.   Berenice Fisher, "Guilt and Shame in the Women's Movement: The Radical Ideal of Action and Its Meaning for Feminist Intellectuals," *Feminist Studies* 10.2 (1984): 185-212; italics added.

29.   Nancy, *Being Singular Plural* 53.

30. "Really love those that hate you," writes Teresa Brennan, "do good to them that perse-
cute you. There is no better escape, no clearer path to freedom. There is also no better
revenge." Teresa Brennan, *The Transmission of Affect* (Ithaca: Cornell University Press,
2004) 134.
31. Paisley Livingston, for instance, argues against the critics who describe Bergman's
films as utterly pessimistic, and proposes an alternative view where Bergman is seen
presenting his cinematic world to the spectators as a platform for an evaluation of
their actions, for a deliberation of how change is possible, or even necessary. Paisley
Livingston, *Ingmar Bergman and the Rituals of Art* (Ithaca: Cornell University Press,
1982).

Mediated Memories

A Snapshot of Remembered Experience

José van Dijck

"Media and memory" was the title of a graduate course that Thomas Elsaesser, myself, and two other colleagues initiated at the University of Amsterdam's department of Media Studies in 2004. After deliberating whether the term "mediation *of* memory" might better cover the proposed contents of this course, we decided upon the juxtaposition of the two central concepts in the course's title: media *and* memory. Nevertheless, the course's underlying tenet was that media and memory are not separate entities – the first enhancing, corrupting, extending, or replacing the second – but that media invariably and inherently shape our memories, warranting the term "mediation." The course covered a range of scholarly perspectives on how personal memory feeds on media technologies, and how collective memory is defined by the media's shaping powers. Over the years of teaching this course, the concept "mediation of memory" gradually evolved into a more precise theoretical framework for analyzing the co-construction of memories and media. Through a series of conceptual refinements, I worked the premises of the course into a book which eventually settled on the concept of "mediated memories."[1] Elsaesser's theory played a substantial role in the development of the book's main argument. This essay reconstructs "the making of" a concept. It is the academic equivalent of the director's cut on DVDs – scenes which reveal how the film came into being. In this story, media and memory finally come together, due to the intervention of many actors (students, colleagues, and scholars) who shaped the plot. The happy ending to this story is captured in a snapshot. A sample analysis of this photograph will illustrate the functionality of the concept of mediated memories.

Media and Memory

Memory and media have conventionally been regarded as a hierarchical binary. Since the days of Plato, who viewed the invention of writing and script as a degeneration of "pure" memory (meaning: untainted by technology), every new means of outsourcing our physical capacity to remember has generated resentment.[2] Most scholars acknowledge the continuation of memory's "technologiza-tion" – a term powerfully argued by Walter Ong – from manual and mechanical means of inscription, such as pencils and printing presses, all the way to modern electronic and digital tools.[3] However, these scholars often only refer to the more recent stages as "technologically mediated."

With the advent of photography, and later film and television, writing was tacit-ly transformed into an interior means of consciousness and remembrance, whereupon electronic forms of media received the "artificial" label. The rise of electronic images is often blamed for the decline of the printed word, while writ-ing began being considered a more "authentic" container of past recollection – an irony likely to recur with each new generation of technologies.[4] The rise of elec-tronic "external" memory has, however, also been applauded, an appreciation of-ten based on the very same bifurcated models. Marshall McLuhan's influential theories on electronic media considered these technologies as the "extensions of men," which signaled the unprecedented enhancement of human perceptual ca-pacities: photography and television were augmentations of the eye, whereas audio technologies and radio extended the ear's function. Similar dualities can be observed in more recent debates, particularly in those that discuss how mass media infiltrate collective memory. To this disjunction we should add the ten-dency to define memory in ambiguous media terms: either as tools for inscribing the past or as an archival resource. For instance, when French historian Pierre Nora laments the enormous weight of media versions of the past on our historio-graphy, he basically regards collective memory as a giant storehouse, an archive, or a library.[5] Jacques Le Goff takes exception with this conceptualization by point-ing out that media representations form a filter through which the past is artifi-cially ordered and edited – manufactured rather than registered.[6] It is simulta-neously a means of inscription and an external repository, so that media are considered apparatuses for production and storage, modeled on the mind's sup-posed capacity to register and store experiences or impressions.

The vision of printed and electronic media as *replacements* for human memory reverberates in expressions like this one by historian Raphael Samuel: "Memory-keeping is a function increasingly assigned to the electronic media, while a new awareness of the artifice of representation casts a cloud of suspicion over the documentation of the past."[7] Even if unarticulated, dichotomies often inform scholarly assessments of the media's role in the process of remembrance. On the one hand, media are considered aids to human memory, while, on the other hand, they are perceived as a threat to the purity of remembrance. As an artificial prosthesis, these technologies can free the brain of unnecessary burdens, thus creating more space and energy for creative activity; but as a replacement, they can also end up corrupting memory. Media are thus paradoxically defined as invaluable yet insidious memory tools – a paradox that may arise from the tendency to simultaneously insist on the division between memory and media, and yet conflate their meanings.[8]

Mediation of Memory

Wading through the classics of media theory, we missed out on an important line of scholarly thinking that reflects on the innate intertwining of media and memory. A distinct number of scholars, primarily from the cognitive and social sciences, but also working in anthropology and cultural history, have done research in the area of the *"mediation of* memory." For a better understanding of how memory and media interact, it was necessary to weigh the strengths and weaknesses of this concept, which is used both in relation to personal reminiscence and collective memory. Psychologists point to the inextricable interconnections between acts of remembrance and its specific mediated objects through which these acts materialize. Annette Kuhn claims that photographic images, "far from being transparent renderings of a pre-existing reality, embody coded references to, and even help construct, realities."[9] Photographs never represent a fixed moment; they work to fix temporal notions and relations between past and present. Steven Rose, a British scientist who discusses the physiological complexity of human memory and consciousness at length, makes the case that mnemonic aids, such as photos or videos, are often confused with our individual memories to such extent that we can hardly distinguish between the two.[10] And anthropologist Richard Chalfen, in his study of how home media help communicate individual perceptions of self to others, argues that our "snapshots are us."[11]

A similar notion of "mediation" can be found among historians discussing the infiltration of mass media in collective memory. British sociologist John Urry, in his essay "How Societies Remember the Past," explains how electronic media intrinsically change the way we create images of the past in the present.[12] Mass media, according to popular culture historian George Lipsitz, embody some of our deepest hopes and engage some of our most profound sympathies; films, records, or other cultural expressions constitute "a repository of collective memory that places immediate experience in the context of change over time."[13] Media like television, and more recently computers, are devices that produce, store, and reshape earlier versions of history.

We can witness this contrived interlocking most poignantly at the metaphorical level; the "mediation of memory" refers equally to our understanding of media in terms of memory, as illustrated by the historians' aforementioned accounts;

and our comprehension of physiological memory in terms of media, evidenced by the many metaphors that relate to various aspects of human memory. Ever since the invention of writing tools, but most noticeably since the emergence of photography in the nineteenth century, the human capacity to remember has been indexed in daily language by referring to technical tools of reproduction. Dutch psychologist Douwe Draaisma, who researched the historical evolution of memory metaphors extensively, notes that media are a special conceptual category for envisioning memory's mechanics.[14] For instance, the term "flash bulb memory" – the proclivity to remember an important moment in full detail, including its circumstances, time, and place in which the message was received – derived its signifier from the realm of photography. In the twentieth century, the terminology of film and video began to invade the discourse of memory and memory research: life is said to be replayed "like a film" in the seconds prior to death, and psychologists have extensively examined the phenomenon known as "deathbed flash." By the same token, we are now firmly grilled by the media's convention of visualizing a character's recollection of past experiences as a "slow-motion replay" or as a "flash back." Metaphors are not simply a way of saying something, but conceptual images that structure and give meaning to our lives.[15] As media have become our foremost tools for memory, metaphorical reciprocity signals their constitutive quality.

Mediated Experience

While co-teaching the course on media and memory, I gradually came to understand that, however compelling and valid the "mediation of memory" concept was, it hinged on a few premises that seriously restricted its explanatory scope. First, an exclusive focus on either home media or mass media often presumes a symbiotic union of home media with personal cultural memory, and of mass media with its collective counterpart; such rigid distinctions hamper a fuller understanding of how individual and collective memory are shaped in conjunction. Second, even though most theories acknowledge the convergence of memory and media, the "mediation" concept frequently favors a single vector: media shape our memories, but we seldom find testimony of media being shaped by memory, indicating an implicit hierarchy. Let me address each of these conceptual deficiencies in more detail.

It is practical to assume that personal cultural memory is generated by what we call "home media" (family photography, home videos, and tape recorders), whereas collective cultural memory gets produced by "mass media" (television, CDs, DVDs, and professional photography). But that simple division, even if it is functional, is also conceptually flawed, as it obscures the fact that people derive their autobiographical memories from both personal and collective media sources. Media sociologist John Thompson, who highlights the role of individual agency in media reception, explains the hermeneutic nature of this relationship.[16] He argues that "lived experience," in our contemporary culture, is interlaced with "mediated experience." Mediation, then, comprises not only the media tools we wield in the private sphere, but also the active choices of individuals to incorporate parts of culture into their lives. Experience is neither completely "lived" nor entirely "mediated," as the encounter between the two is a continuously evolving life-project to define the self in a larger cultural context. What makes mediated experience different from the lived experience of two hundred years ago is the fact that individuals need no longer share a common locale to pursue commonality; the growing availability of mediated experience creates "new opportunities, new options, new arenas for self-experimentation."[17] If we accept a preliminary distinction between home and mass media, we not only fail to account for media shaping our sense of individuality *and* collectivity in conjunction, but we equally obscure how individuals actively contribute to the collective media that shape their individuality.

The second deficiency in the "mediation of memory" concept concerns the implied hierarchy between external and internal memory, or in plain terms, between technology and the mind. Understandably, our metaphors often explain the invisible in terms of the visible and knowable; that is why the mysteries of mental processing are often elucidated in terms of media technology – technology that is at once transparent and mechanically predictable. But how about turning the vector back on its arrow: could our development and use of various media technologies be informed by the perceptual mechanisms, the sensory motor actions that underlie memory formation?[18] An intricate aspect of remembering is that mental perceptions – ideas, impressions, insights, feelings – manifest themselves through specific sensory modes: sounds, images, smells. The media we have invented and nursed to maturity over the years incorporate a similar tendency to capture ideas or experiences in sensory inscriptions, such as spoken or written words, still or moving images, recorded sounds or music. One memory rarely encompasses all of the senses, because we tend to remember by selecting particular ones. For instance, we may recall a mood, locale, or era through a particular smell (e.g. Marcel Proust's madeleine, or the smell of apple pie in the oven that may trigger the image of your mother's kitchen on Saturday afternoons), or we may remember a person by his nasal voice or her twinkling eyes.[19] The same holds true for memories captured through media technologies. Rather than exhaustive recordings, we commonly select a specific evocative framework within which we store a particular aspect of memory – a still photograph to store visual aspects, or a diary entry to retain interpretative details and subjective reflection, a video to capture the movement of baby's first steps. We have a large variety of preferred sensory and medial modes at our disposal to inscribe specific memories, but the intriguing question is: do the media technologies available dictate which sensory aspects of an event we inscribe in our memory, or do our sensory perceptions dictate which medium we choose to record the experience?

Mediated Memories

After I had come to dismiss the notion of memory's "mediation," I needed an alternative concept. One of Thomas Elsaesser's articles offered the missing link in my theoretical concatenation of mind, technology, and culture. Thus far, I had argued that instruments of memory inscription privilege particular sensorial perceptions over others and, to some extent, define the shape of our future recall. And yet, even if media technologies privilege a particular sense (photography prefers sight, tape recorders sound) that does not mean there is a one-to-one relationship between the sensorial aspects of memory and the preferred recording instrument. On the contrary, a still picture may invoke the sound of a child's laughter long after that child has grown into an adult. Most people have unconscious preferences for a particular mode of inscription. For instance, they favor moving images over still pictures or oral accounts over written ones. Although part of that propensity is undoubtedly rooted in individual mindsets, another part is inevitably defined by the cultural apparatus available and socially accepted at that time. But this apparatus is far from static. Each time frame redefines the mutual shaping of mind and technology as one is always implied in the other. The brain stipulates the camera as much as the camera stimulates the brain. Mediated experience, as Elsaesser notes, has become a generalized cultural condition:

> In our mobility, we are "tour"-ists of life; we use the camcorder with our hands or often merely in our heads, to reassure ourselves that this is "me, now, here." Our experience of the present is always already (media) memory, and this memory represents the recaptured attempt at self-presence: possessing the experience in order to possess the memory, in order to possess the self.[20]

In other words, memory is not mediated by media, but media and memory mutually constitute our everyday experiences. Media and memory inscribe and transform each other.

It was at this point that I decided to replace the term "mediation of memory" with "mediated memories," a term that offered a more comprehensive prism for understanding the mutual shaping involved in personal and collective cultural memory. Based on Elsaesser's insight, I defined mediated memories, the key concept of my book, as "the activities and objects we produce and appropriate by means of media technologies, for creating and recreating a sense of past, present, and future of our selves in relation to others."[21] Mediated memory objects and acts are crucial sites for negotiating the relationship between self and culture at large, between what counts as private and what as public, and between individuality and collectivity. As stilled moments in the present, mediated memories reflect and construct intersections between past and future – remembering and projecting lived experience.

Indeed, people deploy media technologies to create a repository of autobiographical reflections of self, of family, and perhaps of larger circles beyond the immediate private sphere. They wield photo and video cameras, computers, pens and pencils, audio techniques, and so on, to record moments in which "lived" experience intermingles with "mediated experience." During later stages of recall, they may alter the mediation of their records so as to relive, adjust, change, revise, or even erase previously inscribed moments as part of a continuous project of self-formation. Concrete mediated memory objects stand for encompassing acts of memory; collections of mediated objects, stored in shoeboxes, often become the material and symbolic connection between generations whose perception of "family" or "self" changes over time, which is in part due to social and cultural changes, and in part dependent on the intergenerational continuity each family member brings into this heritage. Beyond immediate family circles, material inscriptions may become part of a larger project, for instance, a documentary, and thus add to a shared collective remembrance.

Through the looking glass of mediated memories, I could magnify the intersections between personal and collective, between past and future, and between mind, technology, and culture. Mediated memories involve individuals carving out their place in history, defining personal remembrance in the face of larger cultural frameworks. Individuals make selections from a culture that surrounds them, yet they concurrently shape that collectivity we call culture. Cultural memory, hence, is not an epistemological category – something we can have, lack, or lose – and neither is mediation the inevitable effacement, distortion, or enhancement of human memory. Rather, cultural memory can be viewed as a process and performance, the understanding of which is indispensable to the perennial human activity of building social systems for cultural connectivity. Mediated memories reflect this cultural process played out by various agents – individuals, technologies, conventions, institutions, etc. – whose acts and products we should examine as confrontations between individuality and collectivity.

Snapshot

The "making of" a concept elucidates how a theory came into being – a concatenation of insights building on each other and shaping a new concept that can subsequently be challenged by other scholars. Such is the nature of academic knowledge building: a theoretical universe in which all phenomena are connected through the combined eyes and brains of people making connections. After a journey that took me through various disciplines, I finally settled on mediated memories as a useful concept to theorize why and how people use media technologies to remember. The marriage of two distinct themes into an inextricable knot is not the happy end of a simple story; on the contrary, the union remains volatile, prone to new insights, to social and technological developments. In the meantime, I can only show the value of a concept by elucidating how it yields specific new insights.

There is a widely distributed picture showing Thomas Elsaesser standing amidst a group of some ten colleagues and PhD students from the Amsterdam Department of Media Studies. Their smiling faces and their clothing betray a happy celebration of which Elsaesser is clearly the focus. It was taken on 6 September 2006, in the reception hall of the Maagdenhuis, the University of Amsterdam's main building. The photograph was taken just after the opening ceremonies for that academic year. Elsaesser had just received the Queen's Medal of Honor in appreciation for his work as a distinguished film scholar. Still a little befuddled by the unexpected honor bestowed upon him, he let us take the picture. We cleared the area, grouped around him, gave him flowers, and all smiled for the photographer. This picture obviously connotes a staged act, a ceremonial posing for the eye of a camera that was arranged to inscribe this glorious moment.

As an act of memory, the digital photograph connotes more than a stilled moment in the past, as it actually connects Elsaesser's individual experience of this moment to the collective experience involved in the staging of this act. My memory is distinctly defined by that collective act, but needless to say, my reconstruction of it remains highly idiosyncratic. Preparations for this ceremonial photo-op had already commenced years earlier. Since we wanted to extend our appreciation for Elsaesser's work beyond the informal circuit, we followed official guidelines that pushed our application all the way up to the Queen. Many known and unknown hands were implicated in this process, and when the word finally arrived, our biggest concern was to keep the positive decision and preparations for the ceremony a secret. When we arrived at the ceremony site, on a pretense involving the university's chancellor, Elsaesser still had no idea what was about to happen. The goal of all this fuss only began to dawn on him when he was called up on the stage. Everything was scripted, including the photograph taken at the end of the ceremony, and Elsaesser found himself playing a lead role in a film he had never seen. His and our experience of the present was already a (mediated) memory, as the cameras were ready to roll and turn a private experience into a public event.

As an object of memory, the photograph (perhaps more than the Queen's medal itself) signifies a token of our appreciation. When I look at it again, I see a smiling Thomas Elsaesser surrounded by a grinning group of colleagues who have managed to bring a secretive process to a happy end and keep the surprise party a surprise. I also see a guru standing among his disciples, a teacher leading his pupils. Moreover, I see a man fathering a new generation of children and grandchildren – in the metaphorical sense; a functional family that even during its dysfunctional moments maintains a strong sense of unity with regard to the outside world. It reminds me of a typical family photo I keep stored in one of my old shoeboxes. The photo has many symbolic levels, which trigger a number of memories of a collective past that leads up to this single moment. I am sure the snapshot will have an impact on future memories. Every time I look at this photo, my memories of the moment will change, simply because the present projects altered interpretations of self and the world upon the stilled object. Memories, like the self and the world, are always in transition, and that is why media are transitory even if they are static.

This particular snapshot is possessed by many different people, as it was distributed widely via the Internet. But those memories are exclusively mine; they are not Elsaesser's, not those of my colleagues. To my mind, the *mediatedness* of this memory stands out more than anything. Citing Elsaesser again: "this memory represents the recaptured attempt at self-presence: possessing the experience in order to possess the memory, in order to possess the self."[22] Our lives are not mediated by media, nor are they simply informed by media. Pictures, videos, and other artifacts do not replace, distort, or confirm memories. We are who we are because we have constructed our experiences and our memories through and in media. Those media are part and parcel of our selves. We do not take photographs to help us remember (or, seen from a different angle, to prevent us from forgetting) our past; we take and use pictures to construct a past. Each time I look at this picture of Elsaesser and his colleagues, the past whips up a story of "me, now, here." Every picture is a still in the "making of" the present.

Notes

1. José van Dijck, *Mediated Memories in the Digital Age* (Stanford: Stanford University Press, 2007).
2. Francis Yates, in *The Art of Memory* (Chicago: Chicago University Press, 1966), points out the significance of photography in the devaluation of memory. The advent of mechanically reproduced images was thought to lead to the destruction of truth, and was therefore thought to undermine human memory.
3. Media theorist Walter Ong, in his renowned book *Orality and Literacy: The Technologizing of the Word* (London: Routledge, 1982), argues that a memory stilled in words, whether spoken or written, is just as "technologized" as memory packaged in electronic images; both combine external technologies and internal techniques to help structure our remembrance.
4. See, for instance, Mitchell Stephens, *The Rise of the Image, the Fall of the Word* (New York: Oxford University Press, 1998), who argues that the popularity of the image was only able to soar at the expense of the written word. Elsewhere, I have extensively countered Stephens's and other arguments that writing and imaging should be defined as opposites in a communicative system. See José van Dijck, "No images without words," *The Image Society: Essays on Visual Culture*, ed. Frits Gierstberg and Warna Oosterbaan (Rotterdam: NAi, 2002) 34-43.
5. Pierre Nora, "Between Memory and History: Les Lieux de Mémoire," *Representations* 26 (1989): 69-85.
6. Jacques Le Goff, *History and Memory*, trans. Steven Rendall and Elizabeth Claman (New York: Columbia University Press, 1992).
7. This quote is taken from Raphael Samuel, *Theatres of Memory*, vol. 1: *Past and Present in Contemporary Culture* (London: Verso, 1994) 25.
8. This double take is not unlike the modernist tendency, observed by Bruno Latour in *We Have Never Been Modern* (Cambridge: Harvard University Press, 1993), to simultaneously insist on hybridity and purification – holding on to the ontological division between human and nonhumans (things, machines) while also canceling out their separation. The invincibility of this argumentation is possible only because they hold on to the absolute dichotomy between the order of Nature and that of Society, a dichotomy which "is itself only possible because they never consider the work of purification and that of mediation together" (40).
9. Annette Kuhn, "A Journey Through Memory," *Memory and Methodology*, ed. Susannah Radstone (Oxford: Berg, 2000) 183.
10. Steven Rose, *The Making of Memory* (London: Bantam, 1992) 91-96.
11. Richard Chalfen, "Snapshots 'R' Us: The Evidentiary Problematic of Home Media," *Visual Studies* 17.2 (2002): 144.
12. John Urry, "How Societies Remember the Past," *Theorizing Museums: Representing Identity and Diversity in a Changing World*, ed. Sharon Macdonald and Gordon Fyfe (Oxford: Blackwell, 1996) 45-68.
13. George Lipsitz, *Time Passages: Collective Memory and American Popular Culture* (Minneapolis: University of Minnesota Press, 1990) 5.

14. For an interesting historical exploration of the notion of time in individual remembering, see Douwe Draaisma, *Waarom de tijd sneller gaat als je ouder wordt* (Groningen: Historische Uitgeverij, 2001). For a specific study on the (historical) use of metaphors in relation to memory, see Douwe Draaisma, *Metaphors of Memory: A History of Ideas About the Mind* (Cambridge: Cambridge University Press, 2000).

15. I am referring here to George Lakoff and Mark Johnson's renowned theory of metaphors as described in *Metaphors We Live By* (Chicago: Chicago University Press, 1980).

16. John B. Thompson, *The Media and Modernity: A Social Theory of the Media* (Cambridge: Polity, 1995).

17. Thompson 233. Thompson is obviously concerned with the double bind that constitutes the process of self-formation in modernity, where the self is caught between an increasing dependency on media and an increasing need for self-reflexivity, to define themselves as part of a larger world.

18. In a way, Gilles Deleuze applies this view to cinema: his adage "the brain is the screen" espouses his idea that there is almost no difference between the mind perceiving someone walking in real life and seeing someone walking in a film. In *Cinema 2: The Time Image* (London: Athlone, 1989), Deleuze theorizes that movies embody the material aspects of our perceptual subjectivity: both brain and cinema are capable of constructing and reconstructing, remembering and *imagineering* the past. For a detailed explanation of Deleuze's theory of the brain, see Patricia Pisters, *The Matrix of Visual Culture: Working with Deleuze in Film Theory* (Stanford: Stanford University Press, 2003) and Gregory Flaxman, ed., *The Brain is the Screen: Deleuze and the Philosophy of Cinema* (Minneapolis: University of Minnesota Press, 2000).

19. Besides sight and sound, other sensory perceptions, such as smell and touch, can trigger subsequent recall. Few contemporary theorists have stressed the role of the senses in cultural memory. See, for instance, C. Nadia Seremetakis, ed., *The Senses Still: Perception and Memory as Material Culture in Modernity* (Boulder: Westview, 1994).

20. Thomas Elsaesser, "Cinephilia or the Uses of Disenchantment," *Cinephilia: Movies, Love and Memory*, ed. Marijke de Valck and Malte Hagener (Amsterdam: Amsterdam University Press, 2005) 40.

21. Van Dijck 21.

22. Elsaesser 40.

Running on Failure

Post-Fordism, Post-Politics, Parapraxis, and Cinema

Drehli Robnik

Yesterday's Misfits: Post-Fordist Mind-Game Cinema

In the Foucauldian section of his reading of THE SILENCE OF THE LAMBS, Thomas Elsaesser interprets the Buffalo Bill character as a kind of over-achiever who:

> literalizes the invitation to self-improvement and "self-storage" which contemporary society addresses to its subjects as consumers. ... Bill becomes a subversive, because wholly dedicated, worker at the site of body- and self-commodification. By taking the system more seriously than it takes itself, he is in the vanguard of a particular form of consumption, that of self-expression turned "self-fashioning," engaged in the permanent bricolage art of identity formation.[1]

The Foucauldian move here is the shift from a notion of power as repressive to a conception of power as productive, mining populations and subjects for ever new energies, and as modulating, i.e., flexibly adapting to any aberrations in the behavior of the governed, and thus as capable of integrating such disturbances into an expanded, intensified system. Thus, highlighting the usefulness and dutifulness of Bill's acts of self-observation and self-perfection, Elsaesser arrives at the conclusion that "[t]he line between the criminal (the extreme embodiment of the system itself, which takes the system at its word) and the resister/contester of the system ... becomes a fine one indeed."[2]

This logic according to which the transgression enriches the norm and expands its rule is also at work in other recent studies of Elsaesser on what, for some duration, he labeled "post-classical cinema." In two essays on different incarnations of Hollywood's ambiguous "newness," the emphasis is on logics of production (rather than docile self-commodification, as in Bill's case), placing two moments in the recent history of American mainstream cinema within the genealogy of the regime of capitalist accumulation known as post-Fordism. First, in his introduction to the reader on New Hollywood Cinema, Elsaesser proposes an alternative to the canonical, fetishizing critical/cinephile view of New Hollywood as oppositional to the main current of American cinema. He suggests seeing maverick or underground filmmakers and cinematic practices as "pilot fish," as an avant-garde preparing and rehearsing Hollywood's move from an overall Fordist logic, which restricts film images – what they render perceptible as well as their production and consumption – to routinized disciplines, into a post-Fordist logic capable of valorizing deviations and rule-breaking, for instance, by way of the paradoxically standardized exception called the "blockbuster." In this view, not only did the "counter-cultural" experimentation within American popular cinema help to modernize a Hollywood in crisis (however vaguely), it also "played" – rather than worked – through its images new, more flexible norms of meaningful subjectivity and sociality. With his outlook on cinema as a site for the rehearsal and capitalization of social productivity, Elsaesser writes of Hollywood circa 1970 as "harvesting and harnessing the counter-cultural energies (including their antisocial excesses) for new kinds of work, especially in those sectors where, according to Hardt and Negri, economic and cultural phenomena can no longer be distinguished" and as "giving, for instance, the psychopath (as well as other marginalized, pathologized or criminalized existences, including 'hippies') a potentially valuable function in periods of transition."[3]

Second, there is the cultural logic and epistemology of the "mind-game film," a recent phenomenon within Hollywood as well as global mainstream cinema.[4] Elsaesser cautions against a – cognitivist/narratological – reduction of these films' textual bifurcations, phenomenological ambiguities, and retroactive dynamics (the built-in necessity to [re-]read them from their surprise endings, as in Shyamalan's THE SIXTH SENSE). Not to reduce the playful weirdness of mind-game films to mere deviations from the norms and normality of commonsense story-telling is a precondition to Elsaesser's interpretation that sees the mental states of protagonists, largely unframed and encompassing all of the film's articulation, as "productive pathologies." Reading films here opens up an ethos of confronting sense-making potentials of insane thinking. The overall "'avant-garde' or 'pilot' or 'prototype' function [of mind-game films] within the 'institution cinema'" is "to train, elaborate and, yes: 'test' the textual forms, narrative tropes and story motifs that can serve such a re-negotiation of the rules of the game."[5] Pathologies such as paranoia, understood as a hypersensitivity to changes in the environment, or the amnesia of MEMENTO's protagonist who practices self-programming by inscribing his body – and even Buffalo Bill's compulsive self-observation and self-fashioning – manifest their productivity as tactics and subjectivities suitable for the labor and power regimes of post-Fordist network and control societies.[6]

If we regard these points as amounting to the formula that yesterday's disturbances and failures are today's assets and high-level performances, then Elsaesser also gives us his second thoughts on these schematics. The assessment that

New Hollywood's "misfits, rebels and outsiders were necessary for 'the system' to first adjust and then renew itself," he intimates, "may be too neat – or cynical"; and he hopes that it is "not too cynically [put]" to state that Hollywood's "auteurs drew their self-understanding from identifying with the ideology of the European artist (or the freewheeling spirit of the Corman operation and the various counter-cultures), while at another level they also played the role of the pilot fish."[7]

Cynicism is a term and a stance worth pondering in the context of Elsaesser's writings on cinema's role within mediatized social life; we reencounter it (in brackets) in his dense 2001 essay on trauma theory: "[T]rauma theory would be called upon to rescue interpretation and hermeneutics from the relativism of 'there is no *hors-texte*,' from the fundamentalism of the 'authentic experience' but also from the (cynical) tyranny of the 'performative,' since trauma poses the enigma of interpretation as a negative performative."[8] The cynicism which Elsaesser has in mind here is the "genealogical" appropriation and reworking of pasts in the service of the successful performing and fashioning of present media-cultural identities. As an antidote to this, Elsaesser's philosophy of cinema and media history offers an "archeological" ethos willing to encounter the irreducibly insisting, irritating virtualities of non-appropriated pasts and presents.[9]

There is also a certain cynicism that Elsaesser's own argument seems to be willing to risk. To quote again from the essay on the mind-game film: "Read 'politically,' in the light of Foucault, mind-game films would show how perceptual or somatic faculties released or manifest by illness are ... 'socialized': ... the illness is made to work, fitting a body (through its mind no longer 'in control') around a new set of social tasks and political relations."[10] Elsaesser's position certainly differs from the American pop sociology he refers to, in which, under the headline "Everything Bad Is Good for You," sophisticated HBO series and mind-game films are advocated as educational tools for the young, effective "in adapting the working population to the social technologies that promise their economic survival, maintain civic cohesion and assure America's hegemonic position in the world."[11] Pointing to such instrumentalist notions of pedagogy-through-media as well as to Foucault's theory of governmentality and Deleuze's concept of the control society, Elsaesser, at the end of his essay, wants to leave open the question of whether cinema is "part of the solution" or "part of the problem."[12]

In avoiding a formalist reductionism of cinema's social role as well as a cinephile/film-critical longing for a film art untainted by capital, Elsaesser, however, emphasizes cinema's usefulness to a post-Fordist, flexible adaptation to a degree that his argument seems to feed into an "economistic" determinism ("culturalistically" rearticulated as it may be) which pertains to neo-liberal ideology as well as to Hardt and Negri's ultra-left celebration of the skilled, knowing "multitude."

What is evaporated in this system-theoretical affirmation of weird cinema train-
ing people to be normal according to new rules is the very category of politics
which Elsaesser invokes with his claim to read mind-game films politically with
Foucault. One can object to this claim with Jacques Rancière's philosophy of politics as a "subjectification in disagreement," that the management of the well-
ordered knowledge and productivity of subjects is not an issue of politics, but of
the "police," in the expanded, Foucauldian sense of government and bio-power
which Rancière draws on.[13]

Trauma as Metaphor and Failure Taken at Its Word

Elsaesser's project to highlight the successful contribution of cinema to a well-
performing machinery of post-Fordist capitalism comes quite close to that unlim-
ited capacity for revaluation and appropriation which is labeled "cynical tyranny
of the performative" in his trauma theory essay (cf. supra). In order to draw a line
here and to dissolve an all-too neat equation of the pragmatics of cinema with the
smooth functioning of social energies, one can, however, turn to another Elsaesserian concept outlined in his writings on trauma and terror. The concept of
"failed performance," loosely derived from the Freudian *Fehlleistung* and expanded into a cinematic/mediatized "poetics of parapraxis," points to a pragmatic
orientation which differs from the mere functioning and "success stories" of genealogical identity-formation.

Looking at mind-game cinema's "productive pathologies" from the vantage-
point of the parapraxis – that which, etymologically, is not yet a praxis or is a
praxis besides itself – what comes to the foreground is what these concepts have
in common. They both act as media for rendering a problem visible, sensible – as
"early warning systems" with respect to the way in which mental insanities fulfill
in an excessive way demands made by governmental power (which, Elsaesser
notes, also gives Buffalo Bill's efforts their "subversive" edge) and as a mode of
reading media images in constellations, as in the following quotation: "[The med-
ia] culture of confession and witnessing, of exposure and self-exposure ... has
made trauma theory the recto, and therapeutic television (also disparagingly
called trash TV) the verso of democracy's failure to 'represent' its citizens' personal concern in the public sphere."[14] Turning a metaphorical media image (TV
culture's notorious "survivors" of experiences ranging from political violence and
natural disaster to childhood consumption habits or long periods of illness and
even to the time spent in jungles or in re-created 1950s school environments as
candidates of TV shows) and a metaphorized concept (trauma) into each other is
the becoming-thought-image of a question which in Elsaesser's writing comes up

almost as frequently as the "recto/verso" diagram: What is the problem or trauma to which this or that media image offers itself as a solution or symptom?

Reading media through trauma means deciphering a crisis of political belonging. All the self-confessed "traumatized" and self-stylists of reality-TV who, sobbing or screaming, display a survived life crisis or a frivolous enjoyment indicate, in Elsaesser's perspective, not a genealogical "carnival of identities," but a loss of possibilities for democratic representation. It is exactly there that we find a trauma, or (which amounts to the same thing) the blind spot of a perception which sees trauma everywhere. Or, as Elsaesser puts it in connection with media images of recent German history, while trauma culture might have become the most comfortable way for German society to speak to itself, there is a genuine trauma, an unrepresentable absence, to be deciphered in the 1968 generation's obsession with working through (the Nazi past) and the 1989 generation's fancy for playful appropriation (of images left behind by history, including periods of political violence): the widespread loss of any belief in the possibility to contribute to a changed world through individual or collective public action.[15] Instead of this lost pragmatics, the present metaphorical extension of the notion of terror serves to label as "terrorist" various attempts to reclaim public activity (swallowing up what once was called "resistance"); at the same time, the universalization of trauma has firmly established the idea that history and politics (or rather: historical experience driven from a well-policed course by the immodesty of politics) produce nothing but victims. For this situation, Elsaesser introduces the image of terror and trauma as "Siamese twins" of political discourse – the semblance of a pre-given, complementary opposition, into which, however, the concept of parapraxis can intervene. Failed performances in politics and in cinema (which we will turn to in a second) are successful in that they, however inadvertently, avoid the extremes of traumatic paralysis and excessive terrorist action, while at the same time marking and keeping open the site which these extremes attempt to occupy: that of meaningful, purposive action. Thus, parapractical action testifies to the still existing, or rather insisting, hope that public action and politics can be possible (again).[16]

Although Elsaesser intimates a perspective on terrorist acts reminiscent of Slavoj Žižek's messianistic invocation of the 9/11 attacks as stand-ins for a genuinely revolutionary rupture in the continuum of neo-liberal policing, his analysis is far more complex and reflexive in confronting head-on terrorism as a phenomenon of media culture.[17] In his study of two semi-documentary German films on the legacy of the RAF, the West-German *Rote Armee Fraktion* (Red Army Faction), and its political terrorist acts during the 1970s, he marks politics as exactly that which insists beyond the closure of a "post-Fordization" logics. The argument goes as follows: First, there is the "double failure" of the RAF, "as artists and as

political activists." Politically, the RAF failed because, instead of mass mobiliza-
tion, they were "merely able to engender 'imaginary' identifications around
either bank robberies, prison break-outs and killing sprees, or designer labels,
rock music and fast cars."[18] Artistically, they failed because their "conceptual art"
version of a politics of the street, while attempting to render intelligible (post-)
urban security spaces cleansed of democratic activity, ended up producing spectacles of a "dangerous lifestyle" that served as blueprints for today's playful pop-
appropriations of left-wing militancy and terrorism (as in Che Guevara or "Prada
Meinhof" clothing). There is even the cynical view, which Elsaesser cites, in
which the RAF appears as outright useful, an invention of the bourgeois state in
its move towards the "information society," legitimizing all sorts of "curtailment
of civil liberties."[19] As he points out:

> What this "mirroring" of the state by the RAF flattens is the underlying dynamic of
> identification: not the kind of imaginary identification ... on the part of the RAF's
> political or pop sympathizers, but the act of symbolic identification ... [T]he RAF took
> the state at its word, mirrored the demand made upon the individual by the state,
> accepted the symbolic mandate that is implied in being a citizen.[20]

This is how a mere post-Fordist logic – failed performances become useful to a
system renewing itself through integration of disturbances – gives way to a parapractical argument. Seeing the RAF as taking the state at its word points towards
the performance of a failure, the exposure of a problem (similarly, reading Buffalo Bill as taking the system at its word exposes the coercive dimension of self-
perfection). What becomes visible-as-legible in this thought-image of the RAF
performing the state through failure is, for instance, the "missing people" (a notion put forward by Deleuze), the absence of the manifestation of a legitimizing
popular will on the part of the terrorists as well as on the part of the state, both
proclaiming themselves as representatives of the people. In the face of such a
crisis of representation, Elsaesser's concluding argument aims at the formation
of a political subject via a failure of belonging:

> It must have seemed to the RAF that it was only by putting themselves outside the
> law that they could constitute a "political group," and again, not in the practical sense
> of organizing a non-authoritarian *Wohngemeinschaft*, or in the formal sense of regis-
> tering as an extra-parliamentary opposition, a sort of NGO for internal affairs, but in
> the sense of being political subjects and constituting a "we."[21]

It is important to note that what counts in the RAF's "making the act of becoming 'criminals' the founding gesture of its group identity"[22] is not its embracing
of a rebel lifestyle, but its very breaking with lifestyle, its tearing loose from a
culturalist and identitarian definition of subjectivity – in this case: from the post-

1968 counter-cultures of hippie collectives and student communes and their sense of being on the right side by virtue of their organization and stylization of the everyday. So, "what sort of 'we,' what group identity, is symbolizable in a civic, political sense?"[23] With this question that Elsaesser raised in the conclusion of his RAF essay, especially when faced with foundationalist attempts at nullifying the very question in the form of identity politics and new nationalisms, the connection of Elsaesser's concept to Chantal Mouffe's and Jacques Rancière's theories of democracy comes to the fore (the latter being explicitly referenced in the formulation of the question). In order to trace that connection, it is rewarding to turn to Elsaesser's early writings on the politics and aesthetics of mainstream cinema; in them, we retrospectively, perhaps even retroactively, re-encounter the issue of a performative "we" that impersonates a rupture, the subjectification of a failure, a "we" that "blew it."

Failure and Fuller

In 1971, in the first issue of the film magazine *Monogram*, Elsaesser already pondered the question of what mainstream cinema teaches people. Under the headline "Why Hollywood?," he opposed the contempt which then-current counter-cultures had for American movies and argued in favor of Old Hollywood. In its classical period, American film served as an "education of sensibility," taking characters as well as audiences "from simple impulse to experience of complexity" and to acknowledging "the impossibility of instantaneous gratification." In contrast to classical Hollywood's teaching of sublimation, contradiction, and – as a category of experience more resonant in his "traumatological" writings – delay, Elsaesser detected a celebration of "outbursts of unmotivated and wholly irrational violence" in contemporary American cinema as "evidence of an unsublimated energy" (THE WILD BUNCH), as well as an artistically nihilistic opportunism in which "essential contradictions are being slurred over by a cult of the aesthetically pleasing" (BUTCH CASSIDY AND THE SUNDANCE KID).[24]

The latter critical point reappeared four years later in a better known *Monogram* article, which already in its title seemed to announce a future key concept: "The Pathos of Failure" was diagnosed as the predominant narrative and ethical stance of Hollywood's youth-oriented road movies circa 1970; these films reflected "the experience of a rebellion whose impulse towards change aborted" and "the moral and emotional gestures of a defeated generation," increasingly resorting to the self-pity of those who feel their identity denied by the establishment.[25] Apart from the recurring critical verdict on Hollywood's catering to hip(pie) audiences by undialectically glorifying a rebel-as-loser habitus, there is also a similarity in the concluding arguments of the two *Monogram* articles. In 1971, Elsaesser wrote about EASY RIDER:

> And just as in the classical movie, the hero learns something from his quest about himself and about the world, so Billy and Captain America learn the lesson of total failure – that they cannot live among the hippies, that the American South is murderous, and that, in short "we blew it." Given the present ideological climate, such an admission may seem the sign of a new realism.[26]

Elsaesser was quick to add that such a bitter, self-devastating "realism" had been the very starting point for films by Nicholas Ray in the classical Hollywood and was therefore not something invented by New Hollywood. Even more significant in this context is how the "Pathos of Failure" article ends on a note similar to this realism implied in the admission of total failure. In his 1975 text, Elsaesser sees the slow-motion car race that becomes a "burning" of the image in the projector at the end of TWO-LANE BLACKTOP – the road movie planned by its producers as a successor to EASY RIDER's triumph and ending up as a huge commercial failure – as a "revaluation of physical reality," with "the momentum of action [giving] way to the moment of gesture and the body." The last sentence of the article reads: "[T]he unmotivated hero and the pathos of failure will be the two negatives that result in a positive."[27]

Two negatives under whose sign a new, post-heroic but also post-political valorization of reality announces itself, with the body in its action-thwarting *givenness* acting as a "positive": we can see this pair as early – dare I say embryonic – incarnations of Elsaesser's "Siamese twins" trauma and terror. On the one hand, we have the embracing of universalized traumatization, resulting in passivity, paralysis, and self-pity. On the other hand, we have the terrorist perversion of the genuine act, corresponding to, well, if not the moment of gesture and body, then certainly to those WILD BUNCH-like outbursts of unmotivated, unsublimated energy and instantaneous fulfillment which in 1971 Elsaesser saw as taking the place of Hollywood's temporalization of image and experience by way of delay. What at the time appeared to be nihilistic is in retrospect legible as an "early warning sign" of the formation of a new socio-aesthetical regime of revaluating reality and revalorizing its profitable energetic potentials, a post-Fordist logic centered on ("repressively") desublimated self-enjoyment, on the authenticity of rebels and on the "wild" productivity of band- and bunch-like teams in creative industries.[28] Or should we, taking the masculinity crisis and psychotic violence of THE WILD BUNCH's Westerners as an optical device, even see a link between EASY RIDER's self-pitying hippie cowboys biking across the prairies dressed in suede and leather, and a self-fashioning post-Fordist Buffalo Bill dressed in women's skin?

Wherever this takes us, it seems that the detour – from the ethical act of political subjectification via breaking with social and cultural belonging to New Hollywood's unmotivated heroes – has brought us to a dead end: It seems that the "We" that impersonates a failure has taken us, more inescapably than before, into the closed circuits of a genealogy of a post-Fordist subsuming of any-life-whatever. Again, one should call upon the poetics of parapraxis to wrest, rescue, and reclaim the dimension of the political in its non-givenness from this closure. I suggest turning to an even earlier Elsaesser text to find the concept of a film aesthetic of performed failure that goes beyond both the cultural habitus of self-victimization and the ethos of a self-realization so anxious to be "fully" expressed. What is beyond the full is Fuller, the American filmmaker of that name, portrayed as a subject of political cinema in an essay first published in 1969 by the then 26-year-old Thomas Elsaesser.

In his essay, simply titled "Sam Fuller's SHOCK CORRIDOR," Elsaesser starts out with finding in Fuller a concept of subjectivity that contrasts with the classical American movie hero. Instead of an individualist relationship to the self and the world, there is in Fuller's protagonists

> a sense of inquisitiveness which often gives way to a kind of obsessive fascination. ... the logic of their actions is that of a strictly internal, existential purposiveness: to penetrate into unknown territory, to go behind enemy lines, or to desert to the enemy altogether. ... Parallel to the action, we therefore witness a process in which [an] external necessity (the mission, the goal) is validated existentially. For what do these characters care about Communism, the war in Indochina or Korea, the American Civil War, the Sioux nation – if not because invariably their fight becomes purely and simply a question of survival?[29]

Fuller's 1957 RUN OF THE ARROW is Elsaesser's implied reference when he mentions the Civil War and the Sioux, and although his essay has Fuller's SHOCK CORRIDOR as the main object of inquiry, this western is a good example of the kind of political existentialism it was aiming for. RUN OF THE ARROW is about a Southern rebel soldier who, right after the Civil War, joins the Sioux nation – not, however, for any "foundationalist" reason, such as a culturalist fascination with an allegedly *unalienated* fullness of Indian life, as invoked in DANCES WITH WOLVES. Rather, the "Johnny Reb" character becomes a Sioux because he refuses to accept the surrender of the Confederacy to the United States; he prefers separation to union, splits from his people who have decided to make their peace with the enemy, lives in the desert as a traveling one-man-war, and only joins the Sioux – as a white man and thus their enemy – after being captured by them and surviving the ordeal which gives the film its title. Being granted a Sioux identity as a reward for not having died at their hands, he accepts it because they are the enemy of his enemy (the US military). Nevertheless, he gives up his Indian life and wife at the end when he finds himself unable to bear the sight of the tribe torturing a captured Union officer and relieves his sworn enemy from his suffering by shooting him. So the outlaw is an Indian because he refuses to be a US citizen and ends up being part of the United States, as his Sioux wife tells him, purely because he is unable to remain a Sioux. Significantly, he is not a self-pitying, New Hollywood-style outsider; rather, the way in which Rod Steiger plays him makes him appear as unlikable in his high-pitched, self-pitying hate-sermons. Devoid of any positive qualities to found a rebel identity or imaginary identification upon, he becomes a political subject according to a logic similar to the RAF's founding rupture: by not-belonging, by tearing himself loose from a cultural habitus. In this he accepts the symbolic mandate of being a representative. As Elsaesser writes (with regard to SHOCK CORRIDOR's split-subject protagonist): "The schizophrenic, traitor to reality, is the true hero of America, because he alone is representative by taking upon him the cross of contradiction."[30]

Elsaesser's point on heroic schizophrenia (a version of "productive pathology" – or a verso to its recto?) is the result of an argument about America's rational, freedom-desiring impulses demonstrating the irrational and oppressive nature of that society. We might read here a philosophy of history in the vein of the *Dialectic of Englightenment*. Actually, it is Herbert Marcuse whom Elsaesser quotes regarding the concept of the American "enemy within." The reference to Marcuse, a key thinker of the events of 1968, can be seen as a theoretical linkage from Critical Theory to a Deleuzian/Guattarian ethics of the "schizo," which Elsaesser, from today's perspective, seems to invoke by in fact anticipating it.[31] Let us, however, retrace at this point the connection between Elsaesser's political aesthetics of cinema and philosophies of (radical) democracy: It is vital that the quest for self-knowledge on which the Fuller hero embarks and his representative role – his readiness for a position which the RAF took up as an impossible one – that, in short, Fuller's politics are not based on a liberal phenomenology of the rational pursuit of individual interest. Elsaesser writes that in Fuller's films, "communism is not an ideological notion, not even primarily a political one, but an existential one."[32] This political existentialism refutes a reductive understanding of politics as a choice between offerings in favor of a radical concept of politics as a milieu of existence and as the genuine production of a subject. This is a subjectification as the event of a political appearance, to use Rancière's terms, a subjectification in disagreement and disidentification. Or, to put it in Mouffe's ontological vocabulary of "the political," Elsaesser's view of Fuller's cinema as one in which the Western subject positions him/herself in a precarious relationship with, and thus in acknowledgement of, an "enemy" (not an "other," because there is no "self" to presuppose or rediscover) subscribes to an "agonistic" definition of politics in categories of the irreducibility of public passions, or affects, and of the performativity of adversarial we/they distinctions.[33] "[T]here can be no question of Fuller's heroes being 'objective' about Communism. Indeed, I would claim that they *have* to be violently anti-communist, racists, maniacs, etc., in order to encounter the 'other,' the alternative on a sufficiently intense emotional level," Elsaesser writes, and he calls this "the didactic-provocative nature of Fuller's cinema."[34]

The issue of cinematic teaching is brought up here with a focus on neither the rehearsal of flexibilization nor rationalization; in the latter respect, Elsaesser's position in 1969 differs from contemporary critiques of cinematic ideology – from attempts to rationalize images that "naturalize" power relations, a project inspired not least of all by a wish to "sanitize" cinema, to "put it right."[35] Instead, Elsaesser offers a theory of a productively "wrong" and ostensibly "inadequate" cinema, which is later rephrased as the poetic of parapraxis. What Elsaesser's more recent writings on performed failure refer to as "strangely adequate discrepancies," "conceptual slapstick," or "slips of the tongue" as "camouflaged articulations" with respect to New German Cinema, could be analyzed in VERBOTEN!, SHOCK CORRIDOR or other Fuller films. Fuller's B-movies are dedicated to disruptions in the sensible, to non-identitary subjectifications and self-founding "speech-events" (Rancière). This aesthetic of the "democratic act" sheds some light on what passes as "political film" in today's American or German mainstream cinema.[36]

Belonging Twice Over: A Body Too Much

To conclude with a recent piece of "unsane" cinema, let us briefly turn once more to Siamese twins; not exactly to Elsaesser's discursive Siamese twins of terror and trauma, however, but to the protagonist(s) of the Farrelly Brothers comedy STUCK ON YOU (2003). At first sight, the film may seem a mere joyful rehearsal of post-Fordist diversity management, a lesson in flexibilization in which two men conjoined at the hips take the place given to pilot-fish and other hippies in New Hollywood. The twins first perform admirably as high-speed "burger flippers" in their diner, and later one of them (!) has an acting career in a TV detective series, co-starring with Cher and dragging his brother along, who is rendered invisible with the help of blue-screen camera technique. But it eventually becomes clear that the film is less about "productive pathologies" and disabilities functioning as empowerment, or rather, it is so only by way of disturbing the count of parts of the social body: the actor brother's career has no obvious relationship to his handicap (unlike the RAIN MAN model where talent neatly complements a pathology), and, generally, disability in STUCK ON YOU does not translate into an identity with an "evident" foundation. Rather, the status of the twin's "god-given Siamese...ness," as Cher puts it in the film, is precarious with regard to its meaning as a phenomenon: from scene to scene, from one encounter to another, it seems to shift from visible to unnoticed, from significant to negligible.

When, in one dialogue, the twins are addressed as "Siamese twins," and one of them objects: "We're not Siamese! We're American!," we have, in the nutshell of a keyline, the affirmation of citizenship over foundational identity, the embracing of the "United States" in every sense as the manifestation of a political subjectivity. Performing a failure in this case implies insisting on the urgency of the question of what it means to say "We" politically, to refuse "having understood" what the adequate, well-founded, culturalizable group identity is. It means taking the system, or rather its irreducible democratic dimension, at its word by taking a meaning literally, thus escaping metaphorization as in Deleuze's aesthetic of "literalness" and parapractically, mimetically, overidentifyingly playing stupid to render a problem visible. Conceived as a political subject or two that cannot be quantified, the non-Siamese twins could be appropached along the lines of Elsaesser's interpretation of Fassbinder's episode in the omnibus film GERMANY IN AUTUMN; instead of a proper symbolization of bodies, they confront, assault us with the gross materiality of "a body too much."[37] This "too much," this embodied excess of being exposed and connected to a community, inescapable being "Stuck On You" as state of the union, is what distinguishes political subjectivity as "belonging twice over: belonging to the world of properties and parts and belonging to the improper community" from a rebel stance of not-belonging to which the economy of cultural identities has so many places (of work) to offer.[38]

Notes

1. Thomas Elsaesser, "Feminism, Foucault, and Deleuze (THE SILENCE OF THE LAMBS)," Thomas Elsaesser and Warren Buckland, *Studying Contemporary American Film: A Guide to Movie Analysis* (London: Arnold, 2002) 275.
2. Elsaesser, "Feminism, Foucault, and Deleuze" 275.
3. Thomas Elsaesser, "American Auteur Cinema: The Last – or First – Great Picture Show," *The Last Great American Picture Show: New Hollywood Cinema in the 1970s*, ed. Thomas Elsaesser, Alexander Horwath, and Noel King (Amsterdam: Amsterdam University Press, 2004) 66. Elsaesser refers to Michael Hardt and Antonio Negri, *Empire* (Cambridge / London: Harvard University Press, 2000).
4. Thomas Elsaesser, "The Mind-Game Film," *Puzzle Films: Complex Storytelling in Contemporary Cinema*, ed. Warren Buckland (Oxford: Blackwell, forthcoming).
5. Elsaesser, "The Mind-Game Film."
6. Elsaesser, "The Mind-Game Film."

7.   Elsaesser, "American Auteur Cinema" 44, 58.

8.   Thomas Elsaesser, "Postmodernism as Mourning Work," *Screen* 42.2 (2001): 201.

9.   Thomas Elsaesser, *Filmgeschichte und frühes Kino. Archäologie eines Medienwandels* (Munich: text + kritik, 2002) chapter X. See also Drehli Robnik, *Kino, Krieg, Gedächtnis. Affekt-Ästhetik, Nachträglichkeit und Geschichtspolitik im deutschen und amerikanischen Gegenwartskino*, PhD dissertation (University of Amsterdam, 2007) chapter 8.

10.   Elsaesser, "The Mind-Game Film."

11.   Elsaesser, "The Mind-Game Film." One is reminded here of the provocation in *October*'s "Visual Culture Questionnaire" which suggested "that visual studies is helping, in its own modest, academic way, to produce subjects for the next stage of globalized capital." *October* 77 (1996): 25.

12.   Elsaesser, "The Mind-Game Film."

13.   Jacques Rancière, *Disagreement: Politics and Philosophy* (Minneapolis / London: University of Minnesota Press, 1999) chapter 2.

14.   Elsaesser, "Postmodernism as Mourning Work" 196.

15.   Thomas Elsaesser, *Terror und Trauma. Zur Gewalt des Vergangenen in der BRD* (Berlin: Kadmos, 2007) 36, 45.

16.   Elsaesser, *Terror und Trauma* 42-47.

17.   Elsaesser, *Terror und Trauma* 47; Slavoj Žižek, *Welcome to the Desert of the Real! Five Essays on September 11 and Related Dates* (London: Verso, 2002).

18.   Thomas Elsaesser, "Antigone Agonistes: Urban Guerilla or Guerilla Urbanism? The Red Army Faction, *Germany In Autumn* and *Death Game*," *Giving Ground: The Politics of Propinquity*, ed. Joan Copjec and Michael Sorkin (London: Verso, 1999) 293, 297. I refer here to the original publication of the essay which, in German translation, became the centerpiece of Elsaesser's *Terror und Trauma* volume and was published in French as *Terrorisme, mythes et représentations: la RAF de Fassbinder aux T-shirts Prada-Meinhof* (Lille: Thousand Augen, 2005).

19.   Elsaesser, "Antigone Agonistes" 292.

20.   Elsaesser, "Antigone Agonistes" 294.

21.   Elsaesser, "Antigone Agonistes" 297.

22.   Elsaesser, "Antigone Agonistes" 297.

23.   Elsaesser, "Antigone Agonistes" 298.

24.   Elsaesser, "Why Hollywood," *Monogram* 1 (1971): 10.

25.   I am quoting this 1975 article from its 2004 reprint: Thomas Elsaesser, "The Pathos of Failure: American Films in the 1970s. Notes on the Unmotivated Hero," *The Last Great American Picture Show* 286.

26.   Elsaesser, "Why Hollywood" 10.

27.   Elsaesser, "The Pathos of Failure" 292.

28.   Some of these points are developed further in Drehli Robnik, "Allegories of Post-Fordism in 1970s New Hollywood: Countercultural Combat Films, Conspiracy Thrillers as Genre-Recycling," *The Last Great American Picture Show* 333-358. For a placing of THE WILD BUNCH, along with other 1960s "teamwork westerns," within the interpretive framework of capitalism's shift to professional élites, see Will Wright, *Sixguns and Society: A Structural Study of the Western* (Berkeley / Los Angeles: University of California Press, 1975). Wright mentions hippies – along with executives and scien-

tists –as one of the social groups that have adopted a self-perception as an élite of the specially skilled (184).

29. I am quoting this essay from a 1976 reprint: Thomas Elsaesser, "Sam Fuller's SHOCK CORRIDOR," *Movies and Methods Volume 1,* ed. Bill Nichols (Berkeley / Los Angeles: University of California Press, 1976) 292.
30. Elsaesser, "Sam Fuller's SHOCK CORRIDOR" 297.
31. Elsaesser, "Sam Fuller's SHOCK CORRIDOR" 295.
32. Elsaesser, "Sam Fuller's SHOCK CORRIDOR" 296.
33. Chantal Mouffe, *On the Political* (London / New York: Routledge, 2005) chapters 2, 3.
34. Elsaesser, "Sam Fuller's SHOCK CORRIDOR" 293.
35. One example would be "Young Mr. Lincoln, texte collectif," *Cahiers du cinéma* (Aug. 1970).
36. Elsaesser, *Terror und Trauma* 32, 132, 187.
37. Elsaesser, "Antigone Agonistes" 281.
38. Rancière 137.

Into the Mind and Out to the World

Memory Anxiety in the Mind-Game Film

Pepita Hesselberth and Laura Schuster

Enter

What would you do if you knew the future? Would you erase me? When you don't have a memory how can you remember who to trust? Change one thing, change everything. Reality is a thing of the past. Remember the future. Some memories are best forgotten. Can you miss someone you don't remember? You are not who you think you are. If you thought it was just a trick of the mind, prepare yourself for the truth. Get ready for the ride of your life. Into your body, under your skin, beyond your senses.

These are just a few of the taglines used to promote a variety of contemporary highly self-reflexive mainstream films – respectively, DONNIE DARKO (Richard Kelly, 2001), ETERNAL SUNSHINE OF THE SPOTLESS MIND (Michel Gondry, 2004), THE I INSIDE (Roland Suso Richter, 2003), THE BUTTERFLY EFFECT (Eric Bress and J. Mackye Grube, 2004), THE MATRIX (Andy and Larry Wachowski, 1999), PAYCHECK (John Woo, 2003), MEMENTO (Christopher Nolan, 2000), CODE 46 (Michael Winterbottom, 2003), DARK CITY (Alex Proyas, 1998), DÉJÀ VU (Tony Scott, 2006), TOTAL RECALL (Paul Verhoeven, 1990), and eXistenZ (David Cronenberg, 1999). These films are thematically as well as aesthetically preoccupied with the rewriting of time, memory, and agency, and they are all well-known examples of the "mind-game film," as this "new tendency" has recently been termed by Thomas Elsaesser.[1] Their scenarios include perceptive delusional disorders, surveillance societies, memory erasure, scientific experiments, virtual reality games, cyborgs, and supernatural phenomena. Despite the variety of the scenarios, however, one binding feature is that all these stories abandon the notion of one reliable, absolute reality, mostly by presenting a non-actual story world such as a future scenario (sci-fi) or by narrating themselves through the perception of a distorted protagonist (psychological delusion/ghost story). Moreover, the films do not fully resolve ambiguities in their story and, with increasing frequency, remain open-ended, which allows for the existence of unconventional phenomena such as paranormal activity or multiple realities. Time is presented

as manipulable, either in terms of chronological or subjectively experienced temporality, and/or as a somehow incoherent or ambiguous time-space continuum.
The past and future are often portrayed as highly subjective domains that can be
accessed, erased, re/designed, or modified.

Many film scholars have tried to get a grip on these films. Some have referred
to them as "non-linear," "parallel," "circular," "disordered," "episodic," "cubist"
and "multiple-draft narratives," "punk" or "puzzle films," "twist movies," and
"techno-cinema," whereas others have approached the issue more in terms like
"neobaroque cinema," "narratography," and "temportation."[2] Corpuses differ
and approaches vary greatly, but a central question seems to haunt academics:
how do we come to terms with this particular trend of films, which are decidedly
self-referential about time and invoke sophisticated media literacy on the part of
the viewer? Although often informed by aspects such as narrative complexity,
circularity, or techno-fascination, the films seem most crucially defined by the
mind-tricks and the games they play on the perceptions of audiences and characters alike, as Elsaesser stresses: "crucial items of information are withheld or
ambiguously presented" to protagonists and/or spectators, for instance when
events are presented through the delusional or otherwise aberrant perceptions of
a character. Many mind-game films do not fully untangle a given mystery, sometimes even allowing for the existence of multiple realities and parallel worlds.[3]

Memory anxiety forms a distinctive preoccupation within the mind-game paradigm. Films like DARK CITY, MEMENTO, ETERNAL SUNSHINE OF THE SPOTLESS
MIND, PAYCHECK, and CODE 46 revolve around the reworking of memory in remarkably explicit ways. Their release and subsequent success suggest a somewhat troubled fascination in contemporary western culture with concerns about
memory and memory loss in the age of omnipresent storage media. This fascination intimates a concern about the media as an assault on or at least weakening of
subjectivity, as if a pervasive media presence disempowers subjects and makes
them passive. At the same time, however, personal memory is often presented as
a unique trait or utility that warrants individuality, spurs desire, and produces
agency under threatening or chaotic circumstances. It is this particular tension,
this trouble with memory within the mind-game "tendency," that we wish to address here.

We will examine MEMENTO and CODE 46 as two extremes of mind-game plots,
in which reality's ambiguity is usually motivated *either* by a protagonist's distorted observations *or* by large-scale deception, technological modifications, or
supernatural phenomena taking place within the filmic diegesis. This distinction,
we will argue, is of particular relevance to those mind-game films concerned with
memory matters. It roughly corresponds with what Elsaesser has termed the die-

getic "in here" and "out there" disruptions, which prompt investigations on the nature of cinematic storytelling:

> [S]uch disruptions, especially when attributed to the world "out there," rather than to our subjective ("in here") perception of it, pose a double challenge to spectators. The films may tell us something about one of the fundamental attractions, but also contradictions that the cinema embodies, namely that it fashions credible worlds by manipulating our perception of time and space (through editing, montage, narration).[4]

There are several other reasons for bringing MEMENTO and CODE 46 together when investigating popular, contemporary explorations of the relationship between media, memory, and agency. First of all, what is striking about both films is their multilayered narrative structure. They are what we could call recollection narratives, as the act of recollection seems to be incorporated into their narrative strategy. The films thus exemplify the preoccupation with the process of memory and the question of agency on a diegetic level.

Secondly, the preoccupation with memory is channeled through apprehensions about memory loss. In MEMENTO, Leonard's condition – damage of his short-term memory system – prevents him from creating new memories. In CODE 46, a subversive romance leads to the medical removal of the protagonists' memories of one another, without their knowledge of the intervention.

Thirdly, the topics of personal memory – materialized in personally imprinted mediated memory objects – and memory loss are examined in explicit relationship to agency. In recent debates about new media, the concept of agency has often been employed to elucidate the aesthetic pleasures associated with so-called interactive narrativity.[5] However, we believe that the films central to this investigation address a more fundamental and philosophical problem of agency, by raising profound questions about the difference between events happening *in* me and *to* me in the "acts of memory."[6] By focusing on memory as an activity, in other words, on *acts* of memory, MEMENTO and CODE 46 offer opposing views as they investigate and debate the difference between event-causation (the view that our actions are caused by prior events which necessitate their occurrence) and agent-causation (the view that we have the capacity to initiate events, the power to cause or to refrain from causing initial events to happen). It is this particular exploration of agency through the films' investigation of memory acts, memory loss and memory objects that we will concentrate on.

And finally, memory and agency in both films cannot be separated from processes of selection and *narrativization*, from recording technologies, or from the body as a recorder and source of information. We suspect that in the way that MEMENTO and CODE 46 present personal and mediated memory, they mimic the ongoing process of *narrativization* taking place in our minds anytime we process personal memories. Here, memory and manipulation travel across various media. As Elsaesser stated during one of his Amsterdam lectures on media and memory, "Memory is essentially discontinuous: not the accumulation and ordering of information but gaps, forgetting, and substitution."[7] Thus, rather than following the common argument that the films first and foremost signify a current concern with the general reliability of our perceptions amidst the continuous creation and exposure of artificial images, the key questions we wish to address are how exactly memory functions within and how it affects these films' narratives, as well as how it relates to issues of media, information, agency, and subjectivity.

In Here

MEMENTO tells the story of Leonard Shelby (Guy Pearce), a former insurance investigator in search of the man he believes has killed his wife and inflicted him with severe head trauma, which prevents him from storing new memories. The film is most renowned for its partially reversed narrative structure. Leonard's investigation is depicted in color sections that are presented in reverse chronological order. Intervening sections in black and white show us clips of Leonard's "authentic" memory prior to the attack, presumably chronologically, as well as fragments of telephone conversations with an anonymous caller in his hotel room, which take place after the attack.

When the character Natalie (Carrie-Anne Moss) in MEMENTO is introduced, it is hard to read her hostility, and we need subsequent scenes to provide us with answers as to what caused this hostility, not to mention answering questions regarding her origins, her role and her interests. It is true, of course, that flashbacks or informative suspense – narrative clues revealed or explained out of chronological order – often fulfill similar functions, and this would have explained Natalie's enigmatic intervention, had the narrative order not been reversed. The point is, however, that there is a distinction between *narrative tenses*. Although a flashback introduces an element of memory, it actually presents us with an event from the past. In contrast, in the case of MEMENTO, the film does not recollect for us but rather provokes anticipation of future past events: instead of triggering a "what happens next," it prompts speculations about "what happened before" this or that event. According to Janet Harbord, this disturbance of the "forward propulsion of cinematic time" is typical for contemporary cinematic play on time's irreversibility. "More than in a flashback, the structural challenge of these films is the twinning of epistemology with ontology: what does it feel like to move back in time, how does retrospective knowledge inform our experience?"[8] The film thus underscores the link between memory and agency in its narrative plot, while simultaneously questioning the nature of that link.

This line of inquiry is staged by means of the conception of recollection that forms the foundation of the film's narrative. Recollection is presented as a conscious act, in which the past is actively tied into present events and, as such, is prolonged into the future. Memory is presented as a dynamic process of appropriation, association and translation of the past (in)to the present. Past events do not remain intact: remembrance shifts their shape, their meaning, and their significance. Memory is thus portrayed as an activity imposed *on* the past – one that can be characterized as a violent intervention. But the relation between the present of such acts and the past that is subjected to them is also reversible.

MEMENTO claims that, in order to act, one needs memories: memories provoke actions, and thus make diegesis possible. But although the mediated memory objects give Leonard agency in the sense that they enable him to act, his greatest exercise of power lies in his ability to distort the objects that facilitate his never-ending story. As such, the film does not simply explore the conditions of memory, but a Sartrean tension between the concept of agency and the idea of total freedom. It opposes post-WWII idealizations of freedom as the most essential feature of human happiness, the view that total freedom results in total chaos, and that, instead, human happiness relies on the limits we set for ourselves on that freedom.

It may seem paradoxical that a film that advocates an active conception of memory would simultaneously criticize an idealized interpretation of agency as total freedom. But the film, thanks to its narrativity and visuality, can do something that for example philosophy cannot do so easily. Thus, instead of presenting a linear argument, it fabricates an argumentative loop around the connection among media, memory, and agency: media facilitates memory facilitates agency facilitates media and so on. It is because Leonard can remember that he can act, and, because he can act, he can create mediated memory objects, and mediated memory objects, for their part, trigger memories.

One of the key concerns of MEMENTO is the paradox of memory and amnesia as simultaneous means of dealing with the world around us, a paradox pointedly addressed by Andreas Huyssen in his reflection on contemporary memory culture, *Present Pasts*. According to Huyssen, our (western) obsession with public and private memorization must be read as an attempt to come to terms with our growing sense of a temporal instability and spatial fragmentation of the world we inhabit.[9] We counteract the ever-increasing informational and perceptual overload with acts of memory, while simultaneously, "the more we are asked to remember in the wake of the information explosion and the marketing of memory, the more we seem to be in danger of forgetting and the stronger the need to forget."[10]

There is a scene in which Leonard is frantically looking for a pen to write something down, something that will remind him of what has just happened. Outside we hear a car door shut, Leonard looks up, and Natalie walks in, severely beaten. He freezes and asks her what happened. When she tells him that she has been beaten up by some guy named Dodd because of something Leonard told her to do, he tends to her bruises and assures her he will take care of the situation – a future event to which we have at that point already been a witness. We find out only later that it was actually Leonard himself who beat Natalie up, an assault to which she provokes him when he refuses to act as her hit man. Only Leonard's hesitant glance at his own bruised hand in the following scene hints at the incident that preceded this.

This example is one among many that shows how the film challenges the equation of agency equaling total freedom. It is Leonard's amnesia that allows other characters in the film to manipulate him into doing things, while still allowing him to believe that he is acting of his own free will. Although his amnesia may not prevent him from acting, it does prevent him from having control over his own actions. Simultaneously, however – and again this is emphasized by the film's reverse narrative structure – it is suggested that events other than the ones presently conceived in his own mind have no effect on him, simply because they have ceased to exist. When Natalie asks him what the use would be to kill the man who murdered his wife and "took away his fucking memory," since he will never remember it anyway, Leonard points out that "Just because there are things that I don't remember, doesn't make my actions meaningless. The world doesn't just disappear when you close your eyes, does it?" However, it is precisely the opposite that is suggested, because it is due to the fact that there are some things that Leonard cannot remember that his actions actually become meaningful.

This is underscored by the film's appalling final scene, which renders all of Leonard's subsequent – for us previous – actions and decisions morally corrupt. He has just been confronted by Teddy (Joe Pantoliano) with the possible but probable idea that he has fabricated his long-term recollection of his wife. She may, in fact, not have been murdered, and he has probably made the whole thing up to cover up a truth he cannot handle, and further provide him with a vengeful purpose in his life. He leaves behind some clues that will eventually lead him to killing the man called Teddy, as we know from the opening scene. After that he willfully destroys the photo of another man he has just killed, a man he initially thought was his wife's murderer. He then heads out in his car and contemplates: "I have to believe in a world outside my own mind. I have to believe that my actions still have meaning, even if I don't remember them. I have to believe that,

when I close my eyes, the world's still here." He closes his eyes, the image flick-
ers and we see fast-moving images of the streets around him, his eyes still closed,
interspliced with images of his wife leaning against his shoulder, a tattoo with the
words "I've done it" clearly visible on his chest as he continues: "Do I believe the
world's still here? Is it still out there?" He opens his eyes, with earlier events by
this time probably already deleted, he looks around and states simply "Yeah."

The notion of trauma needs to be considered at this point. Leonard's loss of
memory was caused by a violent event that appears to have traumatized him.
According to Leonard, he was hit in the head, which fractured his skull, as he
attempted to prevent the rape and murder of his wife. According to Teddy, his
wife survived the assault but subsequently lured Leonard into helping her commit suicide by repeatedly asking him to shoot her up with her daily doses of
insulin as she could no longer handle Leonard's condition. In either case, the
amnesia or damage to Leonard's short-term memory system is thus caused by
and is constitutive of his trauma. It is both fuelled by his so-called authentic
memories of "her," as much as it is a safety valve for keeping these "false" true
memories from breaking the surface. As such, it is a classic example of traumatic
recall.

In the case of Leonard's version of the story, the *repressed* traumatic event of the
rape and murder of his wife is mechanically re-enacted as drama in the staging of
his investigation and his vengeance. In the case of Teddy's version, the traumatic
experience of killing his wife is not so much repressed as it is *dissociated*: it is
split-off into the story of Sammy Jenkis, a story Leonard keeps repeating over the
phone to someone unknown.[11] Although, if it is placed "outside" himself, it can
be re-enacted, it cannot be re-incorporated into his own story. As Thomas Elsaesser asserts, Leonard's trauma is a *prosthetic* trauma and as such, a *protective* trauma that serves as a shield against another trauma.[12] In both cases, the traumatic
event – regardless of whether it was John G. or Leonard himself who killed his
wife – cannot lose its hold over its subject, Leonard. Traumatic events cannot
become a memory because they resist *narrativization*, and they persist in the
present because Leonard lacks narrative mastery. But ultimately it is Leonard
who turns it into a solitary event: he kills his only witness, Teddy, and in a newly
inscribed tattoo, he instructs himself never to answer the phone again. So, even
though MEMENTO makes explicit statements about the necessity of memory as a
device which enables you to live and defines who you are, memory loss is presented as an act that also facilitates rather than negates agency.

Thus, even though the film suggests that one needs memories in order to act,
memory loss is not necessarily presented as a form of de-agenting. On the contrary, it is presented as a skill, as a unique way of dealing with information, which
Thomas Elsaesser has referred to as a "productive pathology" for dealing with

contemporary culture's "stripping of long-term memory" and the "program-ming" of short-term memory.[13] Within the mind-game film, time and agency, memory and identity "become an issue, not only because of an abundance of data, but because an apparent pathological, somatic or 'sick' response to complex-ity, coincidences and chaos proves to be the more successful strategy."[14]

Out There

In contrast to MEMENTO, CODE 46 enlarges the "condition" of inconsistent mem-ory into a futurized technocracy, where authoritative control and intervention in-terfere with its efficient use, and where the possibility of manipulation extends the unreliability of personal memory into the field of objective information. Furthermore, the film posits memory as a substitute or fix for diegetic incoher-ence, but at the same time, takes a highly ambivalent stance toward the possibi-lity of memory as a source of agency.

In a brief synopsis of its over-packed plot, CODE 46's "near future"[15] scenario presents an American corporate fraud investigator, William (Tim Robbins), tra-veling to Shanghai to put an end to the forgery of travel documents at an interna-tional visa-issuing organization. His instant attraction to the culprit, Maria (Sa-mantha Morton), however, causes him to ignore her crime, and the two embark on a brief romance. Weeks later, William is sent back to Shanghai because the fraud activities have continued, and he discovers that Maria has been hospita-lized. An investigation reveals that their fling resulted in a pregnancy which, un-beknownst to her, was aborted along with her memories of William because the two are unfit genetic partners for sexual reproduction. Their intuitive love, how-ever, continues, and the couple makes an unsuccessful attempt to flee the sys-tem. By the end of the film, William has returned to his (married) life, and Maria has been expelled from society to live as an outcast in a vast desert wasteland, presumably the result of global warming.

CODE 46 is an interesting mind-game film because it very ostentatiously blurs the distinctions between memory and information, subjective and objective re-gistrations, coherence and fragmentation. The constant interplay of remembered and recorded events renders any distinction between the two problematic, and perhaps irrelevant. Both systems follow a similar logic of fragmentation and se-lection, and together produce the coherent tale of an illicit love affair in a society where risk minimization motivates genetic engineering, social exclusion, and in-vasions of privacy. The film itself comprises an unusually large selection of narra-tive fragments. Cinematography, editing, and mise-en-scène add to a collage-like collection of imaginative sequences. Knowledge, then, is manufactured and proclaimed rather than being inherently true. In this sense, the inhabitants of CODE 46's world are subject to pre-selected and fragmented information as much as the film's spectators are.

What happens to memory and information in CODE 46 could be called *cross-memory*, a term also used for remote-access ICT solutions, where it denotes systems and capabilities that can exchange information or operations and access virtual memory beyond the range of a simple network.[16] With regard to CODE 46, this principle serves to indicate not only that memory functions mostly as information, but also that personal memories extend well beyond the individual mind. In the film, memories and the "codes" of identity are dispersed throughout the body: in the eyes, the fingertips, even tone-deafness. Intrapersonal exchanges of memory and information are equally common; William carries an "empathy virus" (a biological-software add-on enabling a degree of mind reading) that opens other people's subjective minds and memories for him to scan for information.

Memories can be stored into fully external "address spaces." Even after an involuntary, unnoticed abortion and memory erasure (in itself an act of cross-memory intervention, effaced by the "relocation" of Maria's childhood memory of surgery), Maria's intuitive love for William remains stored within a prescient dream, to which she regains access only much later. Maria has a memory album into which she uploads precious memories from the vantage points of her physical presence in their actual locations. It is this album that allows her to regain her memories of William after their medical removal – firstly, because through the album, William can prove his previous presence in her life. Digitally stored moments are able to prove subjective recordings, which become objective documentation again, while abortion and amnesia go hand in hand. All information is manipulable, thus making the subjective nature of personal memory irrelevant. Both information and memory are equally absolute or equally subject to change.

The embodied mind, then, becomes a medium, a recording technology with its own mode of data processing, compatible with other forms of information. Moreover, memory does not reside solely in the mind, but also manifests itself throughout the human body. The circumstances provided by the peculiar information/control society sketched in CODE 46 perfectly support N. Katherine Hayles's suggestion that "in certain contexts the body itself becomes a medium at the same time as it is in-formed by other media."[17] In Winterbottom's film, memory is essentially de-localized from the brain where we tend to position it, and not only travels across the body but also across media.

In CODE 46, both objective information and subjective or personal memory are unstable and instantaneous. As much as this threatens conventional demarcations, it also prohibits a clear sense of agency. Individual agency and choice are only possible if an agent has enough information to act in a meaningful and effective manner. For both Maria and William, ubiquitous supervision by insurance authorities (the downside of cross-memory practices) largely determines the distribution of agency. If necessary, individual memories will be altered in order to better meet international policies of risk minimization. Memory and desire motivate individual acts, but both become permeable as soon as they collide with society's rules and interests.

All the same, CODE 46 defers to such dystopian pessimism with a great belief in the agency of the human soul and its partial immunity to technology-induced tampering: the romance between William and Maria survives even after her memory of him is erased. Love thus becomes the one possibility for total freedom, and serves as a major cause for individual agency in the age of memory manipulation. Eventually, however, the system has its way. Maria loses her citizenship and retains all of her memories, with full private autonomy but no power to act whatsoever. William is restored to his prior life as a married fraud investigator, oblivious to the fact of his affair with Maria.

Through CODE 46's cross-memory practices, memory distortions, connections, and utilities run from "in here" to "out there," across media, and across bodies. This can empower and/or disempower depending on the context, or concomitantly, as in the various conflicting sorts of agency presented. Prior to the romance, Maria embodied subversive agency by forging travel documents in her employer's laboratory, mostly to the advantage of others. Her choice of a freedom to act results in the authorities removing her from society and denying her any sort of practical agency, which results in her spending her days re-living the past and repeating "I miss you." Maria is left with her memory intact, full autonomy, and a position outside society. In contrast, by erasing his most recent memories, the authorities have decided that William should return to his previous life, with his social agency restored but with a restricted freedom to act. Agency in CODE 46 cannot be defined as something one has, lacks, or desires. And if a rebellious romance is regarded as the ultimate act of agency possible within the parameters of this society, it comes at a dear price.

In fact, Maria's agency arguably manifests itself at an entirely different level. The filmic information facilitates an alternative reading in which she imagines the entire story as a defensive fantasy screen against her near-unlivable actual life, as an outcast of society, wandering through the desert (Baudrillard's "Welcome to the Desert of the Real" is at least as salient here as it is in THE MATRIX). Maria's remembering or perhaps imagining a past romance would then motivate the entire film, which at least grants her the indisputable agency of a narrator. This, in turn, reminds us that film itself is as discontinuous and fragmentary as personal memory, and that, moreover, both arrive at coherence only by their very discontinuity.

With information becoming increasingly unreliable, personal memory becomes a troublesome motivation for agency. Though memory can constitute a sense of agency even under the circumstances of CODE 46's control society, the result is always contingent and dependent upon the approval of authorities. Memory here contaminates and interferes with a clear sense of agency: it always has a hidden agenda, and sometimes proves counterproductive.

However dependent upon the specific parameters of its story, CODE 46's attention to memory interference does have a greater relevance. Without heeding its dystopian warning, we may simply observe that by presenting distorted memories in a fashion mimicking these distortions (the experience of characters whose perceptive systems have been altered by either mental or technologically induced trauma), the film reminds us not to take memory for granted. Media, memory, and agency are all presented as matters dealing with information, selection, and choice. As a consequence, all three are susceptible to alteration or distortion. A porous memory here may reflect contemporary uncertainties regarding the omnipresence of intrusive and sometimes fabricated information; it thus becomes a protective shield for the traumatic impact of information overload. As such, the film demonstrates that what we think we objectively remember is always already informed by memory, desire, or the mind's eye, and possibly by external agents imposing their purposes onto ours, regardless of whether or not a camera – or any other kind of manipulative technology – has had anything to do with it.

Exit

The diegetic differences between the "in here" and "out there" distortions of perception and memory largely account for the varying impact and results of memory disorder in MEMENTO and CODE 46, respectively. Whereas MEMENTO's "in here" structure of memory distortion allows for an efficient and opportunistic use of memory processing, the same tactic proves a poor substitute for coherence in the "out there" manipulability of people's lives in CODE 46. There, personal memory is a specific kind of information which is beholden to the same conditions of digital memory or information so that manipulation (permutation, relocation, duplication) is easy, and its implementation in goal orientation only further dismantles the fixed notions of subjectivity and agency. Moreover, memory in MEMENTO offers both protagonist and spectator an escape from the harshness of time-space causality and an ambiguous refuge in the sense of causality that is entirely subjective and synthetic, whereas, in CODE 46's society of control, subjectivity is synthetic to begin with. The manipulability of subjects' entire lives prohibits any effective use of personal memories, goals, or desires; the pursuit of these inevitably leads to one's ostracism from organized society.

In their epistemological and ontological disruptions of what we generally assume a causally ordered reality, governed by the rules of time and space, both films somewhat betray the gain we expect from narrative fiction cinema: the pleasurable ordering of staged events to which we can relate but from which we always remain at a safe distance. The destabilization of precisely these factors in films such as MEMENTO and CODE 46 creates particular subjectivities. The frailer a film's diegetic reality, the more subjective experience and memory are pushed forward as sources of information. Memory steps in where time-space causality loses ground, but never quite makes up for the loss. Thus, perhaps memory is crucial to subjectivity here simply because time-space causality fails to deliver in these chaotic, fragmented story-worlds.

Furthermore, in both films, memory interrelates with the body, with external objects, and with recording technologies – from handwritten remarks, tattoos, and Polaroid photography in MEMENTO to a wide variety of audiovisual gadgets, flat screens, and surveillance recorders in CODE 46. What is interesting about these materializations of memory vis-à-vis the films' explorations of memory acts and memory loss is the fact that they propose *fiction* as the ultimate tool for recollection and our conceptions of time and memory. This corresponds with the suggestion that human beings need the fiction of time and space, of cause and effect, in order to imagine agency, which is brought to the fore, as we have tried to demonstrate, by the films' narratively fixed focus on remembering and forgetting as reciprocal activities. Memory acts, memory loss, memory objects, and cross-memory practices are thus presented as the *sine qua non* of subjectivity in the age of omnipresent storage media.

And so we circle back, via Elsaesser's hint that cinema fashions credibility out of manipulation, to an earlier discussion on fragmentation and discontinuity in memory and film. In the late 1980s, Friedrich Kittler famously proclaimed the demise of individual memory under the increasing omnipresence of electronic storage media: "Once storage media can accommodate optical and acoustic data, human memory capacity is bound to dwindle. Its 'liberation' is its end."[18] Kittler notes that, in any transcriptive process of media storage, and probably without our awareness, something is inevitably lost; not only is there a decline in our faculty to remember, but also a loss of fullness and detail due to the threshold logic of binary information. This notion basically pervades our two films on the simplest levels: both ponder the pseudo-truths produced by the imperfect storage of information or experience, in the human mind and so too in recording media.

In their concern about the importance and unreliability of personal memory, these two – but also other – mind-game films involving memory matters tell us something about cinema and recording by enlarging the possible manipulations of inconsistent memory: they show how recording and personal memory can interfere with, or be a substitute for, one another. In the selection and *narrativization* of fragmented events, they zoom in on a "technical" aspect that relates the cinema to the mental processing of information and memories, the impossibility of a full account, and the necessity of fragmented perceptions.

Mary Ann Doane poses a related argument specific to early cinema. Benjamin and Freud, she states, have shown how consciousness reveals its function in modernity as a "stimulus shield" against rupture, shock, and contingency that "would, of course, be tougher, more impenetrable, in a highly developed techno-logical society."[19] Doane argues that in modern societies, *cinema* functions as a protective buffer against information overload, which is far more effective than our own minds.[20] Because cinema only records brief intervals of (staged) time and often adds the selective process of *narrativization*, "time is produced as an effect, at least in part to protect the subject from the anxieties of total representation generated by the new technological media."[21]

In a similar vein, Thomas Elsaesser has stated that cinema contains the potential infinity and contingency of modern-day informational data-flows, and as such, functions to mask the epistemological impact of modernity on the Cartesian subject. Narrative cinema, and classical narrative cinema in particular, can create a buffer against the shock or trauma of real-life disorder(liness). The mechanisms of narrative and cinema are of equal and supplementary importance here: both arguably please us simply by virtue of their merit of turning random chaos (the Lacanian Real, or the arbitrariness of reality) into order and causality by implementing demarcations in time and space. Narrative generally promises to "make sense," cinema adds the comfort of a very concrete pre-selection in a seemingly continuous reality: the recording of moving states and energies in time.

Yet, Elsaesser notes that somehow this principle has begun to fail us. Classical narrative cinema at once masks and admits to producing the Cartesian subject, as representation has become "the phantasm of the subject, needed to maintain a semblance of identity (Žižek), in order to protect the 'schizo-subject' (Deleuze) from 'noise' (Kittler)."[22] In contrast, the contraventions and aberrations of contemporary mind-game films *reveal* the symptoms of the strains of classical representation and the kinds of (goal oriented) agency associated with it. The mind-game film, Elsaesser asserts, corresponds to a different modality of agency and in particular with a *parapractic* agency ("the poetic justice of '*Fehl-Leistungen*'") in which the locus of agency is ambivalent and multitudinous, oscillating between the subjects' consciousness and consciousness-less images endowed with agency.[23]

In the figure of Leonard, however, the divide between subject and object collapses. He is both subject *and* object, both a goal-oriented *re*-action hero whose goal lacks a clear-cut indexical referent *and* an "action"-image, a data-processor, a memory object. As such, MEMENTO – still departing from the "safe" place of representation – reflects on the "performative presence" of the cinematic image itself, where every performance is liable to loss of control, contingency is productive (or fatal) and every performative act risks the resistance of both objects and subjects.

MEMENTO's closed circuit, or the fact that there is no "out there" to the "in here" reality of the medium, resists resolution or closure. Leonard's repetitive reprogramming of his own mind constitutes something of a causative feedback loop. His status as a medium *within* the filmic text in a way transgresses all the blurred boundaries between the subjective/objective registrations and the mind/body or mind/machine relations in CODE 46. These blurred boundaries indicate the fluidity of information streams and suggest a "near future" filled with fascinating interactions between all of the above. However, the insistent belief in a truth outside mediated consciousness or memory ensures that the ubiquitous technological mediation in CODE 46 will remain somewhat externalized. MEMENTO more fully exploits the convergence of mind and medium. Leonard's peculiar presence and agency in the film testify to any medium's capacity to chart and problematize subjectivity through the phantasmatic subjectivities it produces – a capacity that the mind-game film in particular is endowed with.

Notes

1. Thomas Elsaesser, "The Mind-Game Film," *Puzzle Films: Complex Storytelling in Contemporary Cinema*, ed. Warren Buckland (Oxford: Blackwell, forthcoming).
2. Jamie Skye Bianco, "Techno-Cinema," *Comparative Literature Studies* 41.3 (2004): 377-403; David Bordwell, "Film Futures," *SubStance* 31.1 (2002): 88-104; David Bordwell, *The Way Hollywood Tells It: Story and Style in Modern Movies* (Berkeley: University of California Press, 2006); Edward Branigan, "Nearly True: Forking Plots, Forking Interpretations: A Response to David Bordwell's 'Film Futures,'" *SubStance* 31.1 (2002): 105-114; Sean Cubitt, *The Cinema Effect* (Cambridge: MIT Press, 2005); David Denby, "The New Disorder: Adventures in Film Narrative," *The New Yorker* (5 March 2007); David Scott Diffrient, "Alternate Futures, Contradictory Pasts: Forking Paths and Cubist Narratives in Contemporary Film," *Screening the Past* 20 (Dec. 2006); Bruce Isaacs, "Non-Linear Narrative," *New Punk Cinema*, ed. Nicholas Rombes (Edinburgh: Edinburgh University Press, 2005) 126-135; Erven Lavik, "Narrative Structure in *The Sixth Sense*: A New Twist in 'Twist Movies'?," *The Velvet Light Trap* 58.1 (Fall 2006): 55-

64; Murray Smith, "Parallel Lines," *American Independent Cinema: A Sight and Sound Reader*, ed. Jim Hillier (London: BFI, 2001) 155-164; Garrett Stewart, *Framed Time: Toward a Postfilmic Cinema* (Chicago / London: University of Chicago Press, 2007); Fiona Villella, "Circular Narratives: Highlights of Popular Cinema in the '90s," *Senses of Cinema*, Jan. 2000: <http://www.sensesofcinema.com/contents/00/3/circular.html>. Last visited 9 Aug. 2007.

3.   Thomas Elsaesser, "The Mind-Game Film."

4.   Thomas Elsaesser, "Contingency and Agency: Cinema after the Image," unpublished paper, 3.

5.   According to Janet Murray, for example: "Agency is the satisfying power to take meaningful action and see the results of our decisions and choices." Janet Horowitz Murray, *Hamlet on the Holodeck: The Future of Narrative in Cyberspace* (New York: Free Press, 1997) 126. Also see Marie-Laure Ryan, *Narrative as Virtual Reality: Immersion and Interactivity in Literature and Electronic Media* (Baltimore: Johns Hopkins University Press, 2001).

6.   Mieke Bal, Jonathan V. Crewe, and Leo Spitzer, eds., *Acts of Memory: Cultural Recall in the Present* (Hanover / London: Dartmouth College / University Press of New England, 1999).

7.   Thomas Elsaesser, *Classic Texts in Media Theory*, Research Master Media Studies, University of Amsterdam, 30 September 2005.

8.   Janet Harbord, *The Evolution of Film: Rethinking Film Studies* (Cambridge: Polity, 2007) 127.

9.   Andreas Huyssen, *Present Pasts: Urban Palimpsests and the Politics of Memory* (Stanford: Stanford University Press, 2003) 16-17.

10.   Huyssen 18.

11.   For the distinction between repressed and dissociated memory and narrativity, see Mieke Bal's "Introduction" to *Acts of Memory* vii-xvii.

12.   Thomas Elsaesser, "Was wäre, wenn du schon tot bist? Vom 'postmodernen' zum 'post-mortem'-Kino am Beispiel von Christopher Nolans *Memento*," *Zeitsprünge. Wie Filme Geschichte(n) erzählen*, ed. Christine Rüffert, Irmbert Schenk, Karl-Heinz Schmid, and Alfred Tews (Berlin: Bertz, 2004) 122. Elsaesser's work on trauma is extensive and thought provoking. Particularly relevant texts for further reading include one recent and one forthcoming publication in which he develops a theory of trauma related to media's narrativity, (retroactive) temporality, (negative) performativity and inherent referentiality that goes well beyond traumatic recollection itself, towards what he has referred to as a post-ontological approach of contemporary media. See Thomas Elsaesser, *Terror und Trauma. Zur Gewalt des Vergangenen in der BRD* (Berlin: Kadmos, 2007) and Thomas Elsaesser, *Melodrama and Trauma: Modes of Cultural Memory in the American Cinema* (London: Routledge, forthcoming).

13.   Elsaesser actually argues that Leonard's amnesia is a productive pathology primarily *for others*, i.e., Natalie and Teddy, who manage to transform Leonard into a hit man and drug dealer by giving him false information in his quest for revenge. Given the fact, however, that the film also hints at the function and – perhaps contingent – agency of ignorance for Leonard himself, we think it is safe to suggest that Leonard's

amnesia is also presented as an appropriate pathology *for himself* and as such, for the recipient. Thomas Elsaesser, "The Mind-Game Film."

14. Thomas Elsaesser, "Contingency and Agency" 16.

15. For a definition of the "near future" film, see Richard Koeck and François Penz, "Screen City Legibility," *City* 7.3 (Nov. 2003): 364-375.

16. "With proper setup of the operating system, it is possible for a program in one standard address space to communicate with programs in other address spaces. A number of cross-memory capabilities are possible, but two are commonly used: [t]he ability to call a program that resides in a different address space [and] the ability to access (fetch, store) virtual memory in another address space." In "Controlling Cross-Memory Communication," from IBM infocenter database, <http://publib.boulder.ibm.com/infocenter/zoslnctr/v1r7/index.jsp?topic=/com.ibm.zsecurity.doc/zsecc_072.html>. Last visited Oct. 2007.

17. N. Katherine Hayles, *My Mother Was a Computer: Digital Subjects and Literary Texts* (Chicago: University of Chicago Press, 2005) 36.

18. Friedrich Kittler, *Gramophone, Film, Typewriter* (Stanford: Stanford University Press, 1999 [1986]) 10.

19. Mary Ann Doane, *The Emergence of Cinematic Time: Modernity, Contingency, the Archive* (Cambridge: Harvard University Press, 2002) 13.

20. Cinema's dependence upon fragmented intervals works on several levels. One film usually consists of a compilation of sequences with large amounts of diegetic time passing in between; one scene is itself often a composition of edited shots already; the single shot is generally perceived to be the smallest coherent component of film, but even a shot is composed of an astounding number of frames, each lasting less than 1/24 second due to the black intervals separating them.

21. Doane 68.

22. Elsaesser, "Contingency and Agency" 10.

23. Elsaesser, "Contingency and Agency" 11.

A Critical Mind

The Game of Permanent Crisis Management

Jan Simons

Crisis Management

If one were to run Thomas Elsaesser's almost uncountable number of publications through a tag cloud generating program, chances are that one of the items to emerge most prominently and dominantly would be the noun "crisis." At first glance, this might be the logical and unavoidable consequence of the increasingly faster pace of changes in the very subject of his writings. Over the last few decades, cinema first became inextricably intertwined with television and electronic media and was soon engulfed by the so-called digital revolution. This is well documented by the *Cain, Abel or Cabel?* book, which Elsaesser co-edited with Kay Hoffman in 1998. Its subtitle already hinted at a possibly altogether different future for *The Screen Arts in the Digital Age*.[1]

These changes are reflected in the large variety of names that film studies have had over the last two decades: from film studies; to film and television studies; to film, television and new media studies; to eventually – but probably not finally – simply media studies. These nominal changes also brought a number of more substantial changes in theories, methods, and paradigms: semiotics, narratology, textual analysis, and psychoanalysis gradually gave way to other approaches like cognitive theories, post-structuralism, deconstructivism and postmodernism, feminism and gender studies, visual studies, cultural studies, phenomenology, identity politics, "new" film history, ethnography, and even network theories and game theory. The "digital revolution," moreover, transformed film (and photography) from media that were supposed to represent reality into objects of skepticism and distrust. And all this happened within a period of less than two decades, and to many a skeptic, it made media studies look like a discipline desperately seeking an object, a theory, and a method. One of the most academic disciplines that has flourished the most over the past two decades is at the same time also one of the most crisis-ridden.

For Thomas Elsaesser these circumstances proved to be a fertile ground to develop a unique style of intellectual crisis management because, in his view, a crisis is not a disturbance of an ideal course of events by external causes (i.e., adverse parties or simply ignorant outsiders) but rather a productive force to be exploited in order to enhance the actualization of possible futures that are virtually present yet repressed in the actual state of affairs. From this perspective, crisis management is not a kind of emergency policy necessitated by external events beyond one's control, but instead a productive method necessary to unleash the potentialities enclosed within a given state of affairs. Elsaesser embodies the "critical" politician for whom crisis management means that one should not only always be on one's guard for the possible causes of a crisis in order to prevent it, but that, in quiet times when there are no apparent reasons for concern, one should be prepared to actually provoke a crisis oneself. For him, the term "crisis management" itself has a fairly unusual meaning: it is not the management *of* a crisis, but rather management *by* crisis. In this approach, crisis is not an emergency one must get under control, or an anomaly that must be intellectually mastered. On the contrary, a crisis is not the *object* of management but an *instrument* of management, a management tool. A crisis is a state of affairs that should be precipitated or even provoked in order to open a Pandora's box. Management by crisis seems to draw upon the lessons of chaos theory in the sciences, from which it has learned that the most interesting and vital processes in nature occur "far from equilibrium."

This sort of crisis management is first and foremost an intellectual endeavor. For a "management-by-crisis" approach, a crisis is not an objectively given state of affairs but the result of a particular reading of that state of affairs. Since a crisis is not independent of how a state of affairs is being perceived, conceptualized, and discussed, a critical crisis manager is quite capable of detecting the symptoms of a crisis where others only see order and stability, or to locate a crisis at another location than others might, and to define it in altogether different terms. Since a crisis is above anything else a clash of concepts, it entails the promise that it can be intellectually and politically managed; the critic's crisis is an intellectual construction.

Management-by-crisis is by no means a negative enterprise. On the contrary, it is productive because its aim is the discovery and unleashing of unexpected futures in the present and the rewriting of the past in the process. Management-by-crisis thus gives way to new "possible futures" as well as yet uncovered "virtual histories" that become visible only from the vantage point of these possible futures. For management-by-crisis, then, the present is always pregnant with multiple futures and at least as many pasts. In order to sense these potentialities, the critic must approach the present as an archaeologist approaches an excavation site. Like the latter, who only has fragments, shards, and ruins to work with to (re)construct the possible histories that came before and after the moment the excavation site became frozen in time, the critic must be prepared to scatter the superficial and apparent coherence that received notions and traditional narratives seem to guarantee and start from scratch.

Since the futures and histories the critic discovers are only possible and virtual and not necessary and factual, management-by-crisis can become itself an easy target of criticism. Its readings are necessarily speculative and, to a certain extent, beyond criticism itself, because it can answer any objection by proposing other possible readings and by pointing out that the consensual description is just one of many possible accounts. Because the management-by-crisis approach scatters an agreed upon coherence and offers no alternative solid foundations on which to build a new consensual narrative, it is often perceived as a negative and even destructive meeting of "terror and trauma."[2] This criticism, however, denies the fundamentally ludic dimension of management-by-crisis: it is first and foremost a "mind game."[3]

Complex Crises

According to the OED, the word "crisis" basically has two meanings: it can be used to refer to "a turning point," "a watershed," "a point of no return," "a moment of truth," as well as to more negatively charged situations such as "an emergency," "a disaster," "a catastrophe," or a "calamity." Both meanings are, of course, not mutually exclusive but rather complement each other. Disasters, calamities, and catastrophes are generally the outcome of chains of events that have reached "a point of no return"; a "turning point" is often the point at which a chain of events takes a dramatic turn, usually for the worse, or it is the point at which one is inevitably forced to face the "truth" and make a decisive choice or else accept "disaster." Crises are generally points at which major interests are at stake, either because they have come under the threat of external dangers or because they are in the grip of opposing forces. In its common sense, the word "crisis" carries connotations of fate, inevitability, threat, danger, and awe, which inspire extreme events. It is no coincidence, for instance, that in narrative theory, a "crisis" is the result of a disturbance of a disturbance of a balanced initial state usually brought about by forces of "evil," which has to be overcome by the intervention of a hero whose mission consists of restoring the initial equilibrium.[4] If one is right in assuming that narrative structures are part of the cognitive equipment with which human beings try to come to grips with the world,[5] this canonical narrative structure is a sufficient indication that in a common sense understanding, a state of stable equilibrium is "good" and desirable, whereas the disturbance of an equilibrium is being experienced as something "bad" and undesirable.

This common sense and consensual feeling about equilibriums and crises is not shared by everyone. In chaos theory, for instance, a crisis is the point where a chain of small and often hardly perceptible events become magnified and turn into a major turbulence. Such a turbulence often manifests itself as a disaster in the commonsense meaning of the term "crisis," such as a hurricane, an earthquake, an avalanche, or a flood. But it can also be the symptom of a phase transition in which a system enters a new state in which it acquires new properties, as when, for example, under certain conditions a system changes from a gas (e.g., steam) into a fluid (e.g., water) and under yet other conditions into a solid (e.g., ice). More interestingly perhaps, these crises or phase transitions are also often bifurcation points at which a system can choose to go in one of two directions, with either choice inaugurating a new state in which the system's properties have irreversibly changed.[6] These bifurcation points correspond to the "turning points," "crossroads," "watersheds" and "points of no return" that make up the first of the two broad senses of the word "crisis." But, because a crisis can force a system into a new state in which it reorganizes itself and acquires new properties, these bifurcation points can be "sources of creativity and innovation," as Nobel Laureate and pioneer of complexity theory Ilya Prigogine calls them.[7]

Since creativity and innovation occur at crisis points where a system is driven "far from equilibrium," systems that are "close to equilibrium" are not the most interesting ones for complexity theorists.[8] What makes bifurcation points interesting is first of all that the "choices" a system will make are not predictable because they are sensitively dependent on the minutiae of the initial conditions that can never be fully known (as captured by the famous Butterfly Effect according to which the small changes created by the flapping of a butterfly's wings in Beijing in April may cause a tornado in the Atlantic in August[9]). Second, the new properties a system will assume are not reducible to its properties in the previous state. The system may display dramatic transformations at a macroscopic level (e.g., a fluid changes into a solid) while at the microscopic level, few changes occur at all. And thirdly, since the changes a system undergoes during the transition of one phase into another are irreversible, the system's itinerary through the "state space" of all possible configurations it might assume can be reconstructed: a system thus produces its own "memory." However, the past that the system records depends on the futures it has "chosen" at successive bifurcation points. At bifurcation points, the "arrow of time" (Prigogine) does not necessarily point in one single direction.

Complexity theory has come up with a model for understanding and reasoning in regard to the dynamics and effects of a crisis that is quite different from traditional common sense notions of crisis. In spite of its analogies with the scientific theories and models of complexity theory, this model is expressly not an expert theory of complex phenomena. It is rather what the cognitive linguist George Lakoff would call an "Idealized Cognitive Model" (ICM).[10] ICM's are "quick and dirty" ways of defining what is accepted as the most representative case of an experiential domain, and most of the time they do their job.[11]

Management-by-crisis also seems to be based on an idealized cognitive model which represents a folk theoretical version of complexity theory. In the format George Lakoff devised for ICM's, it goes roughly like this:

THE ICM OF COMPLEX CRITICALITY
1. A crisis is the result of the interaction of multiple chains of small events.
2. Small changes can have great consequences.
3. A crisis is a transition to a new state with new properties.
4. The properties of the new state depend on the changes that caused the crisis.

How does management-by-crisis bring to bear the ICM OF COMPLEX CRITICALITY on domains as divergent as film theory and history? In order to see this, it might be convenient to summarize the management-by-crisis approach in a few rules-of-thumb:

THE CRISIS PARADIGM
a. An equilibrium is an exceptional state; change, noise, and interference are part of a system's normal state of being.
b. Crises are brought about by the non-linear effects of multiple interactions and unforeseeable feedback-loops between small, ordinary and unremarkable events.
c. Crises cannot and ought not to be prevented but should instead be welcomed – and if necessary even fostered – as opportunities for innovation and change.
d. Since the future is not a given, the past is not either. History, therefore, does not provide lessons for the future, but, instead, the future imposes the necessity of reconsidering the past.
e. Crisis management is itself part of the system in crisis; in order to come to terms with a crisis, crisis management must reconfigure itself, its intellectual toolkit and its view on a system's future and past development.

A Crisis Paradigm for Media Studies

One could point out the structuring effect of the ICM of complex criticality and the crisis paradigm in many of Elsaesser's numerous, wide range publications. One could demonstrate how it operates in his writings on the digital revolution, the crisis of representation, the European Cinema and the Hollywood blockbuster, the Holocaust and contemporary German culture. How precisely does it apply to Elsaesser's approach to the most hotly debated crisis in cinema, the "digital revolution"?

For a long time, the "institution cinema," as Christian Metz once called it,[12] seemed to be a relatively stable system. Once it had learned "to speak its language,"[13] with its technological apparatus maturing with the introduction of sound, and its modes of distribution and exhibition, the system changed very little for almost a century. According to the grand narrative of cinema history – nowadays revised by "new film historians" of whom Thomas Elsaesser is a prominent representative[14] – the system cinema found itself at a bifurcation point at the very beginning of its history when it had to "choose" between the illusionism of Méliès or the "realism" of the Lumière brothers. After a short period of "turbulence" in the era of the "cinema of attractions,"[15] the system cinema settled into an "equilibrium state" of the classical narrative fiction film with its propensity for verisimilitude, linear causality, and narrative closure.

According to this consensual account, this "homeostasis" was broken exactly one century after its mythic birth in Paris with the arrival of new digital technologies. These technologies severed the indexical bond between the photographic image and its referent and dissolved cinema's (and photography's) ontological realism, thus pushing the system "far away from equilibrium" and throwing it into a crisis from which it was hard to imagine that it could ever recover. According to Lev Manovich, cinema had again become "a particular branch of painting."[16] Others saw a "waning" of classical narrative and verisimilitude and a "reloading" of the cinema of attractions in the resurgence of special effects techniques prompted by digital technologies.[17] After this first century, or so the story went, the magician Méliès had finally moved center stage and had pushed the documentary-oriented Lumière brothers to the margins of cinema, in other words, this was the end of cinema "as we knew it."

This canonical version of the history of cinema's first century is obviously structured by the commonsensical model of crisis. In this story, the cinema system's normal state is an equilibrium (the dominance of classical cinema), major changes are caused by major events (the invention of the *cinématographe*, the introduction of sound, the rise of television, etc.), and major events are bound to cause major crises (digital technologies were predicted as the end of cinema).

The response to this perceived crisis is accordingly that either one tries to prevent the imminent crisis by totally rejecting anything digital (the Dogma 95 Manifesto was generally hailed as a response to the special effects Hollywood blockbuster[18]), or one accepts the unavoidable, imminent end of cinema (as, for instance, Lev Manovich seems to have done), or one simply denies that anything of importance has actually happened at all, as David Bordwell does, for instance.[19] How does this perceived crisis look from the point of view of the crisis paradigm?

One might start by challenging the assumptions that cinema is a stable system and that a major event like the coming of digital technologies should have such a major impact. In the midst of the upheaval around the "digital revolution," Elsaesser pointed out that "much of the digital revolution around the cinema has at its heart a familiar commodity, the narrative feature film, mainly identified with Hollywood," which was "still the 'killer application' for many of the new developments." Instead of precipitating the end of cinema, the digital revolution was, according to Elsaesser, "the totem-notion around which a notoriously conservative industry is in the process of reorganizing – and this usually means reinventing – itself, in order to do much the same as it has always done."[20] This last sentence goes further than merely observing that the film industry kept doing business as usual. Elsaesser points out that the "digital revolution" did not disrupt the state of equilibrium of cinema because there had never been such a state in the first place because what is meant by the conservative film industry "doing the same as it has always done" is actually always "reorganizing" and "reinventing" itself. The system cinema has always been "away from equilibrium" and it has always had to respond to major and minor crises by acquiring new properties. Therefore, the "digital revolution" is not an "exceptional state" but a new opportunity for the system to re-create and reinvent itself.

The assumption that the advent of digital technologies is the major cause of the turbulent state that cinema currently finds itself in needs to be qualified. As a technology, an industry, a service, a commodity, a mass medium, and global cultural artifact, cinema is, after all, at the crossroads of many "chains of events" that not only affect cinema itself, but also interact with each other through numerous connections and feedback loops. For instance, Elsaesser points out that television played as important a role in boosting the "art of the record" as film and photography, that in an age of media conglomeration, the cinema experience has become part of a larger "event-scenario" (what nowadays would be called a "cross-media event"), that "going to the movies" has become part of a larger leisure time experience, and one could add to these developments the processes of globalization, the collapse of Communism, deregulation policies, demographic shifts affecting cinema audiences, the rise of new digital supports and distribution channels, the rise of the "home cinema," the emergence of computer games, the coming of YouTube and other DIY film sites, and many more developments, shifts and transformations that affect cinema in one way or another and keep it "away from equilibrium." To single out the advent of digital technologies as a single or major cause for the onset of a new phase transition is nothing but an arbitrary reduction of the complexity of the very system cinema.

Instead of asking what lessons can be learned from the history of cinema in order to be able to better predict its future, Elsaesser turns the question around and asks what the ongoing transformations teach us about cinema's past.[21] This rethinking of the past from the point of view of the present is not aimed at reconstructing in hindsight a new teleological explanation of cinema's current state. Elsaesser's idea of rethinking the past is, on the contrary, an invitation to go time traveling "back to the future,"[22] not to revisit the past with today's knowledge of yesterday's future, but rather to look back from that past into its future from the vantage point of today's uncertainties. In a bold gesture, he reinvents the figure of Louis Lumière by locating him at the junction of technological, industrial, cultural and aesthetic developments in the nineteenth century, while in passing reminding the reader of the doubts he and other pioneers of the moving image had about the future of cinema. At the same time, he confronts the Lumière brothers' films with the expectations of their contemporary audience as well as with a formalist reading suggested by late-twentieth-century avant-garde filmmakers and film critics like Burch. With this "non-linear" methodology, and the reminder to his readers of Lumière's obsession with stereoscopy and symmetry, Elsaesser manages to turn Louis Lumière, the patron saint of documentary realism, into a magician, or rather, in today's terms, "the cinema's first virtualist."[23] Contrary to a common sense belief that digital technologies had made Méliès the master of the new media, Elsaesser argues that Lumière had always been a Méliès-type.

The question mark in the title of the Lumière essay is not without its significance, however. Elsaesser has no intention of proposing his construction of Louis Lumière as cinema's first "virtualist" as the correct alternative to the erroneous icon of cinematographic realism. If the latter image of Lumière is the result of a retrospective projection of later developments of the cinema system as its "destiny," then so is Elsaesser's "virtual Lumière."[24] The "ghost" evoked by Elsaesser's nonlinear methodology is a Lumière that was unknown and even unknowable to the historical Lumière himself, because the latter found himself at the watershed of numerous past "event chains" he could not possibly have been aware of, on the one hand, and numerous possible yet unknown futures, on the other. For this same reason, this virtual Lumière is necessarily a conjectural and speculative Lumière since not only are all of the histories that converged in his persona unknown to this historical Lumière, but they will also continue to remain partially unknown to the future historian. The reconstruction of Lumière can only be virtual, provisional, and conjectural.

However, as Elsaesser once wrote, even though "everything connects, not everything goes."[25] As historian Niall Ferguson has noted, virtual histories are "not mere fantasy: they are simulations based on calculations about the relative probability of plausible outcomes in a chaotic world."[26] The lesson to be learned from this virtual Lumière are not the possible alternative choices and alternative futures he was confronted with, but rather that nowadays in the era of the digital revolution every critic, theorist, filmmaker, and new media artist finds himself in the position of a virtual Lumière. Therefore, there is more to be learned from the uncertainties of the virtual Lumière than from his no less virtual counterpart in traditional teleological accounts of film history.

Elsaesser's crisis paradigm, then, does not look back into the past in the hope of finding answers to contemporary problems in other periods that were faced with similar questions. Instead, his nonlinear methodology creates positive feedback loops that make the uncertainties of today reverberate with those of the past to conjure up the once possible futures that are today's virtual histories, in order not only to stress the precarious and contingent nature of the present, but also to open up the state space of the future as a playground with numerous trajectories to choose from.[27]

Management-by-Crisis as a Mind Game

The crisis paradigm requires a certain intellectual mindset which can perhaps best be characterized by what Elsaesser calls "productive pathologies."[28] What these pathologies, that manifest themselves in contemporary "mind-game films" as paranoia, schizophrenia, and amnesia have in common is a mental state that "suspends our usual categories of sane/insane and enables patients/agents to discover new connections, where ordinary people operate only by analogy or antithesis," endows them with "special insights into patterns, where ordinary mortals see nothing but chaos or contingency" – a feature that Elsaesser has pointed in A BEAUTIFUL MIND (Ron Howard, 2001). These pathologies "seem to liberate and create new connections, establish new networks," but these new networks are not random but "contained and constrained within a protocol."[29]

As Elsaesser has pointed out, these pathologies in mind-game films are often connected to a traumatic incident in the protagonist's personal past. Since these "productive pathologies" are a response to an experienced or perceived emergency they provide a model for management-by-crisis. After all, these pathologies keep their patients/agents permanently on their guards for the returning, repeated or renewed manifestation of a traumatic incident and makes them perceive and experience their environments as permanently "under crisis." But they are also productive because "by shifting perspectives and generating horizons with a higher degree of complexity, [they] can lead to new kinds of knowledge."[30] These pathologies, then, fit the ICM OF COMPLEX CRITICALITY and the CRISIS PARADIGM based on it perfectly.

As the context in which Elsaesser discusses these productive pathologies already suggests, they also have a ludic – though not always necessarily funny – dimension. In mind-game films, either a disturbed character "is being played games with without knowing it," or a pervert protagonist plays games with other characters, or "it is the audience that is played games with."[31] These are the characteristics of the critical crisis manager who must always suspect that unknown forces will play tricks on him but who must also be willing to play games with others and to surprise his observers.

In order to play his mind game, the critical crisis manager must clear his view of perceived narratives, theories and explanations of a situation that might prevent him from detecting the symptoms of an imminent crisis in a timely fashion. The first idea he has to get rid of is the "intentional stance," which explains actions in terms of the psychological, ideological, or political motives of the agents involved.[32] Since the critical crisis manager is fully aware that he is himself the playing ball of unknown forces, he must realize that this also goes for everybody else. If the crisis manager fosters a healthy dose of paranoia, his suspicion is not directed at others personally, but rather at the forces moving their actions behind and beyond their intentions. The critical crisis manager does not assess a situation in terms of subjective goals and desires, but rather in terms of forces that are translatable in terms of codes, programs, and strategies. Instead, the actions of others should be seen as moves in a game the actors might not even be aware of that they are playing and to which the crisis manager must calculate his best response.

Because the critical crisis manager calculates his actions as moves in the game he suspects are happening behind the actions of his counterparts, he is often seen as not responding to the intentions, wishes and beliefs of those who have to deal with him. Thus, the strategic actions of the critical crisis manager are sometimes experienced as traumatizing and even terrorizing, and this perception is partially justified. Since he makes moves in a game other players are often not aware that they are playing, his moves may catch others unawares and leave the latter incapable of interpreting and explaining the situation at hand. It leaves them speechless, so to speak, and with the feeling they are being played with. However, if the critical crisis manager causes shock and awe, he does so to make their perspectives and attitudes shift as well, in order to liberate the field for new possible futures.

The policies of the critical crisis manager are sometimes a source of pity and fear, but more often, also of amusement and entertainment. To the critical observer, they contain the lesson of permanent uncertainty and the expectation of infinite opportunities for possible futures. Paraphrasing the conclusion of the Lumière essay, in one of these futures we will call upon Thomas Elsaesser's "ghost, his virtual self, whom we summon, finally, only in order to help us better know ourselves."[33]

Notes

1. Thomas Elsaesser and Kay Hoffmann, eds., *Cinema Futures: Cain, Abel or Cable? The Screen Arts in the Digital Age* (Amsterdam: Amsterdam University Press, 1998).
2. Thomas Elsaesser, *Terror und Trauma. Zur Gewalt des Vergangenen in der BRD* (Berlin: Kadmos, 2007).
3. Thomas Elsaesser, "The Mind-Game Film," *Puzzle Films: Complex Storytelling in Contemporary Cinema*, ed. Warren Buckland (Oxford: Blackwell, forthcoming). The "mind-game film" was the theme of the PhD seminar "Belief in the World, Presence, and the Body" that Thomas Elsaesser conducted in the academic years 2006-2007 and 2007-2008, together with Joseph Früchtl.
4. See Wallace Martin, *Recent Theories of Narrative* (Ithaca: Cornell University Press, 1986) 85. See also Patricia Pisters, *Lessen van Hitchcock: Een inleiding in mediatheorie* (Amsterdam: Amsterdam University Press, 2002) 64.
5. See Edward Branigan, *Narrative Comprehension and Film* (New York: Routledge, 1992).
6. See James Gleick, *Chaos: Making a New Science* (London: Vintage, 1997) 77-80. See also Philip Ball: "In the 1950s and 1960s Prigogine and his collaborators suggested that dissipative structures are reached when a non-equilibrium system is driven to a crisis point, called a *bifurcation*." Philip Ball, *Critical Mass: How One Thing Leads to Another* (London: Arrow Books, 2004) 131.
7. Ilya Prigogine, *The End of Certainty: Time, Chaos, and the New Laws of Nature* (New York: Free Press, 1997) 71.
8. Ball 131.
9. Gleick 22-23.
10. George Lakoff, *Women, Fire, and Dangerous Things: What Categories Reveal About the Mind* (Chicago: University of Chicago Press, 1987) 126.
11. Lakoff 129.
12. Christian Metz, *Le signifiant imaginaire: psychanalyse et cinéma* (Paris: 10/18, 1977) 13.
13. Christian Metz, *Essais sur la signification au cinéma*, vol. 1(Paris: Klincksieck, 1968).
14. Thomas Elsaesser, ed., *Early Cinema: Space Frame Narrative* (London: BFI, 1990). See also Thomas Elsaesser, "The 'New' Film History," *Sight and Sound* 55.4 (Fall 1986): 246-251.

15. Tom Gunning, "The Cinema of Attraction: Early Film, Its Spectator and the Avant-Garde," *Space Frame Narrative* 56-62.

16. Lev Manovich, *The Language of New Media* (Cambridge: MIT Press, 2001) 295-308.

17. Wanda Strauven, ed., *The Cinema of Attractions Reloaded* (Amsterdam: Amsterdam University Press, 2006). See also Andrew Darley, *Visual Digital Culture: Surface Play and Spectacle in New Media Genres*, (London / New York: Routledge, 2000).

18. See Jan Simons, *Playing The Waves: Lars von Trier's Game Cinema* (Amsterdam: Amsterdam University Press, 2007).

19. David Bordwell, *The Way Hollywood Tells It: Story and Style in Modern Movies* (Berkeley: University of California Press, 2006).

20. Thomas Elsaesser, "Digital Cinema: Delivery, Event, Time," *Cinema Futures: Cain, Abel or Cable?* 203. See also Thomas Elsaesser, "The Blockbuster: Everything Connects, But Not Everything Goes," *The End of Cinema As We Know It: American Film in the Nineties*, ed. Jon Lewis (New York: New York University Press, 2001) 11-23.

21. Elsaesser, "Digital Cinema" 220.

22. Elsaesser discusses the film BACK TO THE FUTURE in Thomas Elsaesser and Warren Buckland, *Studying Contemporary American Film: A Guide to Movie Analysis* (London: Arnold, 2002).

23. Thomas Elsaesser, "Louis Lumière – the Cinema's First Virtualist?," *Cinema Futures: Cain, Abel or Cable?* 45.

24. Elsaesser, "Louis Lumière – the Cinema's First Virtualist?" 61.

25. Elsaesser, "The Blockbuster: Everything Connects, but Not Everything Goes."

26. Niall Ferguson, ed., *Virtual History: Alternatives and Counterfactuals* (New York: Basic Books, 1999) 85.

27. This methodology can be seen as a variety of what Elsaesser in the context of a discussion of trauma theory called the "negative performativity" of traumatic experiences. Assuming that a trauma is experienced through its forgetting, a trauma manifests itself paradoxically by the absence of any symptom. Elsaesser, *Terror und Trauma* 203.

28. Elsaesser, "The Mind-Game Film."

29. Elsaesser, "The Mind-Game Film."

30. Elsaesser, "The Mind-Game Film."

31. Elsaesser, "The Mind-Game Film."

32. See Daniel C. Dennet, *The Intentional Stance* (Cambridge: MIT Press, 1990).

33. Elsaesser, "Louis Lumière – the Cinema's First Virtualist?"

SCHOLARS, DREAMS, AND MEMORY TAPES

by
Catherine M. Lord

FADE IN:

INT. SMOKE HAZED BAR, SOMEWHERE DOWNTOWN - NIGHT

Rain razors the windows. TE enters the bar, disseminating the water droplets from his trilby hat. He examines the hat like a man in a dream. He loosens the belt of his oversized raincoat. Looking around the black-and-white environment, his wide-angled eyes focus on Venetian blinds that shake in the wind. Different shadows attach to the frames of cocktails and leather bar stools.

TE sees the regulars propping up the bar - a figure in a cloak, a fat man with a bald head, and a thin man with 30s hair, horn-rimmed glasses and a tightly-knotted tie, reading a hard-backed book entitled, *Tradition and the Individual Talent*.

Working behind the bar is an appetizing, classy blond with a 40s hairstyle, tight dress, fishnet stockings and golden stilettos (BARBARA STANWYCK). She stands at the other end of the bar and sends a glass of whiskey whizzing across the wooden surface towards TE.

                    TE
               (barely catching the glass)
          That was a touch too western for a
          film noir.

BARBARA freezes. The thin man with the book pulls the copy over his face. The cloaked figure flutters in the wind. At fifteen frames a second, the fat man (ALFRED HITCHCOCK) swivels on his stool towards TE and looks at him straight in the eyes.

                    HITCHCOCK
               (in a growling British accent,
               his mouth stuffed with MacGuffin)
          How dare you!

                    TE
          How dare I what?

                    HITCHCOCK
          Screenwriters do not tell me or my
          set designer what to do.

                    TE
          But I wasn't.

                    HITCHCOCK
          Off with his…!

                    TE
          Now look here, don't get semiotic
          with me. It's a question of signs,
          you see. Am I the dreamer or are you
          the dreamed?

The fluttering cloak turns on its stool to reveal DEATH
(from *The Seventh Seal*) emptying pills from a bottle
marked 'Prozac' into his glass marked 'deadly
nightshade'. Next to DEATH is his chess set. From the
set, DEATH picks up one of the pawns which squeals out as
it is held up in TE's line of vision.

                    TE
                (to DEATH)
          I'm really not a chess player. And I
          don't think you want to rake me up on
          your publication list just yet!

                    BARBARA
                (to TE)
          Of all the bars in all the world, you
          had to come into mine.

                    TE
                (to the room)
          I think we all have a relatively good
          idea of what is going on here. I'm
          participating in a dream, well, yes,
          I'm dreaming. Perhaps this is all
          helping me to write my next book. The
          mise-en-scène suggests a displacement
          of some kind. It's a question of
          metaphors, of metonymies. Perhaps
          it's a question of a historical
          imaginary, national cinema, and male
          subjectivity. A Lacanian twist, *esse
          est percipi*. The melancholia of the
          digitalized gaze? From where to
          where? Not quite sure where the index
          is pointing…

BARBARA comes in front of the bar, her cleavage under
angle point lights.

                    BARBARA
          Suppose you get down from your high
          horse.

                    TE
          Suppose you tell me about your
          current context.

                    BARBARA
          Suppose you tell me why I should.

                    TE
          Suppose you tell me when you finish
          your shift.

                    BARBARA
          Suppose I bust out crying and put my
          head on your shoulder.

                    TE
          Suppose we go into the next scene and
          aim at an unveiled imaginary.

                    DEATH
                    (his long, cloaked arm and
                    whitened hand around TE's
                    throat)
          Hey wise guy…
                    (in heavy Swedish accent)
          k-e-e-p o-f-f m-y c-h-i-c-k.

DEATH continues to choke TE, and in throwing him to the
floor, the edge of DEATH's cloak catches HITCHCOCK's gin
and tonic as its smashes to the floor. TE falls to the
ground, the shards of glass bouncing in "slomo" as TE
chokes then coughs and slowly regains his breath, his
hands cut on the glass. He watches as DEATH puts his arms
around BARBARA and escorts her into a silvery distance.
She looks back at TE, longingly.

                    BARBARA
                    (to TE)
          I guess I don't have to tell you. But
          I'm the kinda girl that only gets to
          be the MacGuffin.

The man in the suit and tightly knotted tie, with his
copy of *Tradition and the Individual Talent* (T.S. ELIOT)
gets off his bar stool.

                    ELIOT
                    (to TE)
          Don't forget time present, time past
          and time future.

                    HITCHCOCK
                 (to TE)
          Don't forget you won't be able to
          wake up until your bladder is full.
          And don't forget, you must finish
          your mission before Maria Braun
          lights her cigarette.

ELIOT and HITCHCOCK both find their own window frames and
disappear. TE lies on the floor and groans.

The pieces of glass from the gin and tonic glass glisten
in a kaleidoscope of colors that break through the
dissolving noir of the scene. The pieces of glass then
flatten into pools of colored water that start to form
shapes, a corduroy trouser leg, a 70s woolly jumper, a
woman in a dark, 70s haircut (LAURA MULVEY).

                    TE
          Laura, thank God. A friendly face!

                    MULVEY
          Visually pleasuring your fetish
          Thomas?

                    TE
          Oh, please.

                    MULVEY
          You'd better go and chase after your
          dame.

                    TE
          Why, why should I?

                    MULVEY
          Because that is what you desire.

                    TE
          There's more to it than that. What
          does the desire signify? Where does
          the signifier of the desiring
          signifier point? Please. Give me a
          clue.

                    MULVEY
                 (floating on cardigan air into
                  the distance)
          That's your job.

                    TE
      No it isn't. I do other things now.
                (Pause, while extricating pieces
                of glass from his hands)
      This is all so passé.

A MIDGET from David Lynch's *Mulholland Drive* (or any
other Lynchian "Scene of Midgetism"), dressed in a black
shirt, white suit and tie approaches TE, still lying
breathless on the floor, and takes TE by the collar,
dragging him along with tracking shot precision. He pulls
up TE's head and forces him to face a wall in which is
set a MIRROR to the left and a WINDOW to the right. The
MIDGET waives his over-sized hand, indicating that TE
will have to choose between the MIRROR and the WINDOW.

                    MIDGET
                (to TE)
      Now choose….

                    TE
      I don't think I care for either,
      right now. I mean, it's one thing to
      write about perceptual concepts, it's
      another thing to…

The MIDGET sits on top of TE's chest.

                    MIDGET
                (in eunuch-like high-pitched
                voice)
      Choose you must. Is it Cain or is it
      Abel? Abel or is it Cain? Cain-Abel,
      Abel-Cain, choose you must or die you
      must.

                    TE
                (out of breath again)
      How about something digital like the
      Internet?

The MIDGET now starts to ride TE's chest.

                    MIDGET
      Mind-games through the mirror,
      Mind-games through the window,
      Professor Professor on the Wall,
      Choose you must or Die you must

                         TE
          Don't get abject with me… LET… ME…
          GO….

                         MIDGET
          How would you like it if I cut off
          your ear and put it next to the
          coffee machine in the Teacher's Room
          at the New Media Department?

                         TE
                    (in surrender)
          No, no, please no.

The MIDGET now bounces up and down on top of TE's chest.

                         TE
          All right, all right… whatever you
          want. I'll go through the mirror.

The mirror in front of TE wobbles and liquefies. In
diaphanous underwear, BARBARA's reflection waves onto its
surface.

                         BARBARA
                    (to TE)
          Put your lips together and blow.

TE puts his lips together and blows. He flaps his arms.
The MIDGET pushes TE's feet through the liquid mirror.

                                        DISSOLVE TO:

INT. THE UNDERWORLD BEHIND THE MIRROR OF JEAN'S COCTEAU'S
ORPHÉE (with some adjustments of mise-en-scène) - ANY
TIME OF DAY

The ruins of Berlin after World War II, the fallen Berlin
Wall, the ravages of burning cars and toppled Persian
buildings in Iraq, melting ice caps, flooded European
cities and in the Hollywood hills, whirling up behind the
HOLLYWOOD logo on Beverly hills, the smoke of forest
fires.

TE floats down into the underworld with JEAN COCTEAU
pulling him along.

                         TE
                    (to COCTEAU)
          Your mise-en-scène is a bit of a pile
          up?

                    COCTEAU
          Ah, oui. My films are petrified
          fountains of thought.

                    TE
          Delightful to meet you Jean. Am I
          spotting an updated postcolonial
          motif? Wouldn't like to let me in on
          a secret would you? Like, *where* are
          we going and can you deal with that
          midget?

The entire frame starts to move to jump cuts. LOLA RENT
sprints past TE and COCTEAU, jump cutting as she runs.
FOREST GUMP jump cuts behind everyone, carrying a box of
chocolates.

                    TE
          I was supposed to be coming to my
          retirement party, not running for my
          life.

                                        CUT TO:

EXT. THE FRONT DOOR OF TE's HOUSE IN AMSTERDAM - NIGHT

Two nineteenth century gaslights on either side of the
door, just like the famous Magritte painting.

                    COCTEAU
                  (to TE)
          The Judges of the Dead Await.

COCTEAU dissolves into the dark.

                    TE
          Great. Just great.

TE's front door opens.

INT. TE's HOUSE - NIGHT

Everything is empty inside. The door at the end
of the corridor opens.

INT. TE's DESCENDING SPIRAL STAIRCASE TO BASEMENT - NIGHT

TE descends.

INT. BASEMENT - NIGHT

The basement is simply lit with one electric bulb. There is a table. Behind are three judges - SLAVOJ ŽIŽEK, INGMAR BERGMAN, and HITCHCOCK.

HITCHCOCK has discovered the joy of an Apple Computer and an editing program. He is absorbed in digitally undressing TIPPI HEDREN and adding silicone breast implants of varying sizes.

> BERGMAN
> (to TE)
> I don't want to make films anymore. I gave myself limits. I was a modernist. I was precise. My films. They were supposed to be fun to make. They were. They were not. Then I made all these films. Then I watched them. All of them. But I could not watch them. My films - they made me so depressed. In fact, I cannot watch any of my films. They depress me so much. I thought when I died that I would be free. That in death there would be no depression. But what do I do every day? I think about my family, on the other side of the mirror. They are still making films. If I pass through the mirror, I will watch their films. Then I will be depressed. Again.

> TE
> (to BERGMAN)
> I know, I know. Haven't you read my chapter on your work in my *European Cinema?*

> ŽIŽEK
> (wearing very 70s beard and jumper, to TE)
> Thomas, how wonderful to see you! Don't worry about him, he's still in post-death anamorphic denial.

> TE
> (to ŽIŽEK)
> Hold on, you are still alive, aren't you?

                    ŽIŽEK
Of course I am. But as you pointed
out, I'm no Lacanian, I am a Lacanian
subject.

                    TE
Which means… oh, I see. You can
actually…

                    ŽIŽEK
I can jump through mirrors.

                    TE
So that's where you get all your
ideas!

                    ŽIŽEK
In a manner of speaking. But apart
from always enjoying my symptoms, I
am a genius, Thomas.

                    TE
Uhhm.

                    ŽIŽEK
Esse est percipi. My next project is
to get Jacques to meet Hitch. Do you
think they will strangle each other?

                    TE
Slavoj, nothing personal. Really, I
greatly admire your work. But Hitch
strangling Jacques is my idea. In
fact, it's in that chapter in
European Cinema, the one I wrote
about your work. You've obviously
read it.

                    ŽIŽEK
Thomas, you left the gas on.

                    TE
What?

                    ŽIŽEK
Just smell it…

                    TE
          I couldn't have left the gas on. I
          haven't been here for weeks. I've
          been in Cambridge, New York, LA…

                    HITCHCOCK
          I need to go to the bathroom!

                    ŽIŽEK
               (to TE)
          This is your house, right? Just smell
          the skin of this film, it's gas!

TE and ŽIŽEK sniff together.

                    TE
          Oh, my, God.

TE dashes through the basement door.

Montage follows in which TE jump cuts through parts of
his house, until, he reaches:

INT. KITCHEN - NIGHT

In TE's kitchen, in all her glory, MARIA BRAUN
desperately tries to light her cigarette with a lighter,
the sound of hissing gas permeating the entire
soundscape.

Close up of TE's face.

                                        FADE OUT

FADE IN:

INT. PARTY IN TEACHER'S ROOM AT MEDIA DEPARTMENT - EARLY
EVENING

LECTURERS FROM MEDIA AND CULTURE DEPARTMENT, all drinking
and pocketing crisps. TE opens his eyes as wide as
possible as though he has just woken himself from a
dream. He discovers a glass of red wine in one hand, and
a sausage on a stick in another.

                    LECTURER AND MEMBER OF PHD SEMINAR
               (to TE)
          So you must be looking forward to
          your retirement.

                    TE
Uhhm, yes.

                    LECTURER
And what are you going to do with it?

                    TE
Not quite decided.

                    LECTURER
Exciting about your next book. Mind
games right? I love all those films,
Minority Report, *Eternal Sunshine of
a Spotless Mind*, *Memento*...

                    TE
I haven't decided if I am going to
write *that* book. In fact, I've
written an enormous amount in my
life.

LECTURER waits expectantly.

                    TE
In fact, I was thinking of opening a
bar.
A film noir bar.
With special costumes.
And actors.
And mirrors.
And midgets...
And a dame.
Yes, a dame.

                              FADE TO NOIR.

ACT II

Europe-Hollywood-Europe

The Cheetah of Cinema

Floris Paalman

Bochum, 10 December 2004. Evening. We took the same train back to Amsterdam after we had attended a workshop on industrial films. This is how I *went* home, while Thomas Elsaesser *was* already at home. When we got on the train he apologized for taking a separate seat, as he had to prepare something. However, after a while he approached me, to discuss something of "strategic importance." He asked me if I was still interested in swarms, emergence, and systems, as I had indicated when I applied for the position of PhD candidate. When I joined the Cinema Europe research project at the end of 2002, the group was working on new methodologies. Much attention was being paid to "cutting edge" insights from other scientific disciplines. We got to explore "big theory," concerning such issues as globalization and network theory.[1] In this perspective Elsaesser handed me some print-outs from the website of an organization called Calresco, which deals with complexity theory. I said that I did not yet know how to connect it to my work on film and architecture. Think about it, he said, and if it seemed interesting, I could use the material for a presentation at the PhD seminar.

Complexity and Systems

Calresco turned out to be an international think tank and platform for the promotion of complexity theory as a multidisciplinary concern, directed by the British physicist and computer scientist Chris Lucas. Complexity theory emerged partly from system theory, which was first developed within the natural sciences, but to some extent within the social sciences as well, as, for instance, in the work of Niklas Luhmann.[2] According to Luhmann, societies are systems, with various subsystems, which regulate their input and output through preconceived channels. As such, Luhmann also frames media. The function of media is to provide knowledge about the world. Observations are checked and channeled through protocols and routines, in order to become news, entertainment or advertisement. However, media do not merely (re)present, but actually *create* their own world. At the center of Luhmann's theory is the issue of *autopoiesis* (i.e. self-creation), which is at stake when a system functions as a black-box, that is, blind to its own environment. Its output is its input. Luhmann offers a way out of subject-centeredness and representation, into the domain of functions. This escape encompasses functions within the system and functions of media within larger environments (i.e. other systems). In one of his last articles, written in 1997, Luhmann describes the world as an autopoietic system as follows:

> [A] re-entry leads to an unresolvable indeterminacy. The system cannot match its internal observations with its reality, nor can external observers compute the system. Such systems need a memory function (i.e. culture) that presents the present as an outcome of the past. But memory means forgetting and highly selective remembering, it means constructing identities for re-impregnating recurring events. In addition, such systems need an oscillator function to be able to cross the boundaries of all distinctions they use, such as, being/not-being, inside/outside, good/bad, male/female, true/false etc.[3]

Culture is for society what memory is for an individual. To be able to remember, identities need to be made, which means images and forms, in other words, cultural expressions such as cinema and architecture among many others. To create these forms, the (collective) mind needs the oscillator function. Luhmann continues:

> To be able to separate memory and oscillation, the system constructs time, that is, a difference of past and future states, by which the past becomes the realm of memory and the future the realm of oscillation. This distinction is an evolutionary universal. It is actualized by every operation of the system and thus gives time the appearance of a dimension of the 'world'. And if there are sufficient cultural guarantees for conceptualizing time, the distinction of time re-enters itself with the effect that past and future presents, too, have their own temporal horizons, their own pasts and futures.[4]

Luhmann's view seems to correspond to the ideas of physicists like Julian Barbour who argue that time basically does not exist[5]. According to Luhmann, it is simply created by the system, and ultimately by the human mind, which becomes manifested through culture. Luhmann did not really emphasize this argument, but it seems to be of crucial importance. It differs from a mere functionalist understanding of society, of which system theory has often been accused, offering latitude to a theory of change. Luhmann died shortly after writing this article, so he was unable to elaborate on his own thoughts. The idea of the oscillator function actually allows for elaboration in terms of complexity theory.

Attractors, Bifurcations, and Iterations

Some of the premises of complexity theory are very different from system theory. Whereas system theory frames preconceived channels to regulate the operations within a system, almost mechanistically, complexity theory, on the contrary, deals with issues of adaptation, change, and chaos. Random events and "noise" stimulate the emergence and development of things, and consequently complex organizational forms come into being. Moreover, the behavior of individual actors can have major effects on the entire system.[6] These things together create certain development paths, which are irreversible, leading to entropy, which in turn generates its own sense of time.

A crucial notion within complexity theory is that of "attractor." It is a "preferred position for the system, such that if the system is started from another state it will evolve until it arrives at the attractor, and will then stay there in the absence of other factors."[7] A major risk of "borrowing" conceptual tools from other disciplines is that it remains simply a matter of translation, and so does not develop insights or elaborate new concepts. However, to some extent, the act of translation is necessary to recognize certain patterns and to be able to connect certain phenomena to others. To that purpose, one could call the convention of classical Hollywood cinema the main attractor of American filmmaking. A film follows a narrative format, based on individual desire and an oppositional force that is overcome (the protagonist – antagonist structure). It usually goes together with continuity editing that respects the axis of action. Foreign filmmakers that come to Hollywood will most likely adapt to these conventions. Similarly, the primary attractor of Bollywood, to give another example, is the convention of Masala, which is the mix of at least one star, six songs, three dances, action and comedy based on a love story following a protagonist-antagonist structure. Film genres are also systems with their own attractors, like thrillers with their obligatory suspense.

In the development of a system, attractors change, which in their turn change the whole system. Again, we face the risk of translation, which may simply result in a confirmation of existing paradigms by dressing them in new conceptual cloths. We should therefore wonder what it means to speak of a "phase" and a "phase change." Could we say that experimentation and technological innovation were the attractors of early cinema, as a system,[8] and that a phase change occurred when narrative cinema became the new attractor? We should also consider what it means that different kinds of systems developed next to that of narrative cinema, like that in the Soviet Union. In this case, we might identify the Kuleshov montage principle as an "attractor" to generate meaning by association rather than by narrative. After the definitive establishment of sound film in 1929, the entire system of cinema, including that of the Soviet Union, gradually evolved. Different systems developed in the USA, Europe, India, Japan, and elsewhere. We could also indicate other moments of "phase change," for example, when television was introduced. In such cases, we could possibly also use other complexity theory concepts , like "bifurcation," which is the ongoing splitting of a system. This leads to chaos in "terms of entropy, where chaos and complexity are hard to distinguish."[9] Bifurcation is fundamental for the emergence of complexity. In the case of the introduction of television, several types of production that had previously been the realm of cinema, such as news reports, travelogues and city impressions, educative and informational films, among others, became the realm of television.

Bifurcation also seems to be at stake when considering the various kinds of audiovisual programs, genres and styles that have appeared and which have deliberately used the various audiovisual media that became available over time. This continued when video was introduced, ranging from home videos to art video production and video installations to new distributional modes for feature films. Cable television should be mentioned here as well. Nowadays, with the availability of digital media, cinema has, above all, become "home cinema." However, movie theaters will also continue to exist, for the release of new films, for social events and festivals, and as an alternative distribution circuit (the reverse of what it had once been). Cinema has become more diverse in format and reception, and so have its form and language. It allows new visual cultures to emerge, for example, the popular cinema of West Africa (on video/DVD), with Lagos as its epicenter.[10]

Several transitions that can be observed here are the so-called "iterations" that cycle "between the available behaviors," which is a phenomenon associated with bifurcation. If we take the documentary, for example, we can clearly see that it has continued to move between cinema and television. But also feature filmmaking has shown this type of pattern. It might be through these concepts that we are able to frame cinema in a different way than we used to do, by looking at the relationship between different media and between different kinds of productions, by taking into account different ways to address audiences and for different purposes. By looking at these connections we can consider the way that television stations support cinema by showing films and co-producing them. Television also sponsors film festivals; the Dutch VPRO, for example, has been one of the main sponsors of the International Film Festival Rotterdam for many years now, as well as the daily newspaper *De Volkskrant*, among others. From the perspective of complexity theory, we should consider whether this situation of television supporting cinema could not have ended up the other way round, historically, with the development of television being supported by cinema, if the system had developed according to other attractors. What kinds of perspectives can be generated via complexity theory, as an alternative to the linear evolution that relies on technological, economic, or even political determinism? Is it possible to consider other histories that could also have happened, but just did not happen – by coincidence, or for structural reasons?

Environment and Interconnected Media

At this point, we should establish a connection with the concept of *Medienverbund*, which Elsaesser developed with respect to the cinema and architecture of Frankfurt in the 1920s and 1930s.[11] In addition to manifestations of architecture and urbanism, city planner Ernst May used media like film, photography, and graphic design to promote the ideas of *Das Neue Frankfurt*. Instead of merely dealing with specific avant-garde expressions, it encompassed an avant-garde strategy in which different media fulfilled complementary or additional functions, serving a similar purpose and reinforcing each other. We could learn about their common agenda if we took one medium and analyzed its connections, to discover its relationship to the built environment and to the social institutions that inhabit it. To that end, Elsaesser has argued in favor of researching "AAA": *Auftraggeber* (commissioner), *Anlass* (reason), *Anwendung* (use). This strategy allows networks come to the fore, instead of just the aesthetic virtues of avant-garde cinema and architecture. These networks cross various media, genres, and categories. Hence an "ecology" that encompasses cinema and urbanism is drawn. This ecology, one can imagine, is itself a kind of *Medienverbund*. Eventually, as Lev Manovich has argued, there may even be a "convergence" of various media, and of media and space, which he has called "augmented space,"[12] which could be considered a radical instance of *Medienverbund*.

To some extent, this relies upon ideas from "media ecology," but instead of drawing a media landscape, I would explore the promises of complexity theory by linking the content of media productions to their conditions, that is, to consider functions of media within a broader socio-cultural environment. To that end, we should consider the more specific notion of complexity theory, that of "stigmergy," which, according to Calresco, is:

> The use of the environment to enable agents to communicate and interact, facilitating self-organization. This can be by deliberate storage of information (e.g. the WWW) or by physical alterations to the landscape made as a result of the actions of the lifeforms operating there (e.g. pheromone trails, termite hills). The future choices made by the agents are thus constrained or stimulated dynamically by the random changes encountered.[13]

Stigmergy is first and foremost about random changes, but self-organization occurs when "stigmergic local knowledge" is used to coordinate the behavior of a collection of agents, which is the definition of a swarm.[14] This means that self-organization takes place when the environment is molded to accommodate cooperation. This can also be understood as an infrastructure that is created by and under the control of the system itself.

We can compare it to approaches based on the notion of "habitat." According to Ulf Hannerz:

> The habitat offers both resources and constraints; it is defined with reference to particular agents, so that the habitats of different agents may overlap either more or less, within the landscape as a whole; and the habitat is emergent and transitory. It is not by definition linked to a particular territory. To what degree it actually turns out to be so depends on the conduct of the agents concerned. In more sociological terms, the habitat of an agent could be said to consist of a network of direct and indirect relationships, stretching out wherever they may, within or across national boundaries.[15]

Hannerz, in elaborating on habitat, frames the global society by employing the concept of "global ecumene" as "an open fairly densely networked landscape."[16] This notion is based on the work of the anthropologist Alfred Kroeber, who referred to the ancient Greek term "ecumene" (*oikoumene*), which means "the entire inhabited world as the Greeks then understood it."[17] Through the notion of "global ecumene" it is possible to frame various kinds of networks, each with its own scale and features, while cross-connections between them are not excluded.

Cultural Ecology

The link between Ulf Hannerz and Alfred Kroeber could be elaborated through the notion of "cultural ecology" that was coined by the anthropologist Julian Steward in 1955.[18] Steward had been a student of Alfred Kroeber. In a similar way, he took the environment into consideration as a major factor in the emergence and development of culture. Although it was an important current until the 1980s, it disappeared as soon as global issues came to the fore. It is, however, akin to complexity theory, and it makes it possible to link the work of social scientists like John Urry and those working in the field of media ecology to a firm tradition within cultural anthropology.[19] This is not only to anchor socio-cultural development in spatial practices and to emphasize the role of the environment, but above all to establish the interrelationship between different institutions and other kinds of actors, within a system, and between different systems.

To understand cinema as a global phenomenon, it is not enough to merely identify the attractors of each system separately. It would be more fruitful to think in terms of interdependencies and co-evolution. To that end, we should look at ecosystems. At the beginning of the 20th century, for example, the Polish started to reduce the number of lynxes in the forests of Bialowieza because they thought that lynxes were too harmful for the rest of the wildlife. The consequence was that too many herbivores now survived, so that much of the vegetation was destroyed, and animals such as the deer began to degenerate.[20] Another example is the cheetah and the Thomson's gazelle in East Africa, which are two of the world's fastest animals only because of co-evolution.[21] As the gazelle became faster, so did the cheetah. In comparison, Hollywood can also be considered a predator. It eats Europe's talent, but in order to do so it also has to invest in it. This creates a relationship that is both competitive and cooperative. However, a cheetah has to rest for about twenty minutes after it has chased its prey at top speed, and it is during this time that a lion or hyena might come along and steal its prey. If Hollywood is the lion, who would be the cheetah? Film theory? Or should we keep it to the lynx, which has upon occasion been spotted in the Netherlands since the 1990s. Is it coming from Germany?

The example of the lynx has revealed its function in a larger environment. We could similarly identify the functions of cinema as a cultural system within society at large. A common point, following Walter Benjamin in the 1930s, is the assumption that cinema has provided a model for modern life. Moreover, it has been a catalyst of modernization through the modes of perception.[22] It links up with a vast discourse on cinema in relationship to aesthetics as well as cognitive functions. One of the most radical theories in this respect is that of Fredric Jameson, who framed cinema as a geopolitical aesthetic mapping of the political unconscious.[23] Here economic functions come to the fore as well; cinema is a factor in the development strategies of cities and countries, and a factor within globalization as well.[24] Recalling Luhmann, cinema is also a matter of collective structural coupling. In comparison, a more orthodox view within film studies frames cinema as an alternative for reality, but Arjun Appadurai has, probably unintentionally, refreshed it by connecting it to the reality of migration.[25] While cinema may lead to new life patterns, Appadurai has addressed the notion of the media informing daily life, to simultaneously control and to redress it. This is related to the notion of "monitoring,"[26] which can be applied to understand where we are going and how. This brings us back to Luhmann; like culture in general, cinema has both a memory function and an oscillator function. This allows us to live in a timeless universe to explore irreversible destinies, to understand that humans get older, revolving around the sun, while we try to make sense of the innumerable other turns we make in life.

Social and Material Factors

The functions of cinema in society at large are interrelated with the attractors of that society. In fact, there might be a complex set of different interconnected attractors and functions; since a "complex system can have many attractors and these can alter with changes to the system interconnections (mutations) or parameters."[27] Hence, it is also necessary to find the cultural equivalent of ecological parameters. It seems problematic to maintain the biotic-abiotic dichotomy, since the abiotic usually also implies human involvement. It could, however, serve as a starting point by replacing the dichotomy with "social" and "material" factors. Some of the social factors may include: population density, the labor force, age, education, cooperation, competition, incorporation, and migration. Some material factors may include: source material, capital, facilities, technology, environment (city), and infrastructure. If one of these factors changes, it affects the cultural ecology as a whole. This is merely a preliminary outline of a possible direction, and to make these factors conceptually productive they should be tested and refined. Nevertheless, we should, by way of hypothesis, think of the possible implications of such a theoretical perspective.

With regard to social factors, density usually guarantees a high level of interaction, but connectivity may be the actual factor involved here. Population numbers nevertheless have an effect on the level of the labor force. A very important demographic factor in cultural ecology is age. Youth, for example, can provoke the emergence of important new movements within cinema. After age comes education, which implies different kinds of (output) values and interactions. Is it true that Hollywood produces mostly films for average audiences in both the USA and Europe, and elsewhere, while European cinema produces relatively more films for the elite among them? Would Hollywood begin producing more art films if European cinema stopped?

After that we have professional education and professional exchange. This concerns both cooperation and competition. Competition seems an important stimulant, but only to cause more cooperation in the next phase, which could eventually lead to incorporation. These dynamics are, at least to some degree, at work in the relationship between Hollywood and Europe, as Elsaesser has suggested in different terms in his book *European Cinema: Face to Face with Hollywood*. Here he has problematized the paradigm of "national cinema." As a notion, it is challenged by international (co)productions, but also by shared markets for distribution. According to Elsaesser, European cinema is usually defined in contradistinction to Hollywood, with the latter being framed as an antagonistic entity with mainly commercial aims, which seeks to monopolize the market and spreads bad taste, whereas European cinema is often considered to be "art."[28] This, according to Elsaesser, obscures the dynamics between the systems of European and American cinema. Rather than thinking in terms of "national cinema," Elsaesser proposes the notion of "double occupancy": belonging to two entities or powers at the same time.[29] "Double occupancy" not only clarifies the interactions between systems, but also the particular phenomena related to these systems, such as migration.

Migration could be added here as a factor, either as a cause of competition or to encourage cooperation, whether we are dealing with migrating professionals or ethnic communities. Furthermore, migration also seems to be an important factor for the generation of "source material." This can be illustrated within contemporary European cinema by the relatively large numbers of successful filmmakers with a mixed background.[30] When we are dealing with source material we are already in the realm of material factors, which concerns not only images, ideas, and values, but also funding, as well as the provision of other facilities, which can also generate new developments. An example is the emergence of Rotterdam as a media city after the introduction of funding regulations and the establishment of accommodations in 1995. Technology is related to the factor of facilities. Technological changes are usually paralleled by other developments that may constitute either the reason or the result of these changes, or both. Finally there is the physical environment. Ideas emerging from different cultural and social realms may circulate within a given environment. Big cities usually serve in this capacity, but smaller cities and various different urban configurations, albeit ones with sufficient infrastructure, can also be included. While big cities remain centers of film production, the other smaller urban areas may cause a gradual shift, either by the forces of co-production or by organizing festivals, workshops and conferences – like we did in Amsterdam in June 2005 with the conference *Cinema in Europe: Networks in Progress*. Are there other significant factors that should be considered and does an approach like this offer a more profound understanding of cultural emergence and the role that media play in it? Furthermore, how do media-specific features relate to these factors?

The outline of cultural ecology should be further explored and tested, both conceptually and empirically. To that end we should continue to research film in connection with various kinds of institutions, with varying articulations of, for example, social institutions, economic exchanges, political strategies, or cultural values, that are somehow embedded in a certain environment, but with the option for the lynx to cross borders, and practice double occupancy. In my own research, I have first of all articulated the environment itself, in spatial terms, through the relationship between film and architecture and urbanism, in a specific location, which is Rotterdam. Other cities may come under consideration in this way as well, along with different geographical entities. Elsaesser has already done this for Frankfurt, in connection with other nodes of a larger network. It now seems that he is interested in the Netherlands, not just as an empirical case, but as conceptual merchandise with a considerable value that allows space and image to converge into an "augmented medium."

Spring 2006. Elsaesser asked me to tape the television program TE KOOP: NEDERLAND / FOR SALE: THE NETHERLANDS, (Kees Brouwer, 2006), which was part of the VPRO series DE TOEKOMST / THE FUTURE.[31] The program focused on an imagined future in which cities are sold as a package deal of real estate objects – a matter of extrapolated current city marketing practices. I put the tape in his pigeonhole. After a month or so he wrote me back (2006/05/03): "Floris, // many thanks for the tape of the City for Sale! // Just discovered it in my huge pile of mail. // Thomas." I replied a couple of minutes later: "a nice sample of poetry you have sent me," to which he immediately reacted: "As to the rhyme, it's like Molière, but in reverse: I didn't know I spoke verse." By way of conclusion, let's subject this reverse (or re-*verse*) to a *subversive* close reading, in the tradition of ASCA and in the spirit of Molière.

In Molière's comedy *Le Bourgeois Gentilhomme* (1670), a shopkeeper has made a fortune and wishes to seduce a pretty aristocratic woman. To cultivate his mind he has employed a professor of philosophy, who asks him what kind of letter he wants to write her – in prose or in verse. The shopkeeper, Monsieur Jourdain, wonders if there are any other options besides prose or verse; what is it called, for example, when we have ordinary conversations? It is prose, the professor answers. Monsieur Jourdain is astonished: "Upon my word, I have been speaking prose these forty years without being aware of it; and I am under the greatest obligation to you for informing me of it." In the reverse, Elsaesser is the shopkeeper. For his shop, he is interested in cities for sale, like Berlin, London, Amsterdam, Vienna, Stockholm, and New York. He has sold the old cinematic city and wants to buy new ones (after Frankfurt). Since he has made a fortune, he now flirts with the higher echelons of capitalism, which is to some extent of an anthropological nature. What actually ends up happening we will only know when the cheetah of cinema enters the city. (What about Amsterdam's zoo Artis, can we expect it there at a certain moment? The conditions are promising, with film producer Haig Balian being its current director...)

Notes

1.   E.g. Manuel Castells, *The Rise of the Network Society* (Oxford: Blackwell, 2000 [1996]); Bruno Latour, *We Have Never Been Modern* (Cambridge, MA: Harvard University Press, 1993).

2. In February 2004, within the context of the PhD seminar, Malte Hagener gave a presentation on Niklas Luhmann's sociological system theory. One of the issues Hagener brought to the fore was that of *autopoiesis* (cf. infra).

3. Niklas Luhmann, "Globalization or World Society: How to Conceive of Modern Society?," *International Review of Sociology* 7.1 (March 1997): 67-79; <www.generation-online.org/p/fpluhmann2.htm>. Last visited 6 April 2008.

4. Luhmann.

5. Barbour explains his ideas in the documentary KILLING TIME (IJsbrand van Veelen, VPRO-television, 2002).

6. Calresco, "Self-Organizing Systems (SOS) FAQ," <www.Calresco.org/sos/sosfaq.htm>, version 2.95, September 2004, §7.2.

7. Calresco §2.8.

8. See Thomas Elsaesser, *Early Cinema: Space Frame Narrative* (London: BFI, 1990).

9. Calresco §6.5.

10. See Obododimma Oha, "Visual Rhetoric of the Ambivalent City in Nigerian Video Films," *Cinema and the City: Film and Urban Societies in a Global Context*, ed. Tony Fitzmaurice and Mark Shiel (Oxford: Blackwell, 2001) 195-205.

11. Thomas Elsaesser, "Die Stadt von Morgen: Filme zum Bauen und Wohnen in der Weimarer Republik," *Geschichte des dokumentarischen Films in Deutschland*, vol. 2: *Weimarer Republik (1918-1933)*, ed. Klaus Kreimeier, Antje Ehmann, and Jeanpaul Goergen (Stuttgart: Reclam, 2005) 381-409.

12. Lev Manovich, "The Poetics of Augmented Space," *Visual Communication* 5.2 (2006): 219-240; <http://vcj.sagepub.com/cgi/content/refs/5/2/219>.

13. Calresco §6.12.

14. Calresco §6.13.

15. Ulf Hannerz, *Transnational Connections, Culture, People, Places* (London: Routledge, 1996) 48.

16. Hannerz 50.

17. Hannerz 7.

18. Julian Steward, *Theory of Culture Change, the Methodology of Multilinear Evolution* (Urbana / Chicago: University of Illinois Press, 1976 [1955]).

19. See, for instance, John Urry, *Global Complexity* (London: Polity, 2003) and "The Complexity Turn," *Complexity*, spec. issue of *Theory, Culture & Society* 22.5 (Oct. 2005): 2-14. For a historical overview of media ecology, see Lance Strate, "A Media Ecology Review," spec. issue of *Communication Research Trends* 23.2 (2004): 3-48.

20. Information from Artis Zoo, Amsterdam, 2005.

21. For a short explanation on co-evolution with the given example, see Thorsten Schnier, "Co-Evolution," 2002; <www.cs.bham.ac.uk/~txs/teaching/2002/evo-computation/13-CoEvolution/13-CoEvolution-4up.pdf>. Last visited 6 April 2008.

22. See, for instance, David Clarke, ed., *The Cinematic City* (London / New York: Routledge, 1997).

23. Fredric Jameson, *The Geopolitical Aesthetic, Cinema and Space in the World System* (Bloomington / London: Indiana University Press / BFI, 1992) 3.

24. Mark Shiel, "Cinema in the City in History and Theory," *Cinema and the City: Film and Urban Societies in A Global Context* 10; see also Allen J. Scott, *On Hollywood: The Place, The Industry* (Princeton: Princeton University Press, 2005).

25. Arjun Appadurai, "Grassroots Globalization and the Research Imagination," *Globalization*, ed. Arjun Appadurai (Durham: Duke University Press, 2001) 6.

26. See Urry, *Global Complexity*.

27. Calresco §2.10.

28. Thomas Elsaesser, *European Cinema: Face to Face with Hollywood* (Amsterdam: Amsterdam University Press, 2005) 487.

29. Elsaesser, *European Cinema* 109.

30. For instance, Fatih Akin (Turkish-German), Ferzan Özpetek (Turkish-Italian), Alejandro Amenábar (Chilean-Spanish), Abdel Kechiche (Tunisian-French), and Hany Abu-Assad (Palestinian-Dutch).

31. TE KOOP: NEDERLAND can now be seen at <www.vpro.nl/programma/detoekomst/afleveringen/27521919/>. Last visited in February 2008.

Bear Life

Autoscopic Recognition in Werner Herzog's GRIZZLY MAN

Dominic Pettman

Love and Death in the Grizzly Maze

> To recognize oneself in the other, who appears alternatively as one's
> opponent, one's accomplice and one's double, is almost *the* cinematic theme
> par excellence.
> – Thomas Elsaesser[1]

The year 2006 was a big year for snuff movies. Not only did Australia's self-
appointed "crocodile hunter" Steve Irwin find himself on the wrong end of a
stingray barb, but Werner Herzog's remarkable GRIZZLY MAN debuted on the
Discovery Channel.[2] In the first case, the footage of the fatal moment has been
safeguarded by Irwin's widow and daughter, who together continue his dubious
legacy in plucky showbiz style. In the second case, the footage of the deathly
instant is missing for two reasons: the lens cap over the camera was not removed
during the attack, and Herzog decided not to include the audio itself in his own
film (although, in a crucial scene, he does show himself *listening* to the gruesome
soundtrack on his headphones).

Herzog's documentary explores the life and death of Timothy Treadwell, who
styled himself as a "samurai" and "kind warrior": a champion and friend of the
grizzly bears in the Alaskan hinterlands. Treadwell spent thirteen summers
camping alone in the Katmai National Park; five of those summers he brought
along a video camera, capturing over one hundred hours of raw footage. After
Treadwell's death (usually flagged as "tragic"), Herzog – who has always been
drawn to people on the periphery of their species-being – then carefully edited
this footage of the "grizzly" man interacting with the camera, with the local fau-
na, and with his own inner demons. These often manic monologues were then
spliced with Herzog's own interviews and commentary from friends, family and
other people who crossed Treadwell's path.

Herzog's voice-over notes:

Having myself filmed in the wilderness of jungle, I found that beyond a wildlife film, in his material, lay dormant a story of astonishing beauty and depth. I discovered a story of human ecstasies and darkest inner turmoil. As if there was a desire in him to leave the confines of his humanness and bond with the bears. Treadwell reached out and seeked [sic] a primordial encounter. But in doing so he crossed an invisible borderline.

Several critics noted the dramatic irony inherent in this project; namely, that Herzog functions as a kind of omnipotent, semi-visible bard, shaping the material he has been given into a narrative with a particularly queasy and uncanny momentum. "I will die for them," says Treadwell, gesturing toward a group of bears early on in the film. "But I will not die at their claws and paws." And yet our protagonist is far from oblivious, as on other occasions, when he seems to relish flirting with his own possible violent end. "Love ya, Rowdy," he says to of his favorite bear. "Give it to me, baby." Then to the camera: "I can smell death all over my fingers."

As this potent quote suggests, Treadwell (and we must also note the irony of such a last name, given his rather reckless foray into a landscape where even anglers fear to tread) was at the mercy of a psyche pulled in two different directions: the life force of the libido, and the siren song of the death drive.[3] Indeed, I would add two other agonistic elements at work here: that of the confessional, and the spectacle (spliced together, in what Thomas Elsaesser calls "autoscopia"[4]). This fused form of knowing-as-looking, or vice versa, stems from "the narcissistic and nostalgic pleasures derived from the cinema as cinema."[5] In other words, autoscopia is a modern form of introspection, highly mediated by cinematic images, whether the viewer-subject is actively engaged in producing these images or not. Clearly this process is complicated further when the protagonist is also in some senses the director, who in turn is the initial audience – as is the case in Grizzly Man.

The viewer is tempted to psychoanalyze Treadwell, to discover the mystery of motivation. Why would anyone give up the "creature comforts" of Los Angeles for the creaturely discomfort of a tent in Alaska every summer, in order to commune with a nature which at any moment could tear you to pieces? Herzog tactfully resists this temptation, or at least never voices his opinion concerning psychology explicitly. Instead, he leaves it up to the editing process to make connections between Treadwell's statements, his often bewildering behavior, and troubled relationship with other humans.

In one revealing scene, Treadwell walks and talks to his camera, clearly needing to unload certain issues regarding his sexuality:

I don't know why girls don't want to be with me for long. I'm very good in the . . .
you're not supposed to say that. But I am. . . . I always wished I was gay – would've
been a lot easier. You know. You could just *ping ping ping*. Gay guys have no problems.
They go to restrooms and truck stops and [laughs] perform sex, and it's so easy for
them. And stuff. But you know what, alas, Timothy Treadwell is *not gay*. Bummer. I
love girls. Girls need a lot more, you know, finesse and care and I like that a bit.
When it goes bad and you're alone . . . you can't rebound like when you're gay. I'm
sure gay guys have trouble too. But not as much as one goofy straight guy like
Timothy Treadwell. Anyway, that's my story.

Herzog is quite discreet in allowing Treadwell to speak for himself here; and yet
the evidence accumulates that the guardian of the grizzlies "doth protest too
much." Indeed, Treadwell's contradictions and mood swings qualify him as a
classic "unreliable narrator."[6]

Homosexuality is never mentioned again in GRIZZLY MAN, and yet it is flagged
in the rather camp antics of Treadwell (an obsession with his hair, diva-like voice
and attitude, references to STARSKY AND HUTCH, etc.), and the biographical details which emerge as the film unfolds. One cannot help but wonder if an attraction to men, and a revulsion of this attraction, led Treadwell to flee his family in
Long Island, change his name, abuse alcohol and other drugs, and ultimately
seek spiritual solace in the wilderness. Indeed, the vulgar interpretation would
be that Treadwell is simply displacing his repressed homosexual urges on to larger hairy creatures than you find in the West Village – after all, the label "bears"
refers to a hirsute subdivision within gay male culture.

It would be a mistake to discount old-fashioned denial as part of the equation.
However, this is not by any means the end of the story. Rather, the key to understanding Treadwell's fascination with animals, and indeed the general public fascination which greeted GRIZZLY MAN, is the slippage or overlap between human
sexuality and bestiality, *under the gaze of the camera*. "I love you. I love you. I love
you," says Treadwell, to not only the bears, but also the bees and foxes. Indeed,
this mantra – spoken emphatically, as if his life depended on it – is what struck
me most when first viewing Herzog's film. Love is pronounced over and over,
dozens of times. "I'm in love with my animal friends," says Treadwell. "I'm very,
very troubled. It's very emotional. It's probably not cool even looking like this.
I'm so in love with them, and they're so f'd over, which so sucks." In another
scene, Treadwell is clearly aroused by a fight between two bears who he knows as
Mickey and Sergeant Brown, over Saturn, "Queen of the Grizzly Sanctuary" (aka,
"the Michelle Pfeiffer of the Bears"). On another occasion, our intrepid environmentalist is excited by the fresh feces of Saturn, as he grasps it in his hands. "I

can feel the poop," he says, in ecstasy. "It's warm. . . . It was just inside of her. It's her life. It's her."

It is necessary to register the interplay between sexuality and technology on this invisible borderline between humans and (other) animals. In other words, I seek to designate Treadwell's camera as not only the recording instrument which allows us access to his remarkable story and experiences, but as a catalytic agent on equal footing with this grizzly man and the grizzly bears themselves.

Herzog is extremely sensitive to the different Treadwells who inhabit the film's footage. There is Treadwell the director, Treadwell the actor, and Treadwell the narrator, to name just three. In one scene, our protagonist seems to lose his grip on his own sanity, as he violently curses and denounces the park authorities and other visitors, who he believes are actively pursuing and persecuting him. "His rage is almost incandescent. Artistic," waxes Herzog, in a voice-over. "The actor in his film has taken over from the filmmaker. I have seen this madness before on a film set [referring to Klaus Kinski]. But Treadwell is not an actor in opposition to a director or a producer – he's fighting civilization itself. It is the same civilization that cast Thoreau out of Walden, and John Muir into the wild."

At other moments, Herzog is deeply touched by Treadwell's ability to capture unexpected and resonant images of the environment: "I too would like to step in to his defense," says the documentarian in his German accent, "not as an environmentalist, but as a filmmaker." He then goes on to sing the praises of someone who can coax cinematic moments from the natural world "that the studios and their union crews could never dream of." Indeed, as a wild fox and her cubs seems drawn to the camera, Herzog notes: "There is something like an inexplicable magic of cinema."

Herzog is not interested in magic for its own sake but in people; but only insofar as they skirt and often plunge over the edges of their race and place. Thus, he shares the conviction of his compatriot, Peter Sloterdijk, that the real question is not *what* the human is (since this posits an unverifiable essence), but *where* the human is.[7] This twist on the usual formula can be read either spatially or temporally. Or rather, at the intersection between this now inherently technical continuum.

Where indeed is the human? Is it something that flares up during moments of compassion, only to disappear when self-interests are compromised? Is it an ontological property found nesting in condominiums, or slums, or space stations, or caves? Or is it an unstable element which needs precise criteria and conditions to emerge? Does it, in fact, cut across current taxonomic species lines, as is the case when we seem to communicate with dogs, horses, or elephants? Are we, as the philosophers might ask, merely simulating these conditions of emergence in a controlled experiment? Moreover, is that which we call "the human" really confined to the invisible souls of *Homo sapiens*? Is it projected onto the historical development of these souls, as relentlessly figured in speech, text, and (moving) image? And finally, if humans are the tool users *par excellence*, then has our quintessential property not been outsourced to objects (as Bruno Latour suggests)?

When approached from the perspective of these broader questions, Herzog's valorization of the cinematic apparatus, *qua* "nature," leads to a kind of media Zen problem. If a human dies in the forest, was he or she really a human? In other words, if something isn't captured on film, did it really happen? (One wonders, for instance, if Treadwell talked as much during the first eight expeditions to Alaska when he didn't have a camera.)

"Sometimes," the director notes,

> images develop their own life. Their own mysterious stardom. Beyond his posings, the camera was his omnipresent companion. It was his instrument to explore the wilderness around him, but increasingly it became something more. He started to scrutinize his innermost being, his demons, his exhilarations. Facing the lens of a camera took on the quality of a confessional.

Treadwell refers several times to a pantheon of deities from world religions, praying for rain so the grizzlies can find fish, and also praying for forgiveness (or at least validation), from above. "If there is a God," states Treadwell confidently, "He would be very pleased with me. If He saw how much I love them. ... It's good work. ... I will die for these animals. I had no life. Now I have a life." (Soon after he adds the caveat: "Lord, I do not want to be hurt by a bear," suggesting that Treadwell would rather have died by the bullet of a poacher or ranger, as a martyr, than by the claws of those he adores.)

At this point we might return to the structuring absence of the film: the gruesome mauling by "bear 141" on a bleak October day in 2003. In fact, there is another significant aporia here; namely, the presence of Amie Huguenard – Treadwell's girlfriend, whom Herzog calls "the great mystery" of the one hundred hours of film footage. The traumatic soundtrack of the attack tells us that she bravely tries to fight off the bear which has grabbed Treadwell in his hungry maw. (The fact that the camera was on, but the lens cap still in place, suggests that the device was always poised to record, and yet this attack was too swift and unexpected to capture visually.) Huguenard thus both complicates and reinforces the autoscopic semiotic square which I'm attempting to set up between sex, death, confession, and spectacle; since she clearly shied away from the last two, in order to morally support Treadwell's embrace of all four.

On Reserves and Resemblance

> Man is nothing other than technical life.
> – Bernard Stiegler[8]

During the First World War, Sigmund Freud made the following observation in a lecture at the University of Vienna:

> [I]n the activity of phantasy human beings continue to enjoy the freedom from external compulsion which they have long since renounced in reality. They have contrived to alternate between remaining an animal of pleasure and being once more a creature of reason. Indeed, they cannot subsist on the scanty satisfaction which they can extort from reality. ... The creation of the mental realm of phantasy finds a perfect parallel in the establishment of "reservations" or "nature reserves" in places where the requirements of agriculture, communications and industry threaten to bring about changes in the original face of the earth which will quickly make it unrecognizable. A nature reserve preserves its original state, which everywhere else has to our regret been sacrificed to necessity. Everything, including what is useless and even what is noxious, can grow and proliferate there as it pleases. The mental realm of phantasy is just such a reservation withdrawn from the reality principle.[9]

I take this quote from an essay by Hubert Damisch, who provides the timely reminder that "the creation of a psychic realm of 'fantasy' and the institution of national parks are perfectly analogous," since "both satisfy the same need, topographical if ever one was, to see constituted, as a reaction against the exigencies of the reality principle as manifested in mental life as well as in geography, a domain and a field of activities free of its grip." Nature reserves and national parks are thus, spatially liminal zones, cartographic states of exception, which allow citizens to "experience" the Great Outdoors. Significantly, this experience must be without any violent disjunction from the daily movements and rituals of urban or suburban life. Which is why Damisch notes the important caveat, that "the 'animal of pleasure' to which the parks were meant to appeal is supposed to cohabit peaceably with the 'rational animal'."[10]

In contrast to "the wild," reservations and parks are nature tamed; like bears which have been caught, trained and forced to dance. Of course, there is a difference between the simulations of Olmsted and Vaux, and the annexed territories of somewhere like Yellowstone or Katmai: a difference based on the qualitative effects of scale. Whereas the former is domesticated through design, the latter is processed through the lens. Since national reserves and parks are, on the whole, too large or too costly to sculpt into aesthetic functionality, it is left up to the postcard industry and photographers like Ansel Adams to document and "capture" the pristine and indifferent beauty of the landscape.

Treadwell's instinct to bring his camera to the Katmai National Park can be traced back through the plethora of nature documentaries which have helped narrate the nation since the invention of film. It is in such places, "reserved" for our civilization's fantasies of freedom (like a table "not too close to the band"), that we enframe ourselves in the *camera lucida* of the outdoors.

Indeed, it is relatively easy for "civilized" men to reflect upon their human qualities in the asphalt jungles of the naked city. That is to say, even in the dehumanized environments of film noir, the dilemmas in which the characters find themselves speak to the pathos of self-consciousness and meta-cognition. We may sometimes *behave* like animals, but the story is only worth telling to the degree that we're tormented by a surplus or exceptionalism to the animal state. We may be poor, but we are not poor-in-world. And thus, we are responsible for the worlds we make, and the situations we therefore find ourselves in. Remorse and sarcasm are the twentieth-century urban coping mechanisms, providing a metallic sheen to the more bucolic modes of mourning and melancholy.

In contrast to the metropolitan lens, a camera in the wild bears witness to the human extracted from his natural (i.e., artificial-cultural) element. We asked earlier, "where is the human"? And now we can answer this question: *wherever there is a constitutive technology of self-recognition.* Whether that technology is a camera, a gun, a broken-in horse, a wife, or the US Constitution itself matters less than the capacity to register, record and transmit this recognition. (Remembering Freud's dictum that we never learn something new, but remember something we have forgotten. A comment that becomes even more apposite on the collective level of culture.)

Bernard Stiegler notes that there are three forms of memory for living beings. The first is genetic (DNA), the second is individual (experiential), and the third is technical (inscriptive or prosthetic). This last type is obviously the kind that humans excel at, being the foundation of pedagogy and other key modes of cultural transmission and reproduction. "Technics," insists Stiegler, "is a process of transmission: from the flint to the video camera."[11]

What Giorgio Agamben calls the "anthropological machine" – that is, an optical mechanism of perpetual self-questioning affirmation – would be impossible without the interlocking of these three types of memory. According to Agamben, one of the most important engineers who worked on the maintenance and upgrading of this machine was Carl Linnaeus, "the father of modern taxonomy." It was Linnaeus's ongoing, neo-Aristotelian "division of life into vegetal and relational, organic and animal, animal and human" elements that created a "mobile border" within vital humans, "and without this intimate caesura the very decision of what is human and what is not would probably not be possible."[12] Historically, the anthropological machine fuses various incongruous or oxymoronic elements together: the soul and the body, the pulse and language, the natural and the supernatural, the terrestrial and the divine. It is a complex soldering operation, which proceeds through capture and suspension. Agamben's vital task is to unhinge these rusting articulations, and "ask in what way – within man – has man been separated from non-man, and the animal from the human?"[13]

Speaking as a "naturalist," Linnaeus concludes that he "hardly knows a single distinguishing mark which separates man from the apes, save for the fact that the latter have as empty space between their canines and their other teeth."[14] In other words, even the inventor of the Dewey Decimal system for sentient creatures could find no "generic difference" between "us" and our evolutionary cousins. This leads to something of a paradox, since the human sciences are usually credited with rationalizing and standardizing important differences, and sweeping away the fanciful overlaps of more superstitious times, in which "the boundaries of man are much more uncertain and fluctuating than they will appear in the nineteenth century."[15] And so Linnaeus is obliged to class *Homo sapiens* as a "taxonomic anomaly, which assigns not a given, but rather an imperative as a specific difference."[16] According to Agamben, this results in a maxim: "man has no specific identity other than the *ability* to recognize himself." In other words, "*man is the animal that must recognize itself as human to be human.*"[17]

Thus, *Homo sapiens* "is neither a clearly defined species nor a substance; it is, rather, a machine or device for producing the recognition of the human." Further, "the anthropological machine is an optical one ... constructed of a series of mirrors in which man, looking at himself, sees his own image always already deformed in the features of an ape."[18] The underlying principle of the modern anthropological machine is that the human "resembles" man, and must recognize itself in a non-man in order to fully identify with that resemblance.[19] This "transience and inhumanity of the human" traces the same border that Timothy Treadwell flirted with and eventually succumbed to: a border "at once the separation and proximity – between animal and man."[20]

Agamben finishes his meditation on a supremely enigmatic note, linking the current crisis of the anthropological machine with the immanently sexual transcendence of its operation. For Agamben, sexual fulfillment is "an element which seems to belong totally to nature but instead everywhere surpasses it."[21] Sex, along with food, is a key area where the human is forced to acknowledge its animalistic aspect. Hence the amount of effort lavished on "sexuality" and "erotica" (not to mention "cuisine"), in order to convince ourselves that we are in the realm of the cooked, rather than the raw. Cameras are increasingly penetrating the previously sacrosanct, domestic spaces of the kitchen and the bedroom. Eat-

ing disorders and sexual pathologies emerge out of the modern apparatus identified by Foucault; that being the constant managerial pressure for the subject to
articulate, delineate, interrogate and sublimate their own subjectivities. Just as
bears were said to lick their young into shape, humans do the same, although
not with their actual tongues, but with language (which, in French at least, is the
same word, *langue*). And, increasingly, with cameras.

Sex is no longer something we do, but something we *have*. Something we *are*.
A burden. A stowaway in the modern soul.

Walter Benjamin wrote that "technology is the mastery not of nature but [the]
mastery of the relation between nature and humanity."[22] Confession is a social
technology with a long and effective history, a device which became increasingly
detailed and codified by the new professions which appropriated its economical
approach to information gathering and population control. Confession moved
from the confessional to the clinic, the courtroom, the couch, and – eventually –
the movie camera, and now the webcam. One cannot remove sexuality from the
equation, since, as I have argued elsewhere, the historically produced libido is
"the goat in the machine."[23] Moreover, as Žižek argues, the camera "not only
does not spoil *jouissance*, but enables it."[24] This observation stems from the case
of pornography, but can be extended to any domain where the sexual is enhanced
or encouraged by the spectacle; since "the very elementary structure of sexuality
has to compromise a kind of opening towards the intruding Third," towards an
empty place which can be filled in by the gaze of the spectator (or camera) witnessing the act.[25]

Taking his cue from Walter Benjamin, Agamben looks forward to a disman-
tling of the anthropological machine through a novel form of erotic ontology:
"the hieroglyph of a new in-humanity." This rather messianic configuration
would usher in "a new and more blessed life, one that is neither animal nor human," saving us from our cosmic agoraphobia; allowing us to play out in the
open without fear.[26] But this is to play the dangerous – or at least rather passive
– waiting game of the "to come."

My own theory is that Timothy Treadwell was driven to the open of the Grizzly
Maze not only in a futile attempt to escape his repressed sexuality (i.e., his humanness), but because he was rejected by the warm and sticky embrace of the
Spectacle. Treadwell's parents trace their son's most significant trauma to his
most bitter disappointment at the hands of his own kind: coming in second for
the role played by Woody Harrelson in the 1980s sitcom CHEERS – this, after
appearing as a contestant on LOVE CONNECTION. "That is what really destroyed
him," says the father somberly in GRIZZLY MAN. "That he did not get that job on
CHEERS." This may sound glib. And any good psychoanalyst would not trust a
word parents say about their children. However, I hope it is clear that this piece

of the puzzle makes perfect sense in the light of my argument that gives equal status to the camera as the creatures it enframes.

A mere ten years before the unveiling of the first movie camera, Nietzsche wrote: "To breed an animal that is entitled to make promises – surely that is the essence of the paradoxical task nature has set itself where human beings are concerned? Isn't that the real problem of human beings?" Mnemotechnics, and the violence they entail for the subject obliged to remember, can stretch in both directions. It can go backwards, as a married person who has promised fidelity well knows. But it can also go forward, in the promise of a glorious and triumphant future. Great expectations, like all things human, have a technical basis.

Walking Out of the Black Forest

> [Herzog] admits no ordinary victims, merely super-victims.
> – Jan Dawson[27]

Finally, we return to Thomas Elsaesser, who has provided us with one of the most useful maps for circumnavigating Herzog's films in his book *New German Cinema*. For while this study was published in 1989, and the director has since made several significant films, the fundamental argument – that Herzog's protagonists are usually "overreachers" or "underdogs" or a combination of both – holds true for the continuing trajectory of his oeuvre. In that sense, Treadwell's imbrications of loneliness, homelessness, isolation, and fear make him a classic protagonist for a Herzog movie. Elsaesser is concerned with contextualizing Herzog's obsession with the extreme, the marginal, and the outside, within the extended German Romantic-historical tradition, and its particularly troubled culmination in the mid-twentieth century. His insights, however, are applicable to the more ontological register that I have been focusing on, especially since Treadwell is not burdened with the same cultural baggage as Kasper Hauser or Stroszek, and yet he is a kindred spirit to these figures, with a similar set of symptoms.

Elsaesser writes: "Herzog's characters are unattached and total individualists."[28] We have seen that Treadwell's onscreen persona fits this description, despite the repressed presence of his girlfriend. What is more, his attempt to integrate with the world of the grizzly bears was not only a "heroic effort and endeavor in a mockingly futile situation,"[29] but perhaps "a necessary spiritual exercise"[30] in the face of existential and sexual panic. Elsaesser links this panic to a nationalist-Oedipal drama concerning bad father images and good father surrogates; most clearly with the human *tabula rasa* of Kaspar Hauser (an inverse Enlightenment figure, acting as a foil for the complete collapse of Enlightenment ideals after the Second World War). However, Herzog seems to have "worked through" this crisis configuration during the 1970s and 1980s, to a more inclusive, global perspective on hubris and overreaching in the years since. LEKTIONEN IN FINSTERNIS / LESSONS OF DARKNESS (1992), RAD DER ZEIT / WHEEL OF TIME (2003), THE WHITE DIAMOND (2004), and, of course, GRIZZLY MAN all attempt to capture humanity at the intersection between the heroic and the banal, the sublime and the hopeless. This is not to claim that Herzog has somehow transcended his Germanness, along with the heavily mustached dead that weigh like a nightmare on his own brow, since artists will never escape the radioactive half-life of the culture which created them. (Unless they are indeed Kasper Hauser.) Rather, it is to observe that in terms of chosen protagonists and scenarios, Herzog asks the same set of questions concerning identity, *akrasia*, meaning making, and survival strategies of people of different backgrounds.

Elsaesser observes:

> Herzog's heroes do not merely exclude the world of the ordinary, the space where most human beings organize their lives, but exist in a void because of a determination to investigate the limits of what it means to be human at all. Between man-as-god and man-as-beast, Herzog's films oscillate in a perpetual search for an existential and metaphysical truth which can only be a divided or dialectical quest. For the neat division between super-man and sub-human in his films is only apparent; there is a constant communication between the two poles.[31]

If Herzog's films are indeed "the haunted quest for the paternal image," then Treadwell found this image not only in the grizzly bears, but in the camera eye which rarely blinked as it watched – and perhaps judged – his confession. (Like any compassionate father, it could not watch his son be killed. It covered its eye, rather than its ear.)[32] The God-Father that Treadwell prays to, while simultaneously disavowing, is reincarnated inside the machine which allows him to autoscopically recognize his own accursed humanity.

Timothy Treadwell fled the trappings of culture for the trap of nature. But he could not resist bringing his teddy bear and his camera; both of which create a far bigger footprint than any eco-tourism operator could measure.

Notes

1.   Thomas Elsaesser, *New German Cinema: A History* (New Brunswick: Rutgers University Press, 1989).
2.   Thereby finding a much wider audience than a year earlier when it was released in art-house cinemas.

3. Strangely, the lead character in the B-movie CHERRY 2000 (Steve De Jarnatt, 1987) is named Sam Treadwell. This film is also about a man who prefers the eroticized company of non-humans; albeit a cyborg female, rather than a grizzly bear.
4. Elsaesser 209.
5. Elsaesser 209.
6. It is tempting, albeit rather uncharitable, to see in Herzog's title a sly pun, in which the "grizzly man" refers to the protagonist's tendency to grizzle or whine.
7. Peter Sloterdijk in a talk at the Cardozo School of Law, 18 April 2005.
8. Bernard Stiegler. Quote taken from THE ISTER (David Barison and Daniel Ross, 2004).
9. Freud in Hubert Damisch, *The Skyline: The Narcissistic City* (Stanford: Stanford University Press, 2001) 132.
10. Damisch, *The Skyline* 143. The reservations inhabited by Native Americans or Aborigines expose the projected status of indigenous peoples, caught between the chthonic and the cultivated.
11. Stiegler in THE ISTER.
12. Giorgio Agamben, *The Open: Of Man and Animal*, trans. Kevin Attall (Stanford: Stanford University Press, 2004) 15.
13. Agamben's paradigm is crying out for the injection of gender dynamics.
14. Agamben 24.
15. Agamben 24.
16. Agamben 25.
17. Agamben 26.
18. Agamben 26-27.
19. I refer the reader to Agamben's book for the more intricate Heideggerean aspects of his argument, especially in relation to captivation, revelation and *Dasein*, especially chapters 10-14.
20. A useful analogy might be that of the border town, which is often ironically more "patriotic" than the capitals of any given nation, since the latter are nestled in the bosoms of secure identities. That is to say, identity reinforcement occurs and radiates more vigorously from the threatened edge, rather than emanating outward from a perceived geo-political center. Of course, it is also the place where blending and promiscuity are likely to occur.
21. Agamben 83. Thus we are in a position to posit various Dantesque levels of "the open" in terms of the anthropological machine. On the first level we have the openness of Rilke's animals (the "pure space" of the outside). On the second level we have Heidegger's reinterpretation of the open as "the unconcealedness-concealedness of being." On the third level – the one we have been dwelling on thus far – there is the opening of the human to the non-human, as a form of autopoiesis or auto-interpellation. On the fourth level we have the opening of the self to the other, in the most figural, transductive sense. Then, on the fifth level, there is the opening of the camera to the open mouth, confessing itself into being via the moralistically charged *logos*. The sixth and seventh levels are the openings of the vagina and the rectum: signifying the alpha and omega of the body politic, and thus the world.
22. Quoted in Agamben 83.

23. See Dominic Pettman, *After the Orgy: Toward a Politics of Exhaustion* (Albany: SUNY Press, 2002).
24. Slavoj Žižek, *The Plague of Fantasies* (London / New York: Verso, 1997) 178.
25. Žižek 178.
26. Agamben 187.
27. Quoted in Elsaesser 221.
28. Elsaesser 218.
29. Elsaesser 222.
30. Elsaesser 224.
31. Elsaesser 220.
32. There is a structurally similar moment in THE WHITE DIAMOND, where Herzog manages to secure some footage behind a sacred waterfall, which has only ever been seen before by birds. He chooses not to use this footage, respecting the feelings of the local Guyanese people, who claim that this kind of visual knowledge simply courts catastrophe. (A situation which replicates the string of problematic and asymmetrical postcolonial encounters which follow in the wake of Herzog's technical apparatus.)

Constitutive Contingencies

Fritz Lang, Double Vision, and the Place of Rupture

Michael Wedel

Inside Film History

With the notion of the "historical imaginary," Thomas Elsaesser has suggested a forceful figure of thought to re-conceive of cinema's place in and contribution to the formation of history and cultural memory. More specifically, the notion has helped to overcome a number of conceptual deadlocks in rethinking the history of German cinema, beset as this national cinema is by questions of continuity and discontinuity, ideological over-determination and political representation, historical trauma, and new beginnings. Thomas Elsaesser takes Weimar cinema, the most celebrated period of German film history in view of its peak artistic achievements but also its most controversial period with regard to its social impact and political meaning, as the looking glass through which German cinema's complex correlations to national (and international) society and culture at large are reconsidered: "Unique among film movements, Weimar cinema came to epitomize a country: twentieth-century Germany, uneasy with itself and troubled by a modernity that was to bring yet more appalling disasters to Europe." In looking at films from the Weimar period through the prism of the historical imaginary, a "Möbius strip is forming before one's eyes, which catches a nation's history in a special kind of embrace" whose powerful grip seems to have the alluring power of renewing its strength for every subsequent generation of cinephiles and film historians alike. As such, Elsaesser contends,

> Weimar cinema is not just (like) any other period of German cinema, it is this cinema's *historical imaginary*, which suggests that it is "the German cinema and its double": in fact, it became a *Doppelgänger* of its own pre-history: foreshadowed in the "kino-debate" of the 1910s, it shadowed the Nazi cinema that selectively tried to (dis) inherit it in the 1930s. On the other side of the Atlantic, in the 1940s, it legitimated – almost equally selectively, as film noir – the work of German émigré filmmakers, before it was dug up again in the 1970s, to lend a historical pedigree to the New German Cinema of Syberberg, Herzog and Wenders.[1]

Among the many merits of Elsaesser's elaboration of the notion of the "historical imaginary" as a cultural temporality evading traditional notions of chronological progress or retrospective teleology, one may notice, on the one hand, that its particular logic of self-definition and otherness cuts across the art cinema / popular cinema divide that has always been such a strong stratagem in writing the history of German cinema; and, on the other, that – rather than discarding the basic assumptions from Siegfried Kracauer's *From Caligari to Hitler* and Lotte Eisner's *The Haunted Screen*[2] – it consciously builds on, works through, and takes further the conclusions to be drawn from their two seminal accounts of Weimar cinema. A central insight taken from Kracauer and Eisner, and easily one of the greatest conceptual achievements of Elsaesser's notion of the "historical imaginary," can be seen in its capacity to locate Weimar cinema's cultural influence, its historical meaning and socio-political dimension, in the specific aesthetic form of the films themselves. It is not (only) on the level of their narratives and modes of production, taken to be symptomatic, but in the concrete cinematic articulation and the degree of self-reflexivity that

> the films usually indexed as Weimar cinema have one thing in common: they are invariably constructed as picture puzzles. Consistently if not systematically, they refuse to be tied down to a single meaning. ... Kracauer's Möbius-strip effect is ... due to a set of formal and stylistic devices, whose equivalences, inversions and reversals facilitate but also necessitate the spectator constructing "allegories of meaning." ... Apart from the ambiguity after which all art strives, Weimar cinema's rebus images – readable, like Wittgenstein's duck-rabbit picture as either the one or the other, but not both at the same time – have to do with mundane matters of film economics and marketing, with the film industry and its objectives and constraints. These function as the "historical symbolic," the limits and horizons that outline and yet vanish in the historical imaginary.[3]

Far beyond qualifying merely as some descriptive term for the aesthetic complexities and manifold cultural inscriptions and re-inscriptions of Weimar cinema, the "historical imaginary" as it is conceived by Elsaesser also forms a meta-theoretical horizon, the fantasy formation and dialectical contraption, to hold more common empirical modes of film historiography in check. The duplicity restored to the films also folds itself onto the heuristic efforts of the film historical discourse it has given rise to. The latter in turn appears less authoritative or objective and closer to its object, affected – as much as it may seek to deny it – by cinema's phantasmagorial powers and therefore becoming part of a mutual historical logic and cultural formation.[4] In its meta-theoretical implications, the idea of a "historical imaginary" offers an effective tool for deconstructing the implicit myths and underlying fantasies behind film historical reasoning and causation, the building of traditions and the formation of a cultural heritage, while, at the same time, it acknowledges their very determining power as the founding impulse and ultimate justification of why we should care for not only writing but "doing" and even "living" and "experiencing" the history of the cinema: "The cinema is part of us, it seems, even when we are not at the movies, which suggests that in this respect, there is no longer an outside to the inside: we are already 'in' the cinema with whatever we can say 'about' it."[5]

In what follows, I would like to trace the reverberations of this conceptual shift in film historiographical thinking and consider some of the consequences that can be drawn from it. With the example of one of Weimar cinema's iconic directors, Fritz Lang, I will use the theoretical framework of the "historical imaginary" in order to point towards the degree to which it transcends not only traditional ideas of cinematic authorship as a revelation of the artist's personality (e.g., in Patrick McGilligan's biographical study of Lang), but also adds an important dimension to accounts of the auteur as textual effect and discursive agency, most recently and most vigorously put forward in relation to Lang by Tom Gunning.

The Enigma of Fritz Lang

The spell of fascination emanating from the figure and the films of Fritz Lang has remained one of the most forceful and enigmatic.[6] Elsaesser characterizes Lang as "the most flagrantly intelligent as well as self-reflexive representative of the enlightened false consciousness," which philosopher Peter Sloterdijk has identified as the ultimate index of the Weimar culture's quintessential modernity: "Lang could have been on Sloterdijk's mind when he says that we need a 'logical and historical "cubism," a simultaneous thinking and seeing in several dimensions' if we are to understand 'the Weimar symptom.'"[7]

On an international scale, neither Alfred Hitchcock nor Jean Renoir, with whom Lang is often compared and whom he both influenced and was influenced by, have proven as difficult in having their artistic signatures recognized in traditional terms of stylistic continuity or biographical self-reference.[8] There are just too many shifts and outright breaks that seem to mark Lang's career: from his silent epics DER MÜDE TOD / THE WEARY DEATH (1921) and DIE NIBELUNGEN / NIBELUNGEN (1924), his science-fiction fantasies METROPOLIS (1926/27) and DIE FRAU IM MOND / WOMAN IN THE MOON (1929), crossbreeding popular kitsch sensibility with stark symbolism (and therefore often improperly associated with German expressionism[9]) through his experiments with early sound technology and the thriller genre in M (1931) and DAS TESTAMENT DES DR. MABUSE / THE TESTAMENT OF DR. MABUSE (1932) to the almost classical, but increasingly bleak

American genre pieces of the 1940s and 1950s, the West German remakes: DER
TIGER VON ESCHNAPUR / THE TIGER OF ESCHNAPUR (1959) and DAS INDISCHE
GRABMAL / THE INDIAN TOMB (1959); and sequels: DIE 1000 AUGEN DES DR.
MABUSE / THE THOUSAND EYES OF DR. MABUSE (1960). For the majority of
critics, especially in Germany and Great Britain, Lang's career appeared to describe the parabola of a decade-long decline after he left Germany (and his second wife and co-author of most of his German films, Thea von Harbou) at the
peak of his creative power. What followed is commonly characterized as a dramatic loss of artistic vision and control within the constraints of the Hollywood
studio system, culminating in nostalgic pastiche and self-parody towards the end
of his filmmaking life.

Film scholars have not ceased to hunt for a common denominator unifying
this body of work, looking for the hidden key with which to unlock the mysterious core of the Langian universe. Along the lines of traditional auteur theory,
Patrick McGilligan, in his recent biography, believes to have found Lang's "Rose-
bud" in a personal trauma caused by the violent death (was it suicide or a covered-up murder?) of his first wife Elisabeth Rosenthal, which occurred after she
had caught Lang and Von Harbou in the act of making love in Lang's Berlin
residence. For McGilligan, this early incident pre-shadowed Lang's obsession
with love triangles, covered-up murders, and personal guilt, which pervades almost all of his films.[10]

Only a few years after the publication of McGilligan's book, the curators of the
Fritz Lang exhibition held in Berlin in 2001 were able to present new pieces of
evidence regarding the circumstances of the death of Elisabeth Rosenthal on 25
September 1920. These were still unknown to McGilligan at the time he was
writing his biography and include a document confirming police registration of
Rosenthal's funeral, issued by the criminal investigation department on 29 September, and the application form for her burial at the Jewish cemetery in Berlin-
Weißensee dated 1 October, which records the cause of death as "shot in the
chest, accident." To the curators of the exhibition and the authors of the accom-
panying book, this entry, in connection with the conspicuous absence of other
official documents, suggests neither murder nor suicide, but a third scenario:

> The word "accident" in connection with such an unusual death caused by a shot in
> the chest might also mean: there was a struggle in the apartment during which one
> party tried to prevent the other – who in the heat of the moment was about to commit
> a crime – from pulling the trigger, but the gun went off, firing the fatal shot.[11]

Whatever the traumatic impact of this early experience might have had on Lang's
artistic development, McGilligan's spectacular re-grounding of Lang's major
themes and cinematic obsessions in an incident occurring early in his "real" life

can be seen as being driven by exactly the opposite logic of a (cinematic) effect desperately seeking its (real life) cause. All too clearly, this temporally inverted logic of "life imitating art" seems to be shaped by an imaginary that wants to identify the biographical "origin," "historical reality" and psychological *Ur-Szene* of the key dramatic triangulation of pleasure, violence, and guilt that Lang's cinema has been working through and made to be felt so "real" over and over again. The irony behind this particular historical imaginary lies in the fact that it ultimately corresponds to Lang's repeatedly stated desire to survive in his films alone. Lang has always refused to reveal too much of his personal life to professional interviewers and film historians - a behavior which has led to infinite speculations based on a handful of biographical legends carefully planted by Lang himself.[12] "Tell her some nice lies about me," he once suggested to an old lady friend whose daughter was interested in what kind of a man he was. This stance might well come to represent Lang's motto regarding all things personal.[13]

Double Vision

In another recent attempt to unravel the conundrum posed by trying to bring together Lang and his films, constructing, as Foucault would call it, the "fundamental" but always imaginary "unit of the author and his work,"[14] Tom Gunning has rooted his speculations not so much in biographical research, but in theoretical reflection. Following a structuralist approach to the idea of the cinematic auteur, he is less interested in Lang as a biographical person than in the artistic persona "Fritz Lang" inscribed in and to be read from his films. Thus reconstructed and placed within the cultural context of 20th-century media modernity, Gunning's "emblematic" Lang re-emerges with a historical agency of much wider implications than reflected by any study of his artistic background or personal surroundings. For Gunning, the imprint Lang has left behind in his work consists above all in the invitation to closely read and reflect on his films, whose representational economy and mode of address are consequently defined as allegorical, in the sense given to the term by Walter Benjamin and Siegfried Kracauer: hieroglyphic images to be contemplated and deciphered by the reader beyond their literal (narrative) meaning.[15]

Gunning's analysis of Lang's cinematic meditations on modernity's basic effects – the commodification of culture and the alienation of subjective experience – looks beyond the traditional level of thematic or stylistic continuities. What Gunning identifies as the driving force behind Lang's cinema is the concept of the "Destiny-machine" which over the years has taken on various narrative forms and audiovisual materializations: Gunning's catalogue of instantiations includes the hourglass and the watchman's cry in THE WEARY DEATH; the *"Gesänge"* fatefully sub-dividing the two-part NIBELUNGEN; Moloch and the recurring steam whistle in METROPOLIS; the false bottoms, spinning wheels and locked doors in DR. MABUSE, DER SPIELER / DR. MABUSE: THE GAMBLER (1921/22); the urban cobwebs of criminal control systems, counter-information highways and intersecting phone calls in M, THE TESTAMENT OF DR. MABUSE, and THE BIG HEAT (1953); the media dissemination of individual identity in FURY (1936), YOU ONLY LIVE ONCE (1937), or WHILE THE CITY SLEEPS (1955); Chris Cross's gold watch timing his manipulation of the electricity circuit in SCARLET STREET (1945); the eternally returning, floating corpse in HOUSE BY THE RIVER (1950); the "unholy" architecture of the ancestral house in SECRET BEYOND THE DOOR (1948) and of the Hotel Luxor in THE THOUSAND EYES OF DR. MABUSE.

According to Gunning, the ultimate image of the Destiny machine in Lang's films is the clock, a machine whose rationale is by definition beyond the control of individual characters.[16] As much as his famous master criminals and media moguls, obsessed painters, novelists, and architects believe in their intellectual and technological mastery of the Destiny machine and the course of the narrative, all of Lang's characters are inescapably caught in the workings of a cinematic system controlled by Lang alone. This hidden hierarchy is built into every single Lang film, introducing a struggle between different narrational agencies, which traps not only its characters but also its audience in a complex game of deception and recognition. Here, Gunning seems to align himself with Elsaesser, for whom: "To see, to know, to believe ... is the triad whose contending claims on perception and reason the radical skeptic in Lang never ceases to play off against each other."[17]

Whereas, according to Gunning, Lang's films occasionally grant glimpses into the structure of the Destiny machine in rare "visionary moments," both characters and viewers of a Lang film find themselves in an unreliable world scattered with false traces and misleading tracks, plunged into an unstable universe full of black holes sucking the individual onto ever deeper layers of contingency.[18] Along a parallel line of thinking, Elsaesser relates the "mesmerizing or hallucinatory effects on spectators so often attributed to Lang's film" to be the result of two kinds of violence: "the film viewer's interpretative violence, and the violence of the film's resistance to interpretation."[19]

The emblematic place of the individual – character *and* viewer – within Lang's cinema would therefore exactly *not* be that of Mabuse at the switchboard of power and control. As Gunning suggests, the signifier of the real power behind Lang's narratives is rather to be found in the many images of rooms emptied out of individual characters by a Destiny machine executing a dark scenario of modernity to which they have fallen victim. Hence, these images of absence in Lang's cinema would also be the moments where the presence of the director is most strongly felt.[20] Gunning's re-readings of Lang's major films re-conceptualize an understanding of the prominent features that have made them classics, but they do not turn the terms of the debate – evolving around fatality and paranoia, ornamental abstraction, narrative duplicity and identity in disguise – completely upside down. His fascination with Lang's films, as that of most of his predecessors, still revolves around what Elsaesser also identifies as their "overriding concerns ...: the relation of vision to knowledge, of knowledge to power, of power to falsehood, and of duplicity to the pleasures of complicity, of 'being in the know.'"[21]

In other respects, it is also interesting to note the degree to which Gunning's paradoxical dialectics of authorship relate to Elsaesser's reading of Lang. But even more instructive are the subtle, yet essential differences. On the one hand, Gunning's notion of a negative authorship seems to be in tune with Elsaesser's observation that in Lang's films "it is artifice that triumphs even more than 'evil,'" and that it is this "underlying doubleness of gesture," the high degree of artifice and stylization, mimicry and parody, that both hides and reveals the author's signature under/in a layer of self-reflexive disguise.[22] On the other hand, with the mechanical and anonymous Destiny machine put in place of any *enunciative* act directly attributable to Lang, Gunning seems to re-introduce another instance for which Lang's cinema is bound to become "the ultimate metaphor"[23] – not of tyranny, as for Kracauer, and not even of the cinema experience itself, as it was for the French critics of the 1950s and 1960s, but of technological modernity. It is precisely in order to avoid this notion of metaphorical or negative unity that Elsaesser introduced Sloterdijk's "enlightened false consciousness" as the "place of rupture" itself, which "implies that the opposite of disguise is not truth, immediacy or 'authenticity,' but rather, whatever it takes to instantiate this symbolic, that is, the condition of possibility of discontinuity, disjuncture, non-identity."[24]

The Place of Rupture

The idea of authorship has always been one of the most prominent shapes that the "historical imaginary" can take in order to convey upon a group of films a certain sense of meaning and coherence. The attempt, famously suggested by Michel Foucault, to recognize the mark of the author in "the singularity of his absence," to "locate the space left empty by the author's disappearance ... follow the distribution of the gaps and breaches, and watch for the openings this disappearance uncovers"[25] has led to the question of Lang's authorship anew in the paradoxical terms of the performance of disguise and permanent deferral, residing, for Gunning, in the allegorical lure of modernity's in-between-spaces of mediation, and, for Elsaesser, in the interstices, the fissures and frictions of cinematic discourse itself: places of rupture and instances of contingency which mark what one could describe as the "historical real" and instantiate the epistemological horizon for all possible figurative meanings and imaginary investments.[26] This shift in emphasis and perspective would suggest an interpretation of Lang's films not so much as emblems of modernity as such, but rather to study the material fabric from which their *textualities* emerge as "allegories of their own problematic existence,"[27] archaeological layers indexical of their concrete time and place in history beneath the level of the symbolic.

That these historical markers, on the level of their material composition, are also openings towards the possible futures of a film and its director has been demonstrated by Elsaesser perhaps nowhere more compellingly than in his book on METROPOLIS. The film was shown in Lang's intended (and now lost) version only once to a select audience on 10 January 1927, before it was immediately dismembered, cut, and re-edited into different national and international release versions. As Elsaesser suggests, it is exactly the uncertain, "un-authored," and "un-authorized" material and thus textual status of METROPOLIS that has turned the film into something like a "ruin-in-progress," re-sampled and re-appropriated by almost every new generation ever since, renegotiating, reinventing, and reinvesting, paradoxically enough, the status of its director as auteur along the way.[28]

By way of conclusion, I would like to take my clue from a moment of rupture occurring in a less prominent example from Lang's oeuvre. It is to be found midway through THE THOUSAND EYES OF DR. MABUSE, Lang's last film as a director. The film's central couple, the American millionaire Henri B. Travers and Marion Menil, the woman he loves and who has fallen in love with him but who is still (if involuntarily) part of a criminal scheme devised against him, sit at a table in the bar of the Hotel Luxor where most of the film's action takes place. Their conversation, held in front of the conspicuous backdrop of a wall decorated with rectangular wooden panels and buzzing ornaments of dots and broken lines producing a moiré effect of smaller rectangular units, is exposed to and monitored by the film's master criminal via a system of surveillance technologies originally installed in the hotel by the Gestapo before World War II, as we learn towards the end of the film. This fact, known to Marion, is revealed to the spectator in a cutaway to the monitor in the secret catacomb of the hotel. Here, the TV image briefly collapses and breaks down into lines and dots of static interference, strongly reminiscent of the designs on the wall behind the couple. Via a zoom into the reconstituted image on the monitor, the camera view jumps back to the hotel bar. Marion and the millionaire briefly go for a dance, before they return to their table, this time captured by the camera from a position inside the decorated wall that has previously been seen behind them. The disorienting rupture occurs when we next get a shot of Marion from her soon-to-be lover's point of view with a completely different pattern of more harmonic and body-like, though angular and abstract, shapes surrounding her face and upper body.

It is easy to discover in this sequence of shots the typical Langian labyrinth of subjective looks and uncanny gazes, the self-reflexive *mise-en-abyme* of *Jugendstil*-design and the tyranny of mediated perception. In the logic of the film itself, the workings of this cinematic labyrinth are bound back to the double legacy of the Nazi past and the criminal energy of the Weimar period's Dr. Mabuse: the temporality of a historical imaginary, superimposing political and cinematic history, is literally turned into the spatial arrangement of a "double occupancy" defining the state of the present as the uncanny *Gleichzeitigkeit des Ungleichzeitigen* and mutual interference of a multitude of (audio)visual regimes.[29] But rather than to simply understand this sequence as being structured around the frozen space and static architecture of the Hotel Luxor as Destiny machine, it could also, and perhaps more productively, be interpreted as the moment of rupture itself: the instant of contradiction and epistemological shock in what first appears to be a blunt instance of false continuity on Lang's part but which may very well form what Elsaesser, in a passage already quoted, describes as "the condition of possibility of discontinuity, disjuncture, non-identity" in order to "instantiate [a new] symbolic."

To "follow the distribution of the gaps and breaches" and "watch for the openings" the disappearance of the author uncovers, as Foucault suggested, would then mean to think of the internal and the external, the contingent effect and its transcendental point of reference and coherence as being caught in the differential image of self and other, co-existing in the spacing between them but never coinciding: a "double vision and a dialectical reflex,"[30] the spatial design and temporal configuration of a parallax non-identity.

From the constitutive ambivalence of the place of rupture as such, an oeuvre's authorial "identity" can only emerge as the vanishing point of a "historical imaginary" that constantly renegotiates and ultimately suspends the levels of the "historical symbolic" (the norms of textual articulation imposed by the industrial structure) and the "historical real" (the materialities of cinematic discourse). Within this logic, the idea of authorial identity, therefore, needs to be considered in terms of its "constitutive outside,"[31] both in relation to its historical "others" of industrial norms and media materialities, but also in respect to its temporal dislocation as the hegemonial reading strategy of an interpretive community, freezing chaos, as Lang himself envisioned, into a formula.[32] As with all sedimented hegemonial articulations, one might conclude, this mode of understanding film history is, however, not only *constitutive* in providing some primary meaning and significance to a cultural practice and body of work. It is also *contingent* insofar as it necessarily remains inside its own fantasy formation and open to be over-turned by others.[33]

Notes

1. Thomas Elsaesser, *Weimar Cinema and After: Germany's Historical Imaginary* (London: Routledge, 2000) 3-4. Also see his "The New German Cinema's Historical Imaginary," *Framing the Past: The Historiography of German Cinema and Television*, ed. Bruce A. Murray and Christopher Wickham (Carbondale/Edvardsville: Southern Illinois University Press, 1992) 280-307.

2. Siegfried Kracauer, *From Caligari to Hitler: A Psychological History of the German Film* (Princeton: Princeton University Press, 1947); Lotte Eisner, *The Haunted Screen: Expressionism in the German Cinema and the Influence of Max Reinhardt* (London: Thames & Hudson, 1969), originally published in French 1952.

3. Elsaesser, *Weimar Cinema and After* 4-5.

4. Elsaesser's prime example for this phenomenon is film noir, a genre invented after the fact in a particular historical situation. See *Weimar Cinema and After* 420-444.

5. Thomas Elsaesser, "The New Film History as Media Archaeology," *CiNéMAS* 14.2-3 (2004): 76. The concept of the "historical imaginary" can, then, be brought into a fruitful constellation to Elsaesser's more recent writings on early cinema, new media, and archival politics, his ongoing critical engagement with the "New Film History" and his programmatic model of "Media Archaeology," first formulated in his general introduction to *Early Cinema: Space, Frame, Narrative*, ed. Thomas Elsaesser (London: BFI, 1990) 1-7; and later fully explored in *Filmgeschichte und frühes Kino. Archäologie eines Medienwandels* (Munich: text + kritik, 2004).

6. Elsaesser speaks of "the enigma of Lang," *Weimar Cinema and After* 148.

7. Elsaesser, *Weimar Cinema and After* 10.

8. See Thomas Elsaesser, "Too Big and Too Close: Alfred Hitchcock and Fritz Lang," *Hitchcock Annual* 12 (2003): 1-41.

9. Lang's relationship to German expressionist film has always been a vexing issue; for a revisionist account which situates Lang opposite to the expressionist movement and closer to the aesthetics of "Jugendstil," see Elsaesser, *Weimar Cinema and After* 185-188.

10. Patrick McGilligan, *Fritz Lang – The Nature of the Beast: A Biography* (New York: St. Martin's Press, 1997) 76-80. Also see Thomas Elsaesser's review essay on McGilligan's book, "Traps for the Mind and the Eye: Fritz Lang," *Sight and Sound* 7.8 (Aug. 1997): 28-30.

11. Rolf Aurich, Wolfgang Jacobsen, and Cornelius Schnauber, *Fritz Lang – His Life and Work: Photographs and Documents* (Berlin: Jovis, 2001) 60-61.

12. Most exemplary in this respect is perhaps Lang's autobiographical note published in Lotte Eisner, *Fritz Lang* (London: Secker & Warburg, 1976) 9-15.

13. Quoted in Bernard Eisenschitz, "Flüchtlingsgespräche: Die Briefe von Fritz Lang an Eleanor Rosé," *Filmblatt* 6.15 (Winter/Spring 2001): 55.

14. Michael Foucault, "What is an Author," *Aesthetics, Method, and Epistemology*, ed. James Faubion (London: Penguin, 1998) 205.

15. Tom Gunning, *The Films of Fritz Lang: Allegories of Vision and Modernity* (London: BFI, 2000). Lang's films have previously been related to the idea of "allegorical cinema" from various interpretative vantage points by, amongst others, David Levin, Catherine Russell, Tom Conley, Garrett Stewart, and Jacques Rancière. Elsaesser's first suggested such a reading in a series of essays on Weimar cinema written in the 1980s, most elaborately perhaps in "Cinema – The Irresponsible Signifier or 'The Gamble with History': Film Theory or Cinema," *New German Critique* 40 (1987): 65-89.

16. Gunning delivers an almost encyclopedic account of the many instances in which clocks of all shapes and sizes assume central roles in Lang's oeuvre. One important figuration of the clock as Destiny-machine in the opening sequence of *M*, however, is not identified by Gunning, but finds its precise description in Anton Kaes, *M* (London: BFI, 2000) 10-11.

17. Elsaesser, *Weimar Cinema and After* 149-150; see Gunning 416.

18. Gunning 476.

19. Elsaesser, *Weimar Cinema and After* 153.

20. Gunning 480.

21. Elsaesser, *Weimar Cinema and After* 150.

22. Elsaesser, *Weimar Cinema and After* 146, 153.

23. The phrase is Raymond Bellour's. See Elsaesser, *Weimar Cinema and After* 148.

24. Elsaesser, *Weimar Cinema and After* 185.

25. Foucault, "What is an Author" 207, 209.

26. The category of the "Real" here understood, of course, in the (post-)Lacanian sense given to the term in the context of film and media theoretical thinking by Friedrich Kittler and Slavoj Žižek.

27. Thomas Elsaesser, *New German Cinema: A History* (New Brunswick: Rutgers University Press, 1989) 75.

28. Thomas Elsaesser, *Metropolis* (London: BFI, 2000).

29. Thomas Elsaesser, "Double Occupancy and Small Adjustments: Space, Place and Policy in the New European Cinema since the 1990s," *European Cinema: Face to Face with Hollywood* (Amsterdam: Amsterdam University Press, 2005) 108-130.

30. Elsaesser, *Weimar Cinema and After* 152.

31. The term "constitutive outside" has been coined by Henry Staten, *Wittgenstein and Derrida* (Oxford: Blackwell, 1985).

32. "... our chaotic age, when it will have frozen into a formula long ago." Lang cited in Elsaesser, *Weimar Cinema and After* 145.

33. I am here drawing on a view of political hegemony developed by Ernesto Laclau and Chantal Mouffe. For a summary of their ideas, see Chantal Mouffe, *On the Political* (London / New York: Routledge, 2005), chapter 2.

Lili and Rachel

Hollywood, History, and Women in Fassbinder and Verhoeven

Patricia Pisters

Although the films of Fassbinder, Herzog and Wenders in the seventies were as vital and formative a film experience as Godard, Sirk and Minelli had been during the 1960s, they were also a shock. They returned me to the country I had left the year the *Oberhausen Manifesto* was published, but they opened wounds, memories and regrets that reached beyond cinema and brought a dissatisfaction and restlessness which I soon recognized as the depressive disposition of a whole generation. The book is dedicated to those who know the intellectual rewards and emotional ravages of such disposition, and who believe in the cinema, nonetheless.[1]

In the introduction to his seminal book on New German Cinema, Thomas Elsaesser confesses that the subject of this book is of more than scholarly interest to him and that the images from this important film movement are not just an event in film history but also relate in complex ways to German history itself, and therefore to the personal life of (German) spectators and film scholars alike. A few years later, Elsaesser would return to New German Cinema and questions of history and identity, this time more specifically through the lens of Rainer Werner Fassbinder's oeuvre. In *Fassbinder's Germany*, one of the (many) networks of complex relations that Elsaesser connects Fassbinder's films to is the threefold relationship between European cinema and Hollywood, German history and the representation of women.[2] When I saw Paul Verhoeven's ZWARTBOEK / BLACK BOOK (2006) in a theater in Amsterdam, appreciating it much more compared to its critical reception in the Netherlands, Elsaesser's Fassbinder came to my mind, and I was struck by the similarities between the German and the Dutch director's ways of dealing with history through their female protagonists: Lili and Rachel, but also Maria and Agnes, Lola and Fientje.[3] In this essay, I will argue that in spite of their considerably different film styles and different national backgrounds, Fassbinder and Verhoeven meet where Hollywood, history, and women come together.

Europe-Hollywood-Europe-Hollywood-Europe

Fassbinder and Verhoeven are both European filmmakers with a great admiration for Hollywood. Although Fassbinder often repeated that he wanted to make Hollywood films *in Germany*, and he expressed his admiration for Douglas Sirk's melodrama both in writing and in his own films, actually moving to Hollywood became a serious consideration after his international co-production DESPAIR (1978) and the international success of DIE EHE DER MARIA BRAUN / THE MARRIAGE OF MARIA BRAUN (1979).[4] When Fassbinder died in 1982 this option was to remain an unrealized desire forever.[5] Paul Verhoeven is bound to Hollywood in several ways. Ever since his short film about the Dutch navy, HET KORPS MARINIERS / THE ROYAL DUTCH MARINE CORPS (1965), which was shot as a 23-minute "blockbuster *avant-la-lettre*," he has been much more interested in the big budget, action-driven type of Hollywood film.[6] Verhoeven moved to Hollywood after the critical acclaim of SOLDAAT VAN ORANJE / SOLDIER OF ORANGE (1977) and the unappreciative film climate in the Netherlands at the beginning of the 1980s. Although the similarities between Fassbinder and Verhoeven at first glance seem only superficial, Elsaesser's analyses of the complex ways in which European cinema and Hollywood mutually influence each other as a sort of "two-way mirror" allows for a more nuanced reading of the Hollywood connections between the German and the Dutch director.[7]

In "German Cinema Face to Face with Hollywood" Elsaesser argues against stereotypical models of influence or counterbalance in which Europe stands for culture and America signifies commerce. He unpacks the ambiguities in the often-quoted phrase from Wim Wender's IM LAUF DER ZEIT / KINGS OF THE ROAD (1976) "the Yanks have colonized our subconscious" and demonstrates how after the success of the revival of 1930s fashion and fascism that started with the film CABARET (Bob Fosse, 1972) and the NBC series HOLOCAUST (1978/1979), Hollywood has played an important role in "profiling German film culture to its own identity."[8] Edgar Reitz most explicitly addressed this issue when he made his television series HEIMAT (1984) declaring that "with HOLOCAUST the Americans have taken away our history."[9] German cinema seems to have a love-hate relationship with Hollywood that changed in the mid-1980s and the beginning of the 1990s, when there was an influx of foreign talent into Hollywood, where they were to make films for a global audience. Now the mirror was reflected back: German and European directors began reading America through a European lens. This was especially true regarding the issue of "fascinating fascism" and Nazism, so deeply and traumatically engrained in German national consciousness and the European history of World War II. Hollywood played a role in "constructing the meaning of Nazism and the Holocaust for Germans them-

selves and between Germany and the rest of the world."[10] But today's blockbusters made by European directors also present a "metamorphosed legacy of the
war and Nazism in today's Hollywood" which can be perceived as another transatlantic cultural transfer.[11]

According to Elsaesser, Verhoeven's STARSHIP TROOPERS (1997) is a very good
example of this metamorphosed legacy of Nazism in Hollywood, where Verhoeven criticizes American superiority and the enjoyment of power in the guise of a
sci-fi monster movie.[12] Obviously this position of the mirror directed towards
Hollywood is not fixed because this mirror of mediated cultural identity continues to flip back and forth across the Atlantic. As Elsaesser indicates, Hollywood-Europe should no longer be seen as an opposition of commerce versus art,
but is better seen as a modality, as an "aggregate of states of varying intensities"
or "states of mind" where Europe and America keep a mutual coded identity.[13] As
I will further point out, with BLACK BOOK's story set in the Netherlands during
World War II but told in Hollywood style, Verhoeven finds himself on the European side of the mirror again.

Relating to History

Elsaesser argues that while time on the American side of the mirror is "real
time," European time is history.[14] Both Fassbinder and Verhoeven have been
marked by the aftermath of World War II. Fassbinder was born at the end of the
war in 1945 and Verhoeven just before the war in 1938. For Verhoeven, childhood
memories of bombardments and occupied Holland have marked his experience
and led him to do extensive archival research about the war, which he first under-
took for a documentary about Anton Mussert, the leader of the NSB, the party of
Nazi collaborators in the Netherlands (PORTRET VAN ANTON ADRIAAN MUSSERT /
PORTRAIT OF ANTON ADRIAAN MUSSERT, 1968). The research continued as he
worked on SOLDIER OF ORANGE, which is a film based on the memories of Erik
Hazelhoff Roelfzema, a resistance fighter who went to England and became the
adjutant to the Dutch Queen in exile. With BLACK BOOK, Verhoeven returns once
more to the history of the war, presenting the story of Rachel Steinn, a Jewish
woman who survives the end of the war by joining the resistance and infiltrating
the German headquarters.

Many of Verhoeven's characters are typically morally ambiguous (perhaps as
part of his European sensibility) or at least less heroic or less villainous than one
would expect. Even Mussert, who after the war was executed for his collaboration
with the Nazis, is presented in a nonjudgmental way. The interviews and archival
material make it clear that Mussert, most paradoxically, was acting out of extreme

patriotism, expecting the Netherlands to become a sort of independent federal
state of Germany (in reality, he was not really taken seriously by the Nazi brass).
In SOLDIER OF ORANGE, the main character, Erik Lanshof, is more an adventurer
than a resistance fighter by conviction. And in BLACK BOOK, Verhoeven shows
how, at the end of the war, the difference between right and wrong had become
completely unclear and that after the liberation, the Dutch demonstrated cruel
tendencies on their part against anyone even slightly suspected of "sleeping with
the enemy." All of the historical events in Verhoeven's fiction films are presented
in a Hollywood action-adventure style that gives the films a dynamic and entertaining energy. BLACK BOOK has been compared to Hitchcock's Hollywood films
(Hitchcock is, of course, another good example of a Europe-Hollywood exchange)
for its effective use of significant details in the mise-en-scène and its play with
elements of suspense and surprise.[15]

In his other Dutch films, Verhoeven also makes use of history, albeit in a less
explicit way. With KEETJE TIPPEL / CATHY TIPPEL (1975) he presents late-nine-
teenth-century Holland via the hardships and survival tactics of a young work-
ing-class girl. SPETTERS (1980), which was controversial at the time of its release,
is now considered a classic and accurate realistic portrayal of provincial youth in
the early 1980s. FLESH+BLOOD (1985), the international co-production that
marked Verhoeven's transition to Hollywood, may not be based on true historical
events (though the historical siege of the city of Münster in 1534 was a source of
inspiration), but Verhoeven did extended research on the customs, morals, and
behavior of sixteenth-century Europeans which he presents in his characteristic
raw realistic style.

Fassbinder's films also have a strong relation to history. Although they are of-
ten read as auteur films, related to the myth of Fassbinder's eccentric personality,
Elsaesser sees Fassbinder as a chronicler of German history. In many of his
films, the references to German history are important, but it is the BRD-trilogy
(THE MARRIAGE OF MARIA BRAUN, LOLA and VERONIKA VOSS) together with LILI
MARLEEN that most strikingly address World War II and its aftermath in the
1950s. On the one hand, these films are – like other films of the New German
Cinema that relate to German history – a response to Hollywood's vision of Nazi
Germany. On the other hand, Fassbinder presents his unique vision of German
history. LILI MARLEEN (1980) is the story of a song, "Lili Marleen," that became
most famous during World War II, and deals with the period 1938-1946. THE
MARRIAGE OF MARIA BRAUN starts with the marriage of Maria Braun during a
bombing at the end of the war and continues until 1954 (the moment when Germany won the soccer World Cup and Maria Braun finally has her husband Herrmann back). VERONIKA VOSS (1981) is set in 1956. Here the war is embodied by
Veronika Voss who had been a famous singer in Nazi Germany (the character is

based on Sybille Schmitz, once a favorite of Goebbels) but has now become ad-dicted to heroin. And finally LOLA (1981) presents the Germany of 1957 when pragmatism and capitalism have brought new economic prosperity for the Ger-mans (Adenauer's *Wirtschaftswunder*).

THE MARRIAGE OF MARIA BRAUN, Fassbinder's most successful film interna-tionally, is also his most classically constructed film. As Elsaesser points out:

> Generically a melodrama, but one whose rise-and-fall structure also gives it the force
> of a morality tale (both might be said to be secular forms of tragedy), MARIA BRAUN
> offers an audience enough generic familiarity to encourage direct identification with
> the heroine's ambitions, goals and disappointments. At the same time, enough mys-
> tery hovers over the ambiguous ending. The retrospective doubt about Maria Braun's
> motivation (whether Maria blew herself up deliberately or by accident ...) can embol-
> den the audience to speculate about the deeper meaning of the story, without leaving
> the cinema baffled or confused ...[16]

As Elsaesser further explains, the particular blend of Hollywood and European art or auteur cinema of MARIA BRAUN invites not just a generic melodramatic reading of a bittersweet tale of a woman who tries to survive in a man's world, it also allows a more metaphorical or allegorical reading where the referent be-comes "the fate of an entire country, rather than of this particular woman."[17] In this reading, Maria Braun becomes Fassbinder's embodiment of the pragmatic, post-Hitler Germany where a woman "picks herself up from the ashes of a war" to become a successful business woman. It can also be seen as a metaphor for the transition that the German nation is undergoing.[18] MARIA BRAUN is a cin-ematic history told from below, through the smaller story of an ordinary person. It is a film that functions as a trigger of memories: "not so much recalling a reality, as setting up a chain of associations, stories remembered from one's par-ents, pictures seen in the family album, the standard version of the 1950s as present in the culture at large of the 1970s."[19] In similar ways, the other BRD-trilogy films plus LILI MARLEEN offer a *mise-en-abyme* of German history through a smaller private story.

It is important to point out that in the films of both Verhoeven and Fassbinder, history is not only represented by referring to historical events or circumstances; but they are also filtered through all kinds of internal references to other media. The references to Hollywood genres have already been mentioned. There are also other films that are alluded to like THE WILD BUNCH (Sam Peckinpah, 1969) in Verhoeven's FLESH+BLOOD, MILDRED PIERCE (Michael Curtiz, 1945) in Fassbin-der's MARIA BRAUN, and DER BLAUE ENGEL / THE BLUE ANGEL (Josef von Stern-berg, 1930) in LOLA. Elsaesser offers an extended analysis of how other media such as popular music, sound effects, and radio broadcasts serve as internal media references in the BRD trilogy. This appears to be important because it indicates how popular culture, and especially media, not only reflect historical realities, but also become a fundamental element of it. However, the most important "medium" for their presentation of history seems to be the way that the female characters embody history, which Fassbinder and Verhoeven have in common.

Woman as "Participating Medium"

Fassbinder believed that women are better "media" for the telling of stories because they have a wider range of emotions, are more in touch with the sensibilities of a period, are less needful of a social façade, and are more flexible and adaptable.[20] Verhoeven has a similar notion regarding the status of the dramatic potential of women. When asked about the best moment in the making of BLACK BOOK, he responded by saying that it was undoubtedly when, after over 20 years of struggling with the script, co-writer Gerard Soeteman called him with the solution that would make the film work: changing the main character from a man into a woman.[21] The second best moment was when he found actress Carice van Houten to play the role of Rachel.

Elsaesser addresses more explicitly the question of why Fassbinder thought that the history of Germany was best told through the fate of women. The possible allegorical readings that women's stories encompass have already been mentioned. However, this is not without its problems since women have very often been used as the symbol of a nation. As many feminists have pointed out, this is very often at the expense of the women themselves who easily disappear in the allegorical picture of collective history.[22] However, Elsaesser points to several elements in Fassbinder's portrayal of women that allow for a more nuanced perspective. First of all, he notices that in crucial scenes in Fassbinder's trilogy and in LILI MARLEEN the women actively give themselves as spectacle. Lola (Barbara Sukowa) presents herself to be seen and acknowledged by Von Bohm, the municipal planning director she wants to seduce. Maria (Hannah Schygulla) checks out how she looks in a bar as she walks up to the soldier who will soon become her lover. Veronika Vos (Rosel Zech) is in love with the image of her former spectacular self. And Willie (Hannah Schygulla) sings "Lili Marleen" in spectacularly staged performances. As Elsaesser indicates: "[T]he women in Fassbinder's films are all too aware of both a power and a presence that they draw from being looked at, and are usually prepared to deploy, knowing full well that it is a weapon that can cut both ways."[23] Elsaesser suggests reading the signifier of "show business" that is so prominent in Fassbinder's historical films as a reference to the power of woman as image. Again, much has been written in feminist film studies about the position of women-to-be-looked-at,[24] but Elsaesser demonstrates that, in Fassbinder's films, a variety of readings are possible:

> the power of self-display, of female exhibitionism, the reification of the image, the society of the spectacle, the woman trapped in her image or using her image to make it in the world of men, and thus using the energy contained in the image as the power of self-alienation. More precisely, the question arises of how in films about women, and about woman as image, the women are nonetheless perceived as strong, rather than as victims, exploited and objectified.[25]

The elements that provide an answer to these questions are related to how the female characters know how to deal with what Elsaesser calls the "stock exchange of impossible equivalences." First of all, this is related to the intelligence of the protagonists involved, which makes Fassbinder's characters so fascinating. As Elsaesser demonstrates in the case of Lola, but which can also be extrapolated to the other (female) characters as well, "it is the sort of intelligence which enables the characters to stand by their own contradictions and inconsistencies, in a manner that energizes their capacity for action rather than blocking it."[26] This makes LOLA not a film about moral hypocrisy, blatant opportunism, and corruption but a film in which characters operate using their political, sensual, and moral intelligence, which allows them to find a *modus vivendi*, which allows them to move on. The other films in the trilogy and LILI MARLEEN are less optimistic, but the intelligence is deployed in a similarly sensitive way.

Two other contradictory elements also need to be mentioned in this respect. The image of the strong woman that puts herself at the center of the spectacle (when politics becomes "show business") is subverted by her capacity to love. At the same time, love leads to a contract, a deal which comes with the love. This seems perverse, or negatively opportunistic, but seen slightly differently it is exactly what makes the women in Fassbinder's films (as well as Verhoeven's as we shall see shortly) such strong and intelligent characters. As Elsaesser notes, all of Fassbinder's films are love stories, albeit very often unconventional love stories. Also the history of Germany is told as a love story: "MARIA BRAUN is predicated on the central relationship remaining unconsummated (but in the minor key there is Oswald's love for Maria), VERONIKA VOSS is a love story between two times two women (with in the minor key, Krohn's love for Veronika), and LOLA is the love story between sex and power (with the minor key provided by Bohm's love for Lola)."[27] The love stories in Fassbinder's Germany films very often lead to some kind of pact or contract. In both LOLA and MARIA BRAUN, many contracts and business deals are made, which recognize a variety of distinct interests. This seems very cold, but as Elsaesser points out, there is an exchange between the strong woman, on the one hand, and a new kind of economic system on the other. For, although the contracts seem to confirm an old tradition where women are traded between two men (for instance, the pact between Oswald and Hermann in MARIA BRAUN), the deals are agreed to so openly, and with so much respect for the woman's own values, it seems that in the end everybody gets a good deal, and exchange values can be transformed into gifts. One of the ways in which the woman maintains her own values is through her intransigence in her demand of love that she fully realizes as an impossible one, but which coexists alongside the contracts being agreed to. This is the "stock exchange of impossible equivalences" which give both MARIA BRAUN and LOLA their dynamics: "for only when human beings no longer need to struggle for their naked survival, only when they possess, besides an intelligence of the head, the body and the heart, also a bank account and a business card, can they enter into and entertain an economy of the gift, as the protagonists of these two films try to create."[28]

The elements that make women such excellent participating media in historical representations, such as the intelligence, love, and pacts that Elsaesser notices in Fassbinder's BRD trilogy, also offer the prospect for comparing the women in Fassbinder's films with those in Verhoeven's films. The similarities between Fassbinder's Maria and Lola and Verhoeven's Agnes (Jennifer Jason Leigh) in FLESH+BLOOD, Cathy (Monique van de Ven) in CATHY TIPPEL, and especially Fientje (Renée Schoutendijk) in SPETTERS are quite striking. These heroines all have been called opportunistic ladies who use their bodies to get what they want. But, upon reassessing them, Verhoeven's women are also quite intelligent, and combine their "to-be-looked-at-ness" with a capacity to love, and they follow their instincts for survival by concluding various contracts that are good deals for everyone involved.[29] A closer look at LILI MARLEEN and BLACK BOOK allows us to compare the female protagonists more elaborately as both are set in the historical period of Nazism.

Lili and Rachel

In comparing Lili and Rachel, one has to start with the names. In LILI MARLEEN Hannah Schygulla plays a woman named Willie, who sings a song about another woman, Lili Marleen. When the song (in reality sung during World War II by Lale Anderson) becomes popular because it speaks to the lonely men in the trenches, Willie signs photos of Hannah Schygulla with "Lili Marleen." Elsaesser has pointed out how Fassbinder here demonstrates the "permanent slippage of actress, character, name and addressee, organized around something [as] ephemeral and banal as a song, albeit one that, like the cinema, commands its own imaginary and mythological space within history."[30]

Meanwhile, Rachel Steinn in BLACK BOOK dyes her hair blond and becomes Ellis de Vries when she joins the resistance. The character Rachel/Ellis is based on the life stories of three different Dutch women who joined the resistance, infiltrated German positions, or had a love affair with various German officers.[31] The dynamics involved in the slippages of names, characters, and events are very different, but like Schygulla, Carice van Houten embodies these different (historic and fictional) women and also manages to create an imaginary space within history that starts operating of its own accord, while maintaining some links with the historical events without letting it become an unambiguous allegory.

Another striking similarity between Willie/Lili and Rachel/Ellis is that they both present the idea of "woman as image," where the woman presents herself as a spectacle quite explicitly through the trope of "show business." As we have already indicated, Willie becomes a great performer for the Third Reich. Similarly, Rachel/Ellis is a singer who, once she has infiltrated a German headquarters, performs for the officers. However, like Fassbinder and Verhoeven's other heroines, Willie and Rachel make the distinction between "lending themselves to others" and "giving themselves only to themselves."[32] Both Willie and Rachel can maintain this non-naive stance because of an impossible love. Willie is in love with the Jew, Robert, whom she continues to see even after she has infiltrated the highest Nazi ranks. Rachel eventually falls in love with the German officer Müntze, after she discovers that they share the fact that they have both lost their entire families and he accepts her despite the fact that she is Jewish. It is this impossible love that allows them to keep themselves for themselves and not deliver themselves completely to the demands of the system. This is clear from the fact that both women are also double agents, working for the resistance and the Nazis at the same time. They do not assume their duties out of idealism or high moral values, but because they want to survive. When Robert asks Willie whose side she is on, she replies: "On your side, as long as I live. But I'm not free to choose how I live in order to survive." Rachel joins the resistance only because, after having lost everything, she has nothing more to lose, except her own life.

Like Fassbinder and Verhoeven's other heroines, Lili and Rachel have to operate in a world where good and bad come in various degrees and disguises, but never in a pure form. In LILI MARLEEN, both the Nazis (with their racial laws) and the Jews (with their severe family laws) are depicted as fundamentalists. BLACK BOOK shows how nobody is transparent, and everybody should thus be distrusted. This fundamental ambiguity in human relations, and the fact that anybody can be a double agent, not out of pure evil or heroic idealism, but because they are forced by historical circumstances, is perhaps the most important of Fassbinder and Verhoeven's insights. By transferring and transforming history through the double mirrors of European and Hollywood cinema, both filmmakers add new perspectives to the historical imagination. However, it is through the fate of their female protagonists that they demonstrate an intellectually and emotionally rewarding belief in the cinema – and perhaps in the world, nonetheless.

Notes

1. Thomas Elsaesser, *New German Cinema: A History* (London: Macmillan, 1989) xviii. The *Oberhausen Manifesto* was declared in 1962 and is usually seen as the beginning of New German Cinema, a vision that is nuanced by Elsaesser in his book by contextualizing the manifesto with greater historical accuracy.
2. Thomas Elsaesser, *Fassbinder's Germany: History, Identity, Subject* (Amsterdam: Amsterdam University Press, 1996).
3. The films I am referring to here are respectively LILI MARLEEN (Fassbinder, 1980) and BLACK BOOK (Verhoeven, 2006), DIE EHE DER MARIA BRAUN / THE MARRIAGE OF MARIA BRAUN (Fassbinder, 1979) and FLESH+BLOOD (Verhoeven, 1985), LOLA (Fassbinder, 1981) and SPETTERS (Verhoeven, 1980). It is very well possible to add Elvira, Veronika, Cathy, and Catherine, to this list of names. These are the names of characters IN EINEM JAHR MIT 13 MONDEN / IN A YEAR OF 13 MOONS (Fassbinder, 1978), VERONIKA VOSS (Fassbinder, 1982), KEETJE TIPPEL / CATHY TIPPEL (Verhoeven, 1975), and BASIC INSTINCT (Verhoeven, 1992).
4. See Rainer Werner Fassbinder, "Six Films by Douglas Sirk," *New Left Review* 1.91 (May-June 1975): <http://www.newleftreview.org>. ANGST ESSEN SEELE AUF / ALI: FEAR EATS THE SOUL (1974) is Fassbinder's most well-known Sirkian melodrama. See Elsaesser, *Fassbinder's Germany* (275-286) for an annotated filmography of his other Sirkian films.
5. The documentary FASSBINDER IN HOLLYWOOD (Robert Fischer, 2002) speculates on how Fassbinder would have fared in Hollywood. It is also known that Fassbinder died on the pages of a treatment of a film on Rosa Luxemburg, which would have been his first American film with Jane Fonda in the leading role.
6. See Rommy Albers, Jan Baeke, and Rob Zeeman, eds., *Film in Nederland* (Amsterdam: Ludion / Filmmuseum, 2003) 190-191.
7. Thomas Elsaesser, "German Cinema Face to Face with Hollywood: Looking into a Two-Way Mirror," *European Cinema: Face to Face with Hollywood* (Amsterdam: Amsterdam University Press, 2005) 299-318.
8. Elsaesser, "German Cinema" 305.
9. Edgar Reitz, quoted in Elsaesser, "German Cinema" 385.
10. Elsaesser, "German Cinema" 312.
11. Elsaesser, "German Cinema" 313.
12. Interestingly, in *Film in Nederland* STARSHIP TROOPERS is referred to as a Dutch movie (334).
13. Elsaesser, "German Cinema" 316.
14. Elsaesser, "German Cinema" 317.

15. Stéphane Delorme, "Showgirl: BLACKBOOK de Paul Verhoeven," *Cahiers du cinéma* (Dec. 2006): 21-22.
16. Elsaesser, *Fassbinder's Germany* 101.
17. Elsaesser, *Fassbinder's Germany* 101.
18. Christopher Sharp, quoted in Elsaesser, *Fassbinder's Germany* 102.
19. Elsaesser, *Fassbinder's Germany* 105.
20. Interviews with Juliane Lorenz, Hannah Schygulla, and Fassbinder himself on the BRD trilogy DVD (Criterion Collection, 2003). See also Elsaesser, *Fassbinder's Germany* 118.
21. Interview on the DVD concerning BLACK BOOK.
22. See Deniz Kandiyoti, "Identity and its Discontents: Women and the Nation," *Colonial Discourse and Postcolonial Theory: A Reader*, ed. Patrick Williams and Laura Chrisman (New York: Columbia University Press, 1994) 376-391; Patricia Pisters, "Refusal of Reproduction: Paradoxes of Becoming-Woman in Transnational Moroccan Cinema," *Transnational Feminism in Film and Media*, ed. Katarzyna Marciniak, Anikó Imre, and Áine O'Heal (New York: Palgrave MacMillan, 2007) 71-92.
23. Elsaesser, *Fassbinder's Germany* 117.
24. This is most famously done by Laura Mulvey, who dismissed the notion of women in cinema as "to-be-looked-at-ness" in her essay "Visual Pleasure and Narrative Cinema," *Screen* 16.3 (1975): 5-18.
25. Elsaesser, *Fassbinder's Germany* 118.
26. Elsaesser, *Fassbinder's Germany* 119.
27. Elsaesser, *Fassbinder's Germany* 122.
28. Elsaesser, *Fassbinder's Germany* 127.
29. Agnes (while keeping her love and affection for her fiancée) chooses both strategically *and* out of desire to make Martin her lover. He is the leader of a gang of mercenaries who kidnaps and rapes her; Cathy's poverty-stricken family forces her to prostitute herself, which gives her the opportunity to climb up the social ladder (in a night club show, the female performers sing about the good life that money can buy). Meanwhile Fientje insists that her love must include these conditions: the ability to earn a living and acquire a house that will allow her to abandon the fish and chips stand she shares with her brother.
30. Elsaesser, *Fassbinder's Germany* 170.
31. Esmee van Eegen, Kitty van Hagen, and Ans van Dijck are the actual names of the historical women who form the basis for the Rachel / Ellis character.
32. Elsaesser, *Fassbinder's Germany* 125.

Amsterdamned Global Village

A Cinematic Site of Karaoke Americanism

Jaap Kooijman

Like Thomas Elsaesser in his introduction to *Hollywood op straat*, I often walk through the Reguliersbreestraat – located between my home and the university – which is the street in Amsterdam where Hollywood's presence is most visible. On one side, there is the Tuschinski Theater, the grand cinema of the Netherlands where all the star-studded premieres take place. On the other side is the Cineac, a former cinema built in 1934 in the style of the *Neue Sachlichkeit*. Thanks to its status as monument, the outside of the building has not been altered, although its function has changed drastically over the years. I clearly remember going to the Cineac as a kid to see Walt Disney movies such as THE ARISTOCATS (1970) and HERBIE RIDES AGAIN (1974), but perhaps my memory is failing me, because the Cineac used to be a newsreel cinema. During my student years, the Cineac became a *knaakbioscoop*, showing old Hollywood movies in continuous rotation each evening, which one could enter at any time by paying a *knaak* (two guilders and fifty cents). I spent many evenings there watching obscure Hollywood genre films in the company of bums who used the cinema as shelter from the rain. In the late 1990s, Arnold Schwarzenegger and Sylvester Stallone converted the Cineac into a Planet Hollywood restaurant, only to see it fail within a few short years. Since then, the Cineac has hosted several trendy clubs like DJ Tiësto's The Mansion, which tend to go bankrupt and start up again somewhere else in the city. However, regardless of its ever-changing interior, the building remains visible in all its architectonic grandeur, and each time I walk by it reminds me of Hollywood.

In *Hollywood op straat*, Thomas Elsaesser takes the Reguliersbreestraat as his starting point to show how "everything is connected" via cinema culture, not only explicitly by the presence of the Tuschinski and the Cineac, and two prominent porn theaters, but also implicitly by the photos of Hollywood stars on the covers of the glossy magazines sold in the kiosks, the Disney action figures included with each Happy Meal at McDonald's, and the hidden presence of surveillance cameras monitoring our every move. Moreover, Elsaesser uses the street to show how its historical depth can be explored. Each building, like the Cineac, tells its own story, often connected to cinema. As Elsaesser points out, the pizzeria was once the office of the Pathé film company, the now-closed flower shop used to be the Nöggerath cinema and recently has turned into a Pathé Arthouse cinema, and just around the corner, on the Rembrandtplein, there was the Rembrandt Theater, owned by the German Ufa film company, which was burned down by the Dutch resistance in 1943.[1] In this way, the Reguliersbreestraat functions as a *pars pro toto* of Hollywood's omnipresence in Amsterdam, rendering visible both its drastic changes as well as its significant continuity, making connections over time and between different cultural spaces and economic sectors.

In this chapter, I will wander beyond the Reguliersbreestraat, through other streets in Amsterdam, by exploring Dutch films that are situated in Amsterdam and which are all, in one way or another, connected to Hollywood. My journey starts with Do Not Disturb (Dick Maas, 1999), a self-proclaimed "dark, off-killer thriller with more twists and turns than the streets of Amsterdam itself."[2] Subsequently, I will race in a speedboat through the canals of Amsterdam in Amsterdamned (Dick Maas, 1988), jump on a bicycle in Turks fruit / Turkish Delight (Paul Verhoeven, 1973), witness an exhilarating Amsterdam streetcar chase scene in Naakt over de schutting / Naked over the Fence (Frans Weisz, 1973), and finally, speed through Amsterdam on a delivery moped in Amsterdam Global Village (Johan van der Keuken, 1996) and in the second sitcom episode of Shouf Shouf (VARA, 2006-2007), the television spin-off of the hit movie Shouf Shouf Habibi! (Albert ter Heerdt, 2004).[3] My theoretical navigator will be the concept of karaoke Americanism, a term coined by Thomas Elsaesser, enabling me to recognize "Hollywood" in Amsterdam in all of its different manifestations, not merely as an imitation of the American generic example, but also as a form of active cultural appropriation, or, citing Elsaesser, "that doubly coded space of identity as overlap and deferral, as compliment and camouflage."[4] This eclectic collection of Dutch films resembles the Reguliersbreestraat in that it can function as a cinematic site, revealing how cinema connects different strands through both time and place, across a variety of genres, thereby providing an entrance into the multilayered cityscape of pop-cultural appropriation and the dominant presence of Hollywood in our everyday lives.

Turn Right at Muntplein

Do Not Disturb opens with the arrival of Walter and Cathryn Richmond, played by the Hollywood actors William Hurt and Jennifer Tilly, and their deaf-mute ten-year-old daughter Melissa (Francesca Brown) at the Hotel de l'Europe, which is located between the Reguliersbreestraat and the Nieuwe Doelenstraat, the first home of the Amsterdam Film and Television Studies department. The street outside of the hotel is crowded with fans of the extravagant pop star Billy Bob Manson, a fictional crossing of the real-life American pop stars Marilyn Manson and Michael Jackson. Inside the hotel, Melissa witnesses the murder of her father's business associate and, while her parents are having dinner in the hotel restaurant, she is kidnapped by the murderers who continuously threaten to kill her as well. Conform to the genre conventions of the Hollywood B-movie, the plot of Do Not Disturb remains thin, predominantly consisting of chase scenes through Amsterdam at night, reaching a climax when one of the villains, driving an ambulance with Melissa tied up in the back while being chased by the police and Melissa's father, causes an Amsterdam streetcar to crash quite spectacularly in the Raadhuisstraat. In the end, the bad guys get punished, and the Richmond family finally gets to enjoy their stay in Amsterdam, although the way the city is depicted recycles the worn-out clichés of excessive sex and drugs, quite similar to recent Hollywood movies set in Amsterdam like Ocean's Twelve (Steven Soderbergh, 2004), EuroTrip (Jeff Schaffer, 2004), and Deuce Bigalow: European Gigolo (Mike Bigelow, 2005).

Both the conventional chase scenes and the clichéd depiction of Amsterdam reinforce the film's imitative character. Unlike other popular movies by Dick Maas such as De lift / The Elevator (1983), Flodder (1986), and Moordwijven / Killer Ladies (2007), Do Not Disturb was not targeted at a domestic audience but at an international one and is an obvious example of a non-American movie that tries to imitate Hollywood. As Thomas Elsaesser notes, very few European films have "the budgets, stars and production values even to try to reach an international mainstream audience," concluding that "often enough these films fail in their aim, not least because they have to disguise themselves to look and sound as if they were American."[5] That Do Not Disturb proved to be a commercial and critical failure may be explained by the plausible factor that its attempt to disguise itself as a "real" American movie is obvious to such an extent that the film becomes even less convincing to audiences and critics alike. A decade earlier, Dick Maas released Amsterdamned, a commercially and critically successful thriller about a serial killer lurking around the canals of Amsterdam. The film's spectacular highlight is the scene in which the hero Eric Visser (Huub Stapel) chases the mysterious killer through the Amsterdam canals in a speedboat, yet its Hollywood allure is comically undercut by touches of Dutch cinephilia. Holland's best-known film critic Simon van Collem peddles by on a water bike, while director Bert Haanstra is conducting a brass band in a jolly boat, a clear reference to his classic film Fanfare (1958). Although Amsterdamned also relies heavily on the often clichéd genre conventions of Hollywood, the film does not, however, disguise itself as American, but explicitly recognizes its local character, appropriating Hollywood within its own Dutch context, rather than trying to be a mere imitation of the American original.

The cultural appropriation of Hollywood in DO NOT DISTURB and AMSTERDAMNED can be discussed in reference to Jean Baudrillard, who has suggested that "America is the original version of modernity," whereas we in Europe "are the dubbed or subtitled version."[6] The use of dubbing and subtitling as metaphor is striking, as the appropriation of Hollywood is most explicitly visible in audiovisual media. Moreover, dubbing and subtitling can be taken quite literally. With the exception of dubbed children's movies, the large majority of the films watched in the Netherlands are subtitled Hollywood genre movies, making Hollywood the standard film language not only for a Dutch audience but also for Dutch directors of feature films. Hollywood equals cinema, both metaphorically and literally. However, this perspective limits the discussion to the question of whether or not the dubbed or subtitled version is a successful copy of the American original. The use of Elsaesser's karaoke metaphor, on the contrary, places emphasis on the performative character of cultural appropriation. Although it may sound rather pejorative, the concept of karaoke Americanism is an effective tool to grasp the slippery distinction between sheer imitation and active appropriation. As a performance based on clichéd pop-cultural conventions that invites creative participation, karaoke Americanism signifies both faithful imitation and playful parody, both mimicry and mockery, enabling an appropriation of Hollywood which leaves room for ambiguity. From this perspective, DO NOT DISTURB is sheer imitation, whereas AMSTERDAMNED is a karaoke performance, which becomes even more overtly pronounced in its international edition, dubbed in English by the original actors speaking with a heavy Dutch accent.[7]

Turn Left at the Dam

In one famous scene in TURKISH DELIGHT, the most popular Dutch film ever, Erik Vonk (Rutger Hauer) bikes across the Dam and through the streets of Amsterdam with Olga (Monique van de Ven) on the backseat. They have just gotten married in city hall (now the luxurious Hotel the Grand, located on the Oudezijds Voorburgwal), and, accompanied by a soundtrack by Toots Thielemans on harmonica, they joyfully play a cat-and-mouse game with a car that is trying to pass them. TURKISH DELIGHT was director Paul Verhoeven's second feature film (he eventually would move to Hollywood) and has been widely recognized as the main representative of a "new wave" in Dutch cinema, in which explicit depictions of sex, bodily functions, and violence were used to attack the Calvinist restrictions of Dutch bourgeois culture.[8] In addition to its celebration of romance, the bicycle scene emphasizes the role of Amsterdam as a bohemian space of artistic and sexual freedom, in stark contrast to the bourgeois small-mindedness as represented by the mundane provincial town of Alkmaar where Olga's parents run an electronic appliance store.

From an auteur film perspective, Verhoeven's TURKISH DELIGHT has been compared to other European films such as Pier Paolo Pasolini's TEOREMA / THE-OREM (1968) and Bernardo Bertolucci's ULTIMO TANGO A PARIGI / LAST TANGO IN PARIS (1972), all of which fit within a tradition of *épater les bourgeois* through sexual liberation. From the perspective of karaoke Americanism, however, TURKISH DELIGHT could also be perceived as a raunchy version of the Hollywood melodrama LOVE STORY (Arthur Hiller, 1970). Like Oliver (Ryan O'Neal) and Jennifer (Ali MacGraw), Erik and Olga fall in love despite their being from different social backgrounds, and like Jennifer, Olga dies of cancer in the end. Moreover, both movies were extremely popular and have become iconic representations of the early 1970s. If one views TURKISH DELIGHT as "the other face of LOVE STORY," as one American critic did, it is tempting to overemphasize the differences between these two popular love stories as part of the traditional divide between Hollywood and European cinema.[9] Accordingly, as a product of the American studio system, LOVE STORY is a tearjerker made to move the audience along the lines of predictable genre conventions, whereas TURKISH DELIGHT is the artistic expression of one individual director, intended to confront rather than please the audience. However, as Thomas Elsaesser shows in *European Cinema*, the two seemingly antagonistic poles of the Hollywood-Europe divide actually complement each other, being two sides of the same coin. European national cinemas have developed not so much in opposition to, but in relation to Hollywood, "existing in a space set up like a hall of mirrors, in which recognition, imaginary identity and mis-cognition enjoy equal status, creating value out of pure difference."[10] Instead of emphasizing the differences, one could also point out the similarities, like how the bicycle scene in TURKISH DELIGHT, intentionally or not, evokes the romantic sentiment of that other famous scene in LOVE STORY in which Oliver and Jennifer playfully throw snowballs at each other in New York's Central Park.

The rigid distinction between Hollywood genre film and European auteur cinema is also challenged by NAKED OVER THE FENCE, the action thriller by the Dutch director Frans Weisz, which was released the same year as TURKISH DE-LIGHT, but never attained the latter's popularity.[11] NAKED OVER THE FENCE tells the story of the Amsterdam pigeon keeper and gambling joint owner Rick (Rijk de Gooyer), who, together with his friends Ed (John Bluming) and Penny (Jennifer Willems), gets entangled in a porn mafia murder scheme. The glamour of Hollywood is embodied by the femme fatale Lilly Marischka, played by the sensual Silvia Kristel, who would later become Europe's most famous porn-chic actress with her starring role in EMMANUELLE (Just Jaeckin, 1974). Amsterdam plays an important role as the film's setting, which is emphasized by the film's opening sequence, which shows the city from a bird's-eye view, lingering over Amsterdam to capture its labyrinthine character. There are several times during the movie that Penny is riding her moped through the crowded streets of Amsterdam while being chased by the mob's twin brothers Jack and Mack (Hans and Lodewijk Syses), whose American convertible keeps getting stuck in the city's web of one-way streets and narrow bridges. The main chase scene, however, takes place on the streetcar tracks. When Jack and Mack hijack a streetcar, Rick and his friends jump on another empty streetcar and chase the twins all over town, eventually forcing them to surrender. Although the chase scene fits the conventions of the action thriller, its "realness" is undercut by the main characters, who are genuinely surprised by the spectacular situation they find themselves in, as they cheerfully wave at stunned passengers who are waiting at the various streetcar stops. For a moment, Amsterdam becomes the location of a "real" movie, and yet, like in the AMSTERDAMNED chase scene, we are immediately reminded that we are in Amsterdam, not Hollywood.

Pass Straight through the Vondelpark

The documentary AMSTERDAM GLOBAL VILLAGE is built around the young Moroccan-Dutch courier Khalid speeding through Amsterdam on his moped delivering developed rolls of film and pictures to photographers like Erwin Olaf. In between these deliveries, he meets his friends who hang around the Museumplein where they chitchat and smoke joints. Throughout the almost four-hour documentary, shot over a period of twenty months, director Johan van der Keuken uses Khalid's delivery route as a thread to connect a wide range of personal stories about belonging and exile, showing various ethnicities, nationalities, subcultures, and lifestyles that exist side-by-side in a relatively small yet international metropolis. In this way, Amsterdam is presented as a multicultural labyrinth in which the experiences of people coming from all over the world are linked over time and space, through both their differences and similarities. As Thomas Elsaesser has pointed out, the cinematic structure of AMSTERDAM GLOBAL VILLAGE was inspired by the circular form of the Amsterdam canals.[12] Van der Keuken shows the city and its inhabitants literally from different angles and spaces in all their heterogeneity, suggesting continuity through disruptive montage, thereby presenting a non-hierarchical structure which makes connections in perpetual motion, of which Khalid is its most prominent personification. Tellingly, the film ends with a shot of Khalid on his moped, saying into the camera that he has had enough of all this filming, before turning around and speeding off, back into the city's labyrinth.

In *European Cinema*, Elsaesser uses AMSTERDAM GLOBAL VILLAGE to discuss his concept of double occupancy, which exemplifies how all Europeans – and not just the most recent immigrants – are hyphenated: "There is no European, in other words, who is not already diasporic in relation to some marker of difference – be it ethnic, regional, religious, or linguistic – and whose identity is not always already hyphenated or doubly occupied."[13] Instead of being just another term for multiculturalism or cultural diversity, double occupancy recognizes the imbalance of political power between different cultural identities, including both the experience of being uprooted as well as the possibility of personal alliances with others in comparable situations. The concept emphasizes the ambiguous multiplicity of identities, which eventually could lead to the rather utopian "point where the very notion of national identity will fade from our vocabulary, and be replaced by other kinds of belonging, relating and being."[14] AMSTERDAM GLOBAL VILLAGE invites its viewers to make such connections between the great variety of city dwellers (including themselves), suggesting a larger collective sense of belonging based on a shared urban living experience. Moreover, as its title implies, the documentary finds the global in the local, while explicitly leaving the national out of the picture.

In addition to AMSTERDAM GLOBAL VILLAGE, Elsaesser mentions SHOUF SHOUF HABIBI! as an example of double occupancy. This Dutch comedy about a group of Moroccan-Dutch and white Dutch youngsters in Amsterdam (which was the box-office hit of the year 2004) closely follows the genre conventions of the Hollywood comedy, making fun of both traditional Moroccan immigrant culture and mainstream white Dutch society. Abdullah (Mimoum Oaïssa) and his friends are continuously failing to achieve their goal of getting rich without too much effort, which allows for, as Elsaesser suggests, "a democracy of bunglers and losers to emerge as the film's political ideal, in the absence of – or while waiting for – better options."[15] Although in a different way than AMSTERDAM GLOBAL VILLAGE, SHOUF SHOUF HABIBI! also opens up Amsterdam as a multicultural space in which diverse senses of belonging can come together. Another link between the two films can be made by looking at the second sitcom episode of SHOUF SHOUF, the hit comedy's television spin-off, in which Abdullah's younger brother Driss (Iliass Ojja) rides his moped throughout Amsterdam to deliver pizzas. In this episode, Driss speeds through the city, going from pizzeria Pastorale on the Haarlemmerstraat to his favorite client on the Lindengracht, a beautiful blond older lady who seemingly wants to seduce him. But before he arrives at her luxurious canal house, Driss rides home to Boutenburg (in Amsterdam West) to groom himself. Here the moped serves as a vehicle that crosses

economic and ethnic boundaries within Amsterdam, moving back and forth between the city's tourist areas, the blue-collar multi-ethnic neighborhoods, and the
luxurious circle of canals called the *Grachtengordel*, home to the (predominantly
white) urban upper class. Even though SHOUF SHOUF is based on the genre conventions of the Hollywood comedy and American sitcom, whereas AMSTERDAM
GLOBAL VILLAGE is part of a Dutch documentary tradition, Driss and Khalid function in a very similar manner. The two young Moroccan-Dutch moped couriers
both race around Amsterdam, constantly making crisscross connections
throughout the cityscape and thereby reinforcing its perpetual transformation.

Go Back to Rembrandtplein

Since the release of AMSTERDAMNED in 1988, film critics and viewers alike have
continued to point out the film's geographical inconsistency, as several shots of
the film's famous chase scene feature the Oudegracht, which is the main canal in
the nearby city of Utrecht. Different than the canals in Amsterdam, the Oudegracht has quays below street level, where people can sit and relax on terraces
alongside the water. Only in Utrecht could director Dick Maas let the speedboats
jump so spectacularly onto the quay and plow through the tables and chairs on a
full terrace, leaving the unsuspecting tourists in awe. This cinematic freedom is
of course quite common and accepted in movies shot in Hollywood, suggesting
that the repeated claim of inconsistency has been inspired by AMSTERDAMNED's
explicit local character. Apparently, the break with the realism of local space (leap-
ing from Amsterdam to Utrecht and back in one scene) undermines the credibility of the film's fictional world. However, although staying within the city limits
of Amsterdam, the other films discussed in this chapter are also geographically
inconsistent, presenting scenes that leap from one specific place to another,
which in the "real" cityscape are often located far apart. Erik and Olga in TURKISH
DELIGHT ride their bicycle from the Muntplein directly onto the Centuurbaan.
The streetcar chase scene in NAKED OVER THE FENCE moves back and forth from
one Amsterdam neighborhood to another in no logical order. In DO NOT DIS-
TURB, the ambulance enters the Vondelpark at the Blauwbrug and exits at the
Raadhuisstraat. Even Khalid in the documentary AMSTERDAM GLOBAL VILLAGE
makes turns along his route that are impossible according to the city map.

Such geographical inconsistencies are not only acceptable in cinematic space,
they also do not alter the way these specific locations function as real-life reference points. Like the buildings in the Reguliersbreestraat represent histories
about cinema's presence in our everyday culture, these films connect me to the
streets of Amsterdam, the city where I was born and have lived most of my life.

Watching these movies brings back personal memories linked to locations that keep changing over time, and yet remain remarkably the same. And vice versa: moving through the city often makes me relive these films, as I find myself humming the theme of TURKISH DELIGHT when biking across the Dam or imagining streetcars chasing each other until they crash when they pass me by on the Weteringscircuit. When Jean Baudrillard traveled through the USA, he experienced how "real" space overlapped with cinematic space: "In America cinema is true because it is the whole of space, the whole way of life that are cinematic. The break between the two ... does not exist: life is cinema."[16] As a cinematic site of karaoke Americanism, life in Amsterdam also equals cinema, even if the actual experience may turn out to be quite different from the American original, repeatedly reminding us that we are not in Hollywood after all.

One explicit moment of both Hollywood's presence and absence brings me back to the Reguliersbreestraat. In 2000, I attended the glamorous red-carpet premiere of the Hollywood movie THE PERFECT STORM (Wolfgang Petersen, 2000) at the Tuschinski Theater, organized by the Benelux branch of Warner Brothers. Although the film's two major stars were supposed to be present, George Clooney called in sick, while Mark Wahlberg was rumored to be smoking pot in some Amsterdam coffee shop. As the paparazzi were taking pictures of Dutch soap opera stars and other locally famous media personalities, I could not help but recognize that we were playing Hollywood in Holland, a true performance of karaoke Americanism. After the film was over, we went to the VIP after party at the Escape, a large discotheque on the Rembrandtplein. Many of the guests probably did not realize the location's historical significance. During the 1920s, the Rembrandt Theater had been the city's most prominent cinema, showing German silent films that were far more popular than the Hollywood movies that were showing at the Tuschinski.[17] Eight decades later, at the exact same spot, we were dancing to celebrate the arrival of THE PERFECT STORM, a Hollywood blockbuster production, in a former cinema now called the Escape. Whether we liked it or not, at that moment, right there at the Rembrandtplein, no escape was possible from Hollywood's omnipresence in Amsterdam.

Notes

1. Thomas Elsaesser, "Inleiding: Hollywood op straat," *Hollywood op straat: Film en televisie in de hedendaagse mediacultuur*, ed. Thomas Elsaesser (Amsterdam: Vossiuspers AUP, 2000) 9-26.
2. As quoted from the back cover of the DVD edition of DO NOT DISTURB.
3. The FilmTrip foundation organizes bicycle tours through Amsterdam for tourists and high school students and also has published a city map that shows all the impor-

tant locations of films shot in Amsterdam, including those discussed in this chapter. See: <www.filmtrips.nl>.

4. Thomas Elsaesser, *European Cinema: Face to Face with Hollywood* (Amsterdam: Amsterdam University Press, 2005) 317.

5. Elsaesser, *European Cinema* 76.

6. Jean Baudrillard, *America*, trans. Chris Turner (London / New York: Verso, 1988) 76.

7. For a more extensive discussion of the cultural appropriation of Hollywood and American pop culture, see Jaap Kooijman, *Fabricating the Absolute Fake: America in Contemporary Pop Culture* (Amsterdam: Amsterdam University Press, 2008).

8. Hans Schoots, *Van Fanfare tot Spetters: Een cultuurgeschiedenis van de jaren zestig en zeventig* (Amsterdam: Bas Lubberhuizen / Filmmuseum, 2004) 99-102; Xavier Mendik, "Turks Fruit / Turkish Delight," *The Cinema of the Low Countries*, ed. Ernest Mathijs (London / New York: Wallflower, 2004) 109-118.

9. As quoted in Mendik 112.

10. Elsaesser, *European Cinema* 47.

11. Turkish Delight holds the #1 spot in the Top 100 of the most popular Dutch films between 1945 and 2003, with an attendance of 3,328,804, while Naked over the Fence holds down 73rd place with 336,909. See Schoots 211-213.

12. Elsaesser, *European Cinema* 197.

13. Elsaesser, *European Cinema* 108.

14. Elsaesser, *European Cinema* 109.

15. Elsaesser, *European Cinema* 113.

16. Baudrillard 101.

17. Ivo Blom, "'Duits gevaar voor onze theaters': Het Rembrandttheater tussen 1910 en 1933," *Ons Amsterdam* (Feb. 2004): 52-56.

Soundtracks of Double Occupancy

Sampling Sounds and Cultures in Fatih Akin's HEAD ON

Senta Siewert

> Just like in German Punk or Hip Hop, what we are doing here is not a cinema of imitation, but rather a cinema of adaptation.
> – Fatih Akin[1]

In *European Cinema*, Thomas Elsaesser discusses Fatih Akin amongst other young contemporary filmmakers who challenge the predominant understanding of national cinema within film studies.[2] Elsaesser's wide-ranging scholarship crosses boundaries and coins terms that have established new discourses in film studies and humanities. One such concept is "double occupancy," which refers to "a filmmaking and film-viewing community that crosses cultural and hyphenates ethnic borders."[3] According to this concept some of the most successful contemporary European filmmakers (Fatih Akin, Gurinder Chadha, Abdel Kechiche), all from different ethnic backgrounds, are doubly occupied, hyphenated Europeans (German-Turkish, British-Indian, French-Magreb). These directors seem best suited to address social problems and identify tendencies of change within European society at large. However, Elsaesser stresses that double occupancy can be applied to "every part of Europe, and to all of us: our identities are multiply defined, multiply experienced."[4] He proposes thinking of a "post-national" Europe and thereby implies that the common practice of identification according to nationality has become outdated and should make way for the possibility of post-national subjectivities.[5]

Alongside films such as LA HAINE / HATE (Mathieu Kassovitz, 2005), TRAINSPOTTING (Danny Boyle, 1996), AMSTERDAM GLOBAL VILLAGE (Johan van der Keuken, 1996), and GOOD BYE LENIN (Wolfgang Becker, 2003), which can be viewed as representing a New European Cinema, Elsaesser also briefly mentions the film GEGEN DIE WAND / HEAD ON by Fatih Akin (2004). As a "post-national subject" Akin explicitly refuses to let his work be reduced to his ethnic roots or to have him typecast as a migrant filmmaker. Akin defines HEAD ON as a European film, in response to media reactions after his film won the Golden Bear prize at the Berlin Film Festival. Both the German and Turkish press claimed the prize as their own success, a reaction which suggested a certain anxiety about defining national identity.[6] In contrast to these critics, Elsaesser focuses on the utopian dimension of double occupancy when he writes that Head On "draws its power, its universality, but also its politics, from the spectator following a human relationship that tries to live by a new socio-sexual contract."[7]

In response, my aim here is to build on Elsaesser's concept of double occupancy and, moreover, add new dimensions to it by focusing on how it works on the level of sound. My hypothesis is that in New European Cinema it is precisely in the music that the double occupancy finds its fullest expression.[8] In order to illustrate this point, I will begin by examining two examples of contemporary European films which depict sampling techniques and technologies in a more explicit manner, before turning to a close reading of Head On, which reveals a shift and amplification from musical sampling technique to sampling as an overall structuring element. In my analysis of these various sampling techniques, my main concern is with specific musical forms, audiovisual relations, musical emotion, sonic memory, and the role of the transnational in cinematic soundtracks.

Sampling

Akin's documentary Crossing the Bridge: The Sound of Istanbul (2005) is connected to Head On, as some protagonists and musicians appear in both films. Crossing the Bridge establishes a central role for music in carving out particular identity patterns and its cultural and geographic implications. It starts with a proverb by the ancient philosopher Confucius, stating that one must understand the music of a country in order to understand its culture. One central theme of the film is the bridging between West and East, Europe and Asia, in terms of spaces, cultures, and different musical styles. The main protagonist is Alexander Hacke, a member of the German avant-garde band Einstürzende Neubauten. He can be seen as a *flaneur*, who tries to capture the diverse sounds of Istanbul with a microphone.[9] In Akin's film, Hacke functions as a mediator who reworks these sounds, samples, mixes, and saves them on his computer in order to produce the soundtrack to the film. Hacke's sampling technique can be understood as a broader aesthetic characteristic that also recurs in the film Head On and other European films such as Trainspotting, Hate, and Dans Paris / Inside Paris (Christophe Honoré, 2006).

In Hate, one particular scene most notably underlines the importance of the music in contemporary films. Here a DJ opens the windows of his housing estate flat in the outer suburbs, and his music reaches down to the main protagonists walking below. The DJ is mixing the song "Sound Of Da Police" by KRS1 with "Fuck The Police" by Nique Ta Mere (NTM) and a loop of Edith Piaf singing

"*Non! Je Ne Regrette Rien.*" The music establishes three cultural backgrounds, with American hip-hop and French hip-hop confronting a French chanson from the 1950s and 1960s. This sampling and cut'n'mix technique together with the lyrics offers a good example for interpreting music in cinema as a form of story-telling. By appropriating different music styles the songs function as a social commentary: Piaf's lyrics of "no regret" provide a justification for attacking the police. Moreover, HATE connects its narrative to real events and layers past and present time through its music.[10]

HEAD ON, like HATE, also constantly blends film and musical traditions by sampling them and thus requiring that the audience provide a special kind of musicality and a way of understanding historical references. Sampling, as a form of discontinuity that is used in hip-hop and drum'n'bass, among others styles of music, can best be described as a way to adapt, appropriate, recycle, and remediate pre-recorded material. In HEAD ON, Akin samples seemingly diverse and contrary musical sounds from different cultures, times, genres, and styles. The music in the film functions as a sound bridge, which transcends cultural borders and reveals a state of double occupancy.

Sound and Image

In order to understand the referential and experiential function of music one must recognize that in film studies there is a tendency to focus more on the visual than on sound and music. One reason for neglecting the music could be that the soundtrack is generally considered secondary since most films are virtually complete before being passed on to the composer for scoring. Traditionally, composed music functions as a tool to underline the narrative and mood; this music is meant to remain "unheard" as film scholar Claudia Gorbman has famously stated.[11] However, this tendency is slowly being reversed as a growing number of contemporary directors have already chosen the songs during the scriptwriting stage; this was also the case with HEAD ON. This phenomenon, which is manifested in the soundtrack practice, suggests a shift in contemporary European films from a reliance on original background scores to foregrounding pre-existing songs. This is also reflected by the fact that the music supervisor of HEAD ON, Klaus Maeck, has become increasingly influential over the years and was even hired as the producer of Akin's latest film AUF DER ANDEREN SEITE / ON THE OTHER SIDE (2007).[12]

Another reason why music has been neglected in film studies could be due to the significant differences between sound and image in film. One important distinction is that, unlike one's eyes, it is difficult to close one's ears to sound. Moreover, the sound vibrations in the space of reception have the potential of going right into a spectator's body. Is this why film theory tends to ignore sound, because sound cannot be easily objectified? Does this originate in the associations of the visual as linked to the rational and the mind, while the auditory has often been linked to the irrational and the body?[13] By contrast, I would like to highlight that sound can affect the body of the audience, with its tone appealing to the emotions, even without the literal elements of the lyrics. This means that music can be seen as a powerful device for reorganizing the affective relationship between film and the spectator and can also convey a kind of presence.

Many critics have agreed that Head On has an intense wrenching effect on its audience. This can be partly attributed to the narrative of the characters' struggle in life and also to the rapid changes in locations, raw digital aesthetics, colors, atmosphere, moods but most of all, to the film's usage of various musical styles. In order to illustrate the dynamics of the music, which stresses the dual background of the characters and the director, I will now introduce several key scenes from Head On in more detail.

The film opens with a postcard view of Istanbul facing the shore of the Bosporus. A band is placed tableaux-like, sitting on top of oriental carpets, looking into the camera and playing the traditional Turkish song "Saniye'M," which is dominated by the sounds of a clarinet and violin.[14] A Turkish singer is wearing a red evening dress, and, as we can read in the subtitles, she is singing about a failed love affair. After seeing these warm exterior colors, a quick cut to an artificially lit nightclub in Hamburg provides a vivid contrast. The protagonist Cahit (Birol Ünel) is introduced via a shaky hand-held camera shot. He is stumbling around, picking up glasses, and drinking leftover beer. He has long dirty hair and a desperate, frustrated facial expression. He seems to be on the verge of an emotional outburst when he begins talking to a friend in Turkish and then to others in German. After he moves to a different club featuring German punk rock, he starts a fight and gets kicked out and then drives his old car head on into a wall.[15]

This scene enacts an episode of the *unexperienceable*, a near-death experience. The audiovisual texture is complex: the squealing tires irritate and the flickering lights on the wall of the tunnel seem to anticipate this moment between life and death. The visual beat sets up an aural beat, which changes into the song "I Feel You" by Depeche Mode.[16] The jump cuts of Cahit's changing facial expressions from hysterical laughter to crying are juxtaposed with POV shots of Cahit driving his car zigzagstyle, to emphasize his drunken, desperate state of mind. While the song can be heard non-diegetically without any ruptures, the editing and the driving increase time's velocity.

The audience has to comprehend a lot simultaneously, moving quickly from Istanbul to Hamburg, from traditional Turkish music to alternative German punk rock and an international song. Apart from the complex negotiations in the dynamic between the crossover of western pop rock music and oriental music, the audience also visually experiences the intensity of Cahit's suicidal behavior. The narrative does not explain the main character's motivations. Instead, the only thing the audience has to go on is the audiovisual texture. For this reason, viewers may have to listen more closely to the sound, which means that the beat and lyrics provide further narrative explanation. The lyrics in "I Feel You" resemble those in the beginning of the Turkish song, in that they tell us about the end of an unfulfilled relationship: "This is the morning of our love, it's just the dawning of our love." Listening to the clash of musical styles opens up facets of the characters, which words and images alone cannot explain.

As Elsaesser has noted about HEAD ON: "After a near-death accident, the male protagonist, having cancelled all obligations even to the proposition of staying alive, eventually agrees to enter into a kind of contract, with an almost equally post-mortem young woman."[17] Like Cahit, the female protagonist Sibel (Sibel Kekilli) is also accompanied by a multifaceted soundtrack. She is introduced in a close-up, not unlike a classic melodrama. However, a single camera pan movement quickly shows the audience her wrists, indicating that she is a psychiatric patient who has also survived a suicide attempt. From the moment she first appears, she offers a strong unapologetic seductive gaze into the camera, which is addressed to Cahit, who is also in the clinic. After she discovers that Cahit is Turkish, she tries to persuade him to marry her so that she can flee her strict Muslim parent's home. Later, at their traditional wedding they take cocaine and dance excessively to traditional Turkish wedding music. Sibel moves into Cahit's anarchic and dirty apartment. She cooks and cleans, but maintains her independence from him while she leads a liberated sex life, with many different partners. Sibel redecorates Cahit's apartment, leaving behind only one single reminder of his past, a poster of the 1980s punk rock band Siouxies and the Banshees on the door. In this way, pop music is also part of the visuals in the form of a poster of a band as a reference to the identity patterns of the male protagonist. Moreover, a hospital doctor attempts to relate to Cahit by referring to a pop band and their lyrics. He asks if Cahit knows the band The The and their line: "If you can't change the world, change your world."[18] This reference to pop music functions as a communication bridge between two people from different cultural backgrounds.

Enhancing Emotions with Diegetic Music

In another scene, the importance that music has for the characters becomes apparent, which one experiences on the level of diegetic music. Soon after their marriage, Sibel comes back to their home and dances to the song "Temple Of Love," joined by Cahit. The song, originally by The Sisters of Mercy, represents the 1980s western rock tradition, and in the film it is mixed with Middle Eastern musical styles, including the haunting voice of Israeli singer Ofra Haza.[19] With her dancing, Sibel combines typical 1980s German head banging with Turkish dance. At the song's climax the image freezes, fixing Cahit in his wildest dance move, resembling the image of a pop star. As the song continues, Sibel and Cahit are now suddenly shown in a nightclub and still dancing to the same song. As Sibel is seen seducing a man, Cahit's jealousy marks the beginning of their passionate yet destructive love affair. When Cahit later becomes aware of his feelings, he is shown dancing in another club with his arms in the air covered in blood.

In the film, these extreme feelings are manifested in alcohol and drug use, in dancing and self-inflicted wounds, and always accompanied by a specific soundtrack. This is illustrated in a later scene, after Cahit has accidentally killed Sibel's former lover in a fight. When Sibel returns home alone after this incident she puts on music that matches her grieving mood and the impossible love relationship she has with Cahit. She now puts on the Turkish song "Agla Sevdam."[20] This enhances her emotions, and she begins to cut herself to feel even more pain. This pain is visualized as she watches her own blood flow all over her and is further emphasized by the melodramatic music. The "empathetic music" matches the mood of the action.[21] Both Cahit and Sibel live a life of ecstatic suffering, which is called *kara sevda* in Turkish, which describes people who are either in ecstasy or agony and who long to see and feel their blood in order to intensify their feelings. This particular behavior is rooted in an oriental tradition of suffering for love, as Feridun Zaimoglu has observed.[22] Based on these examples, which show that diegetic music plays a key role in enhancing feelings, the next section shows diegetic music as a sonic memory device.

Musical Codes / Sonic Memory

After the fatal incident, Cahit is sent to prison, and Sibel flees to Istanbul. There she is seen entering a nightclub, where she takes drugs (this time the "oriental" drug opium), dancing and turning in spirals on her own with her eyes closed. This scene, seems to show her trying to escape the space of the Turkish nightclub by transferring herself to a virtual space via excessive dancing until she collapses and subsequently is violently assaulted. Here the song "I Feel You" by Depeche Mode is played diegetically, the same song that was played as a soundtrack as Cahit drove headfirst into a wall. The song connects two different locations (Hamburg and Istanbul) and two people (Cahit and Sibel), who are both experiencing extreme physical pain and emotional despair. The song, like feedback, functions here as a "cue" for the audience, enabling them to predict an imminent disaster. By this time, the audience can sense what is going to happen next via the soundtrack. The song refers to a particular mood of a previous event and also to a shared sonic memory for audience members. When well-known songs are played in familiar spaces – such as nightclubs or cars – the participation of the audience is at its highest level. In these familiar spaces where everyone has had their own personal experiences with dancing in the past, the sonic memory is the most intense because personal experiences, combined with scenes from the film, blur the lines between actual and virtual, fantasy and reality. Just as the consumption of energetic and hallucinogenic drugs brings one into a non-space, a space outside the body, dancing can evoke a delocalization of the body that suspends normal affective relationships and perception of the self.

When coupled with memory, this sound experience can be described as the sonic equivalent to the déjà vu. Steve Goodman has coined the term "déjà entendu" to describe the sonic memory as something that has resonated before with some part of one's body.[23] He calls it "an unfolded acoustic memory, which is latent, virulent" and is waiting to be activated by a trigger, which stimulates an embodied memory. Déjà entendu implies the enhancement of chronological time by active memory. This goes beyond the somatic experience of the aural and the visual to a deeper personal resonance of the body. Goodman notes that one has to consider both the referential and the experiential function of music.

Transcultural Soundtrack

In HEAD ON it does not matter on what level one understands all the German, Turkish, or English lyrics, because the beat, rhythm, and tone of voice all have an effect regardless of their cultural reference points. This border-crossing quality of music is also described by Simon Frith, who has suggested that "sounds carry across fences and walls and oceans, across classes, races and nations."[24] Musicologist John Sloboda also argues that, as an emotional response, music is transcultural.[25] If one takes into account all of the qualities of music that have thus far been mentioned, then Elsaesser's concept of double occupancy helps us to understand the characters and the director, their affinity with both pop and traditional music from various cultures. Audiences are also doubly occupied or even multi-occupied, as they share certain of the film's musical codes, because they live in, with and through these codes. This means that the viewers can sense what affects the characters in the film. The function of music is to captivate the audience: their bodies are affected by the rhythms that are transmitted via vibrant bodily experiences, which shows that music, enhanced by camera work, recreates and simulates an experience in a way that the mere sequencing of images cannot.

In this way, the music acts as a bridge for the spectator, whose experience of extreme states usually does not involve the slashing of one's wrists, trying to commit suicide or escaping an oppressive Turkish family life, but that via well-known spaces (nightclubs, cars, etc.) – that combine both familiarity and extra-territoriality – the spectator's access is therefore enhanced, which is equal to the extreme emotional states, where ecstasy and agony are so closely commingled. The extreme emotional states denote the particular types of protagonists found in HEAD ON as well as other contemporary European films such as TRAINSPOT-TING, HATE, and INSIDE PARIS. In these films, the protagonists escape the binary narrative of either succeeding or failing; they are neither rebels nor conformists; instead they can be seen as survivors, who live a life with risky cutting-edge experiences like racing at extreme speeds in a car, dancing excessively, or taking drugs. Elsaesser also describes similar contemporary protagonists when he introduces them as "abject heroes" (referring to Julia Kristeva's[26] famous term), here delineating a utopian dimension of double occupancy, because these abject heroes tell us something about "the conditions of [the] possibility of a counter-image of what it means to be human."[27] In the case of HEAD ON, Elsaesser points to a special kind of abject heroes: the post-mortem heroes, who have "cancelled all obligations even to the proposition of staying alive."[28]

In other words, here the extreme states of the characters place them in a no man's land, from which they are brought back to life by the various affective, semantic, and historical references embedded in the music. When "Life's What You Make It" by Talk Talk[29] is heard at the end of the film, it functions as a classic *déjà entendu*, because Cahit had played this same melody earlier in the film on the piano. Here it is obvious that songs can even serve as lifesavers, because through the lyrics, rhythm, and the tone of voice, the song offers a glimpse of hope for the protagonists and for the audience, who have to recover from the tour de force of the soundtrack. This strategy of considering the music in a film shows that the dichotomies of doubleness one first recognizes in HEAD ON (German vs. Turkish, Occident vs. Orient, western pop music vs. Turkish "traditional" music) are undermined and therefore display a post-national Europe. This is linked to the multi-defined identities of all Europeans, whose identities are already hyphenated, with respect to regional, societal, and gender aspects.

Generally speaking, the films of the New European Cinema let the audience experience new perceptual modes, subjectivities along a specifically sonic kind of bodily memory. The concept of double occupancy helps develop an audiovisual analysis that fully apprehends the combination of cinema and popular music, which has either been overlooked or been inadequately classified. Even though the films are situated in and draw on local cultures, subcultures, and patterns of identity formations, these national or regional peculiarities are best understood within broader "European" or even global patterns of identity formation, co-habitation and conflict resolution among the young and their relation to pop music.

Notes

1. "Aber wie im deutschen Punk oder Hip-Hop ist das, was wir hier machen, kein Kino der Imitation, sondern der Adaption. Wir übernehmen etwas, um es auf uns selbst zu übertragen – und dann etwas Eigenes daraus zu machen." Fatih Akin in an interview with Michael Ranze about his film SOLINO (2002): "Heimat ist ein mentaler Zustand," *epd Film* 11 (2002).
2. Thomas Elsaesser, *European Cinema: Face to Face with Hollywood* (Amsterdam: Amsterdam University Press 2005). For other discourses on national cinema, see Andrew Higson, "The Concept of National Cinema," *Screen* 30.4 (1989); Sabine Hake, *German National Cinema* (London: Routledge, 2002); and for concepts such as "migrant and diasporic cinema," *"cinema de métissage,"* "accented cinema," or "border crossing identities," see Hamid Naficy, *An Accented Cinema: Exilic and Diasporic Filmmaking* (Princeton: Princeton University Press, 2001).
3. Elsaesser, *European Cinema* 27.
4. Elsaesser, *European Cinema* 109.
5. He further claims that the concept of double occupancy intends to provisionally succeed that of the *historical imaginary*, by suggesting that "mirror-relations and forms of 'othering' typical of a previous period may be in [the] process of being superseded, as identity politics through boundary-drawing gives way to [a] general recognition of co-habitation, mutual interference and mutual responsibility as necessary forms of a new solidarity and sense of co-existence." Elsaesser, *European Cinema* 27.
6. In Germany, people were proud that a "German" won the Golden Bear for the first time in eighteen years, while in Turkey they celebrated the first success of a Turkish filmmaker in forty years. (There were other critics, who focused on the porn background of the female protagonist Sibel Kekilli.) "I don't do migrant cinema. I don't accept this categorization for my films. They don't talk about migrancy, they talk about me and my life." Fatih Akin interviewed by Asu Aksoy, "Reality: Check," *Vertigo* 2 (2005). Akin later talks about an *identity in motion*. Fatih Akin in an interview with Andreas Kilb and Peter Körte, "Der Islamismus in der Türkei macht mir keine Angst," *Frankfurter Allgemeine Sonntagszeitung* (3 Sept. 2007).
7. Elsaesser, *European Cinema* 125.

8. Some critics refer to different cinematic traditions in connection with HEAD ON and found similarities to Turkish cinema or the New German Cinema. Asuman Suner compares HEAD ON to the films of Rainer Werner Fassbinder. Asuman Suner, "Dark Passion," *Sight and Sound* (March 2005). This reference to Fassbinder is very apparent, especially when we think of the music used in MARTHA (1974) or IN A YEAR OF 13 MOONS (1978) where pop music was already being juxtaposed with classical music and original scores. See Senta Siewert, *Entgrenzung im Film bei Rainer Werner Fassbinder*, unpublished MA thesis (Freie Universität Berlin, 1999). In Akin's film AUF DER ANDEREN SEITE / ON THE OTHER SIDE (2007) one of the main characters plays Hanna Schygulla, a favorite Fassbinder actress. In my current research, I have explored pop music in such contemporary European films as TRAINSPOTTING, 24 HOUR PARTY PEOPLE, VELVET GOLDMINE, LOLA RENNT / RUN, LOLA, RUN, SONNENALLE / SUN ALLEY, LA HAINE / HATE, CLUBBED TO DEATH, and DANS PARIS / INSIDE PARIS.

9. The soundtrack of CROSSING THE BRIDGE is comprised of Turkish hip-hop and Turkish rock music, which refer to the Western tradition; and arabesque and Gypsy music, which relate to the Middle Eastern world. Akin's films not only refer to New German Cinema director Fassbinder; there are also references to Wim Wenders, because CROSSING THE BRIDGE is reminiscent of BUENA VISTA SOCIAL CLUB (1999), where the main protagonist, Ray Cooder, is also a *flâneur*, and pop songs are used as lifesavers (like in Wenders's earlier films).

10. The beginning of the film shows scenes of violence from actual television footage of youth riots against the French police after they shot a sixteen-year-old boy. This montage of found footage is underscored by Bob Marley's song "Burnin' and Lootin'," which seems to connect the images to broader post-colonial struggles against suppression. This sampling of images allows the tragic shooting to become part of the fictional story. Moreover, it is as if the past and the present are simultaneously being experienced through the song.

11. Claudia Gorbman, *Unheard Melodies: Narrative Film Music* (London, BFI, 1987).

12. Klaus Maeck is the founder of the music distribution company Freibank, the manager of Einstürzenden Neubauten, music supervisor for HEAD ON, KEBAB CONNECTIONS (Anno Saul, screenplay by Fatih Akin, 2005), and the producer of CROSSING THE BRIDGE and AUF DER ANDEREN SEITE.

13. This perceived tension has a long philosophical tradition, as seen in *The Birth of Tragedy* where Friedrich Nietzsche describes this conflict, referring to Apollo's victory for the rational control over Dionysus's emotional excess, which shows that a body out of control was considered to be subjected to all types of dangerous excesses, associated with drugs and the sublime. Compare to Friedrich Nietzsche, *The Birth of Tragedy* (Cambridge: Cambridge University Press, 1999).

14. *Saniye'M* (Selim Sesler, Alexander Hacke), Selim Sesler and Orchestra, Idel Üner. See also Fatih Akin, *Gegen die Wand: Das Buch zum Film* (Cologne: Kiepenhauer & Witsch, 2004).

15. This scene refers to the original German title GEGEN DIE WAND, and means literally "against the wall."

16. "I Feel You" by Depeche Mode on *Songs of Faith and Devotion* (Virgin / EMI, 1993).

17. Elsaesser, *European Cinema* 125.

18. "Lonely Planet" by The The on *Dusk* (Sony Music, 1993). Cahit even switches to English in other scenes, citing song titles in order to communicate his feelings.

19. "Temple of Love," Sisters of Mercy, touched by the hand of Ofra Haza. The original song dates from 1983 on *Some Girls Wander By Mistake* (Wea), the remix version with Ofra Haza from 1992.

20. "Agla Sevdam" (Attila Özdemiroglu, Aysel Gürel), Agir Roman. The lyrics of the song refer to her failed love.

21. Michel Chion would call this an experience of "empathetic sound, where the mood of the music matches the mood of the action." See Michel Chion, *Audio-Vision: Sound on Screen* (New York: Columbia University Press 1994).

22. See Feridun Zaimoglu, "Lebenswut, Herzhitze," *Tagesspiegel* (10 March 2004). In Turkey, some ecstatic fans still cut themselves at pop concerts, similar to what Cahit does in the film. This emotion can be described as "an overwhelming condition experienced almost like an incurable illness, from which the 'victim' can never recover." Compare to Asuman Suner "Sex, Suicide, Romantic Abandon and Hard Rock Collide in HEAD-ON, Fatih Akin's Electrifying Exploration of the Changing Dynamics of German-Turkish Identity," *Sight and Sound* (March 2005).

23. Steve Goodman, "Déjà Entendu: On the Virology of Acoustic Time Anomalies." In a presentation on aural virology, at the Sonic Interventions Conference Amsterdam 2005.

24. See Simon Frith, *Music and Identity* (London: Sage 1996).

25. See John Sloboda and Patrick N. Juslin, eds., *Music and Emotion: Theory and Research* (Oxford: Oxford University Press, 2001).

26. Julia Kristeva, *Powers of Horror: An Essay on Abjection* (New York: Columbia University Press, 1982).

27. Elsaesser, *European Cinema* 125: "Abject heroes or heroines in European cinema are not only symptomatic for what they tell us about a society and subjectivity that no longer has a social contract about what count as the minimum conditions of value and use, labor and affective work in a given society or community."

28. Elsaesser, *European Cinema* 125. See also Thomas Elsaesser, "Was wäre, wenn du schon tot bist? Vom 'postmodern' zum 'post-mortem'-Kino am Beispiel von Christopher Nolans *Memento*," *Zeitsprünge. Wie Filme Geschichte(n) erzählen*, ed. Christine Rüffert, Irmbert Schenk, Karl-Heinz Schmid, and Alfred Tews (Berlin: Bertz, 2004).

29. "Life Is What You Make It" by Talk Talk on *It's My Life* (EMI UK 1984). The song is performed by Zinoba in the film.

Hollywood Face to Face with the World

The Globalization of Hollywood and its Human Capital

Melis Behlil

Non-American filmmakers, ranging from Charlie Chaplin and Billy Wilder to Milos Forman and John Woo, have directed some of the most admired classics of Hollywood cinema. During the writing of my dissertation about some of these directors, two articles by Thomas Elsaesser inspired me the most. Spanning a great period of time, the first article "Ethnicity, Authenticity, and Exile: A Counterfeit Trade?" reinvestigates why so many talented European filmmakers from the very earliest days of cinema have ended up in Hollywood.[1] The second article was about contemporary directors, "German Cinema Face to Face with Hollywood: Looking into a Two-Way Mirror," in which Elsaesser proposes an emulation / emigration model which was adopted by German filmmakers to break entry barriers into Hollywood.[2] In this chapter, I will use these two articles as my starting point to develop a new paradigm to look at the world's directorial talents in Hollywood. My aim is to position blockbuster-era global directors within a wider historical context of émigré talent. My use of the term "global" directors instead of "émigré" or "foreign" is deliberate for a number of reasons. I do not use the term émigré because I want to distinguish my work from the research done on the earlier generation of filmmakers who emigrated to the US in the 1930s and the early 1940s, and also because émigré connotes an act of relocating for good or leaving the old country behind. Many of the directors, especially in the post-1975 era, have chosen to move between countries.[3] The use of foreign to describe these filmmakers has been quite common in the last decades, as they work outside of their nation of origin, and to do so they need a special permit to work in the US. Nonetheless, as Hollywood has become global, the paradigms that rely on emigration, whether for political or economic reasons, no longer function.

While the political émigré narrative is insufficient to explain the talent flows of today, it may have already been inadequate as far back as the silent period. In "Ethnicity, Authenticity, and Exile: A Counterfeit Trade?," Elsaesser extends the emigration period backwards to cover those directors from the 1920s, and brings trade and competition into the picture, aiming to "complicate the picture" set forth by the political émigré thesis.[4] This is essential for an analysis of the migra-

tion flows of recent eras, since the political motives have been practically nonexis-
tent since the time of the émigré Czech directors of the 1970s. Even from the
countries that may be considered to be totalitarian regimes, where the state imposes limitations on filmmakers, like China, there has been very little emigration
based on political reasons. Elsaesser's emulation/emigration model proposes that
some European, in this case German, directors such as Roland Emmerich and
Wolfgang Petersen adopted a Hollywood-like style to make it possible for them
to be noticed by American studios. Elsaesser argues that "these directors and
directors of photography … practiced a deliberate and open emulation of Hollywood: their dream was to make films that either found a large popular audience
or pleased an American distributor, in order then to set off and emigrate to New
York and Los Angeles."[5] Although I agree with the emulation aspect of this model, my research has shown that the migration to Hollywood is not a final one, nor
does it always require a physical relocation. Contemporary directors who have
moved to the US in order to work in Hollywood can and do return to their home
countries to make other films. This has been the case for Alejandro Amenabar,
Paul Verhoeven, as well as a number of Hong Kong directors like Ringo Lam,
Hark Tsui, and even John Woo.[6] With the globalization of Hollywood, there have
been changes in the flow of talent which have apparently not been sufficiently
analyzed in the existing literature.

Talent Flows Then and Now

A periodization of Hollywood history in terms of the influx of global directing
talent, not surprisingly, turns out to be parallel to one based on the ups and
downs of the studios. Roughly, the first period corresponds to the "golden age" of
Hollywood, in which studios functioned in a vertically integrated system from the
early 1910s until the mid-1940s. This period can be divided into two periods: the
1920s, when studio heads made regular trips to Europe to hunt for talent like
Murnau and Stiller, and the late 1930s and 1940s, when most of the European
directors came to the US for political reasons. Whatever the underlying reasons,
this period is characterized by an immense number of notable European directors who relocated to Hollywood. The second period is the "slump," when the
studios tried to adjust to the new realities brought on by a combination of forces
such as the Paramount decree and the coming of television. From the mid-1940s
to the mid-1970s, with a few exceptions (Richardson, Reisz, Forman, Passer), the
talent flow to Hollywood not only diminished, but in certain cases (Lester, Ku-
brick) was reversed. The final period is the era with which I am concerned,
namely the New Hollywood era starting in the mid-1970s. During this time,

some of the most renowned names in European art cinema such as Ken Russell and Richard Attenborough from the UK, Louis Malle from France, and Wim Wenders from Germany worked on various projects in Hollywood. This reflects a similar pattern to the 1920s, when importing artsy European directors was a source of prestige for the studios. Similarly, most of these directors did not find critical or commercial success in Hollywood, demonstrating the validity of El-saesser's emulation/emigration model: because their native work was not an emulation of Hollywood movies, their studio ventures turned out to be outsider works as well.

During the so-called blockbuster era which emerged in the mid-1970s, there were quite a few filmmakers who garnered attention, for instance Ridley and Tony Scott (UK), Ang Lee (Taiwan), John Woo (Hong Kong), Roland Emmerich and Wolfgang Petersen (Germany), and Paul Verhoeven (the Netherlands). The cinema-going public might know that BLADE RUNNER (Ridley Scott, 1982), INDE-PENDENCE DAY (Roland Emmerich, 1996), STARSHIP TROOPERS (Paul Verhoeven, 1997), or FACE/OFF (John Woo, 1997) were directed by global directors, even though this is not really an attribute that is highlighted in the marketing of any of these films. It is very unlikely, however, that anyone in the audience would be aware that the following films were debuts by non-American Hollywood direc-tors: the martial arts movie DOUBLE TEAM (Hark Tsui, 1997), the Oscar-nomi-nated racial conflict drama MONSTER'S BALL (Marc Forster, 2001), and the comedy hit LEGALLY BLONDE (Robert Luketic, 2001).[7] These films are only a few of the dozens of Hollywood titles directed by global filmmakers every year, and clearly, they have no thematic or stylistic resemblance to one another, other than their being a part of the Hollywood system.

Looking at the number of non-American directors, one can see that a divide occurred in the late-1970s. Not surprisingly, this divide coincided with New Hol-lywood, as well as the increasing globalization of world economies and film in-dustries. The number of directors who make their first Hollywood film in any given year started to increase during the mid-1970s and reached a level of at least six to eight directors per year by the early 1980s.[8] Many of the directors who arrived in the 1980s continued to work in Hollywood for at least several years, and their numbers increased. The number of Hollywood films made by global directors each year has increased over the last three decades, and occasionally approaches fifty. Out of approximately 450 new films released annually in the US, about 250 are domestic.[9] These figures show that the proportion made by global directors should not be underestimated: it varies roughly between ten and twenty percent. The number of films made by global directors reached an all-time high in the late 1990s and stabilized thereafter. This indicates that there appears to be a large turnover in global talent in Hollywood; if all the filmmakers had continued their careers in Hollywood, the number of films made by global directors would continue to increase, assuming they continued to make films at their usual pace. This turnover is one of the greatest factors that differentiates contemporary non-American filmmakers in Hollywood from earlier generations.

Another major difference in recent years is that the source for new talent is no longer limited to Europe and now covers almost the entire globe. While there was no flow toward Hollywood from anywhere outside Europe until the 1980s, this has changed with the boom in the Australian film industry. The next continent was Asia, which revealed a similar migration pattern. The dominant Hong Kong film industry especially saw its directors move to Hollywood, either early on (Corey Yuen, John Woo) or after the transfer of sovereignty to China (Hark Tsui, Stanley Tong, Ronny Yu). Although most of these directors did eventually return to Hong Kong, their influence on young American filmmakers is still visible. Lately, Latin American directors, especially from Mexico, such as Luis Mandoki, Alfonso Cuaron, and Guillermo Del Toro have begun to claim their share of Hollywood's globalized labor.

These changes over the past few years are the natural results of globalization and technological developments. Technology has also facilitated the ability of directors to move between continents and alternate between production bases. The distance that separates continents has been reduced to a few hours by plane or none at all, if one takes the new communication technologies into consideration. Furthermore, films are now frequently shot on locations in numerous different countries. This mobility allows directors (such as Michael Apted, Marco Brambilla, and Del Toro) to work in entirely different styles in almost the same year. The post-WWII changes within the studio system have also facilitated this mobility. While in the classical studio era the studios kept a director on a payroll, or made multiple-picture deals with filmmakers, they now work on individual projects.

Globalization of Hollywood

In his introduction to *Hollywood Abroad*, Richard Maltby discusses the reception of Hollywood productions by audiences across the globe, and the extent to which these films are construed as American. He argues that throughout its history, Hollywood has been identified as American largely by its competitors, and by European cultural nationalists, while American supporters, as well as critics of Hollywood, "do not perceive these products as part of a specifically national culture."[10] This is a sentiment echoed by more and more film scholars, especially in recent years. Andrew Higson has argued that Hollywood, in addition to being "the most internationally powerful cinema," has been "for many years ... an integral and naturalized part of the national culture, or the popular imagination, of most countries in which cinema is an established entertainment form."[11] And Thomas Elsaesser and Warren Buckland have pointed out that "Hollywood cinema is a world industry, just as much as it is a world language, a powerful, stable, perfected system of visual communication."[12]

As a location, Hollywood is a district of Los Angeles. But with the move of the motion picture industry from the East Coast to the West Coast, the terms "Hollywood" and "American film industry" have been used interchangeably since the mid-1920s.[13] However, not all of these studios are American owned. The Australian media mogul Rupert Murdoch's News Corporation started this trend in 1985, when he purchased Twentieth Century Fox. MCA, the parent company of Universal Studios, was purchased in 1990 by the Japanese Matsushita company, then in 1995, by the Canadian Seagram's company, and subsequently, Seagram's was purchased in 2000 by the French company Vivendi. Universal then merged with NBC in 2004. Sony acquired Columbia Pictures Entertainment, including two studios (Columbia Pictures and TriStar Pictures), as well as home video distribution, a movie theater chain, and an extensive film library in 1989.[14] The last stand-alone studio was MGM, which was also finally purchased by Sony in the summer of 2005. Warner Bros. is a subsidiary of Time Warner, Inc., whose chairman in 2000 stated: "We do not want to be viewed as an American company. We think globally."[15] In view of these changes, Hollywood at the level of ownership no longer equals American either.

While an American film industry does include a large part of the Hollywood companies and is centralized there, Hollywood goes beyond the US and is spread across the globe. Hollywood has become transnational, and its films are distributed globally by the studios themselves or by their subsidiaries. Among the leading distribution companies is United Pictures International (UIP), which is jointly owned by Paramount and Universal, based in London, with offices in twenty-six countries, with representation in twenty-three others, and business involvement in a total of two hundred countries.[16] That the exhibition of these films is also global hardly needs any explanation.

The terms "studios" or "majors" are also frequently used in the same sense as "Hollywood." As Ben Goldsmith and Tom O'Regan proposed in their study of contemporary international studios, a "Hollywood studio" now refers not "to the physical plant but to the 'command and control' distribution and financing operations of the Hollywood majors."[17] Especially since the mid-1970s, when major studios started being acquired by transnational media corporations, it has become almost impossible to call Hollywood films "American." Frederick Wasser argues that Hollywood studios "ceased to be institutions of national culture" around the mid-1970s.[18] He points out that long before Japanese corporations started buying American studios, European producers like Dino DeLaurentiis, Arnon Milchan, and Mario Kassar were producing films in Hollywood, largely funded by European money. These were "'Hollywood' pictures independent of American companies and of American financing."[19] Because these were event films, blockbusters with enormous budgets, they needed to do well not only in the US, but globally as well.

Within this context, what I mean by working in Hollywood is making a film that is being produced by a production company from within the Hollywood system. Working in / with / for Hollywood does not necessarily mean working physically in Southern California. Hollywood studios make films across the globe, and directors who become a part of this world work wherever the production takes place. In this sense, one can employ the term transnational for Hollywood, as analogous to the transnational corporations that own the Hollywood studios. Transnational corporations have been defined by the United Nations using four criteria: size, their oligarchic nature, having a large number of foreign subsidiaries and branch offices, and their origins are in developed countries.[20] The media conglomerates which now own Hollywood studios are transnational corporations, and Hollywood has always employed talent from around the globe and increasingly does so. Hence, despite the current connotations of the term, transnational cinema is also, perhaps even more so, applicable to Hollywood.

In the introduction to their comprehensive transnational cinema reader, Elizabeth Ezra and Terry Rowden define transnational as "the global forces that link people or institutions across nations" and assert that it comprises globalization, "in cinematic terms, Hollywood's domination of world film markets."[21] Similarly, my use of the term transnational aims to draw attention to this domination, aligning Hollywood with transnational corporations and the global capitalist world order. Elsaesser has also made note of this issue, calling Hollywood "an engine of global hegemony" that "propagate[s] and advertise[s] very specific tastes and attitudes"; and posits that Hollywood declares a national agenda as universal.[22] I would argue that this is not a "national" agenda, but in fact a corporate one. Globalization is criticized foremost for allowing corporate interests to take precedence over all else, and Hollywood in its blockbuster era is the manifestation of this corporate capitalist system. Therefore, it certainly makes sense to look at talent flows within this context and to explain them using the same approaches that are used to discuss the mobility of other global skilled labor within transnational networks.

Hollywood functions as a network of connections, and as in most industries – but here more than in others – it is who you know that is the key to survival. In an industry that is primarily dependent on relationships, the producers and the agents play some of the most important roles. In a three-leveled model of administrative, above- and below-the-line labor, the administrative departments are located in and around Hollywood, because that is where the deals are made; it is the command and control center, and directors are among the most mobile of the above-the-line workers. For these members of the filmmaking community, actual presence in Hollywood can be delegated through agents. Membership in the Directors Guild (DGA), which is located in Los Angeles, is another type of delegation. As members, directors maintain a presence in Hollywood, even if they are not there physically. This allows them a level of mobility that is akin to the executives working for transnational corporations, a recognized new professional class that has arisen from within the processes of globalization.[23]

To alter the discussions of the new transnational capitalist class, Richard Florida adds creativity to the definition of this new class, which basically eliminates business executives.[24] Thus we find the global directors of Hollywood in this creative class. Florida explains that the "migratory patterns of the creative class cut across the lines of race, nationality and sexual orientation."[25] Like the nationality of a film, the nationality of individuals is no longer (if it ever was) a simple matter. Recent debates regarding citizenship have centered around the alternative notions of belonging. The internationalization of capital has led to a denationalization process, especially in the larger cities where capital is concentrated. In a world where the nation-state is no longer fixed and immutable, passports become "less and less attestations of citizenship, let alone of loyalty to a protective nation-state than of claims to participation in labor markets."[26] Hollywood's global directors no longer need to make "American" films, as long as they make films that succeed at the box office.

Conclusion

As I stated at the beginning of this article, my aim was to (re)conceptualize the international flow of directors toward Hollywood. I proposed that we look at the global director through the lens of transnational structures. Hollywood has always been international, as the examples from the 1920s have already demonstrated. Nevertheless, its current transnationality extends to ownership, production (including pre- and post-), distribution, exhibition, and reception. Within this global network, filmmakers are more analogous to mobile human capital which is employed by transnational corporations than they are to the émigré directors of the earlier decades. Since the émigré paradigm is no longer valid, and the global mobility of international talent has become the norm, there is no reason why the filmmakers in question should not be treated as any other member of a global, mobile, transnational creative class; or indeed, as CEOs or other lead-

ing executives of multinational corporations. Unlike their émigré-era counterparts, global directors today do not need to be tied down to a single location.
They are denationalized both in terms of citizenship and in terms of workplace.
If they seek to work in the US, all they need is a valid work visa and membership
in the DGA, both of which can be temporary. In transnational Hollywood, questions of nationality no longer work as a paradigm, although they still matter, because they continue to be the point of entry to many debates, including this very
article.

Notes

1. Thomas Elsaesser, "Ethnicity, Authenticity, and Exile: A Counterfeit Trade?," *Home,
    Exile, Homeland: Film, Media and the Politics of Place*, ed. Hamid Naficy (London/New
    York: Routledge, 1999) 97-123.
2. Thomas Elsaesser, *European Cinema: Face to Face with Hollywood* (Amsterdam: Am-
    sterdam University Press, 2005) 299-318.
3. For a discussion of various forms of displacement and mobility among the intellec-
    tual classes, see Darko Suvin, "Displaced Persons," *New Left Review* 31 (Jan.-Feb.
    2005): 107-123.
4. Elsaesser, "Ethnicity, Authenticity and Exile" 98.
5. Elsaesser, *European Cinema* 306.
6. It must be noted that even the earlier generations of filmmakers have often returned
    to their home countries, like the Swedish directors of the 1920s or the French direc-
    tors who worked in Hollywood during World War II.
7. Carson is British, Forster is Swiss, Luketic is from Australia, and Tsui is from Hong
    Kong.
8. For further details and more charts, see Melis Behlil, *Home Away from Home: Global
    Directors of New Hollywood*, unpublished PhD dissertation (University of Amsterdam,
    2007).
9. Motion Picture Association, "MPA Snapshot Report: 2004 International Theatrical
    Market" (2005) 1. This is an average for the last ten years; *Hollywood Foreign Press
    Association Official Website*: <http://www.hfpa.org/aboutus.html>. Last visited 29
    April 2005. One should keep in mind, however, that many of these "domestic" pro-
    ductions are shot outside the US, with international talent, and occasionally, with
    international financing.
10. Richard Maltby, "Introduction: 'The Americanization of the World,'" *Hollywood
    Abroad: Audiences and Cultural Exchange*, ed. Melvyn Stokes and Richard Maltby (Lon-
    don: BFI, 2004) 5.
11. Andrew Higson, "The Concept of National Cinema," *Screen* 30.4 (Fall 1989): 39.
12. Thomas Elsaesser and Warren Buckland, *Studying Contemporary American Films: A
    Guide to Movie Analysis* (London: Arnold, 2002) 4.
13. Allen J. Scott, *On Hollywood: The Place, The Industry* (Princeton: Princeton University
    Press, 2005) 25.

14. Tino Balio, "'A Major Presence in All of the World's Important Markets': The Globalization of Hollywood in the 1990s," *Contemporary Hollywood Cinema*, ed. Steve Neale and Murray Smith (London / New York: Routledge, 1998) 62-63.

15. Quoted in Danny Schechter, "Long Live Chairman Levin!" <http://www.mediachannel.org/views/dissector/chairman.shtml>. Last visited 22 August 2006.

16. UIP web site: <http://www.uip.com>. Last visited 24 January 2007.

17. Ben Goldsmith and Tom O'Regan, *Cinema Cities, Media Cities: The Contemporary International Studio Complex* (Sydney: Southwood, 2003) 64.

18. Frederick Wasser, "Is Hollywood America? The Trans-Nationalization of American Film Industry," *Critical Studies in Mass Communication* 12.4 (1995): 423.

19. Wasser 431.

20. Thomas Guback and Tapio Varis, "Transnational Communication and Cultural Industry," *Reports and Papers on Mass Communication* 92 (Paris: UNESCO, 1982).

21. Elizabeth Ezra and Terry Rowden, "General Introduction: What is Transnational Cinema?," *Transnational Cinema, The Film Reader*, ed. Elizabeth Ezra and Terry Rowden (London / New York: Routledge: 2006) 1.

22. Elsaesser, *European Cinema* 59-60.

23. Saskia Sassen, *Globalization and its Discontents* (New York: New Press, 1998) xxxvi; Leslie Sklair, *The Transnational Capitalist Class* (Oxford / Malden: Blackwell, 2001); Michael Peter Smith and Adrian Favell, eds., *The Human Face of Global Mobility: International Highly Skilled Migration in Europe, North America and the Asia-Pacific* (New Brunswick: Transaction, 2006).

24. Richard Florida, *The Rise of the Creative Class* (New York: Basic Books, 2004) xxvii.

25. Florida 243.

26. Benedict Anderson, "Exodus," *Critical Inquiry* 20.2 (Winter 1994): 314-327.

To Be or Not to Be Post-Classical

Eleftheria Thanouli

Thomas Elsaesser's fascination with word plays and double meanings was what perturbed me the most when I started attending his theory and history classes in the Master's program at the University of Amsterdam. Having no background in film studies at the time and being as pragmatic as I am, I had very little use for terms like "*mise en abyme*," "deep structure" or "sliding signifiers." Gradually, however, as I began to understand the value of metaphors and rhetorical strategies in the theoretical discourse, I found it intriguing to analyze and dissect Elsaesser's own writings with the very same tools he used to analyze films. After a several-year-long practice, I sometimes now feel that I can crack his code and find the algorithms that copiously produce such meandering and far-reaching reflections.

In this article, I would like to venture a decryption by focusing on one of Elsaesser's major areas of interest: Hollywood cinema in the post-studio era from the 1970s to this day. In film studies, this amounts to a highly contested terrain that has traditionally forced scholars to divide into two opposing camps; the one would accommodate those who wished to assert an almost seamless continuity between the classical and the post-1960s Hollywood filmmaking, while the other would shelter those who detected a significant break between the two phases. From the outset, Elsaesser was eager to succumb to the allure of "what is different" in contemporary American films rather than adhere to "what is still the same," and thus chose to take a clear, albeit nuanced, position in the debate at the time.

By 1975, he had already published a seminal essay entitled "The Pathos of Failure: Notes on the Unmotivated Hero,"[1] where he launched a compelling rhetoric that called attention to a number of innovations that the younger generation of filmmakers had brought to New Hollywood. Without the privilege of historical distance and emotional detachment, Elsaesser observed a number of changes that were under way and elaborated on the finer nuances of this transitional period with unprecedented insight. For him, the films of New Hollywood were the instigators of a double play; they manipulated a number of classical signifiers in order to create a meta-cinematic layer where the New could voice a critical reflection on the Old. One of the salient features of this trend was the combination of the classical motif of the journey with heroes that lacked clear-cut motivation. Using examples such as Two-lane blacktop (1971), Five easy pieces (1970),

THE LAST DETAIL (1973) and CALIFORNIA SPLIT (1974), he distinguished a tension between the familiar formula of the journey, which by convention bears a strong logic of purpose and intention, and the characters in these films, who failed to embody a determinate goal. According to Elsaesser, the lack of motive in the characters' actions and the loose progression of the plot were indicative of a skepticism towards the ideals of American society and its traditional belief in personal initiative. Whereas classical Hollywood maintained a solid faith in human agency and the ability to accomplish any mission, the emerging sensibility of New Hollywood adopted a more pessimistic stance about the possibility to solve all problems, to face all obstacles.

However, as the rebelliousness of the 1970s wore off and Hollywood returned to the more familiar paths of studio dominance in a post-Fordist model at this time, the unmotivated heroes soon gave way to diehard males who not only reclaimed their motivations but also reveled in the mass-market fanfare of the conglomerated New New Hollywood.[2] At that point, Elsaesser once more had to face the question of whether there is a difference between these contemporary films and their classical Hollywood antecedents. Again, he responded with a stubborn "yes." It is this response that I would like to scrutinize here in order to serve a twofold goal; on the one hand, I would like to critically engage "the code" used by Elsaesser to theorize post-classical cinema, while, on the other, I would like to verify its validity through the analysis of an example of the most recent Hollywood output.

Inside Post-Classical Hollywood

When Elsaesser decided to conceptualize the developments in American cinema of the 1980s and 1990s, he not only maintained his focus on "what is different" but also sought to craft a consistent method for constructing a post-classical reading of popular blockbusters. In a lengthy chapter entitled "Classical/Post-Classical Narrative" in the book *Studying Contemporary American Film*[3] he carried out a very carefully balanced analysis of a blockbuster hit, John McTiernan's DIE HARD, as a typical Hollywood product of the late 1980s.

The working hypothesis for his investigation was that the film can be both classical and post-classical depending on the analyst's theoretical and conceptual agenda. In order to demonstrate how different questions about the same film can generate entirely different answers, Elsaesser ventured on a rather lengthy exposition of some of the key theoretical approaches to classical cinema, namely David Bordwell's neo-formalist poetics and the structuralist approach inspired by Vladimir Propp and Claude Lévi-Strauss. With these theories and their respective methodological tools in hand, Elsaesser was able to trace all of the traditional classical elements in Die Hard. The thorough reading of the film's narrative construction showed that it constituted a textbook case of classical cinema, as it faithfully incorporated all the norms and principles of classical filmmaking: the three-act structure, the goal-oriented hero who has to accomplish a mission and win the heart of a woman, the oedipal trajectory, the enigmas and the repetitions, to name but a few. Thus, Elsaesser's analysis of this popular blockbuster explicitly confirmed the claims of Bordwell and others about the continuity of the classical formulas in contemporary cinema and the resilience of classical narration over the course of time.

And yet, despite the persistence of formal classicism in contemporary films, Elsaesser's long-standing interest in "what is different" made him test the limits of his intellectual resources in an effort to map a set of differences in a sea of overwhelming similarities. A minute reading of Die Hard with the help of a multifaceted conceptual sieve led him to formulate the following five key observations:

a. The post-classical narratives do not reject the canonical story format, but entail a multiple layering of plotlines and characters that can be readily transferred to a video game format.

b. They express a kind of "knowingness" about the heuristic distinction between surface and deep structure, and in a literal sense they play with these conceptual categories.

c. They address issues of race, gender and the male body more openly and explicitly, although not necessarily in a more progressive way.

d. They acknowledge their presence in a transnational/post-colonial/globalized world and simultaneously provide a commentary on the situation at the same time, thus adopting an inside-outside position.

e. They are replete with sliding signifiers, i.e., verbal and visual puns that denote the sophistication and professionalism of New Hollywood.[4]

All of these aspects constituted different facets of the quintessential quality of post-classical cinema, its "knowingness," described as "a special sort of awareness of the codes that govern classical representation and its genre conventions, along with a willingness to display this knowingness and make the audience share it, by letting it in on the game."[5] In other words, post-classical Hollywood has absorbed the classical rules to such a degree that the only way it can use them anymore is through an excessive mastery and display.

Elsaesser's scheme for constructing a post-classical reading of Hollywood films, despite its sophistication and insight, has thus far not reached a canonical status in film theory. Elsaesser himself has not supported this theory any further in other publications, which is partly due to the fact that he has already moved on to other concepts, like "world cinema" or "mind-game film," and partly due to his own dissatisfaction with the term and his search for a post-post-classical cinema.[6] However, I would like to cling to this "post-classical" a little bit longer. Having built my own academic identity with Bordwell and Elsaesser as my two father figures, I would like to use the former's persistence to support the latter's claims about post-classical cinema.[7] My motivation is not based on any obligation but on genuine belief. In fact, the more I watch contemporary Hollywood blockbusters, the more impressed I am by the acuteness of Elsaesser's observations. For that reason, I would like to examine a recent Hollywood release to see how effective the five-tier method of post-classical analysis holds up after almost two decades of New New Hollywood filmmaking.

Into INSIDE MAN

INSIDE MAN is Spike Lee's latest full-length film released in 2006 by Universal Pictures. It was produced by the Academy Award-winning producer Brian Grazer on a budget of $45 million, which was more than amply recuperated at the box office.[8] Even though Lee has occasionally attempted more alternative formulas, here he delivers a typical crime thriller, featuring an acclaimed cast of Hollywood actors in a story about a bank robbery. The plot is not easy to summarize due to the various generic twists and turns but the main lines of action go like this. Dalton Russell (Clive Owen) leads a group of robbers into the Manhattan Trust bank posing as painters. They take everyone in the building hostage, forcing everyone to wear identical uniforms so that villains and victims look identical for the cameras. The NYPD puts Detective Keith Frazier (Denzel Washington) in charge of the hostage negotiations. Frazier tries to figure out the eccentric plan of the robbers and deal with this critical situation. Parallel to these developments, we see the founder of the bank, Arthur Case (Christopher Plummer), being informed about the heist who then takes things into his own hands. He promptly hires a power broker named Madeleine White (Jodie Foster) to protect the contents of his safety deposit box, which seems of exceptional value to him. These four key players, who all have their own agendas in the case, meet and interact with one another throughout the 129-minute film in order to resolve the situation. Russell's plan works, and he walks out of the bank with his loot, Frazier gets promoted as he solves the case without any apparent casualties, White adds another successful deal to her résumé, while Case is condemned for his sinful past after his secret leaks out.

These main plot elements attest to the presence of a conventional Hollywood formula that builds a suspenseful story through the careful arrangement of classical compositional and generic elements such as character-centered causality, a tight causal chain of events, a series of twists and reversals, a cat-and-mouse chase between the cops and the villains and, finally, a clear resolution or even a happy ending. In other words, if we employed the analytical tool of narrative analysis à la Bordwell, we would be happy to conclude that INSIDE MAN is another instance of classical narration that abides, to a large extent, to the same norms of narrative construction that crystallized in the studio period from 1917 to 1960. There is nothing wrong with this line of reasoning, since it faithfully serves the principles of historical poetics, which strictly measures the poetic elements of a film and the way they evolve in history. But this is not the only thing we should analyze here, and this is where Elsaesser's theory comes in handy. By subjecting INSIDE MAN to the post-classical method of inquiry, its true nature becomes more than manifest. In the following, I will structure my reading of Lee's film based on Elsaesser's five criteria.

a. Narrative Structure

Even though the plot development largely follows the classical trajectory of Exposition, Conflict, Complication, Crisis and Denouement, the film layers its characters and entangles their actions in a way that surpasses the linear logic of the classical storylines and allows the various plot components to relate laterally as if they formed a network with interconnected nodes. The four main characters – Russell, Frazier, Case and White – offer the viewer separate entry points into the story, as the plot allows each one of them sufficient screen time to unfold their plans and claim their stakes in the robbery case, which turns out to be a game rife with opportunities. The plot becomes difficult to summarize precisely because its classical premises can be reconfigured in various ways depending on which character you place in charge and which link you choose to follow every time these four people meet to negotiate. The story can be about an ingenious and self-assured robber who implements the perfect plan or about a decent cop who gets a second chance or about a corrupt banker who is finally exposed or about a ferocious power broker who works on the margins of legitimacy, running immensely profitable errands for the rich and the powerful.

The painstakingly layered screenplay allows the four protagonists to take turns in the villain-victim position, creating a tension that is never fully resolved. Is Russell the real villain, or is he the savior who punishes a Nazi collaborator and even rewards Frazier with a diamond? Is Case the ultimate villain since he built his empire on stealing from the Jews during the Second World War or should years of philanthropy have cleansed him of his guilt? Is Frazier the honest cop, or is he gradually seduced by the cleverness of Russell's plan and thus turned into an accomplice? And finally, is White the one who quintessentially poses the dilemma of agency with her never quite being guilty of anything while she as a hired hand facilitates the dubious activities of people with blood – or at least dirt – on their hands? Overall, the multiple layers in the narrative structure of the film seem to confirm Elsaesser's claim that post-classical cinema might not have abolished the canonical story format but has imbued it with a nodal logic that facilitates the convergence of the filmic narrative with the ones we find in new media and, particularly, video games.

b. Surface Structure and Deep Structure

When we look at INSIDE MAN, the heuristic distinction between "surface structure," which amounts to the characters' actions, and "deep structure," which regards the characters' hidden desires, becomes particularly tangible through the ingenious play between false appearances and hidden truths from start to finish. The notion of a character's oedipal trajectory is here played out in the open, as the plot offers us the obvious plan of the bank robbery as a façade for a deeper and darker story which is not revealed to us until the closing moments. Russell's scheme is not to empty the bank's treasury, as we initially assumed; it is to steal the contents of a tiny portion of that wealth and, at the same time, atone for his crime by uncovering the crime of the respectable, respected banker who stands in for the Law. Thus, the hero almost literally displaces the Father to satisfy his Oedipus complex and then takes his position in the symbolic order, i.e., he serves the purposes of civil society where the good are rewarded (Frazier) and the bad are punished (Case). In other words, a post-classical film like this dares to depict an almost literal realization of the oedipal trajectory by emulating, at the plot level, the distinction between "surface structure" and "deep structure," which in classical films was usually identified at the level of interpretation.

In addition to the oedipal trajectory, Lee's film plays with other psychoanalytical concepts that were applied in the analysis of classical Hollywood cinema. Firstly, there is a post-classical femme fatale, Madeleine White, who bears all the characteristics of her classical archetype, such as charm, elegance and wit combined with a predatory attitude, but the subliminal threat to male masculinity and the fear of castration that she embodies here become verbally exposed on numerous occasions and particularly when the profane Mayor tells her: "You are a magnificent cunt." The same explicitness is brought to the fore regarding Lacan's notions of "voyeurism" and "misrecognition." The use of masks and disguises as well as the staging of a false murder, in an outspoken manner, seems to aid in the investigation of the problematics of the look and the identification process that it instigates. By using the masks or manipulating the surveillance cameras, Russell consciously blocks the gaze of the police and denies them access to the reality of the moment. He as both a hero and as our frame narrator seeks to problematize the deeper issue of identification by preventing the actual identification of the robbers and by triggering off, from the start, a game of constant misrecognition: nobody and nothing in this film are what they appear to be. In view of these dramaturgical strategies, INSIDE MAN seems to display a profound knowingness by performing in a self-conscious way what was previously reserved for the un-conscious.

c. Race, Gender and the Male Body

One of the most salient features of the film is the wide racial palette of its char-acters. The various hostages in the bank, the policemen and the passersby com-prise a broad racial mix, which is regularly foregrounded in the dialogues, espe-cially during the interrogation process. Apart from the fact that the very core of the story – the Holocaust – hinges on the issue of racism, the film relentlessly evokes the problematics of race and stirs up an overt discussion not only about multi-raciality but also the use of politically correct registers. When a police offi-cer begins to tell the story of a shooting using the word "spic" to refer to a Span-ish-American, Frazier asks him to "tone down the color commentary" and forces him to carry on his account using the politically correct hyphenated terminology.

When it comes to gender, the agenda is equally crammed with explicit refer-ences to femininity and masculinity, starting with White's aggressive behavior, which, combined with Jodie Foster's lesbian profile, creates a very ambiguous sexual identity. However, what pervades the entire story is the jocular homoeroti-cism between Russell and Frazier and the sexually loaded phrases they constantly use. The following verbal exchange is indicative.

> Russell: "Soon I'm gonna be sucking down piña coladas in a hot tub with six girls named Amber and Tiffany."
> Frazier: "No, it's more like in the shower with two guys named Jamal and Jesus... and here's the bad news; that thing you're sucking on? It's not a piña colada!"

The selection of names in this quote also confirms the constant slippage or "trade-off"[9] between race and gender in contemporary Hollywood that becomes even more palpable in the following dialogue between Frazier and White:

> White: "Don't take this personally, but I don't think you can afford me."
> Frazier: "Don't take this personally, Miss White, but kiss my black ass."

The characters' preoccupation with their racial and sexual characteristics permeates the creative options in ways that I could not possibly hope to cover in this essay. But it would certainly provide the "race-gender studies" people with a field day, to paraphrase Elsaesser once more.[10]

d. The transnational/Post-colonial/Globalization Theme

If we look at INSIDE MAN through the prism of this fourth analytical pillar, the observations we generate are again copious. Set in a post-9/11 New York City, the film consciously seeks to acknowledge its place in a multicultural and globalized environment where all nationalities co-exist but not without friction or prejudice. In downtown Manhattan, you can find an Albanian-speaking person just around any corner, and anyone wearing a turban is immediately considered an Arab, hence a threat. Lee pays his respect to the 9/11 victims by foregrounding a "WE WILL NEVER FORGET" poster, but he offers a scathing critique of the paranoia against the Arabs that followed this tragedy. In addition to the initial fear that the heist might be an Al-Qaeda job, the film stages another relevant incident with a hostage named Vikram Walia. When he exits the bank, the police start to harass him and take his turban, all the while calling him "a fucking Arab." Walia protests his treatment and demands his turban back, explaining that he is a Sikh and wears it as a part of his religion. Later on, during his interrogation, he is offered the opportunity to voice his resentment against the bias he encounters everywhere he goes.

In general, the characters in the story underline an awareness of the social reality in the era of post-colonialism and globalization, where borders are blurring, where ethnic identities become hybrid and where traditional binaries such as friend/enemy or, most importantly, inside/outside collapse.

e. Sliding Signifiers

The title INSIDE MAN is itself the key sliding signifier of the film, as what is signified keeps shifting as the various narrative twists unfold. Initially, we assume that Russell is a lawbreaker or a blackmailer who wants to rob the bank, but as the plot thickens and Case's dubious past emerges, we begin to wonder whether this "inside man" is not some sort of a double agent. However, the final revelations offer a very different view, attributing to the title a strictly literal meaning, i.e. the man who stays inside. In fact, Russell has prepared us from the very start. In the opening scene, he warns: "Pay strict attention to what I say because I choose my words very carefully." He earnestly describes his whereabouts as a "prison cell" and rushes to explain that there is "a vast difference between being stuck in a tiny cell and being in prison." This wordplay is accompanied by its visual equivalent that shows Russell confined in a tiny space that resembles a prison cell. This image haunts us throughout the film, encouraging us to believe that Russell is eventually imprisoned. It is only in the final moments that we come to realize the "vast difference" between the two places he had pointed out.

This preoccupation with space stimulates various other verbal puns, but I will mention here just two. Firstly, the robbers use a van with a fake company logo which says, "Perfectly Planned Painting: We Never Leave Until the Job Is Done," foreshadowing Russell's escape plan to remain inside until the job is done. Secondly, the line "When there's blood on the streets, buy property" is repeated twice and refers to how Case profited during WWII, while, in fact, its signification slides over another more contemporary figure, namely Bin Laden's nephew, who is supposedly buying a co-op in Park Avenue. This double entendre is particularly difficult to miss, especially given the aforementioned post-9/11 atmosphere in New York.

These few examples indeed denote the sophistication of the professionals in New New Hollywood who, apart from the usual film references,[11] manage to imbue the films' basic compositional elements with multiple signifieds, which ascribe the film with an exceedingly dense texture and flaunt the knowingness of what Elsaesser calls "the classical-plus."[12]

Epilogue

Elsaesser's post-classical method of analysis enabled me to perform a close analysis of INSIDE MAN and bring to the surface a series of elements that would go unnoticed using the standard tools of narrative analysis. The five criteria above function as a conceptual grid that isolates the differences between contemporary American films and their classical origins and further highlights the relation between the cinematic discourse and the wider historical and cultural context. It is important to keep all five of these criteria together and apply them complementarily because, otherwise, we risk undermining their heuristic value and reducing them to minor distinctive features that easily lose their critical value under the pressure of the similarities at the level of narration. This was the strategy that Bordwell deployed to debunk Elsaesser's theory in his latest book entitled *The Way Hollywood Tells It* (2006), where he once again tried to sustain his standard thesis about the stability of the classical Hollywood system to this very day. In his critique, Bordwell concentrated almost exclusively on the issue of "playful knowingness," claiming that this element called "knowingness" was as old as the (Hollywood) hills, as it could be found in many Marx Brothers films or even in Bugs

Bunny cartoons.[13] Ironically enough, neither slapstick comedy nor animation has ever been regarded as quintessentially classical. Quite the contrary. Both of these genres have regularly underlined the weaknesses of the classical mode of narration and its tight cause-and-effect logic. The fact that Elsaesser's argument about knowingness reminded Bordwell of some of the most anomalous instances in the history of classical studio filmmaking is quite indicative of the nerve that the former's theory is able to touch.

At any rate, contemporary Hollywood will continue to be a battleground for some of the most fascinating theoretical struggles, and the line between the classical and the post-classical will continue to be redrawn. With each charting, what matters is the consistency of the methodological tools and the application of the theoretical premises to a sufficient sample of films. Thomas Elsaesser ensured the former with the clarity and precision that characterizes his "Classical/Post-Classical Narrative" account. Hopefully, my analysis of INSIDE MAN will contribute to the latter.

Notes

1. Thomas Elsaesser, "The Pathos of Failure: Notes on the Unmotivated Hero," *Monogram* 6 (1975): 13-19; reprinted in *The Last Great American Picture Show: New Hollywood Cinema in the 1970s*, eds. Thomas Elsaesser, Alexander Horwath and Noel King (Amsterdam: Amsterdam University Press, 2004) 279-292.
2. Elsaesser uses the terms Old, New and New New Hollywood to distinguish three major phases in Hollywood cinema, mainly in terms of production practices. Old Hollywood refers to the studio years from 1917 to 1960 and is characterized by the Fordist principles of industrial production. New Hollywood is a transitional phase that lasts through the 1970s and is characterized by a more personal type of filmmaking. Finally, New New Hollywood emerges in the 1980s and is still the dominant system, signals a return to a strictly industrialized mode of production according to post-Fordist principles. Each phase is also characterized by, even if it is not reducible to, a specific type of film product: with Old Hollywood we find the classical narratives, with New Hollywood we have the unmotivated heroes, while New New Hollywood is dominated by blockbusters. See the introduction to *The Last Great American Picture Show* 37-69.
3. Thomas Elsaesser, "Classical / Post-Classical Narrative," *Studying Contemporary American Film* (London: Arnold, 2002) 26-79. The book was co-authored by Thomas Elsaesser and Warren Buckland, but this particular chapter was written by Elsaesser, as noted in the Preface. Thus, I will attribute this approach to Elsaesser, despite Buckland's contribution to the overall structure and editing of the book.
4. Elsaesser, "Classical / Post-Classical Narrative" 66.
5. Elsaesser, Classical / Post-Classical Narrative" 78. Here we can observe a slight shift in the terms he uses, which can be elaborated as follows; in the article on New Holly-

wood and unmotivated heroes, Elsaesser was discussing a distinction between Old and New Hollywood. In his analysis of Die Hard, the distinction is made between classical and post-classical cinema. The question is where the 1970s films fit in, in the classical-postclassical continuum. Elsaesser never answers this question directly, but what I could infer from his overall argumentation on the topic is that these films would not qualify as post-classical, at least not according to the post-classical method he developed in his chapter in *Studying Contemporary American Film*. They could be deemed as a transitional phase that was in dialogue both with the classical tradition as well as with the films of the European *auteurs* who had their heyday in the 1960s.

6. See, for example, Thomas Elsaesser, "The Mind-Game Film," *Puzzle Films: Complex Storytelling in Contemporary Cinema*, ed. Warren Buckland (Oxford: Blackwell, forthcoming).

7. In my own attempt to demarcate a post-classical cinema strictly in terms of narration, I had to disagree with both Elsaesser and Bordwell for different methodological reasons.

8. Within the first year of its release, the film grossed a total of US$183,960,186 worldwide.

9. Elsaesser sums up Sharon Willis's argument about race in contemporary American films as follows: "Rather than the film translating racially coded issues into gender-coded ones, she sees a constant slippage and reversal, indicative of what she calls the 'trade-offs' between race and gender, from the point of view of masculinity in crisis, which then release different 'erotic economies' that entail the consequence that 'black' and 'female' emerge as incompatible with each other, unable to exist within the same discursive space." Elsaesser, Classical / Post-Classical Narrative" 71.

10. Elsaesser, "Classical / Post-Classical Narrative" 70.

11. Lee's film is rife with explicit references to films such as Serpico (1973), Dog Day Afternoon (1975) and The Godfather (1972).

12. Elsaesser, "Classical / Post-Classical Narrative" 39.

13. David Bordwell, *The Way Hollywood Tells It: Story and Style in Modern Movies* (Berkeley: University of California Press, 2006) 8.

Bumper Stories

The Framing of Commercial Blocks on Dutch Public Television

Charles Forceville[1]

Introduction

In "Reclame: markt en betekenis" ("Advertising: Market and Meaning"), Thomas Elsaesser sketches the pervasiveness and impact of advertising on daily life.[2] He argues that audiences willingly and knowingly surrender to its promise of identity-building novelty and exoticness, suggesting that advertising is ultimately a flattering mirror. Elsaesser also refers to the "Wag-the-Dog" principle, reminding us that, particularly on commercial television, advertising is the tail that wags the dog called "programs" by paying the bills. Although television programs are made to entertain or inform, they are also effective tools to reach a broad audience and to assure that viewers will watch the commercials. Elsaesser cites the notion that "television does not bring programs to viewers, but viewers to advertisers," a quote based on Richard Serra's renowned art video "Television Delivers People" (1973).[3]

In this chapter, I focus on one specific element of advertising on television: the so-called "advertising bumper," the audiovisual logo that brackets a block of commercials, thereby helping viewers to distinguish between commercials and television programs. Although media-literate audiences may believe that they are immune to the persuasive force of commercials, Dutch law finds it necessary to warn television viewers when they are going to see a block of commercials, and when the commercials are over. The prototypical warning, deployed both on public and commercial channels, is the advertising bumper. By analyzing fourteen specific cases of advertising bumpers on Dutch public television, ranging from 1976 to 2007, I will argue that in the course of its (in this case, Dutch) history, bumpers have become systematically less distinctive both visually and aurally and, as a consequence, have lost much of their function of patrolling the borders between commercials and programming.[4] My findings can contribute to a better understanding of the "Wag-the-Dog" principle that Elsaesser recognized in advertising on Dutch television.

Background: "Bumpers" and the Genre of Television Commercials

Dutch television, which had its first complete broadcast (a soccer match) in September 1948, has featured commercial advertising since 1967.[5] The selling and monitoring of advertising slots on the publicly funded television channels – Nederland 1, Nederland 2, and, since 1988, Nederland 3 – as well as on public radio and on any related websites has always been handled by the STER (*Stichting Ether Reclame*). Together with public funding and subscription fees, this has helped pay for programs. From the late 1980s onwards, the publicly funded channels have faced increasing competition from a variety of commercial broadcasting companies, which depend entirely on advertising for their revenues.

Dutch media law specifies a number of criteria that advertising must adhere to. An important regulation is that a commercial block "is clearly recognizable as such by optical and acoustic means from the regular programs."[6] The *Stichting Reclame Code*, founded by the advertising industry itself to enhance self-regulation and to provide a forum for complaints by the public, similarly emphasizes that a commercial must be identifiable as such, forbidding "the use of elements from a radio or TV program in a commercial ... if it can be reasonably assumed that viewers or listeners would thereby be misled or confused."[7] The basic idea is clearly that audiences should be cautioned whether and when they are confronted with advertising, so that they realize that an agency with a financial self-interest is trying to persuade them to buy consumer goods or services. Indeed, people need to be able to "frame" events correctly to be able to respond to them in an appropriate manner.[8] When "events" assume the form of representations or discourses, attributing "genre" is a crucial aspect of this framing activity. Deciding what genre a text belongs to activates certain interpretation strategies.[9]

During the first five years of television advertising, a block was announced by images of ocean waves. From 1972 until halfway into the 1990s, the puppet animation of Loeki de Leeuw (Loeki the Lion), created by Joop Geesink, featured in the opening and closing bumpers of commercial blocks, together with his friends Piep the mouse, lioness Roos, Guusje the little duck, and Filiep the blue elephant. Loeki also played a role in short (4" to 5") separators between commercials in a block.[10] From the mid-1990s onwards, Loeki no longer "bracketed" a block, although until 2004 he still occasionally performed in clips separating commercials. Loeki – a lion because of this animal's prominence in Holland's heraldry – featured in more than 7,000 bumpers,[11] and became a national icon. His disappearance was widely mourned by the television audiences that had grown up with him.

The success of the commercial channels in the 1990s meant that the advertising revenues of the public channels began to dwindle. Loeki's disappearance was part of an extensive restyling and repositioning process of the public channels. This process was completed in 2006, when the three public channels were profiled as catering to the entire family (Nederland 1), providing content and reflection (Nederland 2), and addressing a younger audience (Nederland 3).[12] This profiling also had an impact on the design of the bumpers for the three channels.

While the system of framing a commercial block may be beneficial in activating viewers' alertness to the persuasive nature of the messages they are going to watch, it is not, of course, necessarily in the interest of advertisers. It is a well-known fact that many viewers use commercial breaks to interrupt their viewing. For this reason, the boundary area between what is "regular" television programming and what is a series of commercials is of special interest. I will consider more closely the audiovisual advertising bumpers that Dutch media law insists on to mark the boundaries of a commercial block. More specifically, I will first chart salient dimensions in which bumpers surrounding commercial blocks on public TV may differ from one another. Subsequently, I will suggest how changes in bumpers potentially affect their boundary function. This article can serve as a blueprint for a much larger, systematic project, involving the commercial channels as well; here I cannot do much beyond sketch some contours.

Method of Analysis and Case Studies

The bumpers are analyzed in chronological order, but since they are not widely available, I have made a practical, and hence eclectic, selection. Some samples of difficult to find, older commercial blocks have been located online (YouTube), and these have been complemented with more recent material in my possession. My claims depend on the assumption that a bumper in a given commercial is representative of its use over a longer period. Obviously, I cannot claim to have charted all of the salient changes in the history of advertising bumpers on Dutch public television; I do maintain, however, that the present approach allows for the identification of certain trends. Here are the questions I have asked for each of the case studies, followed by these case studies themselves.

1. How long are the opening and closing bumpers? This is measured in terms of the number of seconds.
2. How can the opening and closing bumper be described? A crucial issue is whether the bumpers are the same visually and/or aurally.
3. Is there a distinctive melody or tune detectable in the bumpers?

4. What other elements, if any, occur within the commercial blocks apart from the commercials themselves that may affect the "framing" of the genre as advertising?

CASE 1 (30 March 1976)[13]

Opening: Loeki, playing the standard opening melody on a trumpet, walks past flowers whose squarish heads change from dark to an eye-like circle. The flowers turn their heads to maintain their gaze on him. At the end, the eye-like circles transform into STER logos. A super, with "Nederland 1," in plain text, is visible for a few seconds (duration: 10").
Closing: Loeki, playing the trumpet, stands in front of the flowers. On the rhythm of the standard closing melody, the flowers' STER logos switch off (duration: 7").
Music/sound: Loeki performs the standard melodic tune, the beginning of which is the same in opening and closing bumpers, while the ending differs.
Notable features: There is the suggestion of the flowers "waking up" in the opening, and "going to sleep" in the closing bumper. In the closing bumper Loeki waves to the viewers. The length of the opening and closing bumpers differs (10" versus 7"). All of the commercials in this commercial block are alternately separated by Loeki mini-narratives (duration: 4-5") or by abstract separators (duration: 2").

CASE 2 (17 May 1983)[14]

Opening: Loeki, in a picnic scene, plays the pan flute, accompanied by seven violin-playing daisies. In the background, the sun containing the STER logo rises. Piep, the mouse, ends the scene by appearing from a picnic basket and sounding the final note on a triangle. Super as in case 1 (9").
Closing: Same picnic scene. The sun is setting as it becomes dark (9").
Music/sound: Same as in case 1 but with different instruments.
Notable features: Beginning and end of a picnic are suggested. In the closing bumper, Loeki and Piep wave goodbye to the viewer. The commercials are separated by (non-Loeki) mini-narratives with live-action characters, taking place on a film set, varying in length between about 4" and 9".

CASE 3 (19 January 1986)[15]

Opening: Loeki, standing on the drawbridge of a castle in medieval attire, plays the trumpet – from which a banner with the STER logo unfolds – accompanied by Piep on the violin. Super "Nederland 2" as in case 1 (10").
Closing: Same scene (10").
Music/sound: With different instruments as in cases 1 and 2.
Notable features: In the closing bumper, Roos appears in a castle window, all three characters wave to the viewer, and Loeki's helmet falls over his eyes on the last notes. All of the commercials within this block are separated by Loeki mini-narratives (4-5"), except once, when a more abstract STER logo separator is used (2").

CASE 4 (February 1987)[16]

Opening: Loeki, Piep and Roos, dressed up as performers, play winding instruments on a theatre stage; the STER logo becomes visible in the background. Super "Nederland 1" as in case 1 (9").
Closing: Same scene (9").
Music/sound: As in cases 1-3.
Notable features: All three characters wave goodbye to the viewers. The commercials within the block are alternately separated by Loeki mini-narratives (4") and abstract STER logos (2"). In one mini-narrative Loeki exclaims "Asjemenou!" ("Well-well-well!"), an utterance that became uniquely associated with him.

CASE 5 (8 September 1989)[17]

Opening: A playground scene in which the camera pans past various familiar Loeki characters enjoying themselves, ending with Loeki on the swing. The STER logo is visible on a rolling barrel. There is no super indicating the channel (10").
Closing: Same scene, different events. There is no STER logo (10").
Music/sound: As in cases 1 to 4.
Notable features: Loeki and Roos wave to viewers. The commercials are separated by Loeki mini-narratives (4") or abstract separators (2" each). Moreover, Loeki and his friends no longer play the music themselves.

Case 6 (May 1992)[18]

Opening: Loeki and Piep are driving a manually operated railroad wagon as they turn the corner on an ordinary road. The STER logo is visible on top of a building. There is no super indicating the channel (4").
Closing: Same scene, but now they go in the other direction.
Music/sound: The standard melodic opening tune and the standard closing tune. The difference from the earlier cases is that now the part of the tune that was the same in opening and closing bumpers has been deleted, so that the two are totally different – and shorter.
Notable features: In the closing bumper, Loeki waves goodbye to the viewers. The commercials are separated by a Loeki mini-narrative (4"), or by a black screen with a duration of less than 1".

Case 7 (20 August 1994)[19]

Opening: Loeki, wearing a white cowboy hat, drives past in a big American car, with Roos in the passenger seat waving (!) at the viewer (4"). There is no indication of the channel and also no STER logo visible.
Closing: Loeki reaches up for a chain to draw the blinds over the STER logo (4").
Music/sound: As in case 6.
Notable features: The opening and closing scenes have no relationship. The closing bumper cues the disappearance of the STER logo. All the commercials within the block are separated by black screens lasting less than 1".

Case 8 (4 January 1997)[20]

Opening: Loeki and Piep are on skates, waiting for Roos to fire the starter's gun, but Loeki falls. No indication of channel. The STER logo appears against a tree (4").
Closing: Same scene, no STER logo. Various Loeki characters wave to viewers (4").
Music/sound: As in cases 6 and 7.
Notable features: The one remaining Loeki mini-narrative within the block retains the skating scene of the opening, but here Loeki falls through a hole in the ice. All the commercials within the block are separated by black screens lasting less than 1", except for one Loeki mini-narrative (4"). "MisterCrash1984," who uploaded the commercial on YouTube notes that this commercial block was broad-

cast immediately before a sports program that showed the finish of the skaters in Holland's most famous long-distance skating race, the *Elfstedentocht*. Almost all of the commercials in the block play on the theme by cueing "skating," "snow and ice," "cold," and Friesland (the province where the *Elfstedentocht* takes place).

Case 9 (22 April 2004)

Opening: A split screen. On the left side, we see people on a moving escalator, going up from left to right. On the right side, a boat, filmed from above, also moves from left to right. The Nederland 2 logo, a "2" in a yellow diamond, straddles the two sides of the split screen bottom center. After some four seconds, this logo disappears, and the STER logo appears instead in the right bottom corner for less than two seconds (6").
Closing: Exactly the same scene as in the opening. The only difference is that the STER logo (which appears now in the left side of the screen) disappears and is replaced by the centered Nederland 2 logo (6").
Music/sound: The same tune occurs in both bumpers.
Notable features: All the commercials within the block are separated by black screens lasting a split second.

Case 10 (17 May 2004)

Opening: An elderly couple, delicately intimate, in a field of grass, against trees. The red Nederland 1 logo appears in pixelized form in the left-hand bottom corner and gives way, during the last two seconds, to the centralized STER logo (8").
Closing: Same scene with marginally different images from the opening bumper. After two seconds, the STER logo is replaced by the Nederland 1 logo (8").
Music/sound: The same tune occurs in both bumpers, but it is a different tune than the one in case 9.
Notable features: All of the commercials within the block are separated by black screens lasting a split second. There are also inserts: an announcement for the program OP REIS MET FELDERHOF; an announcement of programming pertaining to "Europe" on Nederland 2; and a non-commercial exhortation to participate in the National Sponsor Lottery, a charity.

CASE 11 (18 October 2004)

Opening: Man holds woman, both are lying back on a field of grass. Nederland 1 and STER logos as in case 10 (8").
Closing: Same scene. Camera zooms out and reveals the field is full of people. Logos as in case 10 (8").
Music/sound: Tune as in case 10.
Notable features: The closing bumper uses a surprise: the couple is far from alone. All of the commercials in this block are separated by black screens lasting a split second.

CASE 12 (13 February 2007)

Opening: High angle shot of sunny market square in historical center of a Dutch city, people walking leisurely across it. Dozens of the "Nederland 1" logo (a "1" in red diamond) calmly whirl across the upper part of the screen, as if blown by the wind. There is a slightly noticeable pan to the right. During the last 3", the STER logo appears, via quick fade-in, in the bottom right-hand corner of the screen (7").
Closing: Extreme long shot of the lit glass wing of a building, against an evening sky. Nederland 1 logos whirl across the upper part of the screen (with their shadows visible in the glass of the building). The STER logo in the bottom right-hand corner disappears after 3". There is a barely noticeable track-out (7").
Music/sound: The music is a soothing, minimal tune, played partly on guitar, and is the same in the opening and closing bumper, but with marginally different instrumentation. There is no diegetic sound.
Notable features: The swirl of three-dimensional "Nederland 1" logos, the appearance/disappearance of the "STER" logo, and the tune, with its various instrumentations, is a standard recurring feature of all of the Nederland 1 STER bumpers from this era. There are different visuals; sometimes the same visuals are used in the opening and closing bumpers. No fixed combinations between opening and closing bumpers exist either in the visuals or in the tune.

CASE 13 (22 February 2007)

Opening: Long shot of two adolescent pupils sitting in the first row in a classroom. The boy looks out the window at the square outside. At about the place of the window, a big, transparent version of the Nederland 2 logo (a blue "2" in a diamond) enters from screen right, acting as a magnifying glass for the scene outside. The camera pans left, along with the viewing direction of the boy. The STER logo appears in the bottom left-hand corner and is visible for the last 2" (7").

Closing: A beach scene with a young girl and boy playing in the sand. Factory chimneys are visible in the background. The same "magnifying" Nederland 2 logo drifts into the scene, now from screen left. The STER logo in the bottom right-hand corner disappears in about 2" (7").

Music/sound: A soothing tune; the opening and closing tunes are the same, but they differ slightly in their instrumentation. In both cases, faint diegetic sounds are audible.

Notable features: In 2006, the Nederland 2 logo changed from yellow to blue.[21] The magnifying transparent logo, the appearing/disappearing STER logo, and the tune were all recurrent elements in the Nederland 2 bumpers from this period, but were later replaced by the regular logo with the blue "2" appearing in unexpected places. These barely noticeable stable factors combine with a range of different films, in varying combinations – as in case 12.

Case 14 (13 April 2007)

Opening: Using computer animation techniques, the Nederland 3 logo (a green "3" tilted rightward in a tilted-rightward rectangle, with a green border around a white field) disintegrates quickly and turns into a car which bumps up and down a few times, disappears from the screen, re-appears, and drives off into the distance. The STER logo appears in the bottom left-hand corner and is visible for the last 2" (7").

Closing: An animated green track is followed quickly, as if the point-of-view is from a car in a rollercoaster, and ends in the "Nederland 3" logo. The STER logo in the right-hand bottom corner disappears after 2" (7").

Music/sound. Percussion sound effects simulate the movements of the car using Mickey-Mousing effects; there is no tune. Opening and closing sounds are virtually the same.

Notable features: Green is usually the dominant color in this era's Nederland 3 bumpers. Within this particular block, one clip shows a number of Dutch politicians along with soundbites, followed by the phrase, *"Altijd bij 2"* ("Always on 2") – the "2" being the Nederland 2 logo. Although no program is explicitly mentioned, it alludes to political commentary programs on Nederland 2 such as Netwerk and Nova.

Analysis of the Fourteen Cases

Although conclusions must be drawn with great caution because of the nonsyste-
matic nature of the corpus of case studies investigated, the general trend appears
clear: through a variety of techniques, the opening and closing bumpers of commercial blocks on Dutch public television channels have, in the course of their
history, changed in an ever higher tempo, and moreover, have become increasingly interchangeable. Let me briefly recapitulate some aspects of this development.

First, in the long period when opening and closing bumpers used the Loeki
animations, his adventures clearly separated the commercial block from its surroundings. The most important reason for this was that the opening and closing
bumpers were not identical either visually or musically. When their length was
reduced from some 10" to some 4", this distinction was retained. Although
sometimes the two greatly resembled one another, the closing bumper always
had one or more of the characters waving to the audience, something which
usually did not happen in the opening bumper. Moreover, in the early Loeki period, the commercials within the block were often separated by Loeki mini-narratives – and otherwise, by one of a series of abstract or STER logo separators.
Gradually, Loeki became a rarer occurrence within the block – allegedly because
producing the animations was a very costly business and because they occupied
lucrative advertising seconds – while the abstract separators became black
screens. These screens also became shorter than the earlier abstract separators:
at first somewhat under a second, and later a mere split second.

When Loeki stopped bracketing the blocks, things changed even more radi-
cally, no doubt because of the competition from the growing number of commercial television channels. Using a range of subtle devices (specific visuals sometimes used as opening, sometimes as closing bumpers; a variety of different and
identical bumpers used for both opening and closing bumpers; a (near) identical,
unobtrusive tune used for both opening and closing bumper; a wide variety of
different clips for blocks on the same channel, alternation between diegetic
sound/no diegetic sound), the opening and closing bumpers of commercial
blocks on public television became almost indistinguishable, the brief appear-
ance/disappearance of the STER logo (and of the channel logo, in reverse) being
the only remaining distinctive feature.

The indistinguishability of the opening and closing bumpers is significant, I
propose, because of viewers' zapping habits. During the Loeki era, a bracketing
bumper was identifiable as either an opening or closing bumper because of various audiovisual cues, but these cues have now virtually all disappeared. As a
consequence, zapping viewers can no longer be certain whether a bumper they

zap into marks the beginning or the end of a commercial block, with a greater chance that they will see (at least the beginning of) a commercial than back when they *did* know.

The bumper's length has varied over time. It was initially curtailed to match the shorter bumpers of the commercial channels, and then became longer again. Arguably, this lengthening occurred because the bumpers now serve not merely to separate commercial from noncommercial footage, but also act as "brand identifiers": they remind viewers that they are watching one of the three public television channels and help promote, via the bumper film styles, the channel's profile. However, this means that bumpers lose even more of their separator function, also because the unobtrusive STER logo is visible for no more than 2". This tendency is further reinforced nowadays because the blocks on Nederland 1, 2, and 3, unlike in the Loeki era, increasingly contain noncommercial content: trailers for programs broadcast later in the evening on the same channel, or on the other two public channels; brief announcements of cultural events in theaters and museums; public service announcements about national anniversaries (e.g., World War II Memorial and Liberation Day on 4 and 5 May). Since these "inserts" regularly feature presenters and anchors of regular programs, they help further lower the distinction between programs and commercials. There are other, even more subtle devices that appear to achieve this effect. In 2007, a series of bumpers on Nederland 2 displayed familiar institutional settings: a school square, a church, a studio, a court of law. Since there are so many different bumpers to choose from, specific bumpers can be selected to "match" the contents of preceding or following programs (a phenomenon, incidentally, that is also the case for specific commercials *within* a block). On one occasion (17 September 2007), an opening bumper shows people entering a theater and features a poster with the words "new dance." This poster is actually a still from another bumper. Moreover, the commercial block is immediately followed by an announcement for a ballet performance to be broadcast later that evening. Another subtlety is that one bumper from the Nederland 2 series features a journalist, Ron Fresen, who is a regularly commentator on the NOS national news programs. Other devices I have noticed include channel logos remaining in the same part of the screen during the transition from program (announcement) to the opening bumper (e.g., in the lower corner), and the introduction of the opening bumper tune before the bumper has started – or its use during other times of the day, early in the morning, when there are no programs, for instance, when only a clock is visible. All these devices, I claim, are aimed at lowering people's awareness of the transition to or from commercial blocks.

Coda

To what extent such a trend indeed has a "lowering awareness" effect on viewers can only be assessed in experimental research. One could, after all, disagree and argue that over the past few decades viewers have become considerably more visually literate, and thus have learned to signal the persuasive goals underlying the audiovisual styles in advertising bumpers. But even if this should turn out to be true for certain groups of viewers (adolescents, young adults), it may not be true for others (children, elderly people). Moreover, some of the techniques signaled above may even qualify as instances of the "subliminal techniques" in advertising that the Media Law prohibits (*Mediawet*, paragraph 50.8). Their surreptitious effectiveness may become all the greater precisely because of their infinite variety, and their unsystematic and short-lived use: advertising bumpers are continually being altered in a variety of ways, far exceeding the variety of the Loeki era.

Advertising bumpers have become ever less distinctive as warning separators between commercials and programs, and have therefore lost much of their function as guards against unforeseen commercial attacks. Whereas the advertising tail has always wagged the dog of programming, as Thomas Elsaesser pointed out, nowadays the dog begins to look ever more like one big tail itself. In contemporary audiovisual media culture, it becomes increasingly difficult to distinguish between content and advertisement, between television program and commercial. The growing inconspicuousness of the advertising bumper is a telling symptom of this development.

Notes

1.   I am much indebted to Anton Kanis for alerting me to relevant websites, discussing various dimensions of bumpers, and making me more aware of their growing importance in helping to galvanize channel identity. I also gratefully acknowledge Liselotte Doeswijk. She furnished pertinent details, made thoughtful comments, and corrected some errors. I would also like to thank Maarten Reesink for his comments on an earlier draft of this chapter. I alone, of course, remain responsible for the views expressed here, and for any remaining errors.
2.   Thomas Elsaesser, "Reclame: markt en betekenis," *Hollywood op straat: Film en televisie in de hedendaagse mediacultuur,* ed. Thomas Elsaesser (Amsterdam: Vossiuspers AUP, 2000) 183-194.
3.   Elsaesser 194.
4.   I very briefly discussed this thesis in Charles Forceville, "Categorisering, genre en Reclame," *Hollywood op straat* 58-73.

5. See Joke Hermes and Maarten Reesink, *Inleiding televisiestudies* (Amsterdam: Boom, 2003) 253.

6. My translation of: "als zodanig herkenbaar en door optische en akoestische middelen duidelijk onderscheiden van de programma-onderdelen," paragraph 50.8 of the Mediawet, text valid as of 1 July 2007 (last consulted 27 Sept. 2007): <http://www.cvdm.nl/documents/mw%20tekst%20per%201-7-2007%20na%20naamswijziging%20bvdp%20schoon.pdf>.

7. My translation of: "Ook is het gebruik van elementen uit een etherprogramma in reclame op radio en televisie verboden indien redelijkerwijs moet worden aangenomen dat daardoor kijkers of luisteraars worden misleid of in verwarring gebracht." *De Nederlandse Reclamecode*, general section, paragraph 10, version Jan. 2006 (last consulted 27 Sept. 2007): <http://www.reclamecodecommissie.nl/Brochure%20Nederlandse%20Reclame%20Code.pdf>.

8. Erving Goffman, *Frame Analysis: An Essay on the Organization of Experience*. (New York / Hagerstown / San Francisco / London: Harper & Row, 1974).

9. See Rick Altman, *Film/Genre* (London: BFI, 1999); Douwe Fokkema and Elrud Ibsch, *Knowledge and Commitment: A Problem-Oriented Approach to Literary Studies* (Amsterdam / Philadelphia: Benjamins, 2000); Charles Forceville, "Art or Ad? The Effect of Genre-Attribution on the Interpretation of Images," *SPIEL* 18.2 (1999): 279-300; Charles Forceville, "Addressing an Audience: Time, Place, and Genre in Peter Van Straaten's Calendar Cartoons," *Humor: International Journal of Humor Research* 18.3 (2005): 247-278; Siegfried J. Schmidt, "Literary Systems as Self-Organizing Systems," *Empirical Studies of Literature*, ed. Elrud Ibsch, Dick Schram, and Gerard Steen (Amsterdam / Atlanta: Rodopi, 1991) 413-24.

10. See Loeki's Wiki-page (last consulted 30 Sept. 2007): <http://nl.wikipedia.org/wiki/Loeki_de_Leeuw>; and the news about Loeki's move from television to the theme parc De Efteling on Nieuwsbank: Interactief Nederlands Persbureau (last consulted 27 Sept. 2007): <http://www.nieuwsbank.nl/inp/2005/03/25/F011.htm>.

11. <www.loeki.nl> (last consulted 8 Jan. 2008).

12. See "Publieke Omroep vergroot herkenbaarheid" on <http://www.tns-nipo.com/sub_ext.asp?co01&file=persvannipo%5cnieuwe_profilering_p006.htm> (consulted Dec. 2007).

13. Source: <http://nl.youtube.com/watch?v=kAF2O-ZLIy8>. The sources in cases 1-8 were accessed on 14 Sept. 2007.

14. Source: <http://nl.youtube.com/watch?v=C6fqXOaYF8o&mode=related&search>.

15. Source: <http://nl.youtube.com/watch?v=krHlCMFDnQY>.

16. Source: <http://nl.youtube.com/watch?v=MVOX7g6PsPQ&mode=related&search>.

17. Source: <http://nl.youtube.com/watch?v=_PIbZiqVFhc&mode=related&search>.

18. Source: <http://nl.youtube.com/watch?v=bYjy_8oatfk&mode=related&search>.

19. Source: <http://nl.youtube.com/watch?v=InC2hobZdps&mode=related&search>.

20. Source: <http://nl.youtube.com/watch?v=Nj8Qi3ZKMtM>.

21. Liselotte Doeswijk, personal communication.

DEAR THOMAS, HERE'S THE
FIRST DRAFT OF THE STORYBOARD
YOU ASKED FOR. DISNEY AND
WARNER BROTHERS ARE STILL
INTERESTED, BUT THEY ARE STILL
NOT SURE WHO THEY WANT TO PLAY
YOU, I'VE HEARD RUMORS,

Storyboard

by

Bruce Gray

for the production of

"Where Were You When . . . ?";
or,
"I Phone, Therefore I Am"

by

Thomas Elsassaer

BRAD AS THE YOUNGER THOMAS
AND TRAVOLTA AS THE OLDER.
BUT THOSE ARE JUST RUMORS!
WE'LL KEEP IN TOUCH,

BRUCE

PRODUCTION: Where were you when…	DIALOGUE	SOUND	

FADE IN

VOICE OVER THOMAS:
For several years now, walking back from the office to my house in the evening…

…I have been pained as well as reassured by the sight of the resident homeless man on Rembrandt Square.

I am relieved when he is talking to himself…

MAN: (SHOUTING) GET A THEORETICAL GRIP ON LIFE!

…and worry when he gesticulates or shouts, as he sometimes does.

MAN: (SHOUTING) PICK UP THE PHONE! HE'S CALLING YOU, HE'S CALLING YOU!

A few weeks ago, I noticed a man in a pin-striped suit crossing the square, also talking to himself and as apparently lost to the world around him as was the homeless man he walked straight past.

PIN-STRIPED MAN: (IN HIS MOBILE PHONE) SOMEONE IS CALLING ME! SOMEONE IS CALLING ME!

What looked like a scene from a Beckett play was proof that the mobile phone will soon be all but invisible. But it took me a few minutes to realize that my placid or angrily fizzing malcontent on the square was also no longer who he used to be…

SNORING

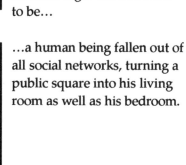

…a human being fallen out of all social networks, turning a public square into his living room as well as his bedroom.

The other man's phone had made the vagrant's behavior normal. More than that, it may have put him in the vanguard of a subtle but momentous cultural change.

That evening, as I felt embarrassed by the comical and even heartless comparison I had made between the two men, it also set me thinking about a problem in my discipline—film studies—that I have not been able to get a theoretical grip on.

CRICKETS CHIRPING

Over the past ten years, we have discarded one type of theory, gradually switching to another, yet to be defined paradigm.

STRIKING A MATCH

Rather than continue to think about the cinema as an ocular-specular phenomenon, whose indexical realism we celebrated or whose illusionism we excoriated (which was the case in classical film theory and, subsequently,

…during the decade when psychosemiotic apparatus theory held sway), scholars now tend to regard the cinema as an immersive perceptual event.

VOICE OF ELECTRICIAN: SOMETIMES YOU HAVE TO SHOCK AN AUDIENCE!

Body, sound, and kinetic-affective sensation have become its default values, and not the eye, the look, and ocular verification.

KINETIC ZAPPING SOUND

The incident on Rembrandt Square gave me a clue about what might be involved,

ACADEMIC TIME WARP SOUND EFFECT

'BACK TO THE FUTURE THEME MUSIC

…but I had to go back some forty years to see the link.

SOUND OF AN AIRPLANE

"Where were you the day John F. Kennedy was shot?" — I was twenty years old, in a dorm at the University of Sussex, and it was the sixth or seventh week of my life as an undergraduate in English and comparative literature.

What I remember is that
22 November 1963 was the day
the Beatles brought out their
second LP, With the Beatles
(known as Meet the Beatles in
the United States)…

SECOND
AIRPLANE
SOUND

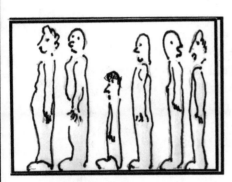

… and I had stood in line
since 6 a.m. to buy my vinyl
(except we didn't call it
that then).

CROSS
FADE:
BEATLES
SONG
'ALL I'VE
GOT TO
DO'

It was a ruinous purchase, but
since we had all been fevering
for the LP's release for months,
my extravagance was part of a
ploy to become somebody
among my fellow students.

There was only one radiogram
in the dorm, and it was installed
in the breakfast room. We were
in the middle of listening to
"All I've Got to Do" ("Whenever
I want you around yeh / All I
gotta do / Is call you on the
phone / and you'll come running
home"),

DOOR OPENS
AND
SLAMS
SHUT

PRODUCTION: Where were you when…	DIALOGUE	SOUND

…when the warden interrupted, ordering us to turn on the radio to hear the news.

PICKUP SLIDES ACROSS RECORD

DIAL TURNING SEARCHING FOR STATION…

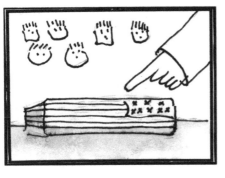

That was the end of *With the Beatles,* and I have to admit that the live broadcast from Dallas would not have been my first choice that morning.
JFK didn't make my day.

RADIO ANNOUNCER: "THE PRESIDENT HAS BEEN SHOT!"

I remember the day of the Challenger disaster less well, although I was in the United States when it happened, teaching at the University of California, Irvine.

MUSIC: THE MAMAS AND THE PAPAS 'CALIFORNIA DREAMIN''

The reason for my distraction at the time was that I thought the NASA space program was part of a peace-threatening arms race, and I disapproved of the cynical way the purpose of this mission was sugarcoated with flag-waving schoolchildren cheering Christa McAuliffe.

CHEERING KIDS

SOUND OF CHALLANGER LIFT-OFF

I also did not have a television in the little sublet where I lived. Instead, I was wrestling with my first computer, which I had brought with me from England, a BBC B, as it was called, with a cassette tape recorder to store data.

SOUND OF EXPLOSION AND BURNING BBC B COMPUTER

Not only was it bulky and delicate to work with (its RAM was enough for a half-page of text, which then had to be transferred to tape), I couldn't find a printer anywhere. But the first six chapters of my book were on the cassettes, and I was damned if I would rewrite them all on the typewriter.

My landlady had a proper IBM PC, with floppy-disk drive and all, but she was so proud and protective of her new possession that she would not let me near it.

WOMAN'S VOICE! (SHOUTING) THOMAS! DON'T YOU DARE TOUCH THAT DOOR!

The day after the explosion, I was teaching my class on Weimar cinema, and—not realizing that the 1970s were definitely over and that Reagan's America had healed its soul, wrapping it in the flag, honor, and pride...

ANNOUNCER: THE PRESIDENT OF THE UNITED STATES... WRAPPED IN HIS FLAG!

…I made a crack about unfortunately not being able to show them The Woman on the Moon, Fritz Lang's sci-fi thriller from 1929.

THOMAS' VOICE: (ECHOING IN THE LECTURE HALL) I'M SORRY I CAN'T SHOW YOU…

It was a feeble joke, flippant, too, and the response was glacial.

SOUND OF SILENT COUGHING

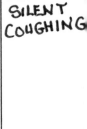

On 11 September 2001, at 3:17 p.m. Amsterdam time, I was in my office at the university, holding tutorials, when the phone rang.

PHONE RINGING

My partner in New York was on the line. She said, "I'm looking out of my window, and I can see smoke coming from the World Trade Center." I said, "I'm very sorry, but I'm in a meeting right now, can I talk to you later?" and hung up.

WOMAN'S VOICE ON THE PHONE

	DIALOGUE	SOUND
	Ten minutes later she rang again: "TheWTC is on fire; I just saw a plane smash into it!" For the next quarter hour we were on the phone.	PHONE RINGING
	While my students waited outside,…	CLOCK TICKING
	…I went to my computer, tried to get to the Guardian's Web site, couldn't, tried again, all the while talking to my friend on the twentieth floor of her building on Washington Square, attempting to focus on her words,…	NASTY COMPUTER VOICE: NO GUARDIAN TODAY, TRY AGAIN TOMORROW… IF THERE IS A TOMORROW… HA, HA, HA!
	…which described how she had gone to the window with her cup of coffee…	

…and what she saw as she talked.

SOUNDS OF SIRENS AND CHOPPERS

I could not picture it, but I heard sirens and choppers through the phone.

DRAMATIC FILM MUSIC

It dawned on me that this would be another of those epochal moments.

Trust New York, I thought, to come up with the millennium event, after 2000 had been such a letdown. I am not proud to have been—yet again—so callous in the face of an American tragedy.

But so strong was this improbable event's real time presence down the transatlantic phone line that cynicism must have served as a shield during that first half hour, before I learned about the hijacked planes and the collapsing towers with their thousands of victims.

CONT: DRAMATIC FILM MUSIC

I hope that my film-historical antennae are more finely tuned than my cross-cultural ones, but I sense that these three events have something in common, beyond their defining role in United States history and American culture.

CABLE GUY: WELL, HI THERE, TOM… CAN I CALL YOU TOM?

Although I am not certain how they relate to my paradigm problem, I believe I can list the correspondents abroad "Where Were You When . . . ?"; or, "I Phone, Therefore I Am" ingredients of what for me constitutes a culture shock and a paradigm shift.

THOMAS' VOICE: HI ME, IT'S ME!

A catastrophic event, happening in and to the United States, at once spectacular and horrific;…

ATOMIC EXPLOSION

…my own sense of having misjudged a mood,…

ANNOUNCE
AND NOW..
HERE'S YOU
HOST FOR
TONIGHT'
MISS JUDGIN
CONTEST..
THE GREATES
MISS JUDGE
OF ALL TIM
THOMAS
EEEE !

…or otherwise been insensitive;…

SOUND OF
PENCIL
SHARPNE
GRINDIN

…and, finally, a new personal gadget, fortuitously connected with the public disaster, itself obscurely linked to a major technology-driven transformation.

MUSIC:
'DON'T
WORRY,
BE HAPPY

In other words, "gramophone, computer, telephone" (to misquote Friedrich Kittler) have successively found me at the cusp of frustrated bafflement,…

ZOOM OUT

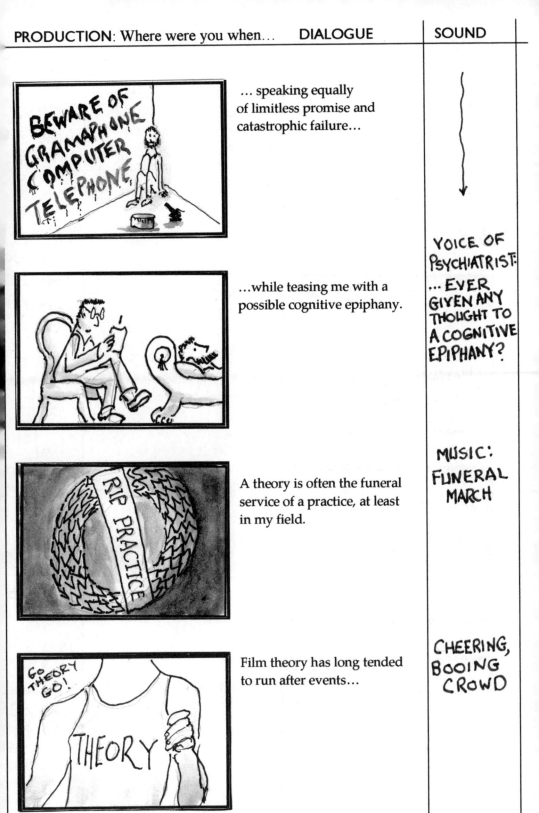

… speaking equally
of limitless promise and
catastrophic failure…

…while teasing me with a
possible cognitive epiphany.

A theory is often the funeral
service of a practice, at least
in my field.

Film theory has long tended
to run after events…

VOICE OF
PSYCHIATRIST:
… EVER
GIVEN ANY
THOUGHT TO
A COGNITIVE
EPIPHANY?

MUSIC:
FUNERAL
MARCH

CHEERING,
BOOING
CROWD

…rather than anticipate them or to declare as theory the brilliant but unsystematic remarks of a practicing critic some decade after he died, as happened with André Bazin,…

SOUNDS OF RIOTING, 'ANTICIPATE ANTICIPATE'

… father of postwar film theory,…

MUSIC BO[X] TINKLE (GODFATHER THEME)

…godfather of the nouvelle vague,…

VOICE OF BAZIN: 'AT LEAST HIS VOICE ISN'T VAGUE.'

…and pope of the neorealist aesthetic

CATHEDRAL CHIMES (CONTINUIN[G] GODFATHE[R] THEME)

Without wishing to push the comparison, I wonder what is the practice that the theory I am groping for might signal as ending?

Or put the other way round: where in these…

…examples of culture shock or tragicomic incongruity is the point at which something new that is already a practice becomes visible before a theory catches up with it?

CROSS FADE

MUSIC: INDIANA JONES THEME

This is why my particular archaeology of the present would start with the question, "Where were you when . . . ?"

History happens, and we, it seems, even more than needing to know why it happened, want to reassure ourselves of our coordinates in space and place when it happened.

TOMTOMVOIC
'YOU ARE HERE'

The Kennedy assassination serves as the watershed because it was the last media event experienced live only on radio,...

RADIO ANNOUNCE
THE PRESIDE
HAS BEEN
SHOT...

GUNSHOTS

...and the first that retrospectively, thanks to the Zapruder amateur footage, has been remastered in popular memory into a televisual media event,...

...which was given (much contested) narrative closure with a defining front-page picture, the Ruby-shooting-Oswald photograph.

GUNSHOTS
AND
SHOUTS

"Where were you when . . . ?" in other words, intuitively breaks with a particular way of picturing oneself in relation to an event.

SOUNDS OF SIRENS AND CHOPPERS

No longer am I at the apex of a triangle in a real time-space continuum as witness or bystander —a role that is implied by a question like "Did you see it happen?" or the forensic "Were you present when . . . ?"

TOM TOM VOICE: 'YOU WERE HERE, OR THERE... OR SOMEWHERE...

Modern media space is not like that, and it clearly requires a different way of situating or locating oneself.

... I SEE YOU, I SEE YOU!'

Television since the 1970s and the Internet since the 1990s are doing away with the mode of representing presence privileged in Western culture since the Renaissance (or, yes, since Rembrandt):...

SOUND OF CAMERA CLICKING

THOMAS POSING FOR PHOTO
FREEZE FRAME : A HAND TURNS THE
PHOTO OVER...

PRODUCTION: Where were you when…	DIALOGUE	SOUND

… AND WRITES ON THE BACK.

…a monocular, unifocal, perspectival projection of space, to which—besides the realist-illusionist arts (including the cinema)—our subjectivity is said to have been in thrall.

SCRATCHIN PEN

No wonder film theory is attempting to draw level with the multivocal surround immersion of space.

VARIOUS FILM SOUNDTRAC FRAGMEN

What is not so clear is how film theory can incorporate the practice so unself-consciously on display in our public spaces: our pleasure in a real-time tracking system that assures us of our existence, even as we are on the move, even as the world turns.

VOICE OVER THOMAS ECHOS IN LECTURE HALL

The universally popular, rapid acceptance of the mobile phone nudges film theory more, it seems, than the existence of digital images or access to the Internet.

MUSIC: SOUND OF MUSIC AND RINGTONE

Crossing Rembrandt Square, whether carrying a mobile phone or talking to myself or, as more often happens, doing neither,…

CONT: SOUND OF MUSIC

…I cannot help knowing I am in the midst of media space. Mobile and local and, like Nicholas de Cusa's God,…

VOICE OF GOD: HELLO, EARTH… GOD CALLING…

…at once at the center of the universe and present at every point of its circumference,…

…BOY, IT'S LONELY UP HERE… GOT ANY OLD MOVIES I CAN WATCH?

…I am the pinpointed set of coordinates in a global positioning system.

NASA LAUNCH VOICE: 'WE'VE GOT HIM PINPOINTED SOMEWHERE IN AMSTERDAM'

I phone, therefore I am

VOICE
 THOMAS:
HI THOMAS
JUST CALLE
TO SAY IT'
ME,
 THOMAS

MUSIC:
DRAMATIC
FILM
MUSIC

Never mind that the celestial grid's technical implementation might still be ten years off and its operational efficacy is for now more in evidence over Afghanistan than Amsterdam.

With the mobile phone, surveillance cameras have been installed in our minds, even before they are fully installed in our malls:...

...it's time we film historians left the cinema to keep an ear on the street and an eye on the sky.

FADE OUT

FADE OUT

ACT III

Archaeology, Avant-Garde, Archive

Reflections in a Laserdisc

Toward a Cosmology of Cinema

Michael Punt

I first met Thomas Elsaesser in 1989 at the University of East Anglia where, among many other things, he was trying to work out what Laserdisc technology could mean for Film Studies. Very soon after, I was helping him and working on a Bellourian analysis of REAR WINDOW as I was also coming to grips with some ideas about cinema and its very early years. Our association continued along these twin tracks in Amsterdam over the next decade and engulfed those rather confused years around 1995 when the cinema had its "soft focus" centenary. Discussions arose about when the cinema was actually invented and by whom, but before satisfying answers were given the celebrations were over and forgotten. In Amsterdam, I wondered not so much who had invented cinema and when, but how and why it was invented in the first place. By 2000, I had come to some conclusions about the necromantic allure of the technology. In his generous response at my defense, Elsaesser reminded us that in choosing to work with Laserdisc we had backed the wrong technology. Well maybe, but maybe not: perhaps the world backed the wrong technology. As a medium for moving image storage, the Laserdisc is far superior to its usurper – the more compact DVD – but, nonetheless, in the same year that I defended my thesis, Paramount (according to legend) released its last title on Laserdisc BRINGING OUT THE DEAD. I could not have asked for a sweeter piece of poetic justice between the beginning and the end of that particular act. Since I am now, so to speak, writing from beyond the grave, it is perhaps to be expected that this essay is a bold, and possibly academically reckless, gift to Elsaesser who always encouraged me to take the "Martian view."

To state the obvious, the priority of the invention of cinema would not be an interesting question if it had not become the movies. Consequently now, after all that work on chronologies, archaeologies, and genealogies, we know that the "when," "how," and "who" of the invention of cinema (as with any technology) are really not the most interesting questions. Thinking about the cinema as technology – before it became the movies, exactly when rather astute men such as Etienne-Jules Marey, Thomas A. Edison, and the Lumière brothers thought "the cinema an invention with doubtful prospects"– suggests more far-reaching questions about the *cinématographe* and its forebears.[1] For example, if they had no idea of cinema as an entertainment form (as clearly they could not have), what on earth could the various inventors, the various promoters, and most of all the audiences have been thinking when they saw the first moving images and found them interesting? How was it that such a simple mechanism attained such a universal interpretation in such a short time? What was it that made the "non-inventors" think that something very special was at stake in the impoverished visual experience that drew audiences over and over again? We know that the imperative of pictorial realism does not coincide with what the cinema was in 1896 or was to become in the future. We know that the delight or shock of a technological attraction is a dubious explanation given the sophistication of the popular understanding of science and technology and the extravagant spectacles offered on city streets and elsewhere. Even the lure of recovering the dead seems, at second glance, to be a late-twentieth-century bourgeois colonization of a technology which was predominantly supported by a working class for whom life was hardly an unmitigated joy. Perhaps we should start again and ask what could Ottomar Anschütz, Albert Londe, Eadweard Muybridge, Marey, Lucien Bull, Georges Demenÿ, the Skladanowsky brothers, and the host of other souls fiddling around with lamps, gears, and ribbons of celluloid have in common with the entrepreneurs and the masses who flocked to the séances over and over again?

In one of his later considerations of some of these questions, Thomas Elsaesser, as ever, raises the ante, suggesting that Louis Lumière may have been the cinema's first "virtualist." He concludes this discussion by asking us to "salute Louis Lumière as one of its [virtuality's] ancestors and begetters." And then (as if the stakes were not high enough) he asks:

> what would this salute mean? That we recognize, and therefore "know" in what ways Lumière and his epoch had, as the German historian Leopold Ranke would say, their own immediate access to God Almighty, or does it signal that we know how to explain Louis Lumière to himself, giving his particular past its own truth – restore him to full knowledge, so to speak, which he could not have had without the historian?[2]

Indeed, a historian may be needed here to restore Lumière to himself; perhaps not a historian of cinema (since that was yet to be invented), but maybe a Martian who, confronted with one of the first films that the clever and sophisticated Lumière brothers made by pointing an early version of the *cinématographe* at their own front door, asks with "naïve" candor: is this the most interesting thing these scientists could think of? These two who sold 15 million photographic plates a year, ran a business in Lyon that employed 300 people, had a worldwide network of agents, who reinvented the structure of a carbon atom, and endowed a university, who consorted with Lippmann, Marey, the Curies, and Bergson in the Collège de France and the Sorbonne and went on to further our understanding of cancer: Were their own factory gates the most interesting thing they could "film" with this brilliant machine?

It is the contention of this essay that the answer to this question is yes it was, and that in doing so, they not only demonstrated the *cinématographe* but also invented the cinema. As Elsaesser suggests, it did have something to do with God Almighty – at least the version of God as something "up there" in the heavens. I want to suggest that the filming of the world and the projection of moving images of that world in an auditorium replicated a technological cosmology that began its life in the emerging science at the start of the eighteenth century. I want to claim, perhaps more boldly, that the origins of the cinema are not found in the infinite regressions of Javanese shadow plays and experiments in ancient Greece with photosynthesis, but can be located quite precisely in 1704, with Prince Eugene of Savoy's commission for a clockwork instrument that was nurtured in the hands of the 4th Earl of Orrery in the following years.

In 1712, John Rowley, possibly with the help of clockmaker Thomas Tompian and copying George Graham's model designed in 1704, built a mechanical device demonstrating the relative positions and motions of bodies in the solar system to the 4th Earl of Orrery, Charles Boyle (1674-1731). According to most histories, by this time the so-called Scientific Revolution sparked by Nicolaus Copernicus and fuelled by Galileo Galilei and Johannes Kepler was well underway and in the safe hands of Robert Boyle, Isaac Newton, and Robert Hooke. Certainly in this baton race to reinstall man as the pivot of the universe, after having been so ignominiously dislodged from the center of God's eye (despite the resistance of the Church and the vigilance and abuses of the Inquisition), the significance of the 4th Earl of Orrery is worth revisiting. Charles Boyle, however, did far more to recentralize man since his clockwork, the orrery, is a three-dimensional schematic which places the observer in a very special position outside the universe, a position later replicated in the subject/object relationship in the cinema.

Science, as it has developed in a post-Baconian world view, is an essentially anthropocentric practice which places man at the center of an epistemological enterprise. Once it became clear that God, as it was understood at the time, could be largely indifferent to human affairs (at least as far as Bacon understood it) – that is, unconcerned with telling us everything that we needed to know – so the task of re-establishing the centrality of man was devolved, not to those qualities that were the undeniable locus of an almighty – omniscience, omnipotence and omnipresence – but to a quality that no self-respecting supreme being could have: curiosity. In this sense the scientific revolution was one in which each new discovery, theorem, and principle was not only a triumph of the intellect but also evidence of the special quality of selfless curiosity that, in the whole universe, was essentially human. As a consequence, the practice of scientific research after Copernicus progressively became an affirmation of a *state of mind* which in the process reveals the supremacy of man quite apart from the useful insights it yields. George Graham and Charles Boyle have a special place in this version of history because the orrery marks a cosmology that insists on the rejection of animism and anthropomorphism, replacing it with a clockwork expression of a new anthropocentrism; one which places the observer outside of the solar system and in the realm of the aerolites and comets.

There were, of course, many ways in which this dynamic schematic could have been represented apart from clockwork. But it was chosen because, apart from being a convenient technology to transfer, store, and release energy in a regulated way, clocks expressed the dominant idea of how the universe and human intelligence coexisted. Public clocks had become widespread in Europe from their inception in the late thirteenth century. However, during the sixteenth century, the mechanism which had been exposed as an intrinsic part of the apparatus was increasingly concealed. At the same time, as Steven Shapin observes, they "became more and more complex in the effects that they could produce and more and more integrated into the practical life of the community."[3] Shapin's argument is that the increasing complexity of the clockwork mechanisms, which often showed celestial cycles as well as the time, was not the inevitable consequence of progressive knowledge but evidence of "the power relations of an early European society whose patterns of living, producing, and political ordering were undergoing massive changes as feudalism gave way to early capitalism."[4] A technological example of this can be found in the changes to the face of the clock from a 24 to 12 hour division. Tompian, Graham, and earlier French and German clockmakers had begun this process by building superior movements with 12-hour dials which ran from midnight to noon to midnight; these overwhelmed the less "accurate" timepieces with 24-hour dials, which ran from sunset to sunset. Superior engineering was the vehicle that detached time from the earth and situated it in the known mechanics of the solar system. This social revolution was also marked by a shift toward mechanical philosophy in which the natural world could be understood as a clock. At the core of this philosophy was the appearance of a purposive agent (the clock) which was known to be the product of a human clockmaker. It was a system in which human ingenuity could produce a mechanism that convincingly appeared to have intelligence. In this system there was a place for both the inquisitive scientist and an omniscient God. The orrery can be regarded, perhaps, as a philosophical instrument which leaves the question of agency open to debate since it simultaneously suggests the supremacy of human curiosity by detaching God's eye and implanting it into the human. What is more certain is that the orrery was not only a description of the solar system, but also a philosophical system expressed in a mechanism.

The genealogy of the orrery in the representation of time duplicates the evidence of the shifting social relations evident in the depiction of space. In the pre-scientific era, European cartography typically narrativized the topography to accommodate both an aerial vision and terrestrial human desire. Fifteenth-century maps overtly told a story of what was significant, what could be significant, and how that sat in a cosmology. Viewing a map was to know a land and enter into the consciousness of the cartographer and his patron by bisecting the angle between man and the almighty. From about the middle of the sixteenth century, maps progressively adopted the point of view of an aerial observer who is (quite fortuitously) always sufficiently distant to provide the appropriate resolution to allow the reader to know what needs to be known. By the seventeenth century, however, the subjective desire of the mapmaker was concealed in the prevailing orthodoxy of an essential discontinuity between mind and body as a guarantee of truth. It formed the foundation for instrumental truth. For Galileo, whose insights derived largely from his own observational drawing, the telescope, which mediates the observer's eye, provided the guarantee of objectivity on which to base his truth claims. With such confidence he could peer up at the heavens and conduct an over-the-shoulder dialogue with God in a rapid shot/reverse shot (to coin a phrase from Hollywood) to depict the heavens as though God was looking at them from Galileo's position. Little wonder that he was shown the instruments of the Inquisition, and little wonder that he changed his point of view when the metaphysical enormity of his gesture was made clear.

Charles Boyle, on the other hand, had no such reservations. His commission to Graham was for heavens that he could look at from the outside as though he were a detached God, the intelligent agent that furnished the illusion of purposive agency to the universe. The paradox of this – a God inspecting his own work which by definition was him – would not have been missed by Boyle who had been a distinguished student at Christ Church, Oxford, and a man of letters. The orrery of 1712 made by Rowley was a copy of an earlier model which was commissioned by Boyle's contemporary, Prince Eugene of Savoy, from George Graham. Prince Eugene was Principal Imperial Commander alongside the Duke of Marlborough in the War of Spanish Succession in which Boyle rose to the rank of Major General. Boyle was also connected with Marlborough through family, and through his academic battles with Richard Bentley. The copy of the orrery, made shortly after his succession on the death of his brother, was clearly not an extravagant whim or a fashionable "toy" but an extension of his academic and worldly activities as a significant intellectual. It supported a mechanical philosophy that was nothing short of a metaphysics which separated matter from life. It refuted naturalist tendencies, which could extend the supernatural powers of a recognized God to include all manner of spiritist forces.

The orrery proposed the contemporary problematic of new science. At the same time, as it clearly acknowledged the possibility of purposive agency in the universe, it simultaneously deprived it of autonomy in a demonstration of the metaphysics of mechanical philosophy summed up by Robert Boyle in the two principles of matter and motion.[5] The cusp of this problem was where to position God in a rational system while at the same time excluding naturalist explanations of the material world. The orrery seemed to satisfy a broad spectrum of interest in and responses to science since, for all its mechanistic appearance, it was an "open" text. Although it appeared to present a precisely scaled model of an observable material reality in reducing the scale of the planets, the causal authority of clockwork detached time from matter with mechanical inevitability and so acquired the license to accelerate the diurnal and seasonal cycles.

The speculative significance of the orrery is illustrated in Joseph Wright of Derby's painting *A Philosopher giving that Lecture on the Orrery, in which a lamp is put in place of the Sun* (1766). Although he painted portraits, landscapes, and genre subjects, Wright is perhaps best known for a few paintings of scientific experiments influenced by Rembrandt's lighting. He was intimately connected with the leading scientists in Britain largely through his membership in the Lunar Society and numbered key scientists among his friends and associates. He also lived close to the clock maker John Whitehurst, and through him it is suspected he was invited to see a lecture similar to the one depicted in his painting. Here, a lecturer has positioned a lamp in place of the sun and is presumably providing a dynamic explanation of an eclipse. Around the orrery are positioned spectators who, with various degrees of fascination, look into the universe while the lecturer observes a man apparently taking notes. As with other Wright paintings the initial impression of scientific triumphalism, conveyed by the dramatic light ("enlightenment") emanating from a mechanical proof, is subtly undermined by a closer inspection of the human participants. The youngest appear to be in the thrall of a spectacle, while a certain passive – even skeptical air is distributed among the rest of the audience. Most curious too is the insecurity of the lecturer overseeing the notes. For all of Wright's association with Enlightenment science, his paintings remind us of the fundamental fragility of the scientific knowledge-base in the eighteenth century. Ultimately, the picture expresses ambivalence and uncertainty in the face of mechanical philosophy. However, what is clear, in this and his other scientific paintings, is that Wright combines art, science, and philosophy in a single gesture and places mortal man in a commanding position relative to nature and the universe.

Wright, it seems, has responded to the orrery as an idea rather than an instrument, and in it he saw a new observer, one who could remove himself from the terrestrial observatory to occupy a place outside the planets in the autochthonic position of their own creator. The paradox and instability of this point of view – observing oneself from outside of the system – formed a key question in the following century. Jonathan Crary has argued that the observer was reconstructed in the nineteenth century to regard perception as a combination of external stimuli and properties intrinsic to the human perceptual apparatus.[6] He cites experiments by Goethe in 1811 (using pressure on the eyes) and Wheatstone's stereoscopic apparatus of 1838 to show how instrumental observation displaced human perception as reliable indices of truth. The photographic camera, Crary claims, became invaluable as an epistemological object not because it replicated the human eye, but because it displaced the act of observation from the human body and devolved it to an external instrument. Instrumentation, personal ambition, and the restriction of legitimate topics became the preoccupations of scientists to the extent that, by the close of the nineteenth century, mainstream scientific enquiry was exclusively confined to professionals who had access to sophisticated apparatus. The predominantly instrumental materialist vision, which excluded lay participation, was countered by an opposition, largely supported by the arts and lay audiences, which manifested itself in a resurgence of the very belief systems that the Enlightenment and rationalism had striven so hard to dispel as superstition. Such a renaissance of an ethereal dimension in the mid-nineteenth century was short-lived. The repression of research into telepathy by scientists and a reinterpretation of the photograph as it entered the public domain as a substitute for reality (as, for example, in portraiture and pictorialism) meant that scientific naturalism penetrated all aspects of life. Nonetheless, while some leading scientists (Davy and Faraday for example) concealed their concern for spiritual matters until much later in life, many in the emerging profession of technologists retained an intellectual engagement with matters that we may now call spiritualist. There were many reasons for this, ranging from an antagonism to professional scientists who had expelled them from their ranks, to the daily engagement with the "stuff" of science as technological conduits for human interaction. The most important was that practical technicians often understood behaviors in advance of their theoretical comprehension. In the technologist's experience, technology, like medicine, was the "art" of science. In chemistry the rationality of physics at the time also did not seem to provide satisfactory explanations for the formation and behavior of atoms.

Carbon in particular seemed to lie outside the laws of physics as they were understood in the last quarter of the nineteenth century. Two scientists who were also accomplished technicians, Auguste and Louis Lumière, became convinced that another dimension was required in order to understand the complexity of the structure of the atom so as to explain the variety of combinations of connections that produced the various carbon forms. Apart from being chemists specializing in dye technologies, the Lumière brothers also had a stake in producing photographic materials for the amateur market. These interests converged in a fascination for three-dimensional photography, and they developed a number of strategies for producing images that were not confined to two-dimensional descriptions. One of these was to photograph in such a way that one of the key perceptual indicators of form (inference drawn from movement and overlap) was perpetually present in the image. Arguably, this network of interests provided the stimulus for the *cinématographe*; a small rat-trap camera (not so very different from the ones devised by photographic pioneer William Fox-Talbot) which could make a photographic record by rapid sampling, print it and project it such that the viewer perceived three dimensionality through apparent movement. In short, it was from a dissatisfaction with two dimensions that the Lumière brothers invented the apparatus now used in the cinema, not (as is often suggested) the imperative of photographic realism.

The innovation and enthusiasm with which their little machine was received surprised them, and within two years there had been more than 880,000 performances of the *cinématographe* alone. The Lumière's machines were mostly demonstrated in the context of a technological wonder, but other machines and other exhibitors integrated them with magic lantern slide shows which were very popular and widespread across Europe at the time. In retrospect, we might see the reception of moving images in a cultural environment in the thrall not of realism but more possibly in what we might now call non-locality and ethereal information (that is, the interconnection of systems and the occurrences outside normal causality). In the context of the magic lantern show, however, it formed an instructional and amusing component of a carefully constructed programme which mixed fantastic narration with travelogues and scientific instruction (which could include mechanical astrolabe slides).

The *cinématographe* and its derivatives laid claim to a cosmology which was as paradoxical, but no less satisfying than the orrery. The viewer regarded events from a point of view outside the universe in which they lived – whether it was the narration of a short story, the passage across a foreign land, or a moving image of the planets. Its special place, in the story told here, is that it technologizes the point of view of a super deity and provides an industrial apparatus in which the pleasures of the distribution of knowledge (in a narrative film for example) have sustained a nearly universal experience – the pleasures and discourses of which can be shared across time and space. The more or less unchallenged interpretation of the *cinématographe* as a "séance machine" which induced a collective experience can be linked to a very particular subject position that kinetic celestial mapping in three dimensions offers. Like the orrery, it produced a fairly particular cosmology, which found popular form in a version of cinema that had an indexical relationship with the everyday perception of the world it was projected into. The Lumière brothers were, after all, scientists at heart, and the little rat-trap box that could take, print, and project kinetic three-dimensional models of the world was a scientific instrument that closely modeled its own epistemology.

This may be just a view from the cosmos by a straying Martian, but one attraction of a cosmological explanation for the invention of cinema is that it does account for the very similar reactions to a technological arrangement that invented the cinema, even though they were experienced in different social and cultural contexts. It may also offer some explanation for the Lumières' decision to point the *cinématographe* at the doors of its origin, as well as the fatal attraction of technological miniaturization and the subsequent relegation of the Laserdisc to the museum of dead media. At very least, regarding the cinema as a cosmology provides us with an opportunity to peer through the rear window and look back in time and space and the universe from which we set off.

Notes

1.   Thomas Elsaesser, "Louis Lumière – the Cinema's First Virtualist?," *Cinema Futures: Cain Abel or Cable? The Screen Arts in the Digital Age*, ed. Thomas Elsaesser and Kay Hoffmann (Amsterdam: Amsterdam University Press, 1998) 51.

2.   Elsaesser 61.

3.   Steven Shapin, *The Scientific Revolution* (Chicago: University of Chicago Press, 1996) 33.

4.   Shapin 33.

5.   Probably for this reason Prince Eugene of Savoy's original commission to Graham is overshadowed in the history of astronomy by Charles Boyles's subsequent copy some nine years later, and the appropriation of his title as the 4th Earl of Orrery as the enduring name for the device (strictly speaking a *tullerium*). In the decades that followed, it became one of the many new instruments that were demonstrated by itinerant lecturers, and even owned by wealthy enthusiasts.

6.   Jonathan Crary, *Techniques of the Observer: On Vision and Modernity in the Nineteenth Century* (Cambridge: MIT Press, 1990).

S/M

Wanda Strauven

A *Schicksalsschlacht* for the Germans, a "miracle" for the French, the Battle of the Marne turned French commander-in-chief Joseph Joffre into one of the most popular figures of the First World War, endowing him with the nickname Papa Joffre. The mythical battle, which took place from 5 to 12 September 1914, forced the Germans to retreat in front of the "apparently almost defeated" French and British armies that Joffre had regrouped. As true counterfactual historians, "many German contemporaries believed that, without that retreat, without the lost Battle of the Marne, the 'Schlieffen Plan' would have worked, and Germany would have won the war of 1914."[1] From the French side, the battle also provides a nice example of deliberate myth building, in that Joffre marginalized the role of his own mentor Joseph Gallieni, the military governor of Paris, to whose strategic offsite perception the victory of the Allies in September 1914 could be largely accredited.[2] But because of his charming personality, it was Joffre who became the "hero of the Marne," not only in the eyes of the French and even the American public, but also – and that is most pertinent for the argument I want to develop in this essay – in the creative writing of the Italian poet Filippo Tommaso Marinetti, founder and leader of the Futurist movement.

In 1915, Marinetti composed a so-called *tavola parolibera* or poster poem, originally entitled *Montagne + Vallate + Strade × Joffre* (Mountains + Valleys + Roads × Joffre), also known as *Après la Marne, Joffre visita le front en auto* (After the Marne, Joffre Visited the Front by Car).[3] Marinetti's free-word homage visualizes Joffre's journey along mountains and valleys in a landscape without horizon and fixed coordinates, as if the poet (or the general) is exploring a new time-space dimension. At least two different, diametrically opposed perspectives are combined: while the curving letters S stand for a path seen from above (bird's-eye view), the form of the letters M suggests the vertical section of mountains and valleys observed from below (frog's-eye view). It is especially thanks to the typographic curves of the S's that motion is introduced into the poem. In some parts of the poster we see the effects of superimposition which are due to the technique of collage, that is, the cut-and-paste of words or ready-made pieces of text on the field of letters. So, the free(d) word VITESSSSSSXXXXXXSSSSS (velocity) is placed over, or rather through, the letters S and M.[4] As a dynamic synthesis of multiple views, *Montagne + Vallate + Strade × Joffre* displays an undeniable cinematic quality, which requires the reader to shift his or her "act of reading" to an "act of viewing." One could also assert that Marinetti's eye is a kino-eye *avant la lettre*, alternating and superimposing high angles, low angles, acceleration, and sound montage, and thus perceiving the front as a filmic spectacle or, better yet, as an alternative cinematic *dispositif*, as a cinema outside the cinema.

More generally speaking, Marinetti can be considered a film practitioner *sui generis*, who intuitively applied and even theorized about montage techniques, cinematic framing, animation, fast motion, and other special effects in his numerous writings, manifestos, and theater plays.[5] Whether or not Marinetti was really, directly influenced by the new medium remains difficult to verify, but – as I will try to point out – some of his cinematic affinities are to be ascribed to the S/M practices of cinema, as identified by Thomas Elsaesser. In one of his various attempts to rethink film history as "media archaeology," Elsaesser states that it is the film historian's task "to map this field as a network, rather than as discrete units." And he confesses to being "struck by the existence of what could be called (but finally are not) the S/M 'perversions' of the cinematic apparatus. Among these normally-abnormal *dispositifs* one could name: science and medicine, surveillance and the military, sensory-motor coordination in the 'movement image,' and maybe [also] 'GMS' and 'MMS,' to include the mobile phone."[6] The benefit of a notion such as S/M practices is that it forces us to think about the existence of cinema (its techniques, technologies, inventions, applications, etc.) beyond the borders of its entertainment (and even artistic) value, that is, beyond the walls of its institution as "movies." Thus, no sex and murder can be expected here, at least not as the (obligatory) ingredients of the screen's story. On the contrary, following Elsaesser's advice to describe film history "as a series of discontinuous snapshots,"[7] I will draw attention to some Italian pioneers who have operated in the various S/M *dispositifs* listed above and, where possible, read them in the light of the Futurist legacy.

Science and Medicine

I would like to begin my inventory with the somewhat forgotten Italian documentary filmmaker Roberto Omegna (1876-1948), who started his film career with reporting sports events – more specifically the first and second Susa-Moncenisio automobile races of 1904 and 1905 – and shooting exotic footage. Omegna is most famous for CACCIA AL LEOPARDO / LEOPARD HUNTING (1908), which he filmed in Eritrea "without telephoto lenses, at a few meters distance from the wild beasts."[8] This film could have inspired Marinetti's statement in his manifesto "Destruction of Syntax" (1913) regarding the cinema's function as multiplier of the sense of ubiquity, as it permits an ordinary person to participate in long-distance events of Futurist bravura. According to Marinetti: "The pusillanimous and sedentary inhabitant of any provincial town can allow himself the inebriation of danger by going to the movies and watching a great hunt in the Congo."[9] See also the manifesto "The Futurist Cinema" (1916), co-signed by Marinetti, where the only contemporary films worth mentioning are "films of travel, hunting, wars."[10]

Years before the well-known French pioneer of scientific cinema, Jean Pain-levé, started filming the wonders of marine life, Omegna made a series of ento-mological documentaries, such as La vita delle farfalle / The Life of the Butterflies (1908-1911), La vita del grillo campestre / The Life of the Cross-Country Cricket (1923-1925), and La vita delle api / The Life of the Bees (1924-1925). In these scientific films, he used time-lapse photography to render the life of several days in a few minutes, to microscopically capture the metamorphosis of the insect, "from the grub leaving its cocoon to the spreading of its wings."[11] Here again, Marinetti's "Destruction of Syntax" can be cited, more particularly the passage where he sentences "the literary I" to death and invites the new generation of poets to explore "matter and molecular life": "To rid our-selves of this obsessive 'I,' we must abandon the habit of humanizing nature, attributing human preoccupations and emotions to animals, plants, waters, stones, and clouds. Instead we should express the infinite smallness that sur-rounds us, the imperceptible, the invisible, the agitation of atoms, Brownian movements, all the passionate hypothesis and all the dominions explored by high-powered microscopes." But Marinetti's aspirations were not purely scienti-fic, as he made clear with the following explanation: "I want to introduce infinite molecular life into poetry not as a scientific document, but as an intuitive ele-ment. It should be mixed in with art works, with spectacles and dramas of what is infinitely grand, since the fusion of both constitutes the integral synthesis of life."[12]

Besides scientific filmmaking, Omegna is also the "first" to make medical doc-umentaries in Italy. In 1908, he filmed La nevropatologia / Neuropathology for the teaching purposes of Professor Camillo Negro at the University of Turin. As observed by the local press at the first screening on 17 February, the film transformed the white screen into a "vertical anatomic table" in order to show "a living sample book of the best neuropathic cases." The reviewer also emphasized Professor Negro's intention to use the cinema as a didactic tool "in smaller uni-versities, where there was a shortage of 'living' clinical material."[13] This filmic experiment became world news when six days later The New York Times pub-lished the announcement "Moving Pictures of Clinics: Prof. Negro Successfully Uses Them in Demonstrating Nervous Diseases," which was telegraphed from Rome to Clifden, Ireland, on 22 February and then transmitted to New York by Marconi Transatlantic Wireless Telegraph. According to The New York Times:

"Particularly striking have been [Prof. Negro's] demonstrations of cases of organic hysterical hemiplegia, epileptic seizures, and attacks of chorea."[14] Furthermore, the American newspaper pointed out that the cinematograph was much more suitable than "a simple photographic plate" since it could render each clinical case "in all the peculiar movements." Thus, in 1908, Omegna's experiment is received as an improvement of Albert Londe's pioneering (chrono)photographic work, undertaken at the end of the 19th century at the Salpêtrière Hospital in Paris at the service of Jean-Martin Charcot's studies of hysteria.

From a more artistic point of view, Giuliana Bruno discusses how, in 1995, Omegna's footage was given an afterlife by Douglas Gordon in his double screen video installation *Hysterical*, performing "two loops – one moving at normal speed, the other in slow motion – whose rhythms occasionally and casually meet up." In this way, LA NEVROPATOLOGIA positions itself in a typical Gordonian genealogy that "exhibits the very representational grounds upon which the filmic bodyscape itself was built and mobilized."[15]

Surveillance and the Military

From Jeremy Bentham's circular all-vision prison model to CCTV and the possible future of Google Earth as a worldwide "electronic panopticon,"[16] applications of the cinematic apparatus as surveillance system are innumerable. As for the Futurist legacy, Marinetti's central concepts of ubiquity and simultaneity can also be seen, to a certain degree, in the surveillance tradition, although they should be considered in terms of (Bergsonian) interpenetration rather than (Foucauldian) power of knowledge. A nice illustration of Futurist omnipresence, connected to the new telecommunication technologies, is found in Marinetti's recently discovered screenplay *Velocità* (Speed, ca. 1918). In the last of eleven tableaux, Marinetti imagines the Futurist man in the future, that is, 100 years later. The Futurist man is a politician who has his office in a high-speed train, equipped with a "telegraphic keyboard and countless telephone receivers." During the telecommunication transmission, one of the receivers transforms itself into a series of remote sites: "the interior of a workshop, a board room, an elegant drawing-room, an astronomical observatory, a room of the Stock market, an arsenal, the tent of a five-star general."[17] This flow of images seems to decode the phone call into a continuous moving from one place to another, into an incessant "zapping" through space. Besides this visual ubiquity, the voice of the Futurist man is instantaneously radioed – via the telephone – across the entire country. It is easy to detect in this description the proto-Fascist motif of demagogic power, which is not so much to be linked to the surveillance (all-seeing, all-knowing) capacities of the telecommunication system, but rather to its materialization of ubiquity (all-being).

Marinetti's cinematic perception in connection with the military, on the other hand, constitutes the most obvious and straightforward S/M lineage of Futurism and could be treated at great length. I will confine myself here to the lesser-known – because it was censored by the major scholars of Futurist cinema – manifesto "The Fascist Morale of Cinema" that Marinetti published in 1934 in *Sant'Elia*, a Futurist journal of anti-Semitic tendencies. Instead of expressing himself on the racial issue (which he never embraced as such), Marinetti discusses the use of the cinematograph in the Fascist school system, listing six "marvelous educational virtues" and four "demoralizing vices," that obviously should be destroyed, hence the launching of seven new virtues, among which "the aesthetics of the war in all its splendor of masses and machines, on the ground and in the air, and in all its excitement of the highest human nobility."[18] It is important to underscore that this military and bellicose aesthetics is regarded by Marinetti as a remedy for the "idiotic aesthetics of the American crime," which he lists among the "demoralizing vices" of contemporary cinema and which might refer to the pre-noir productions of Michael Curtiz, Joseph von Sternberg, Howard Hawks, and so on, that were invading the silver screen during that time. What is intrinsic to Marinetti's aesthetics of the war is not only the visual spectacle of bombardments and explosions, that most modern and dynamic "feast" which reveals the true Futurist nature of things, but also the necessity of heroism and the purification of those in action. Therefore, Marinetti, in the same manifesto, rejects the fake war documentary, or better yet, the war documentary made by "fake fighters who did not know how to control their own fear."[19]

In this respect, attention should be paid to another pioneer of Italian documentary filmmaking, Luca Comerio (1878-1940), labeled by Italian film historian Gian Piero Brunetta as one of the "apostles of the new visual verb."[20] In contrast to many Lumière cameramen, Comerio and his fellow *operatori*, such as Roberto Omegna, Giovanni Vitrotti, Vittorio Calcina, and some others, did not remain in the darkness of anonymity, eager as they were to "transmit the sense of an experience lived in first person."[21] Driven by the demons of risk, ubiquity, and speed, they perfectly embodied the Futurist ideology in formation and awakened the bourgeois audience with heroic "films of travel, hunting, wars" (cf. *supra*). According to Brunetta (and Paul Virilio), Comerio was probably the one "most in tune with Marinetti's spirit," revealing himself as a true artist of the cinematic war spectacle.[22] In 1911, Comerio left for Libya to film the Turkish-Italian conflict; closely participating in the entire expedition, he recorded the various phases, from debarkation to pacification, and made about twenty films documenting the "reality of war," not only its battles, but also "the discomforts and the waiting, the everyday lives of the soldiers and the refugees."[23] Moreover, Comerio mounted his camera on an airplane to record the battlefield, following Marinetti's advice, "from a new vantage point, no longer head on or from behind but straight down, foreshortened."[24] When the First World War broke out, Comerio went again to the front to shoot other violent images, some of which were actually censored because they were considered too raw, too realistic. He lived the war spectacle from inside, as he filmed the battlefield by moving around not only in an armored vehicle constructed for this purpose by engineer Navarro, but also on foot, in the trenches, in the forefront of the battle. A literal avant-garde filmmaker, Comerio, more than anyone else, was pushed by a truly Futurist élan, that is, by "the love of danger, the habit of energy and fearlessness" sung by Marinetti in his founding manifesto of 1909.[25] In other words, he was a real S/M-er *avant la lettre*.

Sensory-Motoring

Two interrelated pre-cyborgian concepts introduced by Marinetti in his literary manifestos are relevant to the sensory-motoring lineage (and possibly also to today's medical and engineering studies on immortality). Firstly, the notion of the "mechanical man with interchangeable parts" that is presented in the "Technical Manifesto of Futurist Literature" as the "beginning of the reign of the machine," can be read in terms of automotive mechanics as well as robotics, preceding Dziga Vertov's formula of film montage by ten years: "From one person I take the hands, the strongest and most dexterous; from another I take the legs, the swiftest and most shapely; from the third, the most beautiful and expressive head – and through montage I create a new, perfect man."[26] Secondly, Marinetti's idea of the "man multiplied by the machine" is to be understood as a first step towards the perfect fusion between the human and the mechanical in a sort of heart-motor that will allow mankind to defeat sleep and, eventually, death: "New mechanical sense, a fusion of instinct with the output of a motor and forces conquered."[27]

A wonderful incarnation of this Futurist "sensibility" can be found on the variety theater stage, more precisely in the figure of Leopoldo Fregoli (1867-1936). World-famous at the turn of the last century, this Roman conjurer dominated the theater scene of many metropolises with his protean art. His variety shows generally comprised more than sixty characters, all of whom he performed himself, by continuously changing his costumes, his voice, and his gender; his success was indeed largely related to his qualities as a female impersonator.[28] Without any mechanical intervention, Fregoli was an unprecedented master of montage. His spectacle unfolded perfectly timed and executed, a non-stop chain of short attractions that were often little exercises in montage themselves. For instance, the attraction of the cake-walk consisted of a cross-cutting between a frivolous young lady and a dandy, like in an early chase film, with the only difference being that both roles were played by one and the same man.[29] Another famous attraction was the so-called "reversed theater," where Fregoli revealed his secret of quick-change artist to the public. This meant performing for a fake audience with his face turned towards the back of the stage (which represented a theater with imaginary spectators); on the proscenium he would then carry out his transformations, before the real audience, with the help of his assistants quickly undressing and dressing him. Unlike Alfred Borden in Christopher Nolan's THE PRESTIGE (2006), Fregoli had no twin brother or look-alike. He was a machine-man, or better yet, a "living cinematograph,"[30] epitomizing the Futurist principles of dynamism, rapidity, and movement. It is therefore no coincidence that Marinetti was among his admirers. The Futurist leader went to visit him in person, during one of his tournées in Naples, and included two direct references to Fregoli in his important manifesto "The Variety Theater" (1913).

After his encounter with the Lumière brothers in 1897, Fregoli also started integrating films in his variety shows. During the projection he would hide in the wings, next to the screen, and recite the lines of the different on-screen characters, thus obtaining a perfect synchronism and the title of the "forerunner of the sound film."[31] Eventually Fregoli decided to make his own films, and with the help of war reporter Luca Comerio (!), he recorded several of his conjuring and transformation tricks as well as the above described "reversed theater" act.[32] The Fregoligraph, as the projection screen was called, turned Fregoli quite literally into a "man multiplied by the machine," provoking a tension between the stage and the screen, the trick-less Fregoli and his tricked double, dismembered and X-rayed in the film FREGOLI DOPO MORTO / LIVING DEAD FREGOLI (ca. 1898), which shows us – by means of white stripes on a black background – the dance of a "joyful skeleton."[33] Thanks to Fregoli's cinematic alter ego, some of his protean grandeur still survives to this very day.

SMS

Lastly, instead of addressing the Global System for Mobile communication (GSM) and its Multimedia Messaging Service (MMS) that together form the last S/M "perversion" listed by Elsaesser, I would like to briefly discuss the popular phenomenon of texting among mobile phone users by means of the communication protocol Short Message Service (SMS). Initially conceived of as a one-way communication system whereby call centers could send short messages such as voice mail notification to their subscribers, the industry could never have foreseen the immense success this protocol would have had as a point-to-point application, turning receivers into senders, talkers into writers. Indeed, "the decidedly unsexy SMS was of little interest to an industry bent on promoting itself as exclusive and futuristic."[34] Yet the development of a new argot – that is, the SMS "shorthand," characterized by the omission of subject pronouns and the use of abbreviations such as CUL8R ("see you later"), acronyms such as LOL ("lots of laughter"), and text-based emoticons such as :-), :-(, :-o, 8-), ;-), not to forget the mathematical kisses (xxx) – seems to follow quite literally Marinetti's Futurist poetics as theorized in the early 1910s. To render life in a more dynamic and synthetic way, Marinetti pleads for the destruction of traditional syntax and the creation of "a living style that creates itself, without the absurd pauses of commas and periods." And he adds: "To accentuate certain movements and indicate their directions, mathematical signs will be used: $+ - \times : = >$, along with musical notations."[35] Marinetti's (theoretical) dislike of nouns "sandwiched" between adjectives and verbs and his preference for a speedy, telegraphic language that has recourse to the "abstract aridity" of mathematical symbols and other "very brief or anonymous" signs sound incredibly modern and progressive in the light of today's media usage. Conversely, thanks to the SMS protocol's restrictions, that is, its limit of 160 characters and its rather complex multi-tap writing method, many (young) mobile phone users across the world have become the Futurist poets of the 21st century, some of them manifesting actual physiological changes in their thumbs.[36]

Hence, SMS can be inscribed in the Kittlerian genealogy of writing systems, from the telegraph and phonograph to the cinematograph and the typewriter, all of which could be read in the light of "Spiritualism and Mediumship," an additional S/M "perversion" already explored by Friedrich Kittler himself and others.[37] Among the 1900 writing systems, special attention should be given to the wireless telegraph, invented in 1895 by Guglielmo Marconi (1874-1937). As Timothy Campbell has pointed out, the wireless must be distinguished from the radio, in that the former is a technology based on the inscription of sounds while the latter is a system of voice transmission.[38] The wireless operation system should therefore be addressed as a process of writing, through the "medium" of the wireless operator, who often trans- or deformed the coded message, due to mishearings and/or misspellings. Marconi's wireless telegraphy, known in French and Italian as T.S.F. (*télégraphie sans fils, telegrafo senza fili*), is at the very source of Marinetti's concept of "wireless imagination" (*immaginazione senza fili*) and a recurring motif in his free-word poetry. Marinetti's abolition of proper syn-

tax and proper spelling can be explained in wireless terms, as suggested by
Campbell: "Spelling will go the way of syntax, conjugated verbs, and the adverb,
mere clutter on the highway to a more abstract symbolic encoding of the real.
Interestingly, previously correct spellings of words also undergo a change, a de-
formation that occurs in the act of transmission by a wireless imagination to the
writing hand. They are the material proof that a transmission is taking or has
taken place."[39]

Z

If I now look back at the free-word poster poem singing the glories of Joffre's
dynamic journey to the Marne, I am struck by the presence of two smaller Z's
that could be "decoded" not only as the zigzagging of hairpin bends in a mountain road but also as misspelled S's. Or is the S a misspelled/mirrored Z? According to Roland Barthes, "Z is the letter of mutilation: phonetically, Z stings like a
chastising lash, an avenging insect; graphically, cast slantwise by the hand across
the blank regularity of the page, amid the curves of the alphabet, like an oblique
and illicit blade, it cuts, slashes, or, as we say in French, *zebras*; from a Balzacian
viewpoint, this Z (which appears in Balzac's name [and in the Dutch spelling of
Alsacian: *Elzasser*]) is the letter of deviation."[40]

In Futurist terms, Z's are preferred over S's, because they combine straight
lines instead of curved lines. In "Destruction of Syntax," Marinetti eulogizes the
straight line for its synthetic visualization of speed and connects it to the movement of trains and cars through tunnels, which could be interpreted as an implicit reference to the early film genre of the "phantom ride."[41] This confirms, once
more, Marinetti's cinematic perspicacity outside the institution of cinema. Molecular life, visual ubiquity, war aesthetics, mechanically multiplied men, telegraphic poetry, and the sharp-edged Z of Zpeed, these are all S/M ingredients of
a true Futurist cinema, an "art-action" *dispositif*, that was never fully achieved during the heyday of Futurism but that appears to have penetrated our present-day
media landscape all the more.

Notes

1.   Annika Mombauer, "The Battle of the Marne: Myths and Reality of Germany's 'Fate-
     ful Battle,'" *The Historian* 68.4 (Dec. 2006): 748.
2.   Robert B. Bruce, "America Embraces France: Marshal Joseph Joffre and the French
     Mission to the United States, April-May 1917," *The Journal of Military History* 66.2
     (April 2002): 411, note 11.

3. The poster poem was renamed *Après la Marne, Joffre visita le front en auto* for its pub-
    lication in the collection *Les mots en liberté futuristes* (Milano: Edizioni futuriste di
    "Poesia," 1919), together with another famous poster poem *Morbidezze in agguato +
    bombarde italiane* (1917), re-titled *Le soir, couchée dans son lit, elle relisait la lettre de son
    artilleur au front.*

4. See <http://www.getty.edu/art/exhibitions/tumultuous/marinetti_marne.html> for
    an on-line image of the poster poem.

5. For a close reading of Marinetti's writings in cinematic terms, I refer to my *Marinetti
    e il cinema: tra attrazione e sperimentazione* (Udine: Campanotto, 2006).

6. Thomas Elsaesser, "Early Film History and Multi-Media: An Archaeology of Possible
    Futures?," *New Media, Old Media: A History and Theory Reader*, ed. Wendy Hui Kong
    Chun and Thomas Keenan (New York: Routledge, 2005) 17. For other media archae-
    ological speculations by Elsaesser, see, among others, "Early Cinema: From Linear
    History to Mass Media Archaeology," *Early Cinema: Space Frame Narrative*, ed. Tho-
    mas Elsaesser (London: BFI, 1990), *Filmgeschichte und fruehes Kino. Archaeologie eines
    Medienwandels* (Munich: text + kritik, 2002), and "Film History as Media Archaeol-
    ogy," *CiNéMAS* 14.2-3 (2005): 75-117.

7. Elsaesser, "Early Film History and Multi-Media" 17.

8. From the last interview with Omegna, quoted in Virgilio Tosi, "Il pioniere Roberto
    Omegna (1876-1948)," *Bianco e Nero* 40.3 (March-June 1979): 14.

9. F.T. Marinetti, "Destruction of Syntax – Wireless Imagination – Words-in-Freedom,"
    Modernism: An Anthology, ed. Lawrence Rainey (Oxford: Blackwell, 2005) 28.

10. F.T. Marinetti, Bruno Corra, Emilio Settimelli, Arnaldo Ginna, Giacomo Balla, and
    Remo Chiti, "The Futurist Cinema," *Futurismo & Futurismi*, ed. Pontus Hulten (Lon-
    don: Thames & Hudson, 1992) 451.

11. Tosi 28. In his 60-page article, Tosi gives a detailed description of the various ento-
    mological documentaries and other nature films made by Omegna in the 1920s and
    1930s. By way of comparison, Painlevé made his first aquatic documentary, titled
    L'ŒUF D'ÉPINOCHE: DE LA FÉCONDATION À L'ÉCLOSION / STICKLEBACK EGGS, only in
    1927.

12. Marinetti, "Destruction of Syntax" 31.

13. Quoted in Tosi 20.

14. "Moving Pictures of Clinics: Prof. Negro Successfully Uses Them in Demonstrating
    Nervous Diseases," *The New York Times* (23 Feb. 1908): <http://query.nytimes.com/
    mem/archive-free/pdf?_r=1&res=9C05E4D81F3EE233A25750-
    C2A9649C946997D6CF&oref=slogin>.

15. Giuliana Bruno, "Collection and Recollection: On Film Itineraries and Museum
    Walks," *Camera Obscura Camera Lucida*, ed. Robert Allen and Malcolm Turvey (Am-
    sterdam: Amsterdam University Press, 2003) 236. Bruno also cites the above quoted
    reviewer from Turin and identifies the source as follows: Mario Dall'Olio, "La neuro-
    patologia al cinematografo," *La gazzetta di Torino* (18 Feb. 1908).

16. This hypothesis is developed by Lærke Rasmussen in her student paper for the
    course Media Archaeology, "Ogen in de ruimte? Google Earth en de nieuwe beeld-
    cultuur" (Jan. 2008).

17. F.T. Marinetti, "Speed," *Fotogenia* 2 (1995): 147.

18. F.T. Marinetti, "La morale fascista del cinematografo," *Sant'Elia* (April 1934); also in Enrico Crispolti, *Il mito della macchina e altri temi del futurismo* (Trapani: Celebes, 1969) 579; my translation.

19. F.T. Marinetti, "La morale fascista" 579; my translation.

20. Gian Piero Brunetta, *Cent'anni di cinema italiano* (Roma / Bari: Laterza, 1991) 91.

21. Gian Piero Brunetta, *Storia del cinema italiano*, vol. 1: *Il cinema muto 1895-1929* (Roma: Editori Riuniti, 1993) 23.

22. Brunetta, *Cent'anni* 90. Brunetta refers to Paul Virilio's "L'aeromitologia futurista," *Velocittà: Cinema & Futurismo*, ed. Paolo Bertetto and Germano Celaut (Milano: Bompiani, 1986) 88-91.

23. Carla Manenti, *Luca Comerio fotografo e cineasta* (Milano: Electa, 1979) 46.

24. F.T. Marinetti, "Technical Manifesto of Futurist Literature," *Modernism: An Anthology* 18.

25. F.T. Marinetti, "The Founding and the Manifesto of Futurism," *Modernism: An Anthology* 4.

26. *Kino-Eye: The Writings of Dziga Vertov*, trans. Annette Michelson, ed. Kevin O'Brien (Berkeley: California University Press, 1984) 17. Compare this to Marinetti's words: "After the reign of the animal, behold the beginning of the reign of the machine. Through growing familiarity and friendship with matter, which scientists can know only in its physical and chemical reactions, we are preparing the creation of the mechanical man with interchangeable parts. We will liberate man from the idea of death, and hence from death itself, the supreme definition of the logical mind." (*Modernism: An Anthology* 19).

27. Marinetti, "Destruction of Syntax" 25.

28. Vittoria Ottolenghi, "Fregoli," *Enciclopedia dello Spettacolo*, vol. 4 (Roma: Le Maschere, 1958). See also Jean Nohain and François Caradec, *Fregoli, sa vie, ses secrets* (Paris: La Jeune Parque, 1968).

29. See Glauco Pellegrini, "Fregoli ou Le premier 'appareil' de projection sonore," *La revue du cinéma* 14 (June 1948): 49: "Le voici: il sort de scène, à droite, sous l'aspect d'une vaporeuse jeune fille à robe de mousseline et ombrelle. Il revient presque instantanément, à gauche, au rythme d'un *cake-walk*: et c'est un frétillant gandin monoclé qui poursuit la demoiselle. Puis on le revoit en jeune fille et, immédiatement après, de nouveau en gandin."

30. This label was used in *Tribuna Illustrata* (18 Dec. 1904) in reference to one of Fregoli's imitators.

31. Mario Corsi, "Fregoli pioniere del muto e precursore del sonoro," *Cinema* 1.11 (Dec. 1936).

32. Actually, there exist two films of this attraction: FREGOLI DIETRO LE QUINTE / FREGOLI BEHIND THE SCENES (ca. 1898) and its remake SEGRETO PER VESTIRSI (CON AIUTO) / SECRET OF GETTING DRESSED (WITH HELP) (ca. 1898). In the latter, the frontal fixed framing is interrupted twice by a shot from a different angle, and fast motion is introduced to enhance the quick-change art of Fregoli. A copy of this film is preserved at the Cinémathèque Royale de Bruxelles.

33. This is the title of a 1898 Lumière film, presenting the same attraction.

34. Alex S. Taylor and Jane Vincent, "An SMS History," *Mobile World: Past, Present and Future*, ed. Lynne Hamill, Amparo Lasen, and Dan Diaper (London: Springer, 2005) 79.

35. Marinetti, "Technical Manifesto of Futurist Literature" 16.

36. "Mobiele telefoon doet duim muteren," *Gazet van Antwerpen* (24 March 2002): <http://antwerpen.gva.be/nieuws-nieuwe-media-wetenschap/2002/03/24/mobiele-telefoon-doet-duim-muteren.html>. An interesting illustration of today's revival of the Futurist poetics is the "160" column in *NRC/Next* wherein SMS poems by readers are published. The column has its proper manifesto with six bulleted rules. See: <http://www.precies160.nl/#pageID=11>.

37. In his introduction to *Gramophone, Film, Typewriter* (Stanford: Stanford University Press, 1999), Kittler observes: "... the invention of the Morse alphabet in 1873 was promptly followed by the tapping specters of spiritistic séances sending their messages from the realm of the dead. Promptly as well, photographic plates – even and especially those taken with the camera shutter closed – furnished reproductions of ghosts or specters, whose black-and-white fuzziness only served to underscore the promise of resemblance. Finally, one of the ten applications Edison envisioned for his newly invented phonograph in the *North American Review* (1878) was to record 'the last words of dying persons.'" (12). See also Jeffrey Sconce, *Haunted Media: Electronic Presence from Telegraphy to Television* (Durham: Duke University Press, 2000).

38. Timothy C. Campbell, *Wireless Writing in the Age of Marconi* (Minneapolis / London: University of Minnesota Press, 2006).

39. Campbell 90.

40. Roland Barthes, *S/Z*, trans. Richard Miller (New York: Hill and Wang, 1974) 106.

41. Marinetti, "Destruction of Syntax" 29: "Disgust for the curving line, the spiral, and the *tourniquet*. Love for the straight line and the tunnel. The habit of foreshortened views and visual syntheses created by the speed of trains and automobiles which look down over cities and country landscapes. Dread of slowness, minutiae, detailed analyses and explanations. Love of speed, abbreviation and synopsis."

Consumer Technology after Surveillance Theory

Richard Rogers[1]

Picture a prison in a Hollywood film, with long lanes of adjacent cells full of prisoners. The prisoners are shouting and smashing their dinner trays against the bars. But then, the Nokia ring tone pierces the corridor. The guard checks his pockets, but his phone is not ringing. All of the prisoners simultaneously reach into their overalls, and one pulls out a ringing phone. The idea of prisoners being called by their friends on the outside or even fellow prisoners is shocking, suggesting that they are completely beyond control.

Aside from the consumer-prisoner scenario described above, affix the word consumer to the otherwise disciplined, and consider some events of the recent past. The consumer-soldier provided the Abu Ghraib torture shots, for example. The consumer-worker writes a blog that criticizes the corporation. The consumer-student uses his own laptop and provider, avoiding the university's server and its log files. The consumer-patient looks at her chart and Googles her condition, checking the prescribed treatment against postings in the patient discussion forum. In other words, the Foucauldian subjects of surveillance now own and use consumer technology, which makes them unruly. Michel Foucault described how surveillance disciplined people in enclosed spaces – the prison, the barracks, the hospital, the factory, and the school. Design as well as techniques (the institution's daily "regime") eventually reformed bodies and made them docile.[2] In the eighteenth and nineteenth centuries, the periods analyzed by Foucault, people will have had consumer technology, or personal objects foreign to the institutional regime. Thus far, however, the personal objects carried and accessed by the subjects under surveillance have barely been considered.

Does surveillance theory currently take the consumer-prisoner, consumer-soldier, consumer-worker, consumer-student, and consumer-patient into account? It does take the consumer into account, at least. According to surveillance theory after Foucault, consumers are enticed into participating in the act of being watched in exchange for product, as Mark Poster and Greg Elmer have noted.[3] Participatory surveillance describes how the consumer must leave traces and thereby becomes subject to dataveillance, as Roger Clarke has termed it, the current state of which is described below.[4] Click-and-agree as well as click-and-buy have an intermediary step, however, where it is noted in the scroll-down what information is collected about you. Michael Stevenson sums it all up in a new media project called "The whatever button."[5] The Firefox extension replaces command confirmation buttons with "whatever." Normally, one simply clicks through the various buttons ("I agree," "I accept," "I confirm"), and receives the product. In response to the interactions in between, one would simply say, "whatever." There is a sense of docility and perhaps futility in Stevenson's notion, which surveillance theorists keep in mind, as well. To participate in consumer society, you have to be watched. It is not so much that resistance is futile. It has more to do with the fact that there is just too much interactivity. Elmer writes that turning cookies off blackens out much of the Web's access for the surfer.[6] Having to confirm every cookie, after setting advanced privacy preferences, unleashes a barrage of browser alerts. Eventually, one yields back to the default setting, and carries on with "whatever." Click-and-buy has one of its finer moments in the patented "1-click" purchasing system by Amazon, which frees the consumer from the "whatever" step. To be able to consume products even faster, in a single click, you must have all your data pre-filled, well formed, and fresh. Thomas Elsaesser has suggested that our data body – the set of stored personal details that grants us access to product or space – must remain well groomed, so as to get it ready for the day, like brushing one's teeth in the morning.[7]

Theorists and consumers alike are already familiar with consuming at a quickened pace. As Manuel Castells points out, for some time now surveillance has allowed the docile to consume not simply products but space, as through airports to the next remote comfort lounge.[8] Docile bodies moving quickly is an unfamiliar image, for we are more accustomed to the Orwellian motion pictures – hordes of the similarly clad, ambulating like sleepwalkers, whether in factory outfits or in late 1940s business suits, hats, and shoes.[9] The backdrop is Pittsburgh's dense smog. Surveillance and disciplining regimes once used to drain energy, and slow commerce. To become human again after mechanization, and to resist, factory workers would "pace" themselves, and perhaps strike. That is to say, the watchful, disciplining regime eventually would slow down money and people. Nowadays, it speeds things up.

As in George Orwell's *Nineteen Eighty-Four,* those worth watching and under the highest levels of surveillance are the "kinetic elite," who are able to consume dedicated flow space by passing quickly through its gateways.[10] The "space of flows," as Castells termed it, consists of three layers: the hardware and its electronic impulses, the network topology of cable links, and the organization of space for the managerial elite.[11] It is the third layer that is of interest in the access society, a term employed by Jeremy Rifkin.[12] Those under less surveillance – like Orwell's Progs who do not merit watching – sadly wait in line by economy class check-in, with too much luggage. Their flow is impeded. They hurry up and wait, caught repeatedly by Deleuzian fencing. Gilles Deleuze took issue with Foucault, saying that the password society has superceded the panoptic society.[13] Surveillance no longer reforms bodies, it grants physical access to bodies of various sizes instead. One need not be in shape, physically, though looks remain important. Those passing through controls most swiftly have their data bodies well formed, like good code. As Peter Adey writes, waiting at customs at Amsterdam Schiphol Airport and watching businessmen arch their necks for the Privium eye-scanner is a Deleuzian moment.[14] It is not so much that a given elite has its own lounges, passageways, and gateways, in a Castellsian sense (like royalty had its own waiting rooms, entrances, and exits at train stations); it is more that flow space is a result of "privileges." One's achieved "level" unlocks free space – as in a computer or video game.

The "data body" was coined by the Critical Art Ensemble, taking a cue from Mark Poster's data double. The Critical Art Ensemble (CAE) defined it as "the total collection of files connected to an individual" – a collection "in service" to corporations and the state.[15] While Poster believes that the data double impoverishes the self by reducing it to fields in a database with character length limits, the CAE actually thinks it becomes far richer. All data are in play: "No detail of social life is too insignificant to record and to scrutinize."[16] Wendy Chun has discussed how the Internet has brought with it not only the idea of a "freedom frontier," but also that of a "dark machine of [state] control." The latter myth, she writes, "screens the impossibility of storing, accessing and analyzing everything... Even the US National Security Agency (NSA) admits this impossibility."[17] In other words, the question nowadays is not so much whether data are collected and stored, but rather how they are indexed and made queriable. Firstly, with respect to its collection, there was the issue of the ephemerality of data. The memory rot that so worries digital librarians and archivists, combined with the maintenance of old machines to view the content in something like its original setting, are less the issue than query machines just stopping, when the scripts break. One normally concerns oneself with exploits, and subsequent inrushes of spam and the editbots, automatically changing Wikipedia pages.[18] Networked content is at risk. Who forgot to turn the filter back on after the re-install? Now look at the mess.

But, secondly, the data sets are becoming increasingly bounded by time in ways different from digital decay. When privacy advocates negotiate data retention durations, they are also creating limited query windows. How long should the police keep video surveillance data? How long should a search engine keep user data? In 2007, Google, for example, agreed to anonymize user data that was over 18 months old, changing an earlier proposal that read "18 to 24 months," as Peter Fleicher, the company's Global Privacy Counsel, writes on the official

Google blog.[19] Whilst the 6-month difference is banal (but may also be a product of Google's organizational culture – their servers also last 18 months), the time-frame creates new urgencies for the query machines seeking, as Fleicher continues in bullet points:

- to defend our systems from malicious access and exploitation attempts;
- to maintain the integrity of our systems by fighting click fraud and web spam;
- to protect our users from threats like spam and phishing; [and]
- to respond to valid legal orders from law enforcement as they investigate and prosecute serious crimes like child exploitation.[20]

The study of anonymized profiles of users is only just beginning, and their current constitution in search engine space is not well interrogated. The famous case of the release of AOL search engine query data in 2006 made news for its "disturbing glimpse into users' lives."[21] Later, it became an item in the US House of Representatives, where the Congressman from Massachusetts remarked: "We must stop companies from unnecessarily storing the building blocks of American citizens' private lives."[22] Here is how Declan McCullagh, the staff writer at CNET News, introduces the story of a person sharing his life in his search strings, including his queries:

> AOL user 311045 apparently owns a Scion XB automobile in need of new brake pads that is in the process of being upgraded with performance oil filters. User 311045, possibly a Florida resident, is preoccupied with another topic as well:
> *how to change brake pads on scion xb 2005*
> *us open cup florida state champions*
> *how to get revenge on a ex*
> *how to get revenge on a ex girlfriend*
> *how to get revenge on a friend who f—ed you over*
> *replacement bumper for scion xb*
> *florida department of law enforcement*
> *crime stoppers florida*[23]

Further questions arise beyond what users may expect from search engines. These now also have to do with the everyday disappearance of the query environment as well as the results. The server logs keep the queries, as well as the clicked-on items (not shown above), but not all of the results that were offered. Moreover, they remain ephemeral; one cannot recreate search engine query results from the past. This allows search engines to shift the blame and responsibility to the users.

But *anonymized*, 18-month-old profiles of exploiters, spammers, phishers, frauds, and other anomalous users also raise somewhat different questions from those previously put forward by database philosophers who were critically concerned with aberrance as a normal outcome of algorithmic queries of large, stored collections of data. Profiles are slices of norms, and generate niches as well as "niche envy," as Joseph Turow writes.[24] The Internet has changed advertising as an art form for the masses (on TV and billboards) back to that of the pedestrian "direct advertising" of the weary door-to-door salesman, lugging product. "Direct," to use the short form, now relies on the collection of individual data, knowing not the customer, as in the past, but the customer type. Demographics, although important, are merely broad indicators compared to the specific purchase histories in what Elmer has termed the personal information economy. "Customers who bought this item also bought..." is one form of recommendation that *thrives* on anonymous users.

Turow's "niche envy" is a concern not so much for the daily grooming of the data body that Elsaesser discussed, resulting in the ability to consume product and space rapidly, but more about people knowing other people's data bodies, and desiring them. The constant uproars amongst Facebook users are cases in point. The social software continues to increase the number of sticky events in the social network. Previously, one's edits to a Facebook page or to friends' pages were not broadcasted, until early September 2006, when a student posting from the Campus Progress blog appeared on Slashdot:

> So-and-so is "no longer single." Someone else removed "the Hubble Telescope" from their interests. Apparently, 10 of my friends "care about the End the Genocide in Darfur campaign issue." For those who haven't logged on, not to mention the poor souls who aren't on Facebook, here's what the networking site introduced just after midnight, California time, last night: The site now records the minutia of everyone's moment-by-moment activities on Facebook, and aggregates them all to a handy "News Feed" page, and a "Mini-Feed" on every profile.[25]

After user protest, the feeds became an option, instead of the default. More recently, another default versus global opt-out episode unfolded. Beacon, introduced by Facebook in December 2007, takes feed analysis to a new level of niche marketing. Whereas in the past one's anonymized purchases were logged on a single site and recommended to others (Amazon), with Beacon a Facebook user is alerted to friends' purchases from multiple sites (via their captured and aggregated feeds). The backlash came from Moveon.org, the online, political progressive organizer, with a campaign and a petition, where one Moveon.org member and Facebook user wrote: "Oh my gosh, my cousin's entire Christmas shopping list this week was displayed on the [Facebook News] feed."[26] Whilst the outcry was smaller (0.1% of users joined the Moveon.org campaign as opposed to 7% joining the earlier protest group, "Students against Facebook News Feed"), Facebook yielded once more, allowing users to opt out of what it describes as organic and social promotion of product – by adding just three lines of code.[27]

What to do? To theorists, artists, activists, and NGOs, awareness may bring change. We should know how much we are participating in the surveillance society, and that not possessing the local supermarket's loyalty card is the equivalent in surveillance thought to being punished (as without the loyalty card one pays more). It becomes expensive when one tries to avoid participating in the surveillance society. To raise consumer consciousness, Michael Stevenson proposes that supermarkets install an additional viewing screen. As soon as the loyalty card is scanned and you are rewarded with your discounted items, you also see the dynamic back-end, or what Lev Manovich has called new media: capture, store, interface, search, to which may be added: algorithm and recommend.[28] Perhaps consumers would like to see their shopper profiles when they check out, and be made aware of how collective profiles shape (shelf) space. Products are recommended (and shelved) on the basis of collective past purchases; new products are "related," in a relational database sense, to ones well consumed by the profiles passing through the supermarket. Corporate research departments also scout awareness-raising projects, which are often initiated by artists. It is in this context that Eric Kluitenberg refers to artist-designer projects as accidental, unpaid beta testing.[29] In December 2007, a Google query for "RFID workshop" Amsterdam returned 880 results, many of which referred to a series of radio frequency identification (RFID) tag events, attended by hackers, artists, thinkers, programmers, and facilitators. For example at the PICNIC'07-event in Amsterdam, people tagged themselves in the hope that an application would be hacked together to enable the like-minded, or similarly interested, to locate each other. Interest fields in the database would network people live. Social life would imitate new media.

Another strategy for dealing with the surveillance society lies in data body self-help. The aware and profiled consumer may try to reassert his idiosyncrasy, becoming less like consumer shop-alikes, or algorithmically social networkers with related interest tags, and more a unique, special individual. Looking at the profiling machine with a transparent back-end, the shopper may ask: "Can I escape from this particular rendering of myself? Can I recompile my *data self*?" First, here's a poignant example of how the self is taken over by data capture, storage, algorithm, and recommendation, and how the consumer tries to reassert himself, armed with knowledge of how his TV and digital video recorder store interactions and subsequently recommend content. In 2002, the *Wall Street Journal* wrote:

> Mr. Iwanyk, 32 years old, first suspected that his TiVo thought he was gay, since it inexplicably kept recording programs with gay themes. A film studio executive in Los

Angeles and the self-described "straightest guy on earth," he tried to tame TiVo's gay fixation by recording war movies and other "guy stuff." ... "The problem was, I over-compensated," he says. "It started giving me documentaries on Joseph Goebbels and Adolf Eichmann. It stopped thinking I was gay and decided I was a crazy guy reminiscing about the Third Reich."[30]

Of course the user may not like what a machine has captured, stored, and algorithmically recommended. He may try to make his data body cooperate with his current preferences, so as to improve his future profile. (There is yourself, and a simulation of a future self, as William Bogard writes.[31] The *simself* is a surveillance product of great value.) The question concerns whether consumer technology will allow him to reestablish himself. For example, can he really clear his history? Previously expressed preferences may cast unwanted shadows on the future.

The larger question for consumer technology has to do with whether it needs to know you in order for you to consume it. This is familiar ground. To consume space, you can no longer simply remain anonymous, like Walter Benjamin's *flâneur* once was.[32] The *flâneur* was able to blend into the urban crowd. Up until the 1950s, one could board an ocean liner, and just disappear. Board an airplane these days and you re-appear. The current impossibility of anonymous movement has been captured in the notion of the "disappearance of disappearance," as Kevin Haggerty and Richard Ericson put it.[33]

The disappearance of disappearance is evident in the consumer safety city, as the *flâneur* and the anonymous shopper are on the verge of extinction. Moreover, in consuming product, as opposed to space, surveillance is no longer limited to the (kinetic) elite. Everyday people, the under-surveilled progs in Orwell's terms, or the data body-challenged queued up in airports, the *dividuals* in Deleuzian terms, are increasingly the subjects of surveillance. The question remains whether the unruly consumer-prisoner, consumer-soldier, consumer-patient, consumer-worker, and consumer-student are using products without surveillance built in. Which consumer technology is still available without it? (Consider buying professional grade technology, and set mode to manual.)

Notes

1.   The original version of this piece was co-written with Sabine Niederer and published in *Cut-Up* 32 (25 Oct. 2006). The authors would like to thank the Databodies research interns, convened in early 2006 by the Institute of Network Cultures, Hogeschool van Amsterdam, and Media Studies, University of Amsterdam: Bas Bisseling, Heleen van der Klink, Jasper Moes, Jerneja Rebernak, Daphne Ben Shachar, Loes

Sikkes, Michael Stevenson, and Esther Weltevrede. This internship was inspired by Eric Kluitenberg's "Databodies," De Balie, Center for Culture and Politics, Amsterdam 2004. Our thanks also go to Pierre Ballings and Maarten van Boven at the Paradiso, Amsterdam for organizing the related event, ParaPlay, on 26 Oct. 2006.

2. Michel Foucault, *Discipline and Punish: The Birth of the Prison*, trans. Alan Sheridan (New York: Vintage, 1979).

3. Greg Elmer, "A Diagram of Panoptic Surveillance," *New Media & Society* 5.2 (2003): 231-247; and Mark Poster, *The Mode of Information* (Chicago: University of Chicago Press, 1990).

4. Roger Clarke, "Information Technology and Dataveillance," *Communications of the ACM* 31.5 (1988): 498-512.

5. Michael Stevenson, "The Whatever Button," <http://www.whateverbutton.com>, accessed on 1 Nov. 2007.

6. Greg Elmer, *Profiling Machines* (Cambridge, MA: MIT Press, 2004).

7. Personal communication with Thomas Elsaesser, 20 Dec. 2005, in Amsterdam.

8. Manuel Castells, *The Rise of the Network Society* (Oxford: Blackwell, 1996).

9. BRAZIL (Terry Gilliam, 1985) and the Apple MacIntosh "Big Brother" TV commercial aired during the Super Bowl, 22 Jan. 1984.

10. George Orwell, *Nineteen Eighty-Four* (London: Secker and Warburg, 1949). The notion of the "kinetic elite" is attributed to Peter Sloterdijk.

11. Castells 1996.

12. Jeremy Rifkin, *The Age of Access: How Networked Services Change the Economy, and Us* (Harmondsworth: Penguin, 2000).

13. Gilles Deleuze, "Postscript on Control Societies," *Ctrl Space: Rhetorics of Surveillance from Bentham to Big Brother*, ed. Thomas Levin, Ursula Frohne, and Peter Weibel (Cambridge, MA: MIT Press, 2002) 317-321.

14. Peter Adey, "Secured and Sorted Mobilities: Examples from the Airport," *Surveillance & Society*, 1.4 (2004): 500-519.

15. Critical Art Ensemble, *Flesh Machine* (New York: Autonomedia, 1998) 145.

16. Critical Art Ensemble.

17. Wendy Chun, *Control and Freedom: Power and Paranoia in the Age of Fiber Optics* (Cambridge, MA: MIT Press, 2006) 2.

18. Alexander Galloway and Eugene Thacker, *The Exploit: A Theory of Networks* (Minnesota: University of Minnesota Press, 2007).

19. Peter Fleischer, "How Long Should Google Remember Searches?," *Official Google Blog* (11 June 2007): <http://googleblog.blogspot.com/2007/06/how-long-should-google-remember.html>.

20. Fleischer.

21. Declan McCullagh, "AOL's Disturbing Glimpse into Users' Lives," *CNET News* (7 Aug. 2006): <http://www.news.com/AOLs-disturbing-glimpse-into-users-lives/2100-1030_3-6103098.html>.

22. Declan McCullagh, "AOL Gaffe Draws Capitol Hill Rebuke," *CNET News* (9 Aug. 2006): <http://www.news.com/2100-1028_3-6104040.html>.

23. McCullagh, "AOL's Disturbing Glimpse."

24. Joseph Turow, *Niche Envy* (Cambridge, MA: MIT Press, 2006).

25. Graham Webster, "Doug Jones Sneezed. 1:23pm," *Campus Progress Blog* (5 Sept. 2006): <http://campusprogress.org/features/1138/big-brother-is-poking-you>.

26. Moveon.org, Facebook Privacy Campaign Petition (Dec. 2007): <http://civ.moveon.org/facebookprivacy/071120email.html>.

27. "Beacon Protests a Hundred Times Smaller than News Feed Uproar," *Valleywag* (5 Dec. 2007): <http://valleywag.com/tech/facebook/beacon-protests-a-hundred-times-smaller-than-news-feed-uproar-330299.php>.

28. Lev Manovich, "New Media: Capture, Store, Interface, Search," lecture delivered at the University of Amsterdam (29 Nov. 2005).

29. Personal communication with Eric Kluitenberg, 2 Oct. 2004, in Riga.

30. Jeffrey Zaslow, "If TiVo Thinks You Are Gay, Here's How to Set It Straight," *Wall Street Journal* (22 Nov. 2002).

31. William Bogard, *The Simulation of Surveillance* (Cambridge: Cambridge University Press, 1996).

32. Walter Benjamin, *The Arcades Project*, trans. Howard Eiland and Kevin McLaughlin (Cambridge, MA: Harvard University Press, 1999).

33. Kevin D. Haggerty and Richard V. Ericson, "The Surveillant Assemblage," *British Journal of Sociology* 51.4 (2000): 605-622.

Migratory Terrorism

Mieke Bal

A fabulous painting by Marlene Dumas titled *Neighbor* (2004) depicts the figure of a migrant.[1] In many subtle ways his migratory status is evoked within the image. The depicted man is not just, say, Middle Eastern. It is not just the *jelabba* he is wearing underneath his western jacket. There is something in his face – a shadow of a dark beard, and it is especially his eyes that suggest "foreignness" or more specifically, "Arabness." Not a beard but the shadow of one; a *jelabba* as well as a jacket. There are more details that indicate the figure of the migrant. One of his bare feet points to the viewer, the other to the side, for example, as if he is either hesitant to leave or stay. Combined with the title – always important elements of the paintings in the case of Dumas – it reinforces the notion that this is an instance of what I have been calling "migratory aesthetics."

This term indicates an aesthetic of migratory culture, which is the term used to indicate a Western European (or North American for that matter) culture that is in constant transformation under the influence of the increased phenomena of migrancy. The neighbor opens his coat with a theatrical gesture of sincerity, in order to show that no bombs are hidden underneath it. The gesture accords well with the straightforward look with which he addresses the viewers. Both are vehicles of a "rhetoric of sincerity." [2] This painting suggests and critiques the conflation of the migratory and the terroristic that is so strong in contemporary mythology in the West. Invoking the paranoia concerning "Middle-Eastern looking" men, the painting tells us that settled people "make" terrorists simply by projecting onto "neighbors" the very media- and state-managed fear of otherness that has congealed around some of the groups of former *Gastarbeiters* at Mercedes Benz and other industrial giants.

Thematically, this is where my interests join those of Thomas Elsaesser; where his work inspires me. When I was invited to contribute to this tribute, I immediately decided that I would focus on the beautiful small publication *Terrorisme, mythes et représentations*, on the RAF (*Rote Armee Fraktion*) and two films about this terrorist group, DEUTSCHLAND IM HERBST / GERMANY IN AUTUMN (Rainer Werner Fassbinder, Volker Schlöndorff, et al., 1978) and TODESSPIEL / DEATH GAME (Heinrich Breloer, 1997).[3] But thematic interest is only part of what brings Elsaesser's work within my orbit. The other part is conceptual – and that is where a more lasting congeniality lies. Elsaesser wisely declined to *define* terrorism. This negative act has already brought the concept closer to my view of the usefulness of concepts for interdisciplinary cultural analysis. I had already been interested in the productive looseness or "traveling" of concepts for quite a while, which is actually a variation on the "weak thought" of the 1980s.[4]

In a similar vein, Elsaesser went through the case at hand, the double case of the history of the RAF and the films devoted to the movement, to list the many varied, often contradictory, facets of that instance of "terrorism." The analysis of the events, the discourses, and the films together as political history and media representation form a third reason why I have taken this as my starting point, and why I consider the essay an exemplary instance of cultural analysis. The passionate commitment to foreground the politics of culture and the culture of politics, as well as the continuity to the present, is a fourth. Thus, Elsaesser makes an utterly convincing and original case for the integration of cultural analysis with the political thinking that should be integral to it but so seldom is.

I am most interested in the conceptual moves in the essay. Clearly, we had a non-concept here; a concept that was best left "traveling," mobile. In the spirit of that productive negativity, I put my interest in the "migratory" and Elsaesser's in "terrorism" together. I will try to develop a connection between his work on terrorism and mine on the migratory. I extend the latter to the conceptual level, as I claim Elsaesser does with the former. "Migratory," then, refers less to the actual movement of people, even if that movement is of crucial social-political importance, but to the qualifications this movement places with the assumed certainties, including conceptual ones, by which we live. Elsaesser's "moving" way, of diffusing the concept of terrorism through mapping its ramifications, is similarly a way of un-fixing. On the basis of this common interest in critically engaging the myths and representations of what the West has been taught to fear, I will peruse his essay not out of thematic interest but primarily for how the "migratoriness" of the conceptual moves helps us to understand "terrorism" as a constructive conceptual tool.

The starting point and justification for this approach are simple. Furthermore, in Elsaesser's essay the concept of terrorism is made to "migrate" over twenty times, bridging an equal number of differences or oppositions. If in the end it offers a clear and analytically helpful meaning, it is because of the restraint of the compulsion to define, to fix and narrow down meaning. Thus, the concept remains open to what the "case" can tell us about it. I will simply follow the migratory line of the article, reconstructing, in terms of migratoriness, the moves Elsaesser makes to do justice to the complexity of the social phenomenon he studies and the artistic manifestations through which we can know it. I will put these moves obliquely in touch with contemporary concerns where terrorism and migratoriness meet.

Generations

The first cluster of migratory moves concerns *generations*. From the vantage point of today, the RAF period in the 1970s is positioned right in between Germany's most problematic period, the 1940s during which the RAF members' parents made their political choices, and the 2000s when "terrorism" has once again become an urgent issue, an excuse for violence, persecution, and a *nouvelle vague* of colonialism. Moving constantly between the beginning and end of these three key decades, and the familial genealogies involved, Elsaesser seeks to understand the multiplicity of the political ramifications to which the brief yet endless history of the RAF points only obliquely: "Neither the films nor a slew of books managed to lay the episode to rest, though ... because they also inscribed themselves in several other histories ... to recover their possible significance for the 1990s."[5]

This generational migration of the kinds of politics that might lead up to terrorism implies two other forms of conceptual migration. First, Elsaesser includes in this reflection on generational tensions a vision of the constant "migration" between "private" situations of children growing up in a country riddled with ambivalence, and "public" history of a country dealing with a past that is literally unspeakable, hence, *traumatogenic* on a collective level. I would maintain that this is a (conceptual) migration rather than a merging because although there is no harmonious integration, there is a constant tension and escape from the one into the other. This is how and why a child can become violent out of anger toward a parent and commit acts of terrorism that kill countless others they have never met. These connections between the two domains of social history – political history and the history of the family – run through the essay inconspicuously but forcefully. For me, they offer a template for understanding the youthful terrorism of today. Only in extreme historical situations do these connections come to the fore strongly enough to inform the political behavior of people who, from the vantage point of others, have everything to live for – whether they come from well-to-do families and have a future as brilliant professionals, or whether they are simply young and "promising," like many contemporary radicals – but prefer to endanger or willfully destroy their lives.

The second generational implication concerns the status of the nation. The RAF happened in the former West Germany, the Federal Republic, which was at that time still strictly separated from East Germany, the DDR (GDR, German Democratic Republic). But the two films Elsaesser discusses were made before (GERMANY IN AUTUMN) and after (DEATH GAME) the fall of the Berlin Wall, that moment when the "great divide" collapsed, and Germany, never quite certain of its unity, became a political unity once again. Hence, the concept of terrorism migrates within the nation, between not only two states of the nation-state(s) but also between two states of the world – the one when the world was divided into capitalist and communist states, and the one when, for a brief moment, it appeared unified. Subsequently, as Elsaesser points out, the *"raison d'Etat"* takes over, and new hostilities fall into place.

In relation to these partial shifts, Elsaesser introduces the myth of Antigone and its importance in GERMANY IN AUTUMN. This myth is often used for political purposes, which is understandable given that it is concerned with just this issue of politics versus family. At the same time, by using this myth as GERMANY IN AUTUMN does, it already tips the balance in the direction of such a *raison d'Etat*. Elsaesser writes:

> The appearance of Antigone in GERMANY IN AUTUMN is thus over-determined: it raises the question whether the film, by pointing to her presence, already specifies a particular reading of the historical-political dimension of the events with which GERMANY IN AUTUMN is concerned.[6]

On the one hand, the object proposes an interpretation that can only follow this very interpretation. On the other, it opens up the conceptual reflection that all too often prescribes and delimits what the object can say.

On the level of content, and to connect this historical shift with my interest in today's migratory aesthetics, I see a heterogeneity-in-continuity here. Between the two moments in which "terrorism" became an acutely real issue – between the collapse of the communism/capitalism divide and the current migratory culture, another collapse of boundaries – the world shifted. And when the traditional enemy vanished, the necessary creation of its us/them divides from communism shifted as well. From the profound, but not-profound-enough changes within Germany(s), we can learn what makes state terror tick, and how individual initiatives emerge within it.[7]

Domains of Thought

A second cluster of moves in the essay concerns the bond, inextricable as much as problematic, between *politics, aesthetics,* and *ontology.* As in the generational issue, this is not a simple merging but a constant back and forth movement, which brings the baggage from one domain into the concerns of the other. Here, the concept of terrorism migrates back and forth several times, demonstrating in the process that Elsaesser's keen sense of the political in cultural analysis is extremely timely.

Elsaesser characterizes with great sensitivity the reception of the two key films he discusses, GERMANY IN AUTUMN and DEATH GAME, as engaged in a sad sympathy for the terrorists, combined with a general feeling of paranoia of being (seen as) a terrorist, and empathy for the perspective of the State and the victims, respectively.[8] This is more than a political characterization. It also indicates an aesthetic appeal that informs the former without becoming one with it. Elsaesser recalls his own, personal *frisson* upon learning of the first RAF events in 1972, the "Bonnie-and-Clyde-ness" of it. Mediated, aestheticized, yet politically real.

Another set of migratory movements between politics and aesthetics can be deducted from Elsaesser's almost casual mentioning of the fact that some of the RAF principals moved with apparent ease from the extreme left to the extreme right politically. To explain this political flexibility, Elsaesser invokes another myth, that of the deeply patriarchal and Oedipal myth of Hamlet:

> Such an emphasis of father-son relations ... was itself symptomatic of the fact that the movement of contestation was anti-authoritarian rather than egalitarian, that despite its Marxist political discourse it was caught in the ruses of patriarchy, which the women owed it to themselves to escape from, perhaps by contesting this "Hamletization" of German history of after the war through "antagonizing" it instead for itself.[9]

In addition to suggesting the political inconsistency of the individuals, this indicates how the divisions between left and right are no longer tenable. The state of the world today confirms this. This does not mean that labor issues and other leftist political issues are obsolete – no more, say, than the silly notion of "post-feminism" makes rape an obsolete issue. Rather, it is no longer consistently on the left that we can hope that these issues will be addressed, or anywhere else on the traditional political spectrum. This need for regrouping around issues redefines aesthetics. Where Elsaesser deploys the tension between the use of the myths of Antigone and Hamlet, I see contemporary artists deploying similar forms of intertextuality to regroup various political positions. One example is a recent video work by Canadian artist Stan Douglas, VIDÉO (2007), which, instead of myths, deploys the classics of film history to do this.

While writing this essay, I was watching this film intensely. Just like Elsaesser's *Terrorisme* book it was produced on the occasion of an exhibition at the Centre Pompidou devoted to a single artist, this time not Fassbinder but Samuel Beckett. Douglas responds to Beckett's FILM, probing and updating the ontological question of being (defined as being perceived). Douglas articulates the ontological question, aesthetically followed through in the way he films consistently from behind, narratively through a reworking of Orson Welles' LE PROCÈS / THE TRIAL (1962).[10] Like Elsaesser in his balancing act on the cusp of Antigone and Hamlet, Douglas thus knots together the individual and the social, the political, the aesthetic, and the ontological questions of our time – the question of whether identity, for example, is ontological or discursively constructed. The main character of the film, a young black woman, whose face we never get to see, is sense-lessly persecuted and perhaps executed, like Kafka's anti-hero. Since the voices are never audible, we fail to know how the harsh demand of identity papers, and its subsequent shrugging off as irrelevant when the woman extends her passport, articulates her identity, and how the latter pertains to the men's attempt at her objectification.

While the scholar deploys such concepts as migratory, the artist uses aesthetics with a similar migratory thrust. But here again, an apparent division fails to hold. In one of the boldest passages of his text, Elsaesser claims an aesthetic function of the RAF members:

> Perhaps the RAF was trying to produce a different kind of "art" altogether: not spec-tacular, but "conceptual," by making visible deeper, irreconcilable contradictions, ar-ticulating a series of "deadlocks" in the body politic, in the fabric of democracy it-self?[11]

Conversely, Douglas is an artist, but his deployment of the intertextual relations to three canonical works from the history of cinema, all three concerned with attempts at objectification, can arguably be seen as equally conceptual, even if the incredibly precise cinematic aesthetic is his tool to achieve this.

In the French version of the passage quoted above, Elsaesser uses the word *"vraiment"* ("truly") – a casual reference to a form of authenticity. He mentions authenticity more explicitly in relation to that preoccupation with Germany and things German. He points out that the loud anti-American and pro-Vietnam dis-course, shibboleths of leftism at the time, were only "authenticated" by turning the attention inward, to Germany itself and its political stocktaking in this post-war period: "Though stridently anti-American and pro-Vietnam, it became 'authentic' only where it referred itself to Germany and its political post-war re-cord."[12] This is right after the confession of his own shivers of the Bonnie-and-Clydeness in the aesthetics of the RAF actions. I am fascinated by this moment in the text, where the author's personal involvement in the historical culture he is describing folds into an authenticity defined as closeness and personal involve-ment, as a form of Germanness. This move points to the need for self-involve-ment indeed – in the wake of Habermas, we called it self-reflection – in an at-tempt to understand "terrorism" in all of the cultural and the political, the aesthetic and the ontological aspects of it together. "Paranoia" may be the key; that emotion, or neurosis that focuses on the individual's response to the world without making any pronouncements on the (ontological) reality of the persecu-tion feared. To be a terrorist or to be considered one becomes a blurry ontological area. Withholding ontological judgments is necessary in order to understand any political action, and terrorism more than any other.

In other words, the knot where politics, aesthetics, and ontology must not be disentangled is the site where the migratory concept of terrorism is at its densest. Importantly, then, the move Elsaesser makes here is a (provisionally) stabilizing one, keeping together in the bargain both past and present, both self and other, but never in harmony. This is why the conceptual metaphor of the migratory is helpful. When thinking about migratoriness, this knot is crucial. Without it, we inevitably fall back into an *exoticizing* form of *othering* – of migrants who are neighbors or of terrorists who are compatriots – that precludes an understanding of contemporary culture, including European culture.

Revisiting Taxonomy

A third cluster of migratory reflections on terrorism congeals around *categories*. Critical of Breloer's simplifications in DEATH GAME of complexities in the emotional responses emerging from the social fabric, Elsaesser points to the streamlining effects of genre, to its inevitable complicities. This is the first among categorical migrations. His sentence "The docudrama exudes the gravity of the reason of state" introduces the notion that genres are always already bound up in politics, whether or not this politics is recognizable as state or party politics.[13] Due to its realistic claims, yet allowance of fiction within it, docudrama is an excellent example of this.

This reflection introduces the section on Antigone's role in GERMANY IN AUTUMN mentioned above, where the "official" opposition between family and state is carefully challenged, so that a hermeneutics of Antigone becomes central to the argument. For me, the *"raison d'Etat"* and its counterpart, the *"raison de famille"* so to speak, are among the most powerful areas of conceptual migration. The earlier reflections on generational tensions substantiate this need to open up the boundary between these two domains because family is itself a *raison d'Etat*, as is the private-public division. Here it becomes clear what they really are: categories as political tools. This is the second taxonomic migration.

Meanwhile, the question of hermeneutics introduces a third migratory move in this cluster, the one between text and interpretation, again a move back-and-forth rather than a merging. This is very important, because the facile merging of these two categories allows for the escape from and the obscuring of the real issue; and this is something Elsaesser would never fall for. Thus, he rhetorically asks, would Antigone be a hermeneutics, a key to understanding GERMANY IN AUTUMN as an allegory of modern German history? Instead, Elsaesser moves between text and interpretation. For example, when he brings in classic categories such as class – when discussing the bourgeois backgrounds of RAF members – he pulls it into the realm of provisional and historically specific indetermi-nacy. Much later, a similar move occurs between history (or History) and herme-neutics, when, with reference to Jacques Rancière, the author reminds us that in the face of history, there always occurs a move that turns us into political sub-jects: "What sort of 'we' is symbolizable in a civic, political sense?"[14]

This, in turn, brings in the moment where migration in the literal sense sub-verts the category from within. Discussing the large percentage of workers with foreigner status in the Mercedes Benz factory (whose director Schleyer was a prominent RAF victim), Elsaesser recalls the connection between this moment in the 1970s and, on the one hand, the requisition of "slaves" during Nazism and, on the other, the "future transformation of those workers into undesirable foreigners."[15] From the RAF activist present, with Nazism as the past, and cur-rent migration policies as the future, a rather bleak blurring of categories appears to occur. Here, in the way Elsaesser complicates that most reliable of historical concepts, class, by merging Nazi slaves, Mercedes Benz workers, and current *"étrangers indésirables,"* the connection between terrorism – the phenomenon as well as the concept – and migratoriness becomes highly over-determined. Cate-gories, then, remain useful only when they are not rigidified in a positivist grid. Instead, phenomena that elude and question categories demonstrate, through the dynamic relationship they maintain and to the taxonomies, that far from un-dermining the production of knowledge, they stimulate it; and far from being evidence of "sloppiness", they help integrate dynamic with rigorous thought.

Domains of Experience

This brings me to the fourth cluster of conceptual migrations, perhaps best char-acterized as domains of *experience*. This most closely resembles my use of migra-tory aesthetics as an instance of a traveling concept. Experience has been a pro-ductive, yet problematic concept in cultural analysis, especially in feminist and postcolonial thought.[16] The experiences of underprivileged and subaltern groups have been systematically under-illuminated in the production of knowledge, but an appeal to identity politics alone fails to explain and remedy this situation.[17] Harking back to his earlier thoughts on generational confusing, Elsaesser's essay moves from the figure of Antigone to that of Hamlet, and further pursues the family metaphor by way of fathers and sons among historical political figures (here, Rommel and Schleyer).[18]

This metaphor is brought to the foreground and developed in GERMANY IN AUTUMN, and Elsaesser is sensitive to its Oedipal overtones and the exclusionary consequences these never fail to generate. As indicated earlier, Elsaesser argues that the film attempts to Oedipalize the political past, by a "Hamletization" (diagonally from father to son) and then argues that the women in the movement owed to themselves a "[re-]Antigonizing" of Germany's post-war history. This is how the two myths inspire a host of analytical moves. But these increasingly complex plays with family metaphors are also anchored in the domains of experience where positions can and must be swapped.

First, the distinction between spectator and spectacle nearly collapses when the machinery of surveillance makes everyone both spectator and spectacle, a theme Fassbinder elaborates in his section of GERMANY IN AUTUMN. The use of that machinery to produce "surveillance effects" in the film turns the director into a figure of complicity, so that the implication of the viewer can be shown in the same move as his or her exclusion. Complicity is itself a category of experience that, when ignored, muddles the political waters while, when acknowledged, can be politically productive, as it overcomes the illusion of the possibility to step outside of ideology. This argument concerning complicity recalls the early cinematic experiments with "phantom rides" where cameras mounted on the roofs of trains would produce an automated recording of a journey, so that cinema became inevitably entangled in conquest and state control.[19]

Later, the distinction between life and theater is the domain of migratory conceptualization. Drawing attention, first, to the RAF members' theatricality as well as their opponents' behavior, the text recalls the public theatricality of the cultural-historical moment, not only of certain suspense films but also of happenings and performances, street theater and other forms of behavior that suspend the firm distinction between fiction and reality. The analysis of the iconography of revolution, the media exploitation of images such as a child carriage pushed in front of Schleyer's car to force the driver to stop, and the police information and disinformation all sensitize the reader in a mere page and a half to the dramatic *mise-en-scène* that frames the events.[20]

The importance of this analysis of the artistic aspects of the phenomenon can be found in a few distinct elements. First, understanding how "art" shapes these real actions helps us be aware of the pre-programmed nature of response as well. The earlier connection between genre and state had already made that clear. Second, utterances such as citation (of Eisenstein's 1925 film BATTLESHIP POTEMPKIN) and invention (scenes of perverted maternity) to suggest the inhumanness of the terrorists are speech acts in the true sense, doing things with words (or images, as the case may be) and hence, at least partly, performatives. This clears space for an endorsement of the performative effect and solicits reflection on the desire to believe. Third, the analysis itself becomes a depiction of the stage, its backdrops, props, and characters, so that we are able to vividly imagine what the scene of terrorism looked like. This concrete quality of the analysis helps us to understand how the migratory movement between the real and the imaginary, belief and enjoyment, acceptance and doubt is continuously wavering. As a result, "we" – the readers of this essay, the users of cultural analysis, and the critics of history – are placed inside the historical "otherness" that is the subject matter of this essay.

Elsaesser also discusses another instance of aesthetical experience related to the notion of the performative. Invoking an autobiographical essay on the RAF by Michael Dreyer, he demonstrates how the RAF was experienced as music: "For Dreyer, the RAF's street violence was not only street theatre, it was a kind of 'music' ('no more/mere words')."[21] With music, he draws attention to the non-signifying aspect of language – its sensate, bodily aspect, which produces what he calls a "new subjective space." Dreyer describes the sensations of the rupture of monotony that the RAF actions caused in children bored by the cocoons of their nuclear families. In this sense, the rupturing of such monotonies by way of public violence becomes a political aesthetization, much like certain kinds of rock music at the time. Signs without proper meaning, although material, the sounds, colors, and forms became a forceful "super band" on which street credibility could be projected as a desirable commodity.

Within this cluster of moves, the migratoriness also plays on the dual level of conceptualization and critical social analysis when the distinction between politics and space is set in movement. Here, when discussing public space and the public sphere, two facets of an entangled whole, the "topography of visual signs" of an "urban theater in movement," the essay is couched in a contemporary vocabulary of ghettoized suburbs. This brings his text ever so close to my own interest in contemporary migratory culture, so much so that its formulation strikes me with a new actuality. Space itself, then, Elsaesser reminds us, becomes a political category.[22]

Mediatizations

This leads to the final cluster of moves in this non-exhaustive list. Here, the moves play out conceptual and social migratory aspects between *spatial categories within the mediatic domain*. One concerns a superposition of interiority and exteriority, when the city becomes the theater of a concerted *in*visibility. Surveillance is an aspect of this superposition, and this is the "natural" environment of the RAF, and so is hiding (the victim of kidnapping). The distinction that is suspended here is the one between "natural" and "critical" – between, that is, belonging and creating an artificial space. When the example of airport security is cited, I cannot help but think of Marc Augé's analysis of airports as non-spaces; spaces where people neither "live" nor "dwell" but merely pass through; and where the quality of not-belonging is so predominant that security as an artificially produced non-habitat overrules the peace of ordinary passers-by.[23]

In this context, Elsaesser raises the question of the symbolic status of terrorist acts – of the possibility of speaking of a "language" in this respect. Many of the moves already mentioned recur here. This additive strategy makes the (non-)concept of terrorism ever denser. At this point, the essay raises what is for me the most important suspension; and here, the use of quotation marks signals Elsaesser's hesitance to define and decide, as well as to escape in conceptual finesse. Recalling the theater, he writes that the "art" of the RAF may very well be of a different kind, namely "conceptual." Thus, it becomes an art of the migratory itself: a form of expression geared toward making visible the most profound, irreconcilable, *aporetic* contradictions at the heart of democracy itself. These include the place of terroristic threat in an over-securitized society, and that of the invention of the information-saturated world; the role of surveillance in relation to civil rights and freedom, and the subliminal tension of historical *Nachträglich-keit*: "[The RAF] involved in a situation of *Nachtraglichkeit*, engaged in making up for something that had been omitted in the past, desirous to assume a role, across a historical gap, that was marked by shame, guilt, self-hatred."[24] As Elsaesser explains, by making up for what the Nation failed to do during Nazism, the RAF was not only attacking the State, but also "addressing" it.

On the basis of this conceptual reflection regarding these contradictions, the position of the contemporary cultural analyst comes into focus. When all is said and done, "terrorism" must remain undefined so that the concept is able to absorb historical change, the mode of staying "inside" – inside Germany, inside the times, then and now, and inside the domain where political and conceptual thinking must remain bound together. This gives *Terrorism, mythes et représentations* the *force de frappe* it has. This is cultural analysis as it should be: critical with complicity, historical in the contemporary, and profoundly migratory in mode of thinking. Terrorism, then, is a concept that can only be productively understood under conditions of migratory interiority. Only then, I contend, can it be a "neighbor" à la Dumas: close by and held at bay at the same time.

Notes

1. The painting is now part of the Stedelijk Museum's collection in Amsterdam.
2. The term "rhetoric of sincerity" refers to a forthcoming volume: *The Rhetoric of Sincerity*, ed. Ernst van Alphen, Mieke Bal, and Carel Smith (Stanford: Stanford University Press).

3. Thomas Elsaesser, *Terrorisme, mythes et représentations: La RAF de Fassbinder aux T-shirts Prada Meinhof*, translated by Noël Burch, (Lille: Tausend Augen, 2005). Unless otherwise indicated, all translations are from an earlier English version of this text, Thomas Elsaesser, "Antigone Agonistes: Urban Guerilla or Guerilla Urbanism? The RAF, *Germany in Autumn* and *Death Game*," *Giving Ground: The Politics of Propinquity*, ed. Joan Copjec and Michael Sorkin (London: Verso, 1999) 267-302. A digital version of this text can be found at <http://www.rouge.com.au/4/antigone.html>.

4. Mieke Bal, *Travelling Concepts in the Humanities: A Rough Guide* (Toronto: University of Toronto Press, 2002).

5. "Mais ni ces films ni une foule de livres ne parviendront à clore cet épisode ... du fait de leur inscription dans d'autres histoires ... fai[t] ressortir leur signification présente." Elsaesser, *Terrorisme* 16.

6. "L'apparition d'Antigone dans L'ALLEMAGNE EN AUTOMNE est donc surdéterminée: elle soulève la question de savoir si le film, en désignant ainsi sa figure, ne prescrit pas déjà une lecture particulière des événements historico-politiques qui font l'objet du film." Elsaesser, *Terrorisme* 27.

7. The term "the great divide" is meant to draw attention to the two-step shifts in aesthetics that, chronologically at least, coincided more or less with this political one. See Andreas Huyssen, *After the Great Divide: Modernism, Mass Culture, Postmodernism* (London: MacMillan, 1988) and *Twilight Memories: Marking Time in a Culture of Amnesia* (New York: Routledge, 1995).

8. See Elsaesser, *Terrorisme* 20, where he says about GERMANY IN AUTUMN: "... les terroristes semblaient constituer une menace moins en raison de leurs actes de violence que parce qu'ils inspiraient ... une certaine tristesse, voire une dose de sympathie. Ils firent apparaître le terrorisme comme contagieux."; "Presque tous les épisodes de L'ALLEMAGNE EN AUTOMNE évoquent un climat de paranoïa: n'importe qui pouvait être un terroriste ou pis, n'importe qui pouvait être pris pour un terroriste." Translation: "To the press [in the 1970s], it was as if the terrorists were a threat less by violent acts than by the fact that they could inspire not just universal revulsion, but sometimes sorrow and even sympathy. Like a virus terrorism seemed contagious."; "Almost every episode in GERMANY IN AUTUMN, for instance, conveys a climate of paranoia: everyone might be a terrorist, or worse still, everyone might take one for a terrorist."

9. "Cet accent mis sur l'axe père-fils ... laisse entendre que le mouvement de contestation en Allemagne était plus anti-autoritaire qu'égalitaire, que malgré son discours politique marxiste, il était pris dans les ruses du patriarcat, ce à quoi le mouvement des femmes se devait d'échapper, peut-être en contestant cette 'hamlétisation' de l'historie allemande d'après-guerre en 'l'antigonisant' pour son propre compte." Elsaesser, *Terrorisme* 38; translation modified.

10. Stan Douglas, VIDÉO, DVD color, 22', 2007. Paris, Centre Pompidou, exhibition *Samuel Beckett*, 14 March-26 June 2007. The third film that Douglas refers to is 2 OU 3 CHOSES QUE JE SAIS D'ELLE / TWO OR THREE THINGS I KNOW ABOUT HER (Jean-Luc Godard, 1967). My analysis of Douglas's work, "Re-: Killing Time" can be found in *Stan Douglas: Past Imperfect. Works 1986-2007*, ed. Hans D. Christ and Iris Dressler (Stuttgart: Hatje Cantz, 2007) 64-93.

11. "Mais peut-être les militants de la RAF cherchaient-ils vraiment à produire un "art" tout autre: non pas spectaculaire mais 'conceptuel', à même de rendre visibles des contradictions plus profondes, plus irréconciliables, d'exprimer une série d'impasses au centre du corps politique, dans le tissu même de la démocratie?" Elsaesser, *Terrorisme* 67.

12. "Bruyamment anti-américain et pro-vietnamien, il ne devient 'authentique' que lorsqu'il se réfère à l'Allemagne elle-même et son bilan politique d'après-guerre." Elsaesser, *Terrorisme* 20.

13. "De ce docu-drama suinte la gravité de la raison d'Etat." Elsaesser, *Terrorisme* 21.

14. "Quelle sorte de 'nous', quelle identité de groupe, peut être symbolisée dans un sens civique, politique?" Elsaesser, *Terrorisme* 75-76.

15. "D'autre part, cela annonce la future transformation de ces ouvriers en étrangers indésirables (futures cibles du ressentiment néo-nazi à partir des années quatre-vingt." Elsaesser, *Terrorisme* 33.

16. See Joan Scott's seminal article "Experience," *Feminists Theorize the Political*, ed. Judith Butler and Joan Scott (New York: Routledge, 1992).

17. The best version of Gayatri Chakravorty Spivak's famous essay "Can the Subaltern Speak?" – a version that addresses critical responses – is in *A Critique of Postcolonial Reason: Toward a History of the Vanishing Present* (Cambridge: Harvard University Press, 1999).

18. Elsaesser, *Terrorisme* 43. The son of Rommel, Hitler's right-hand man, attended the funeral of Schleyer, a RAF victim.

19. With apologies for this shortcut, I must refer to Kaja Silverman's discussion of this issue (and of Althusser's work) in the opening chapter of her *Male Subjectivity at the Margin* (New York: Routledge, 1992). On productive complicity, see Spivak, *A Critique of Postcolonial Reason*. On phantom rides, see Nanna Verhoeff, *The West in Early Cinema: After the Beginning* (Amsterdam: Amsterdam University Press, 2006).

20. Elsaesser, *Terrorisme* 49-50.

21. "Pour Dreyer, la violence de rue de la RAF n'était pas du théâtre de rue, mais une sorte de 'musique'." Elsaesser, *Terrorisme* 60.

22. Elsaesser, *Terrorisme* 52. Elsaesser refers here to the useful collection *The City Reader*, ed. R.T. LeGate and F. Stout (New York: Routledge, 1996).

23. Marc Augé, *Non-Places: Introduction to an Anthropology of Supermodernity*, translated by Hohn How (London / New York: Verso, 1995).

24. "[La RAF] était impliquée dans une opération *Nachträglichkeit* ('après-coup'), de réparation d'une omission passée, elle voulait assumer, à travers le hiatus historique, un rôle marqué par la honte, la culpabilité et la haine de soi." Elsaesser, *Terrorisme* 71.

The Echo Chamber of History

Frank van Vree

> *... uns, die wir vorbeisehen an den Dingen neben uns,*
> *und nicht hören, daß der Schrei nicht verstummt.*[1]

Ambiguities

Early in 2001, Joschka Fischer, Germany's Minister of Foreign Affairs, was almost outrun by history. While acting as a witness in a trial against a former member of the *Rote Armee Fraktion* (RAF), Hans-Joachim Klein, he was severely attacked by Bettina Röhl, a journalist and daughter of RAF-leader Ulrike Meinhof. Working on a critical biography of the leader of the *Grünen* party, Röhl claimed to have discovered some pictures showing Fischer and his radical friends, among them Hans-Joachim Klein, fighting with the police during a demonstration. Although these photographs had been published before by the *Frankfurter Allgemeine* in 1973, she sold them as new to the conservative weekly *Stern* and the *Bild* tabloid. It did not work out well. Röhl lost her credibility and was accused of conducting a crusade against Fischer out of frustration with her own troubled past as daughter of a violent revolutionary who had committed suicide.

In the midst of this commotion a film was released that dealt with this very subject – being the daughter of violent radicals. Die innere Sicherheit / The State I Am In (2000) by the young film director Christian Petzold tells the story of a girl's coming of age while being on the run with her family. Her parents, members of a non-specified terrorist organization, had escaped to Portugal but are forced to return to Germany many years later. The State I Am In aroused few political debates, which is quite remarkable when one compares it to other events related to the memory of left-wing violence such as the fierce debates concerning, for instance, the legitimacy of the exhibition *Regarding Terror* at the Institute for Contemporary Art in Berlin in 2005 and the pardoning and release in 2007 of former RAF members from prison.

According to Thomas Elsaesser, the story of the RAF is a *Vexierbild* of the (media) history of the former West German *Bundesrepublik*: a puzzling picture in which one might alternately and unexpectedly see various images.[2] Although the violent revolutionary movement had entirely lost its political significance and had become part of the German past, memories of the RAF never disappeared, in fact, its name has continued to roam around like a ghost, *"wie ein Gespenst."*[3] The story entered a new phase just before the turn of the century, the upbeat of which took place even before April 20, 1998 – Adolf Hitler's birthday – when an eight-page typewritten letter landed on the desk of the Reuters news agency, signed "RAF" with the machine-gun red star, declaring that the group had voluntarily dissolved, ending its "project of liberation" through urban guerrilla warfare. A few months earlier, the Westdeutscher Rundfunk (WDR) had screened the prize-winning docudrama TODESSPIEL / DEATH GAME (1997), a miniseries by Heinrich Breloer dealing with the bloody events that had taken place two decades earlier during the "German Autumn," but this time from the perspective of the victim and the authorities.[4] Thomas Elsaesser has analyzed this shift in perspective from sympathy for the RAF in his analysis of DEUTSCHLAND IM HERBST / GERMANY IN AUTUMN (Rainer Werner Fassbinder, Volker Schlöndorff, et al., 1978) and DEATH GAME.[5]

DEATH GAME marked a new beginning of a "history returning as art," with a prominent role for the cinema. The memory of the RAF became *fiktionstauglich*, "fit to be fictionalized," as Petzold aptly put it.[6] Volker Schlöndorff – who had already been working on the issue while being in the middle of it, producing two important films, DIE VERLORENE EHRE DER KATHARINA BLUM / THE LOST HONOR OF KATHARINA BLUM (1975) and GERMANY IN AUTUMN – took up the thread in 1999, directing DIE STILLE NACH DEM SCHUSS / THE LEGEND OF RITA. The film, partly based on the life of RAF member Inge Viett, portrays the vanity of left-wing and violent radicalism as well as the failings of the DDR (GDR, German Democratic Republic). THE LEGEND OF RITA tells the story of Rita Vogt, a member of an unnamed terrorist group who manages to escape after a bank robbery and some shooting incidents to settle down in East Germany with a new identity provided by the secret police, the Stasi. Through the eyes of Vogt's "real existing socialism," though not completely depicted in black and white, appears a society ruled by indifference, conformism, and an all-pervading stagnation, while she herself lives in constant fear that her cover will be blown – which happens, eventually, with the fall of the Berlin Wall, when she is mortally wounded trying to escape at a checkpoint.

While THE LEGEND OF RITA evoked critical and even sharp responses – some critics accused Schlöndorff of portraying East Germany and its secret police too positively, whereas others complained that he was too harsh or, on the contrary, too gentle in his judgment of the RAF[7] – THE STATE I AM IN, released only one year later, as mentioned earlier, aroused very little political discussion. Petzold takes a considerably different stand than Schlöndorff does. THE STATE I AM IN chooses the perspective of a fifteen-year-old girl discovering the world and finding her own way, after a childhood with her parents, living underground, in exile among anonymous tourists on the Portuguese coast, conscientiously avoiding behavior that could lead to her being caught. This lifestyle has dramatic effects on the family with the parents vaguely maintaining their old beliefs but living with their back to the world. Meanwhile, Jeanne, their daughter, is cut off from a normal social life at school with her peers. The situation changes dramatically when a small oversight forces them to change their plans, and they have to return to Germany instead of emigrating to Brazil to start a new life. On the run again, hiding in Hamburg, Jeanne starts to make her own way, to discover the world and to establish her own "inner certainty." She falls in love, a forbidden love with Heinrich who she had met earlier in Portugal and to whom she decided to be honest: she tells him about her parents' illegal activities. This turns out to be a sincere and fatal moment for the family.

THE STATE I AM IN aims at a more universal reading, not only through its very theme but also by deliberately avoiding political issues and historical clues, a choice that was partly forced upon Petzold by the broadcasting companies as he himself admitted. Nevertheless, the film was generally understood as related to the history of the RAF.[8] The viewer really didn't need to know anything about the historical background or the key source of Petzold and his co-author Harun Farocki – namely texts written by RAF member Wolfgang Grams, who was shot in 1993 – he could not have missed this interpretation. Critics went on at length about the issue and some insiders noticed more details that pointed to the RAF, in the mise-en-scène as well as some scenes.[9] The way Petzold revealed the gun of the father in his Portuguese hotel room, for instance, was inspired by pictures of the gun that Andreas Baader used to commit suicide. And when the family secretly meets an old acquaintance, they use an old RAF symbol, Herman Melville's novel *Moby Dick*, the story of the heroic hunters chasing the white whale with whom the RAF identified and whose names they adopted – tailing their own whale as a metaphor for the State.[10]

Avoiding historical references and focusing on the private side of life, particularly of Jeanne, a teenager in search of her stolen youth, THE STATE I AM IN finds itself stuck in ambiguity. In that respect, the film illustrates the idea of the German (film) history as a *Vexierbild* perfectly with the film alternately denying and confirming, according to one's point of view, the presence of this history of violence, fear, and sorrow. Although it is obvious that the film could not have been made – or even screened – without these actual events, it appears to attempt to escape from the past and the memories, leaving many urgent questions unanswered.

An Echo Chamber of the Past

The same deliberate ambiguity is encountered in the scene in which Jeanne, after having stolen some CDs, is seen roaming around Hamburg-Bergedorf, when suddenly she finds herself in a classroom. Having asked a girl standing in front of a school for a cigarette, she is taken along into the building and for the first time in her life Jeanne enters a classroom, where a documentary on concentration camps is being shown. Initially, we hear only the music and the voice-over of a commentator, while the camera observes the young spectators in the classroom, for a few seconds, before switching to the screen. We see the end of the film through Jeanne's eyes: an open green field, some scattered bushes, and in the background, some barracks, while the camera dwells for a moment on a broken staircase, then a second sequence showing the remains of a concrete building, followed by pictures of another ruin, shot from the side and below in a long sequence, culminating in rather abstract images. The scene – in total, a little less than ninety seconds – has a quiet ambience, a feeling that is reinforced by the rather melodious music.

The voice-over, however, leaves no doubt about what we are viewing: the remnants of a site of horror, grass growing at the *Appelplatz* and around the blocks, "like an abandoned village, still full of menace."[11] The pile of concrete is the crematorium, a landscape haunted by millions of dead victims. And while another ruined building appears, the voice-over tells:

> Who among us is standing watch and warns us when the new executioners come? Do they really have a face different from ours? ... And there is us, who, when looking at this rubble, sincerely believe that the racial mania is forever buried underneath there, us who see this image vanishing and act as if we were creating a new hope, as if we really believed that all that belongs to one time and one country, us, who look past the things next to us and don't listen that the scream is not silenced. [12]

At the ending of this film, Alain Resnais's NUIT ET BROUILLARD / NIGHT AND FOG (1956), the teacher, obviously the same age as Jeanne's parents, wants to know her name and warns her that he is going to have to talk to her parents, only to burst into complaints about students not attending his classes (except when he shows films) and never learning anything from their history books. And then he asks Jeanne to tell him something about the film: "Was it a color film? Was it a sound film?" Jeanne leaves the class.

The screening of the film is the most explicit reference in THE STATE I AM IN to the history of the representation of left-wing German terrorism. It is *"eine Szene ... die eine Art Archäologie des Terrorismus enthält"*[13]– a kind of archaeology – although of a peculiar kind. The scene refers directly to DIE BLEIERNE ZEIT /

GERMAN SISTERS, Margarethe von Trotta's prizewinning 1981 film, which is
loosely based on the life of Gudrun Ensslin, one of the founders of the RAF, and
her sister Christiane, a feminist journalist. The film parallels the real lives of the
Ensslin sisters, from the rise of the Baader-Meinhof Group through to the suicide
of Gudrun Ensslin in the Stammheim prison in 1977. It avoids any reference to
specific historical facts, however, choosing instead to dramatize the relationship
of the two sisters and their everyday lives.

In a flashback to their youth, halfway through the film, the spectator sees two
adolescent girls, Juliane and Marianne, in a setting that resembles THE STATE I
AM IN, watching the German version of the same documentary, NIGHT AND FOG.
The sisters, who appear to be quite close, are the children of a decent protestant
family, born in the last years of the war, who grow up in the late 1950s and early
1960s. Juliane, who is the main protagonist of the film who remembers, is also
clearly the rebel in the family, provoking her strict father and her teachers with
her choice of clothes, her behavior, and her attitude. She reads Sartre and prefers
Celan and Brecht over Rilke, whose poems she ostentatiously denounces as
kitsch.[14] The younger sister, on the other hand, is more quiet and obedient, a
daddy's girl, at least until that moment, as the film suggests, because seeing
NIGHT AND FOG becomes a turning point in Marianne's life. To the question of
how this soft-hearted and idealistic girl became radicalized to the point of deciding to join a terrorist organization, the film offers just two closely connected
clues: the screening of NIGHT AND FOG and some news footage of Vietnam, with
shocking images of napalm bombings and dying children, people in despair, and
destroyed villages.

The excerpt from NIGHT AND FOG in Von Trotta's film is more than just a
quote: it lasts for more than three-and-a-half minutes, at least as far as the film's
sound is concerned, since the camera turns away several times to the audience
and the two sisters in particular. Moreover, the sequence is relatively long considering the total length of Resnais's documentary (32 minutes). The scene begins
with an overview of the concentration camps, mentioning their immense size
and their exploitation by large German industrial companies. What follows are
horrible images of corpses, skulls, emaciated people with terrified eyes, a bulldozer ruthlessly shoving piles of bodies into a mass grave, SS guards, women and
men taken prisoner – a sequence that leads to images of Nazi defendants on trial:

I am not responsible, says the kapo
["*Ich bin nicht schuld*" in Celan's translation[15]]
I am not responsible, says the officer
I am not responsible
Who is responsible, then?
[*Wer also ist schuld?*]

Piles of corpses again, jumbles of naked, emaciated, mutilated human bodies.

> As I talk to you the water soaks into the death chambers
> Water of marsh and ruins
> It is cold and turbid as our bad memory

"The war only slumbers" – and at this point, we reach the same scene Petzold cited in his film: the remnants of the site of horror, the green grass of the *Appelplatz*, the ruins, with the voice-over reading:

> Who of us is standing watch ...
> [*Wer von uns wacht hier ...*]

Right at this point, in the middle of that sentence, the commentary and the music of NIGHT AND FOG cease, while the image of Marianne's face in front of her sister in the prison meeting room appears. But even before that moment we, the viewers of GERMAN SISTERS, have already left NIGHT AND FOG behind as we only *heard* the last part of the commentary and the music since Marianne, deeply nauseated, escaped to the bathroom at the moment when the voice-over refers to "the water cold and turbid as our bad memory," and is followed by her sister Juliane. While we observe the two girls in the bathroom, we hear the final quote "*Wer von uns wacht hier...*"

Situating the screening of NIGHT AND FOG in the heart of the story, GERMAN SISTERS links the origins of left-wing terrorism directly to a deeply felt guilt and shame about the Nazi past, coupled with a serious vow to never make the same mistake again: "Who of us is standing watch" – in the case of Vietnam, for instance, as the second screening within the film makes clear. In this respect, Von Trotta, with her preference for personalizing conflicts, definitely went beyond "a reduction of the political and social to psychological categories," for which Elsaesser and others have criticized her work.[16] GERMAN SISTERS stresses the notion of the inescapable bearing that the past has on us as much as the idea of repression of memories, lasting from the 1950s till the days of the German Autumn.[17] It even derives its German title from this silence – these were "the leaden years" (*die bleierne Zeit* – a phrase borrowed from a Hölderlin poem), when the children grew up fully aware of Germany's immense guilt, as this scene illustrates. When NIGHT AND FOG is shown, Marianne and Juliane's father, Pastor Klein, is standing behind the projector, watching his daughters, but he is obviously unable to talk about the events portrayed.[18] He does not associate the recent past to his own rather dictatorial behavior toward his children. He is in the same situation of "leaden" silence as Juliane's teacher was, sending her out of the classroom when she ostentatiously demands to read Paul Celan's "*Todesfuge*" and Bertolt Brecht's "Ballade von der Judenhure Marie Sanders," a poem that criticizes the Nuremberg Laws (for which Hanns Eisler, the composer of Night and Fog, also wrote the music). From this perspective, terrorism might seem to be – in the words of Paul Coates – "a cry in the echo chamber of the Nazi past."[19]

At this point, we can return to the episode in The State I Am In where Night and Fog was screened. What at first sight seemed to be a casual though deliberate reference to an earlier film on terrorism – 'eine Art Archäologie des Terrorismus' – turns out to be its opposite. The State I Am In takes up Resnais's documentary at the very moment that Juliane in Trotta's film flees the room, because she cannot bear the images any more. In contrast to German Sisters, the sequences in Petzold's film do not contain any shocking images but only the long tracking shots searching the landscape for ruins and barracks. Through Jeanne's eyes we perceive the most aesthetic and abstract parts of the documentary, a choice that seems to underscore Petzold's refusal to consider the historical source of radicalism[20] and to relate various historical events.[21] It even opens up the way for a more malicious interpretation, suggesting that the new executioners we need to be warned about, according to Night and Fog – "Who of us is standing watch when the new executioners come" – are the radical left itself.

Indigestible Images

While the spectators of The State I Am In are prevented from seeing the horrible scenes in Night and Fog, viewers of Von Trotta's film have no choice but to watch these images, through the eyes of the two sisters and the other youngsters in the late 1950s. Times, however, had changed between these years and the release of German Sisters in 1981. From the 1960s on, the Nazi policy of destruction and annihilation had begun to move toward the center of the prevailing commemoration culture, a process that was broadened and accelerated by the broadcast of the American docu-drama Holocaust (Marvin J. Chomsky, 1978), televised in Germany in early 1979, an event that was breathlessly followed by the rest of the world.[22]

A year earlier in 1978, German television broadcast Night and Fog. By that time, however, the documentary had become part of the collective memory of a whole generation. Following the well-known incident at the Cannes Festival in April 1956, when the film was withdrawn due to German diplomatic pressure, it was widely screened in schools, youth clubs, parish halls, police stations, and at union meetings, particularly in the northern states of Germany.[23] The scene in German Sisters may thus be considered to be illustrative of the experience of those growing up in the late 1950s and early 1960s.

At first sight, the wide distribution of Resnais's film would appear to contradict the generally accepted view that, during these "leaden years," Germany – in the words of Alexander and Margarete Mitscherlich – was "unable to mourn."[24] It should be understood, however, that the Mitscherlichs were criticizing the widespread attitude of sheer materialism and indifference, on a political as well as a personal level, of the German people. They criticized the prevailing tendency to deny collective and personal guilt, to acknowledge the losses, including the loss of millions of killed Jews, and to refuse "remembering, repeating and working-through," which was needed in order to be healed, according to Freud.[25]

But there were, of course, also people who seriously promoted a policy of active denazification and the reinforcement of democratic and humanist values.[26] It was these circles who urged the prompt release of NIGHT AND FOG in Germany. The Berlin Senate took the initiative to have it screened at the Berlinale in early July 1955. Upon this occasion, the president of the Berlin House of Representatives, Willy Brandt, denounced a diplomatic move of the government to ban the movie and argued that Germans "should not forget, to have other people forget what has been brought upon them."[27] The German version of the film used a delicate translation and recording of the voice-over text by the young acclaimed poet Paul Celan and was released in early 1957. However, the original French version had already been shown in Germany before then. There were approximately two hundred copies of NIGHT AND FOG, almost all 16mm and in black and white, available for rental from various government agencies. There is no doubt that these copies circulated widely, particularly in Germany's northern states, where the film was screened in the upper classes of the secondary schools through to late in the 1960s.[28]

Therefore, the key scene in GERMAN SISTERS may have caused a shock of recognition among German viewers of Marianne and Juliane's generation – including their *physical* reaction to the pictures of the *anus mundi* Resnais portrayed: the images were literally *indigestible*, revolting and sickening and eventually forced Marianne to leave the room. The German writer Anne Duden (born 1942) considers the film to be the beginning of a trauma and a turning point in her life. She watched NIGHT AND FOG when she was thirteen years old: "I saw how the piles of corpses in Bergen-Belsen were shoveled away. We were forced to watch the film at school, but nothing was explained." There were rumors, according to Duden, about concentration camps and gassing, and suddenly they saw these horrible images – she would never be able to put them out of her mind.[29] This is also true of subsequent generations: when Christiane Peitz (born 1959), a critic at the *Tageszeitung* newspaper, interviewed Petzold (born 1960), they discussed their shared experience of watching NIGHT AND FOG as sixteen-year-olds: "we were traumatized for weeks."[30]

The obligation to watch these horrors of the past on the screen, to which Anne
Duden and others including Von Trotta refer, was no invention of German anti-
Nazi pedagogues of the 1950s and 1960s. Forcing people to watch was an essential element in the educational strategy of the Allies during the early postwar
years.[31] The inhabitants of Weimar were summoned by a US General and forced
to view Buchenwald first hand immediately after its liberation – and they did so,
thousands of them, in a long row, often dressed in their Sunday best. The same
occurred elsewhere as well. Short documentaries, produced by the Allies, known
in Germany as *Anklagefilme* ("accusation films"), such as DIE TODESMÜHLEN /
DEATH MILLS (Hanus Burger, 1945) – which includes scenes of the Weimar people visiting Buchenwald[32] – and DEUTSCHLAND ERWACHE / GERMANY AWAKE (US
Army Signal Corps, 1945)[33] were screened all over Germany. These measures
were taken by the Allies to convince the German population that these crimes
had actually occurred. This is also why the trials at the International Military Tribunal at Nuremberg were broadcast on the radio and published in the press. This
was certainly not an unnecessary measure, considering the fact that two years
after the war about half of the German population still believed "that National
Socialism had been a good idea badly carried out," while less than one-third
viewed it as a "bad idea."[34]

The screenings of NIGHT AND FOG in the 1950s and 1960s strongly resembles
the forced visits to the concentration camps and the screening of documentaries
such as DEATH MILLS directly after the war.[35] First of all, the viewers were, in part,
shown identical images, since Resnais used many scenes, particularly the most
terrifying ones, from the Allied documentaries mentioned above. Secondly, one
might argue that the postwar generation, being forced to watch the documentary,
underwent a traumatic experience comparable to that of their parents. This is
even documented because DEATH MILLS contains some scenes in which people
literally turn their heads away, unable to view the dead and mutilated bodies right
at their feet; many held handkerchiefs over their mouths, to minimize the effects
of the stench – which is not unlike Juliane's gesture in GERMAN SISTERS when
she leaves the screening because she is nauseated. The horrible scenes of
corpses, skulls, emaciated people with terrified eyes, a bulldozer shoving piles of
bodies into a mass grave, jumbles of naked, emaciated, mutilated human bodies
at the gates of the liberated camps, screened in cinemas in the two or three years
immediately after the war, and then incorporated again into Resnais's documentary and then quoted again two or three decades later – these images did not only
arouse feelings of anxiety and horror but were actually *indigestible* and *unbearable*.

This may have been why these films have largely disappeared from the public
domain. It is true that these and other documentaries can be found online at the
Steven Spielberg Film and Video Archive Collection at the Holocaust Memorial Mu-

seum in Washington DC and even on YouTube, but they are seldom shown to the general public anymore, and similar photographs are sparingly used in books, magazines, and newspapers, even in studies about the death camps.

In contemporary art, a variety of strategies are exploited to keep the memory of the horrors of annihilation and destruction alive without explicitly exposing these images – strategies that aim to preserve the overwhelming and petrifying qualities of the original images. As places of memory, however, these works of art – fictional films, novels, documentaries, exhibitions, monuments – and the indigestible footage are interdependent, as Adolphe Nysenholc has argued in relation to Lanzmann's criticism of NIGHT AND FOG and his plea for withholding these images of destruction.[36] Because in the end, the screening of this footage *in our imagination* is a prerequisite for these works of art to be effective. However, one may wonder whether younger generations, who may not be aware of the existence of these images, will have the same experience. If not, then these images may very easily end up fading into oblivion.

Notes

1. Phrase from Paul Celan's translation in Alain Resnais's NUIT ET BROUILLARD / NIGHT AND FOG (1956).
2. Thomas Elsaesser, *Terror und Trauma. Zur Gewalt des Vergangenen in der BRD* (Berlin: Kadmos, 2007) 27.
3. Wolfgang Kraushaar, cited in Elsaesser, *Terror und Trauma* 20.
4. For a critical analysis of DER TODESSPIEGEL, see Elsaesser, *Terror und Trauma* 53-60.
5. Thomas Elsaesser, "Antigone Agonistes: Urban Guerilla or Guerilla Urbanism: The Red Army Fraction, *Germany in Autumn* and *Death Game*," online version: <http://www.rouge.com.au/4/antigone.html>. Last consulted Jan. 2008.
6. "Nach dem Schiffbruch – Christian Petzold im Gespräch [mit Christiane Peitz]," *Der Tagesspiegel* (25 Jan. 2001).
7. Stefan Steinberg, "Den Finger in die Wunde legen," 17 March 2000, online version: <www.wsws.org/de/2000/mar2000/stil-m17.shtml> (also in English). Last consulted Jan. 2008.
8. Many sponsors, particularly the broadcasting companies (Arte/WDR and the Hessischer Rundfunk), according to Petzold, preferred an apolitical film. "Nach dem Schiffbruch – Christian Petzold im Gespräch [mit Christiane Peitz]."
9. Denise Uijtdewillegen, *Echo's uit de ondergrond: De veranderende representatie van de RAF in visuele media*, unpublished MA thesis (University of Utrecht, 2007) 92.
10. "Terrorismus: 'Aber nicht andere nur, auch uns töten wir,'" *Der Spiegel* 43 (2002); "1. Trailer: Deutschland sucht den Terror-Star," at <www.rafinfo.de>; "Wer die RAF verstehen will, muss *Moby Dick* lessen," interview with Stefan Aust: <http://www.faz.net> (28 Oct. 2007).

11. Freely quoted from the French text of NIGHT AND FOG by Cayrol, the original (and sometimes abridged) English translation as well as Paul Celan's German translation.

12. The translation of Celan for the German edition of the documentary is in many respects a poem of its own, as David Coury pointed out in "'Auch ruhiges Land ...': Remembrance and Testimony in Paul Celan's *Nuit et Brouillard* Translation," *Prooftexts* 22 (2002): 55-76. Quotations are from Coury's translation. See also Ewout van der Knaap, *De verbeelding van Nacht en Nevel* (Groningen: Historische Uitgeverij, 2001).

13. Merten Worthmann, "Leben nach dem Terror. Christian Petzolds Film DIE INNERE SICHERHEIT," *Die Zeit* (1 Feb. 2001).

14. For an analysis of the dense literary references in GERMAN SISTERS in relation to NIGHT AND FOG, see Van der Knaap 98-102.

15. These and the following lines are literal translations from Celan's German version that is actually screened in GERMAN SISTERS. As stated earlier, Celan's translation often implies different connotations, as Coury and Van der Knaap have argued.

16. Thomas Elsaesser, "Mother Courage and Divided Daughters," *Monthly Film Bulletin* (July 1983): 177. See Elsaesser, *New German Cinema: A History* (London: MacMillan, 1989) 235. Charlotte Delorme is even more critical in "On the film MARIANNE AND JULIANE by Margarethe von Trotta," *Journal of Film and Video* 2 (1985): 47.

17. Christ Homewood, "Von Trotta's THE GERMAN SISTERS and Petzold's THE STATE I AM IN: discursive boundaries in the films of the New German Cinema to the present day," *Studies in European Cinema* 2.2 (2005): 94; Anton Kaes, *From Hitler to Heimat: The Return of History as Film* (Cambridge / London: Harvard University Press, 1989) 23.

18. Susan E. Linville, "Retrieving History: Margaretha von Trotta's MARIANNE AND JULIANE," *PMLA*, 106.3 (1991): 453. In this article, Linville loses herself in a bold feminist reading of the film.

19. Paul Coates, *The Gorgon's Gaze: German Cinema, Expressionism and the Image of Horror,* (Cambridge: Cambridge University Press, 1991) 193.

20. Petzold admits this explicitly in the interview with Christiane Peitz in *Der Tagesspiegel*, "Nach dem Schiffbruch": "Ich wollte nicht dass die Eltern ihre Vergangenheit diskutieren."

21. See Merten Worthmann, "Leben nach dem Terror," *Die Zeit* (1 Feb. 2001).

22. Jeffrey Herf, *Divided Memory: The Nazi Past in the Two Germanys* (Cambridge / London: Harvard University Press, 1997) 349; and Kaes 28. For a comparative perspective see Frank van Vree, *In de schaduw van Auschwitz: Herinneringen, beelden, geschiedenis* (Groningen: Historische Uitgeverij, 1995) as well as "Auschwitz and the Origins of Contemporary Historical Culture: Memories of World War II in European Perspective," *European History: Challenge for a Common Future*, ed. Attila Pók, Jörn Rüssen, and Jutta Scherrer (Hamburg: Körber, 2002) 202-220.

23. For a well-documented overview, see Van der Knaap 57-111.

24. Alexander and Margarete Mitscherlich, *Die Unfähigkeit zu trauern: Grundlagen kollektiven Verhaltens* (Munich: Piper, 1967).

25. *Erinnern, Wiederholen und Durcharbeiten* is the title of a publication by Sigmund Freud (1914).

26. At the same time, this attitude did not necessarily have to imply a *personal* resolution.

27. "Wir dürfen nicht vergessen, damit anderen vergessen, was ihnen angetan wurde," quoted in Van der Knaap 73.

28. Van der Knaap 84.

29. Interview in the *Neue Zürcher Zeitung* (29 Oct. 1996), quoted in Van der Knaap 99; also in Stephan Braese, "Das deutsche Objektiv: Der Holocaust im Film und der deutsche Literaturbetrieb 1945-1956," *Die Shoah im Bild*, ed. Sven Kramer (München: Taschebuch, 2003) 7-85.

30. Peitz.

31. Susan Carruthers, "Compulsory Viewing: Concentration Camp Film and German Re-Education," *Millennium* 3 (2001): 733-759; Hannah Caven, "Horror in Our Time: Images of the Concentration Camps in the British Media," *Historical Journal of Film, Radio & Television* 3 (Aug. 2001): 205-253.

32. For a detailed analysis of DEATH MILLS see Fritz Baur Institut Cinematographie des Holocaust: <www.cine-holocaust.de>.

33. These films were reissued in 2006, together with a documentary, in a DVD edition DEMOKRATIE LERNEN: RE-EDUCATION IM NACHKRIEGSDEUTSCHLAND (Göttingen: IWF Wissen und Medien 2006).

34. Herf 205.

35. These films were withdrawn from public screening in 1947, possibly in relation to the international tensions of the Cold War. Jan-Frederik Bandel, "Mit Moos bewach-sen: Ein kleine Rezeptionsgeschichte von Alain Resnais' Film NACHT UND NEBEL," *Jungle World* 18 (4 May 2005), online version: <www.jungle-world>.

36. Quoted in Emma Wilson, "Material Remains: NIGHT AND FOG," *October* 112 (2005) 91, originally published in an issue of *Contre Bande* 9 (2003) dedicated to Resnais.

Displacing the Colonial Archive

How Fiona Tan Shows Us "Things We Don't Know We Know"

Julia Noordegraaf

> Emotions, one could argue, ought to belong to any engagement with matters of life
> and death on the part of both those whom history has given the role of spectators and
> those who are charged with passing on compassion and preserving memory.[1]

In recent years, the archive has become a major trope in the humanities. Archives are no longer simply neutral bodies aimed at collecting, ordering, and storing our documentary heritage, they are now viewed more as cultural artifacts that actively shape the nature of that heritage and its use. From sites of knowledge retrieval, archives have come to be seen as sites of knowledge production.[2] The documents that archives hold – as those that have been lost or neglected – form the basis for the way we remember the past and thus play a crucial role in the formation of individual and collective identity.[3] In this sense, the archive actively shapes the way we see ourselves and how we situate ourselves between past, present, and future. As art historian and critic Hal Foster has pointed out, contemporary artists also have shown a renewed interest in the archive as a source and topic for their work.[4] For these artists, the archive serves as a site for developing alternative memories or reconstructing forgotten pasts. They achieve this by elaborating on the found image, object, and text and presenting them in a new form.

In this article, I discuss the reuse of colonial and ethnographic footage from the Dutch East-Indies (present-day Indonesia) in the film and video installations SMOKE SCREEN (1997) and FACING FORWARD (1999) by Amsterdam-based visual artist Fiona Tan (Indonesia, 1966). The analysis of these two cases aims to investigate how the works situate viewers towards the archival footage and the people and pasts it documents. In doing so, I depart from Thomas Elsaesser's analysis of "subject positions" and "speaking positions" as articulated in his work on post-Second World War representations of the Holocaust and fascism in film.[5] I analyze the installations with respect to the subject positions they create, and the speaking positions from which they articulate their perspective on the Dutch colonial past. Tan's treatment of the colonial footage results in a deconstruction of the unified subject positions assumed in the original films. I argue that her work implicates the spectator in the very construction of the subject positions vis-à-vis the archival footage, eventually with the purpose of establishing an affective relation with the footage and the people it documents. Tan's work thus transforms the subject position into a speaking position, where the spectator becomes the co-creator of the work. In this sense, the analysis of the two cases aims to demonstrate how the reuse of archival footage in film and video installations can offer a different perspective on the dynamics of subject positions and speaking positions in relation to audiovisual media.

Editing as a Window Cleaner

Fiona Tan was born in Indonesia in 1966 to a Chinese-Indonesian father and an Australian mother. She was raised in Australia, left for Amsterdam when she was eighteen and has been living and working there ever since. In her work – mostly film and video installations – identity is a central theme, especially as defined in relation to time and place. Tan often works with "found footage" that she combines into compilation films that are usually presented as film or video projections in the gallery space.[6] Since compilation films use archival material not as illustrations of real events but as images that draw attention to the constructed nature of media productions, these films have the potential to critique, challenge, and possibly also subvert the power of cinematic representation.[7] As Tan puts it: "The recycling of film fragments or photos breathes new life into the images; they are liberated from the harness of their original context. Recycling makes it possible to see images in a new way. Recycling creates new images. Editing as a window cleaner."[8]

With this particular interest in working with existing footage, Tan can be considered an artist working from what Foster has termed "an archival impulse." In his discussion of Thomas Hirschhorn, Tacita Dean, and Sam Durant as exemplars of artists working from this archival impulse, Foster indicates that these artists present their archival materials "as active, even unstable – open to eruptive returns and entropic collapses, stylistic repackagings and critical revisions."[9] The aim of these works is to "fashion distracted viewers into engaged discussants."[10] Artists do so by elaborating on the images, objects, and texts and presenting them in a new order that deliberately avoids the taxonomies of the "official" archive. Tan's film installation SMOKE SCREEN illustrates how the displacement of archival footage from the archive to the gallery can be a means to critically engage viewers with the images and the history they represent.

Deconstructing Colonial Subject Positions

In 1926, the Dutch cameraman Iep Ochse recorded a fascinating scene on the island of Bali, Indonesia: three toddlers cheerfully smoking a cigarette. The brief shot – it lasts eleven seconds – shows three naked children that fill the frame; they are seated facing the camera, the youngest sitting on the eldest boy's lap. The latter vigorously inhales and exhales, creating a cloud of smoke that fills the screen. He then passes on the cigarette to the boy to his right and lovingly grooms the lock of hair of the youngest child.

This shot was first used in a film made by the Dutch newsreel production company Polygoon (NAAR TROPISCH NEDERLAND / A TRIP TO THE TROPICAL NETHERLANDS, 1926) that offered a portrait of the Dutch colony in the form of a boat trip from the Netherlands to Batavia (present-day Jakarta), visiting various parts of the archipelago along the way. The original film is lost, but in the 1940 remake TROPISCH NEDERLAND / THE TROPICAL NETHERLANDS the scene is accompanied by a voice-over that says, "These babies take advantage of the fact that mother went shopping."[11] The scene is thus explained as an example of innocent, naughty behavior that occurs when mothers leave their children unattended.

THE TROPICAL NETHERLANDS clearly refers to Indonesia from the position of the colonizer. The footage was shot by a Dutch cameraman who regarded the Indonesian customs and traditions with interest and affect but was by definition bound to his outsider perspective.[12] Moreover, the film was commissioned by a Dutch company for the Dutch market. It propagates life and work in the colony by alternating scenes of the benefits of colonization – in particular in the field of education and health care – with scenes that emphasize the exoticism of the Indonesian landscapes, people, and local customs, such as the shot of the smoking children, which is edited in between shots of Balinese men and women in a kampong and of a baby rocking in a so-called *slendang*, a baby carrier made of traditionally dyed cloth.[13] This exoticism emphasizes the difference between, on the one hand, the indigenous population and, on the other, the Europeans who live and work there, like the ones who live in the "motherland." The boat trip itself mimics the "discovery" of Indonesia by the Dutch and the visits to the various islands during its subsequent colonization. In that sense, the spectator of this film is witnessing the creation of a colonial empire. The film thus constructs a unified subject position of the inhabitant of the Netherlands as part of a blossoming, colonial nation, where the differences between "East" and "West" remain clearly delineated.

In her film installation SMOKE SCREEN, Tan deconstructs this unifying, colonial subject position. She edited the shot in a short compilation film that is supposed to be played in a continuous loop. In the beginning, her film uses the traditional documentary format: we see the shot, followed by a title card that explains the place and estimated date of the recording: "Indonesia, maybe 1930." The second title card repeats the 1940s reading of the shot: babies taking advantage of the fact that mother went shopping. After that, however, the film becomes more ambiguous. Again we see the toddlers, now followed by the enigmatic title card "Boys will be men." This text seems to suggest that smoking is part of a ritual marking the transition from childhood to manhood, and invites reflections on the fact that these children have since grown up to be men. The following title card offers yet another perspective on the material: "With my own eyes." Whose eyes have actually witnessed this scene? From the first title card we know that the shot is archival footage, so the scene cannot have been witnessed by the artist herself. But then who did see and record it? Or does the text perhaps refer to the viewer, who is confronted by the filmic documentation of the scene and thus sees it "with her own eyes?" Finally, the film shows the artist herself, with a toy camera held before her right eye. She seems to be reenacting the recording of the original situation with a toy camera: we are now watching the artist mimicking the cameraman who filmed these three Indonesian children.

Then the film starts over again, and by now the viewer knows that the texts and images are highly ambiguous. The contrast between the old, archival footage and the new, self-reflexive texts and images invites the viewer to adopt a more distant standpoint. The relation between the camera, the people filmed, the artist, and the viewer is being questioned from this standpoint. Who are these children? Where does the footage come from? To what extent was it staged? What has become of these kids? But also: Why are we looking at it now? How do we relate to these images of colonial Indonesia?

Shared Speaking Positions in the Gallery Space

Obviously, the speaking position in Tan's piece is entirely different from that of the original film. Being herself of Chinese-Indonesian-Australian descent, and having lived in Europe for most of her life, Tan speaks from the position of the migrant.[14] Moreover, she is speaking from the position of the artist, who takes the freedom to rearrange images and texts in a form that deliberately avoids a unified perspective on the archival material, and that underscores her personal involvement in the interpretation of it. As literary scholar Ernst van Alphen states with regards to another of Tan's works, LINNAEUS' FLOWER CLOCK (1998): "This striking juxtaposition of obviously old and new footage emphasizes Tan's act of placing herself in the image. Like Alice in Wonderland she has found access to an imaginary world. She appropriates the old images into her present."[15] The insert of the shot of the artist with a toy camera in SMOKE SCREEN similarly serves to underline the artist's contemporary, subjective perspective on the footage of the toddlers.

In addition, the shot of the artist directs the viewer's attention to the constructed nature of Tan's film and of cinematic representations in general, as to the viewer's active role in making sense of the images. When looking at the artist "looking" at the shot of the three Balinese children, the viewer begins to question his or her own relation to the material, and to the conditions in which it was originally shot: "Tan's videos and films all reflect on how the medium functions as an agent that creates specific relationships between the viewer and the image."[16] The work thus creates an unstable subject position from which the viewer is invited to actively participate in the artist's montage in order to make sense of the images. In this sense, Tan invites the spectator to join her at the speaking position of the artist.

The fact that Tan's works are usually presented as film or video projections in the gallery space further underlines the active role of the viewer in the interpretation of the archival material. Contrary to cinematic spectatorship, where viewers are more or less required to sit still and watch the film as it unfolds over time, in the gallery space both the images and the spectator are mobile. German thinker Boris Groys explains that "a video or movie installation in a museum neutralizes the ban of motion that determines the viewing of these pictures in a movie system. Pictures and spectators are allowed to move at the same time."[17] Consequently, compared to the cinema spectator, the viewer of film and video installations in the gallery switches "from a passive position to a more interactive one, from an observer separate from the apparatus to a participant."[18] According to film scholar Raymond Bellour, installations guide the viewer towards the composing and recomposing of the images and words being presented.[19] In the space of the gallery, then, the physical displacement of the viewer is required to make sense of the work.[20]

Tan's video installation TUAREG (1999) is a case in point. This work is based on a black-and-white shot of a group of twelve Tuareg children posing in front of a tent, which is supposed to be projected on a transparent screen that divides two separate rooms. In that way, the viewer can literally approach the same image from two sides: on the one side you see the image as it is, on the other side of the screen it is reversed. There is a different soundtrack for each side – on the one side, we hear the sounds of birds, flies, and the chatter of children; on the other, the more ominous sound of a howling wind – which emphasizes the changing perspective of the image by the viewer's physical displacement in space.

Facing Forward with Found Footage: Showing "Things We Don't Know We Know"

The displacement of the viewer in the gallery space parallels the physical displacement of the footage, from the geographical location where it was shot, to the original film, to the archive, and then to the gallery space. This displacement in space also entails a displacement in time: from the moment of recording and editing to the inclusion and storage in the archive and the subsequent appropriation of the material in the artist's and viewer's presence. One of the attractions of working with archival material is that it presents the opportunity to investigate the relevance of past events for our present and future. As Foster indicates, the archival elements reused in contemporary visual art works serve as "found arks of lost moments in which the here-and-now of the work serves as a possible portal between an unfinished past and a reopened future."[21] This connection between past, present, and future is achieved through "affective association."[22] In that sense, archival art works refer to the past in a way similar to how memory works: images of past people, places, and events are combined and recombined in constantly changing constellations. As a consequence, our interpretation of the objects and events from the past is constantly changing as well; each time we approach them from a different perspective.

The re-presentation of history as memory is certainly not limited to art works. Elsaesser argues that the traditional conception of history is presently in crisis, in large part because it has become a past that cinema and television "can 'master' for us by digitally remastering archival material." The effect of this constant re-presentation of the past in the form of its audiovisual documentation is that "the line where memory passes into history has becomes [sic] uncertain, and ... the divide is being crossed and recrossed in either direction."[23] He argues that the process of making sense of the past has become a therapeutic activity, where developing a unified story about the past has been replaced by "acts of re-telling, re-membering, and repeating," acts that point towards obsession, fantasy, and trauma.[24] Elsewhere, Elsaesser describes the traumatic dimension of our contemporary engagement with the past as "the things we don't know we know."[25] This category hints at

> a version of the past and our knowledge of it, which includes forgetting, repressing, and disavowal, that is, aspects of the workings of an unconscious, or of a knowledge of which the individual is not in control, where language and memory speak to us, where the discourse determines the subject, and where there is acknowledgment of the discontinuous, shock-like de-contextualizing and re-contextualizing power of both memory and amnesia.[26]

It is precisely this traumatic aspect of colonial history that Tan addresses in her work. In re-presenting and re-contextualizing filmic documents that remind us of the exploitation of the indigenous population in the former Dutch colony, she makes us face a history that we would rather forget – she reminds us of "what we don't know we know." And the preoccupation of the Dutch with their colonial past in Indonesia – and by extension, that of all Western nations and their colonial pasts – certainly is of a traumatic nature. As historian Frank van Vree has pointed out, the culture of memory in the Netherlands has been dominated by romantic constructions of colonial history. Even the more critical documentaries and fiction films display a sense of nostalgia for this "lost paradise" or tend to portray the colonizers as victims (in particular of the Japanese occupation of Indonesia during World War II).[27]

Tan's video installation FACING FORWARD addresses this current preoccupation with history as (traumatic) memory by showing how the past is always present in our audiovisual memory of it. For this work, she chose ethnographic footage from the collection of the Netherlands Filmmuseum and edited it into an eleven-minute film that is usually projected onto a gallery wall. The film opens with a black-and-white shot of a large group of non-western (Indonesian?) men who face the camera as if they were having their portrait taken. In the middle, three white men (missionaries?) are seated, flanked by other white men in army uniforms and leisure wear. This shot is followed by other shots of (Indonesian) men and women staring silently into the camera. This scenario is repeated throughout the rest of the film. We see different shots of people from various parts of the world who appear to be coerced into posing before the camera. This impression is reinforced by the inclusion of shots of a white man operating a film camera who is wearing a headband decorated with four feathers. A shot of two African women wearing face masks epitomizes the contrived nature of the footage: women who do not want their faces to be seen are being forced to "face forward."

The work stimulates a reflection on the relation between past and present by way of a voice-over that narrates parts of the hypothetical conversations between the traveler Marco Polo and the emperor Kublai Khan from Italo Calvino's book *Invisible Cities* – a text about traveling through time and space.[28] In the beginning of the film, the voice-over cites Marco Polo, who explains to Kublai Khan "that what he sought was always something lying ahead, even if it was a matter of the past. Arriving at each new city, the traveler finds again a past of his that he did not know he had: the foreignness of what you no longer are or no longer possess lies in wait for you in foreign, unpossessed places."[29] The film ends with the comment that "By now, from that real or hypothetical past of his, Marco is excluded; he cannot stop; he must go on to another city, where another of his pasts awaits him, or something perhaps that had been a possible future of his and is now someone else's present." In Marco Polo's view, the past, present, and future no longer form a linear continuity; in fact, the past can only be reached in the present or the future.[30] There is a conflation between places from the past and places in the present; in each new city, he finds a past he "did not know he knew."

Marco Polo's reflection on his travels can be seen as metaphoric for the displacement of the footage from the archive to Tan's video installation. Tan uses archival material from other times and places in order to stimulate critical reflection on the viewer's contemporary perspective of the past, and its relevance for his or her future. In that sense, FACING FORWARD demonstrates how "relating to the past as well as to distance is always a matter of alterity (times as well as spaces are different) and a matter of identity (the past, the distance as such, being part of our present culture)."[31]

As in SMOKE SCREEN, the repetition of shots and the use of self-reflexive texts and images here prevent the formation of a stable, coherent subject position. Besides, the almost exclusive use of medium-shots and close-ups of people staring into the camera, such as the inclusion of the shot of the white cameraman with his ridiculous feather headband, instigate a play of gazes, where the positions of the subject observed and the observing subject are eventually reversed. This radical destabilization of the position of the viewing subject opens a space for engaging with the otherness of colonialism. As Elsaesser states: "fracturing the viewers' identity is the very condition that makes the radical otherness of an extreme historical experience representable."[32] In that sense, Tan's installations address "the affect of concern," a concept that indicates "recognizing oneself to be emotionally called upon to respond, act, react." As such, they try "to convey subject positions that ... touch a point where the self itself knows and can experience otherness."[33] The purpose of Tan's works in the end is "to make one see things which are not on screen and listen to voices speaking from within oneself."[34]

Conclusion

As I have argued above, the fact that Tan's film and video installations invite viewers to listen to their "inner voices" has consequences for the positions from which one speaks or is spoken to about the Dutch colonial past. The specific form in which Tan re-presents colonial footage not only deconstructs the unifying subject position of the original films, but makes the formation of subject positions vis-à-vis this material the very center of the work. The fragmented nature of her compilation films, supported by the viewer's mobility in the gallery space, invite spectators to actively construct a perspective on the meaning of those images. The result is that the artist vacates her speaking position for each individual viewer, who becomes the co-creator of the work. The aim of this move is to establish "the affect of concern" that urges viewers to investigate the relevance of the colonial past for their own present and future. In this sense film and video installations based on archival footage can function as forms of cultural memory that try to counter the history of the "winners" by "shifting the balance of power from victors to vanquished, giving voice to the silenced, and admitting mute testimony as evidence."[35]

Notes

1. Thomas Elsaesser, "Subject Positions, Speaking Positions: From *Holocaust, Our Hitler,* and *Heimat* to *Shoah* and *Schindler's List*," *The Persistence of History: Cinema, Television, and the Modern Event,* ed. Vivian Sobchack (London/New York: Routledge, 1996) 149.
2. Ann Laura Stoler, "Colonial Archives and the Arts of Governance," *Archival Science* 2.1-2 (2002): 87-109. The seminal reflection on the archive as a cultural phenomenon is Jacques Derrida's *Archive Fever: A Freudian Impression,* trans. Eric Prenowitz (Chicago: University of Chicago Press, 1996).
3. As Eric Ketelaar contends, "Archives are spaces of memory-practice, where people's experiences can be transformed into meaning." Eric Ketelaar, "The Archives of the United Nations International Criminal Tribunal for the Former Yugoslavia (ICTY): A Joint Heritage, Shared by Communities of Records," unpublished paper delivered at the *I-Chora 2* conference, Amsterdam, 31 Aug.-2 Sept. 2005.
4. Hal Foster, "An Archival Impulse," *October* 110 (Fall 2004): 3-22.
5. Elsaesser, "Subject Positions, Speaking Positions."
6. Jay Leyda was the first to distinguish archive-based films as "compilation films," see his *Films Beget Films* (London: George Allen & Unwin, 1964). These films are also referred to as "found footage films," or "archival films." Michael Zryd distinguishes between found footage films (based on non-archived material, literally "found" in private collections, commercial stock shot agencies, garbage bins, etc.) and archival films (based on material from archival institutions). I do not share Zryd's distinction because I actually doubt whether, as he claims, "the archive is an official institution that separates historical record from the outtake." Michael Zryd, "Found Footage Film as Discursive Metahistory," *The Moving Image* 3.2 (2003): 41. Moreover, film programmer Gertjan Zuilhof has remarked that the use of the term *found footage* is not always appropriate, because most artists are actively searching for specific material rather than just accidentally finding it. Gertjan Zuilhof, "Welt Spiegel Kino/World Mirror Cinema: Gustav Deutsch," *Catalogue 34th International Film Festival Rotterdam* (Rotterdam: IFFR, 2005) 226.
7. William C. Wees, "Found Footage and Question of Representation," *Found Footage Film,* ed. Cecilia Hausheer and Christoph Settele (Luzern: VIPER/Zuklopverlag, 1992) 39.

8. Fiona Tan, "Kingdom of Shadows," *Scenario: Fiona Tan*, ed. Mariska van den Berg and Gabriele F. Götz (Amsterdam/Rotterdam: Van den Berg & Wallroth/NAi, 2000) 127.

9. Foster 17.

10. Foster 4.

11. The shot occurs at about 38 minutes into the film.

12. Much of the footage shot for and used in THE TROPICAL NETHERLANDS was reused in the 1995 feature-length compilation film MOTHER DAO, THE TURTLELIKE (Vincent Monnikendam, 1995). For a detailed analysis of this film, as of Iep Ochse's unique material, see Ylann Schemm, *Moeder Dao: Spectacles of propaganda in the Dutch Indies 1912-1933*, unpublished MA thesis (University of Amsterdam, 1996).

13. In Fiona Tan's film installation CRADLE (1998), this shot of the swinging baby is edited into a continuous loop and projected on a piece of cloth.

14. Tan investigated her position as a migrant in the feature-length documentary MAY YOU LIVE IN INTERESTING TIMES (1997), an attempt to map her cultural identity by visiting all the places where her relatives live, from Europe to Australia, Indonesia and China.

15. Ernst van Alphen, "Imagined Homelands: Re-mapping Cultural Identity," *Thamyris / Intersecting* 9 (2002): 54.

16. Van Alphen 59.

17. Boris Groys, "Media Art in the Museum," *Last Call* 1.2 (2001): <http://www.belkin-gallery.ubc.ca/lastcall/past/pages2/page2.html>. Last visited 13 Jan. 2006. This essay, no longer online, is included (in German) in Boris Groys, *Topologie der Kunst* (Munich / Vienna: Hanser, 2003) 59-76.

18. Anne Friedberg, *Window Shopping: Cinema and the Postmodern* (Berkeley: University of California Press, 1994) 144. While Friedberg here discusses the impact of virtual reality devices on cinema and televisual spectatorship, I think her argument also applies to the context of the gallery space.

19. Raymond Bellour, "D'un autre cinema," *Traffic* 34 (2000): 8.

20. My view on spectatorship as constructed by film or video projection in the gallery space is thus more dynamic than that of David Joselit's, who argues that compared to closed-circuit video installations: "In video projection the viewer is made more passive both in her consumption of spectacular imagery and in her ability to intervene within the space of the screen." David Joselit, "Inside the Light Cube," *Artforum* 42 (Fall 2004): 156.

21. Foster 15.

22. Foster 21.

23. Elsaesser, "Subject Positions, Speaking Positions" 145.

24. Elsaesser, "Subject Positions, Speaking Positions" 146.

25. Elsaesser presents this category as an addition to a statement by US Secretary of Defense Donald Rumsfeld, who, at a February 2002 press conference, enigmatically summarized the state of affairs in US intelligence as: "There are known knowns; there are things we know we know. We also know there are known unknowns; that is to say we know there are some things we do not know. But there are also unknown unknowns – the ones we don't know we don't know." He argues that taken together,

these categories adequately describe the relation between history and memory as we know it today. Thomas Elsaesser, "History, Media, and Memory – Three Discourses in Dispute?," unpublished paper presented at the European Summer School in Cultural Studies, "Witness: Memory, Representation, and The Media In Question," Copenhagen, 23-27 August 2004.

26. Elsaesser, "History, Media, and Memory."

27. Frank van Vree, "Bilder/Gegenbilder: Kolonialgeschichte und visuelle Erinnerungskultur 1945-1995," *Kolonialismus und Erinneringskultur: Die Kolonialvergangenheit im kollektiven Gedächtnis der deutschen und niederländischen Einwanderungsgesellschaft*, ed. Helma Lutz and Kathrin Gawarecki (Munich: Waxmann, 2005) 181-202. Van Vree mentions MOTHER DAO, THE TURTLELIKE as the one notable exception. See also Pamela Pattynama, "Over Gordel van Smaragd: een kampongkind in de nationale herinneringsbeelden," *Beeldritsen: visuele cultuur en etnische diversiteit in Nederland*, ed. Tessa Boerman, Patricia Pisters, and Joes Segal (Amsterdam: De Balie, 2003) 41-52.

28. Italo Calvino, *Invisible Cities* (San Diego: Harcourt, 1978).

29. Voice-over commentary in FACING FORWARD (1999); after Calvino 28-29.

30. Van Alphen 66.

31. Hubert Damisch, quoted in Yves-Alain Bois, Denis Hollier, and Rosalind Krauss, "A Conversation with Hubert Damisch," *October* 85 (Summer 1998): 16.

32. Elsaesser, "Subject Positions, Speaking Positions" 174.

33. Elsaesser, "Subject Positions, Speaking Positions" 173.

34. Elsaesser, "Subject Positions, Speaking Positions" 174.

35. Elsaesser, "History, Media, and Memory."

Found Footage, Performance, Reenactment

A Case for Repetition

Jennifer Steetskamp

> ... in the paradigm of the event, images, signs and statements contribute to
> allowing the world to happen.
> – Maurizio Lazzarato, 2003[1]

Almost everyone with even a slight interest in soccer will remember the moment
in the final of the FIFA World Cup in 2006 when France's star player Zinedine
Zidane gave the Italian player Marco Materazzi his famous headbutt. As such,
the event would have gone relatively unnoticed – bending the rules is somehow
part of the game, and body contact of this kind is fairly common. However, in this
particular situation, the incident turned into what could be called an unpredicted
event, with its reruns in the media becoming unavoidable. Not only did the
images become news, but other television formats, such as sports programs and
talk shows, also evaluated the possible reasons for the action. It was Zinedine
Zidane's imminent retirement and his third-time election as FIFA World Player
of the Year that made what he did even more incomprehensible. The action was
not a strategic foul that served the team, but seemed to be personally motivated.
The speculation of what words were exchanged between the two players to cause
this confrontation kept the images in the media for a long time. On YouTube and
similar websites, one can still find many fragments, often as a parody of the
broadcast images themselves, replacing the figure of Zidane with a video game
monster or questioning national perspectives on the subject matter.[2] There is
even a self-pronounced *Zidane World Cup Headbutt Animation Festival* online.[3]
By relating what happened to the types of action found in video or computer
games, these animations address the game-character of soccer and at once indicate that the event-character of the headbutt is preconditioned by the existence of
another type of game entirely dependent on the digital domain, whose rules –
defining what constitutes a permitted action – differs from most processes that
occur on the pitch. In other words: it seems as if this rash, seemingly unpreme-
ditated moment attains its full meaning and determinacy only in a context in
which the media function not only as a catalyst of actions around the world, but
also as a platform on which formerly incommensurable events turn into compre-

hensible information, precisely by producing as many repetitions as permutations.

At first glance, it seems as if Harun Farocki's adaptation of the match between Italy and France in the context of Documenta 12 is perfectly in line with a paradigm in which the dominance of media representation over other forms of world-disclosure remains largely unquestioned. It may even appear that with *Deep Play* Farocki is carrying this paradigm to an extreme. Whereas the YouTube iterations of the headbutt point to the way the event surpasses the primary rules and expectations of the soccer game, exhibiting the degree to which the game is framed and conditioned by the media, while simultaneously leaving the distinction between actual game and media representation intact, Farocki's installation is apparently an even bolder gesture, seemingly equating game and simulation, reality and digital media representation, perception and analysis. This happens to such an extent that not only do they become inseparable, also they are increasingly identical. On twelve plasma screens in the rotunda of the Fridericianum, television footage of the game and its context was combined with simulations and analyses of the game, including an animation of Zidane's headbutt. To do this, Farocki made use of HALCON machine vision software by a company called MVTec, a major global player in the area of automated vision (also including face recognition software frequently employed in the context of surveillance). The software had been customized by a research group of the Technische Universität München in order to be applied to match analyses.[4] In that way, Farocki not only shows how "traditional" media like television are irreducibly framing the game, but also raises the question of how the perception of sports events has changed and will change in the digital era, thus documenting a process as much as enabling prospective vision. However, this strange intertwinement of the old and the new, what is already there and what is possible, indicates that the equation made above, i.e., between the match and its representation, eventually does not hold in the case of *Deep Play*, including both simulation (projecting the possible) and analysis (reading the existing). In this light, the work does not represent a paradigm carried to an extreme but rather indicates a paradigm shift with respect to the paradigm as such.

Strikingly, the presupposed epistemological distinction between the real event and its mediated appearance is actually maintained *within* the realm of the digital. In an almost paradoxical fashion, the machine vision application as employed in *Deep Play* seems to confirm differences that constitute themselves as distinctions between human perception, human perception framed by the media, automated vision, and human perception determined by automated vision (without necessarily claiming the primordial nature of human vision, that is). The digital does not constitute a fusion of binarisms (like presence and representation) or modes of experience (like human and machine vision), but demonstrates that the differences underlying these abstracted patterns are fundamentally irreducible, even if the binarisms themselves are rendered problematic as exclusive categories. That is not to say that everything is *contained* in what I here call "the digital"; instead, it implies that the digital – from the concrete perspective of a work of art and its reflexive potential – is allowed to address its own limitations on the level of experience. This is not totally unlike saying that there is a difference between the participation in the "live" event in a stadium and experiencing the "live" broadcasting of the event, without confirming an *essential* distinction. The difference does not implode, but exclusive distinction is rendered problematic. A similar irreducibility can be traced on an ontological level, where the different material settings point towards differentiation or differential iteration rather than a confirmation of ultimate categories of what is constituted as immediately given and what appears as its mere supplement. Even more so, because that which is immediately given (the concrete material context) is not a characteristic of a primary event which initiates the series of secondary, "immaterial" representations or media events, but both a condition and effect of every single (singular) event in the series. This is exactly what media events, especially in the context of art or other cultural appropriations, might be capable of: the showing of the continuous discontinuity of these occurrences in an epistemological *and* ontological fashion, as a series of intelligible events that include a fundamental incommensurability with the intelligible. In that respect, *Deep Play* has more in common with the YouTube reenactments of the headbutt than one might think: they both confirm differences as much as they seem to erase them.

This paradoxical movement in *Deep Play* is far from new; even in its apparent technological discontinuity with Farocki's other work, reaching from his early film practice to the later film and video installations, *Deep Play* is somehow symptomatic of a way of working, in which media practice is repeatedly questioned and negotiated. Appearing as a culmination of an oeuvre, in which cinema and art, documentation and assemblage take turns, the digital framing of television and the televised experience of sports events are rather indicative of a more general tendency in Farocki's work, enabling an intertwinement of these layers by affirming their difference. In what follows, I would like to situate Farocki's earlier oeuvre in the art context it leads up to, and show a couple of relations with the art practice of others, taking the ideas of Thomas Elsaesser on Farocki and Johan Grimonprez (another artist presented in the context of a Documenta exhibition) as a point of departure. In this way, I want not only to broaden the perspective of how one could understand the type of work both Farocki and Grimonprez are producing, but to try to reach conclusions that count for other art manifestations as well, such as performance which struggles with a range of epistemological and ontological problems related to the possibility or impossibility of repetition. At this point, I would like to mention that, looking at these problems from the perspective of art, having a specific work – *Deep Play* – in mind (and thus working from within a contemporary context), there is always the risk of brushing both Elsaesser and Farocki (too much) against the grain. However, in the attempt to establish an oscillating movement between the old and the new as well as between art and cinema, I would like to approach a situation in which both sides can benefit each other.

Considering his general oeuvre, Harun Farocki is undoubtedly one of the most important exponents of what is called found footage film (and video), which can be understood in the context of film and cinema as well as in relation to art. Being closely linked to the art historical notion of the *objet trouvé*, found footage describes a method of film (and video) making, according to which already existing material is recombined, re-edited and re-sampled to generate different contexts of meaning. The method as such could be seen as an exemplification of the *montage* principle, reflecting on the avant-gardist tradition of the *collage* (including the reference to Lautréamont's notorious pre-surrealist dictum[5]) as well as on the technological conditions of filmmaking itself (and, more specifically, on certain traditions in the history of film).[6] In this sense, every practice that involves found footage could be called meta-film or, in cases where mainly television material is involved, meta-television or meta-video, according to the medium-specific principles exposed in the rearrangement of the footage (in television-based video works, the editing often simulates the viewer activity of "zapping"[7]). Basically, every medium involves the possibility of re-sampling, drawing either upon pictorial *collage* or upon filmic *montage*, and sometimes upon both. The movement induced by these rearrangement techniques leads to what Nicolas Bourriaud, former director and founder of the Palais de Tokyo in Paris, described in 2000 as a symptom of the more general phenomenon of "sampling culture."[8]

Some of the contemporary practices described by Bourriaud actually relate back to earlier movements, one of which is the "appropriation art" of the 1970s and 1980s. The notion of "appropriation" is not restricted to a specific medium or art form; it applies to photography as much as to installation art. The most important characteristic is the recycling and re-arrangement of already existing imagery, objects, codes, and signs. There were actually (at least) two directions that determined these practices of appropriation. First of all, there were artists who were introducing elements from a non-art context to the domain of art (the Duchampian moment of displacement), and secondly, there were artists who were quoting other artists (to the degree the "copy" became indistinguishable from the "original," constituting the second Duchampian moment, that is, the moment of the "artistic" readymade). It is almost unnecessary to say that the constitutive gesture of these works is the Benjaminian event of reproduction, being based on a more fundamental reproducibility which functions as the general condition of art and media in the twentieth century.[9] Furthermore, appropriation art practices are often embedded in a cultural discourse on the role of the "copy" or "simulacrum," explicitly or implicitly referring to the ideas of Jean Baudrillard.

Hal Foster, in his *Return of the Real* (1996), refers in this context to a short text by the artist Barbara Kruger published in *Screen* in 1982, together with some of her "photo-texts," which was the first time they were reproduced in a British magazine. According to Foster, Kruger's text implies that "appropriation art" had a double bias by moving back and forth between ideology critique and "deconstruction." Its aim was, on the one hand, to expose "reality" as "representation" and to raise issues of "authorship" and "property" (like certain variants of "deconstruction" do) and, on the other, to make an attempt to reveal the "truth" *underneath* or *behind* representation (which is a central concern of ideology critique). [10] If one follows the reading of Foster, it almost seems as if Kruger is taking a "constructivist" stance, by being concerned with or exposing the concern of appropriation art with reality as representation. In a way, the position of philosophical constructivism (not to be confused with the constructivism of Soviet art and cinema) is typical for its time: it signifies a line of thought that, in its most radical mutations, turns out to be almost a reversal of the "quasi-Platonism" sustained by classical ideology critique, postulating the primordiality of "simulation" or "representation." I would like to propose another, maybe more subtle reading of Kruger, as the "deconstruction" she is talking about is not only related to problems of "authorship" and "pastiche" but refers to a mode of repetition that includes "alternation" and the performative act of "making explicit" (announcing itself both as a process of "externalization" and as a "declarative" speech act).[11] This, however, casts a rather different light on the appropriation practices of the 1970s and 1980s, which seem to confirm the "concept" of *iteration* much more than the "constructivist" idea of all-inclusive *representation* – at least in the context of Barbara Kruger's work.

Thomas Elsaesser seems to implicitly react to these earlier discussions in a recent essay on the cultural "doubles" of Alfred Hitchcock, one of the – if not *the* – most quoted filmmaker ever. In that respect, it is important to note that Elsaesser does not ascribe the moment of "doubling" to the Baudrillardian scene, but to (a specific reading of) the Foucauldian relation between words and things. This position acknowledges the difference between images and things, signs and objects, but simultaneously emphasizes their similarity (rather than their resemblance).[12] In this way, the epistemological paradigm of the "copy" (that even after canceling out the "original" still relies heavily on its *presentia in absentia*) undergoes an ontological turn. As much as the thing is an image, the image is a thing (at least as long as one acknowledges the necessity of "hardware" for the image to exist[13]). However, the *difference* between the two is not entirely cancelled out, as an image and a thing – as paradoxical as it might sound – are different things, different images. That is, cinematic reality enters life in a more profound way than just absorbing life into the regime of images: life events actually mimic cinematic events, as much as cinematic events mimic life.[14] The mimicking gesture is already a poetical act.

It is rather significant that Elsaesser redefines the connection between cinema and life as an ontological association (or *Verbund*, to follow Farocki) in the context of the recent work of Johan Grimonprez on Hitchcock, which arises from a fascination with the multiplicity of Hitchcock look- and sound-alikes, including the artist's own father. Not so much because of the LOOKING FOR ALFRED (2005) project itself (the implications of that are rather obvious), but because of an earlier work by Grimonprez that left its imprint on our art historical memory: the found-footage video DIAL H-I-S-T-O-R-Y (1997). As large as its impact was when it was presented at Documenta X, this does not begin to hint at its later, even greater success, which can be ascribed to its apparent prophetic qualities, recapitulating the history of plane-hijackings in relation to terrorism. After a work like this, the 9/11 attacks actually seemed like reenactments of television events and cinematic realities, which seemed to leave philosophers like Baudrillard in a state of metaphysical crisis, because everything suddenly became "so real." At the same time, it is also quite interesting that the media events and the video work not only predict and precede what happened *after*, but that the work, functioning as an archive, constitutes a series of events in itself. It is as if (this type of) found-footage work exemplifies an *iterability* that is already both epistemological and ontological. The 9/11 event, especially when considered as a "media event," is in that sense just another event in this series, whose beginning and end can never be determined definitively, the only criterion of affiliation being a rather indeterminate sense of "family relations," as it were.

Elsaesser's observations concerning Grimonprez are also interesting with respect to Farocki: not only in the context of *Deep Play*, in relation to the reading I have suggested above, but also regarding his earlier work. In his introduction to the volume *Harun Farocki: Working on the Sight-Lines*, Elsaesser states that Farocki is basically working "on realities already constituted: replaying them for the sake of the small differences, the small deferrals, so that something (else) may become visible ... in the repetition."[15] This method is at once connected to the "materiality" of the medium. In reference to Farocki's NICHT LÖSCHBARES FEUER / INEXTINGUISHABLE FIRE (1968/69), which broaches the issue of the American napalm bomb attacks during the Vietnam War, Elsaesser focuses on the radical act the filmmaker exhibits in one of the scenes. Just before the (f)act, Farocki states:

"When we show you pictures of napalm burns, you'll close your eyes. First you'll close your eyes to the pictures. Then you'll close your eyes to the memory. Then you'll close your eyes to the facts. Then you'll close your eyes to the entire context."[16] A moment later and totally unprepared, the spectator becomes a witness to an unexpected violent action, as Farocki extinguishes his cigarette on the back of his hand. In this context, Elsaesser refers to one of Christa Blümlinger's essays in the same volume, in which the relation between this gesture, or rather of the scar that remains, and the indexicality of celluloid becomes evident,[17] an indexicality that is questioned by video technology and the later digital imaging techniques. In this way, Farocki's metaphorical gesture transforms itself into a commentary on the conditions and end of cinema. Hence, it is obviously not the "materiality" of film that becomes visible as an "event," but the loss of its (imagined) purity (paralleled by the absence of the key image of the napalm attacks[18]), exposed by a metaphorical image. At the same time, the image itself is not "immaterial": what seems lost is also contained with its self-difference constituting its self-similarity.

This paradoxical juxtaposition of the "similar" as a relation of difference appears to form the very basis of Farocki's method, also on the level of images combined with each other. As Elsaesser writes:

> Juxtaposing apparent opposites and if necessary, torturing them until they yield a hidden identity or an unsuspected similarity, provide the (temporary) moments of closure for his trains of thought. In this sense, metaphoric equivalence and (almost as often) metaphoric discrepancy (catachresis) establish Farocki's poetics as well as his politics.[19]

"Metaphoric equivalence" (which, in its strictest sense, is a contradiction in terms) and "metaphoric discrepancy" (which is almost as contradictory, referring to an unavoidable failure of images and signs in producing analogies) are synchronous movements in two different directions, two tendencies within one differential domain. It is as if the utilization of metaphor in order to establish medium-reflexivity (rather than medium-specificity) leads to a situation in which the principle of an ontological *iterability* (so to speak) becomes somehow evident as a pattern. It is a constant movement, in which one position is simultaneously stabilized and destabilized by the next with every image – every new image – confirming and at once undermining the previous image. Consequently, the movement between equivalence and discrepancy is mirrored on a formal level: "making connections on the basis of having taken something apart is thus where the rhetoric of the metaphor meets the technique of filmic montage."[20] This is possibly also how the "information feedback loop" that is established in Farocki's work has to be understood. According to Elsaesser, it is a *Verbund*, in which any sudden excess is absorbed by the next cycle of (meaning) production, leading to what he describes as an "uncanny timeliness" of Farocki's work. [21]

The oscillation between equivalence and discrepancy is paralleled by the movement between over- and underexposure on the level of information. INEXTINGUISHABLE FIRE does not provide an actual image of the historical event it refers to (the American napalm bomb attacks in Vietnam). Instead, the metaphorical image functions as a stand-in. In this context, Elsaesser mentions Farocki's comment on the air show disaster at the Rammstein airbase on 28 August 1988, which designates the "cut" to be the "revenge" of television makers trying to deal with the pseudo-events that surround actual catastrophes. In that specific case, there was a cut just before the planes collided, and instead of the accident one could see the image of the press conference. The event as such only exists as an "afterimage," supplemented by the viewer's imagination. In INEXTINGUISHABLE FIRE, withholding images of the actual event is accompanied by the staging of a subversive gesture, whose "inadequacy," as Elsaesser states, "demonstrates the fundamental need for metaphor," and thus the necessity of art and aesthetic practice,[22] turning around what has been constituted as "media reality" in the afterlife of cinema.[23]

However, the interplay of visibility and invisibility can also take a rather different direction in Farocki's work when he uses the effects of "sudden exposure," as in VIDEOGRAMS OF A REVOLUTION (1992, together with Andrei Ujica), a video/film project frequently referred to in the context of art and aesthetic theory. It famously documents the Rumanian revolution of 1989, when demonstrators occupied a television station, thus turning it into a historical site; the work is often discussed in the context of the framing or a presupposed loss of framing. Without going too deeply into the discussions surrounding this work, it is worth mentioning that the dynamics of becoming visible is associated here with an ambiguous answer to the question of what kind of status "visibility" should have in general. Both the leaving-invisible and the making-visible (or even the "involuntary" becoming-visible) seem to be predestined to fulfill their function in the rhetoric of public media events. In relation with this, one could refer once again to Grimonprez' DIAL H-I-S-T-O-R-Y, which includes footage of interviews with plane hijackers, elaborating their motivations. Grimonprez states that, from the Reagan era onward, live images of the terrorists' faces were no longer included in public broadcasts – they no longer had a voice.[24] Tracing these changes was one of the main objectives of the DIAL H-I-S-T-O-R-Y project. Both the rendering-visible and the turning-invisible are always part of the politics of the image. What happens to these strategies depends on the context.

The reason why I am referring to this "dialectics" is the way disappearance in terms of keeping the event invisible has played an important role in the theories and debates related to early performance art. Both performance artists and theorists have prevalently emphasized the importance of the artistic event to be ephemeral, to eventually disappear, which has often been based on a predilection for the "here and now." It has to be considered "unrepeatable" to preserve its "performative" character. In order not to corrupt the "ontology" of the performative event, it has to be kept invisible as an image. Performance documentation is therefore considered unacceptable, or at least problematic.[25] Although a closer evaluation of these – in my opinion rather questionable – assumptions has to take place elsewhere, I would like to focus on one specific aspect of this point of view: the idea that the so-called "dematerialization" of art, which supposedly took place in the 1960s and 1970s, defies the logic of the market economy, which is based on the possibility of exchanging commodity objects.[26] With respect to performance art, video or photo documentation (although it was frequently done and is therefore a fact that cannot be neglected, especially if one wants to be able to talk about the phenomenon anyway) is often regarded as something that would follow the logic of this very economy, which forces difference to become equivalence to safeguard exchangeability. The problem, however, is that not documenting these events often means that they are forgotten, as they are irretrievably lost as moments in which this order could be subverted and, vice versa, the attempt to preserve the "uniqueness" of the artistic event increasingly follows commercial concerns, trying to protect "copyrights." Furthermore, one could argue that documentation is not necessarily subscribing to the order of equivalence and value exchange, because, as it both *includes* and *excludes* what it preserves, it transgresses the possibility of taking one as the other. Instead of erasing difference, it actually exposes difference as similarity (or self-difference as self-similarity): what I see is not the same, but remains somehow recognizable.[27] It is singular as an event, yet "plural" as a series.

In this context, a second strategy of keeping the memory of early performance art alive has to be considered, that of performance reenactments (both "live" and on video or film). It is merely in the non-identical repetition of both reenactment and documentation (including the documentation of the reenactment itself) that staging and restaging are identified as one of the possible strategies of performance art, if not as a core strategy of performance *per se*.[28] Strikingly, the repetition of performances as a specific type of transformative event (which is currently taken as far as the placeless grounds of Second Life) could in that way be seen as belonging to a particular type of "appropriation art," including reenactments of earlier art pieces as well as other historical events.[29] But if reenactments are appropriation art and found footage film and video a subcategory of this art form, could one also speak of found footage in terms of reenactment, then? There are certainly examples of found-footage films and videos that rather explicitly make

342   Jennifer Steetskamp

use of reenactments, cross-cutting between television and film footage and the recordings of reenacted events.[30] But even in the case of Farocki's INEXTINGUISH-ABLE FIRE (which is actually not a found-footage film), one could make this connection, as his self-harming gesture could be seen as a metaphorical reenactment of the napalm bomb attacks in Vietnam. Strikingly, this gesture seems to even establish a rather direct relation with prevailing transgressive performance and body art practices, around the time or the years after INEXTINGUISHABLE FIRE was made. On this level, as well, one could detect *iterability*, understood in terms of non-identical repetition in various contexts. But thinking this through, one could even draw the conclusion that the appropriation of found footage itself is a form of reenactment, since it is also a way of re-staging historical events. By transferring an image and thing from one context to another, its reoccurrence can be seen as an event in itself, as it is reflected in the German word *Ereignis* with its double bind of appropriation (*Aneignung*) and disappropriation (*Zueignung*). Where something is gained, something is lost; where something is similar, something is also different. This event is maybe what establishes the "uncanny timeliness" Elsaesser accredits to Farocki's work. In this way his work establishes an alternative economy, in which the principle of the *Verbund* not only relates to the surplus value created within an economic feedback system, in which every excess is reabsorbed to increase profit, but in which the excess itself exceeds the very idea of exchangeability by exposing a simultaneous loss.

This *Verbund*, which is also between art and cinema, performance and film, is what becomes visible in *Deep Play*, like in the earlier work of Farocki referring to the thematic as well as to the form of the work and to its technological and cultural context. The "arranged marriage"[31] between television and digital image processing is such an associative relationship or circuit that produces surplus value. Thus, one could say, there might even be love in an arranged marriage. Following this conclusion, it may be quite symptomatic that *The New York Times* compares seeing the 2006 movie ZIDANE: A 21ST CENTURY PORTRAIT (made by the visual artists Douglas Gordon and Philippe Parreno) – in some ways the exact opposite of *Deep Play* due to its lack of any "match analysis" – to performance art.[32] In that respect, it is not only cinema and film that supplement performance, but also performance (or whatever image one might have of it) that facilitates experiences appropriated by cinema, which, in itself, is based on the plurality of its performative reenactment in time and space. Maybe there is only one thing left to say, then: if soccer is our life (as Diedrich Diederichsen states in the Documenta XII catalogue),[33] and art is soccer, maybe then art and life have finally come to terms with each other.

Notes

1. Maurizio Lazzarato, "Struggle, Event, Media," <http://www.republicart.net/disc/re-presentations/lazzarato01_en.htm>. Last visited 11 June 2007.
2. See, for instance, <http://www.theregister.co.uk/2006/07/13/zidane_headbutt_outrage>. Last visited 11 Sept. 2007.
3. See <http://www.dashes.com/anil/2006/07/zidane-world-cu.html>. Last visited 11 Sept. 2007.
4. For a demonstration on how the software works see <http://ias.cs.tum.edu/projects/aspogamo/wm2006>. Last visited 11 Sept. 2007.
5. The famous chance encounter of a sewing machine and an umbrella on an operating table.
6. Peter Bürger, *Theorie der Avant-garde* (Frankfurt: Suhrkamp, 1974) 98-111.
7. This especially holds for Johan Grimonprez's work that is discussed later in this essay. For Grimonprez, *zapping* is mainly referring to an attitude or mode of experience, which he calls "zaptitude," and as a "poetic practice" becomes the main principle determining the editing process. A large part of this work is based on research he conducted on the history of television. See <www.zapomatik.com>. Last visited 12 Sept. 2007.
8. Nicolas Bourriaud, *Postproduction: Culture as Screenplay: How Art Reprograms the World* (New York: Lukas & Sternberg, 2002).
9. Walter Benjamin, "Das Kunstwerk im Zeitalter seiner technischen Reproduzierbarkeit," *Illuminationen* (Frankfurt: Suhrkamp, 1955) 148-184.
10. Barbara Kruger, "'Taking' Pictures," *Screen* 23.2 (July-Aug. 1982): 90. Paraphrased and quoted in Hal Foster, *The Return of the Real* (Cambridge, MA: MIT Press, 2002) 118-119.
11. Kruger 90.
12. Thomas Elsaesser, "Casting Around: Hitchcock's Absence," *Johan Grimonprez: Looking for Alfred – The Hitchcock Castings* (Ostfildern: Hatje Cantz, 2007) 136-160.
13. With digital images, the self-evident relation and inseparable intertwinement between image and carrier is rendered problematic, although I would like to argue that even an image based solely on numerical codes is heavily dependent on a hardware-based code-environment that enables both the storage of data and the reading of codes. However, the discussion of status of the image in the digital era exceeds the scope of this essay, which concentrates on pre-digital art, including performance, analogue video and film.
14. A similar reading of Elsaesser's text was mentioned during a live interview by Mark Nash with Johan Grimonprez, 26 May 2007, at the Jan van Eyck Academie, Maastricht.
15. Thomas Elsaesser, "Harun Farocki: Filmmaker, Artist, Media Theorist," *Harun Farocki: Working on the Sight-Lines*, ed. Thomas Elsaesser (Amsterdam: Amsterdam University Press, 2004) 14.
16. The original speech is actually in German, the translation is taken from the subtitles. For the film see <http://www.ubu.com/film/farocki.html>. Last visited 12 Sept. 2007.

17. Elsaesser, "Harun Farocki: Filmmaker, Artist, Media Theorist" 18. See also Christa Blümlinger, "Incisive Divides and Revolving Images: On the Installation SCHNITT-STELLE," *Harun Farocki: Working on the Sight-Lines* 61-66.

18. Elsaesser, "Harun Farocki: Filmmaker, Artist, Media Theorist" 17.

19. Elsaesser, "Harun Farocki: Filmmaker, Artist, Media Theorist" 19.

20. Elsaesser, "Harun Farocki: Filmmaker, Artist, Media Theorist" 19.

21. Elsaesser, "Harun Farocki: Filmmaker, Artist, Media Theorist" 14-16.

22. Elsaesser, "Harun Farocki: Filmmaker, Artist, Media Theorist" 17.

23. Elsaesser, "Harun Farocki: Filmmaker, Artist, Media Theorist" 13.

24. Among other sources, this was mentioned in a recent interview with Grimonprez. See note 7.

25. See, e.g., Peggy Phelan, *Unmarked: The Politics of Performance* (London: Routledge, 1993).

26. See, e.g., Lucy R. Lippard, ed., *Six Years: The Dematerialization of the Art Object from 1966 to 1972* (London: Studio Vista, 1973).

27. The "somehow" is not unimportant here, since the very notion of recognition is as such committed to an order that repetition or *iteration* seeks to undermine, that is, the order of representation.

28. Many examples like Marina Abramovic's SEVEN EASY PIECES (2005) could be mentioned here but that would exceed the scope of this essay.

29. See, for example, Jeremy Deller's THE BATTLE OF ORGREAVE (2001).

30. A typical example from the history of video art would be Ant Farm's ETERNAL FRAME (1976), in which "original" footage of the assassination of President Kennedy is used alongside reenactments of the event.

31. See Thomas Elsaesser, "Cinema Futures: Convergence, Divergence, Difference," *Cinema Futures: Cain, Abel or Cable? The Screen Arts in the Digital Age*, ed. Thomas Elsaesser (Amsterdam: Amsterdam University Press, 1998) 12.

32. Christoph Clarey, "Zidane, the Movie: Soccer Performance as Art," *New York Times* (30 May 2007): <http://www.nytimes.com/iht/2006/05/30/sports/IHT-3ozidane.html>. Last visited 12 Sept. 2007.

33. Diedrich Diederichsen, "Harun Farocki: Deep Play," *Documenta Kassel 16-06 – 23/09 2007* (Kassel: Fridericianum) 242.

Digital Convergence Ten Years Later

Broadcast Your Selves and Web Karaoke

Jeroen de Kloet and Jan Teurlings

Introduction

Almost a decade ago, Thomas Elsaesser co-edited *Cinema Futures: Cain, Abel, or Cable?*, a volume devoted to digital convergence and its consequences for cinema and television.[1] Although techno-optimism was at its highpoint in 1998 – the Internet bubble had not burst yet, and Al Gore was the prophet of the information highway rather than of global warming – the volume is characterized by its rather sober perspective on the "digital revolution" that was then taking place. Media archaeologists are indeed weary of the language of breaks, ruptures, and revolutions, because they know the "new" is always a product of the past. No technology comes into being without first being dreamt up, a point already made in 1974 by Raymond Williams.[2] The media archaeologist also knows that a medium – be it cinema, television, or the computer – does not follow a linear history, with technological innovations preceding actual practices (what Bruno Latour calls the "summing up" of nonhuman and human actors[3]). Rather, history shows that each new medium has many parents, with a fair amount of promiscuity between them. Moreover, media archaeology reveals that a medium is never a singular thing, that its meanings are multiple: depending on the context, a TV set can be a tool for state propaganda, an entertainment device, or a surveillance tool – or all three at the same time, of course.

All this does not mean that digitization and convergence had no consequences for the culture industries. On the contrary, the essays in *Cinema Futures: Cain, Abel, or Cable?* attest to the observation that the culture industries are in constant flux, continuously reinventing themselves, and digitization does have its role to play in the process (which is not the same as saying it is causing these changes). As Elsaesser states in his introduction to the volume:

> Digitization is in fact a contradictory factor: there is no denying that in the film in-dustries it is significantly altering the relation production and postproduction, input and output. But it has not by itself changed the way films are made, nor how viewers understand them. Neither, however, is digitization quite as neutral.[4]

We are now ten years later, and digitization has continued its advance. Accounts in the media claim that we are living in the Web 2.0 age, which assumes a radical break with the 1990s. This seems like a good reason to investigate what kind of impact digitization has had on contemporary media culture. Therefore, we will apply some (Elsaesserian) ideas from the 1998 volume to two contemporary cases: the popular digital video website YouTube and the emergence of interactive technologies in the People's Republic of China. But we would like to start with a brief example that will help to begin the questioning of the possibilities of new technologies to turn audiences into producers.

Producing Audiences

The rise of new technologies tends to be accompanied by utopian and dystopian claims. Dystopian views on new technologies stress assumed dangers: it may isolate people, it may lead to verbal or sexual abuse, and it may alienate the new generation. Utopian readings, on the other hand, point out that new virtual communities will emerge, with possibilities for online activism.[5] The denial-of-service attacks at the WTO site during the Seattle conference in 1999 is just one of the examples of online activism. Both utopian and dystopian readings tend to proliferate during a time when new technologies are being introduced, be it the telephone, radio, video, or the Internet.[6]

While straddling between these two poles, we would like to first zoom in on YouTube, which is, along with companies like Google, Ebay, Amazon, and Myspace, one of the select Internet companies that have become part of the collective consciousness. It has done so, moreover, at a remarkably fast pace. The company was only founded in 2005, which makes it barely three years old at the time of this writing. In 2006, the website was purchased by Google, undoubtedly one of the most talked-about purchases of that year. Nielsen Netratings estimated that in June 2006 the website attracted 19.6 million unique visitors, after being online for only one year.[7] Users can upload their own video movies, rate, subscribe to, and comment upon other users' movies – like little Berlusconis they can create their own "channel" – and users can also post video responses.

It is tempting to interpret the arrival of YouTube as the dawn of a new era, one in which the deficiencies and power relationships of the old mass media have finally been overcome. This is indeed what YouTube's slogan, "Broadcast Yourself," plays on: We no longer need to depend on the media professionals who own and control access to the media; we can now produce and distribute our own content. Thus, YouTube promises to unleash the creative energies of the masses, making everybody producer and consumer at the same time. YouTube did not "invent" this emancipatory discourse. It goes back to a long tradition in Western thought that sees technology as a liberating, empowering force that will set us free from the limitations of today.

One example may help to illustrate the potential of YouTube to turn audiences into producers. Patrick Jered is a Netherlands-based folktronica (a genre combining folk with electronic music) singer. At the beginning of 2008, he released his second CD, titled *Tykhana*. On a song called "Hikikomori," he collaborated online with a Japanese vocalist, Yosshi, and with Mintra, a DJ and visual artist from Thailand who made the corresponding MTV clip. The clip was uploaded on YouTube and used to promote Patrick Jered's work.[8] Simultaneously, he launched a website to sell his work through his own record company.[9] He explains how new technologies have enabled new ways of making music:

> The last few years the possibilities have expanded dramatically. It is a fantastic thing, that one song I put on YouTube could not have been done without Internet technology. The translation and vocals are done in Japan, and also the guy in Thailand I have never met, I got in contact through YouTube. The whole thing is completely created through Internet connections with people.[10]

Furthermore, Jered claims YouTube is more democratic, as AR managers from record companies are no longer listening to demo tapes anymore, but instead they are checking out YouTube and Myspace. He explains: "There is a more democratic thing going on now, AR managers take note of the number of times a song is downloaded, so that serves as a kind of measure for them to assess the impact of unknown artists in the world."[11] Jered is not the only one to take advantage of new web technologies. Other examples come to mind, most notably the Arctic Monkeys, heralded as one of the first cases of a band coming to the public's attention through the Internet, thus paving new ways for the promotion and marketing of music.[12]

Both the Arctic Monkeys as well as Patrick Jered are part of what Henry Jenkins labels "participatory culture," a term "which contrasts with older notions of passive media spectatorship. Rather than talking about media producers and consumers as occupying separate roles, we might now see them as participants who interact with each other according to a new set of rules that none of us fully understands."[13] This, to Jenkins, results in a convergence culture, which will cause a paradigm shift for the media industry. Convergence is "both a top-down corporate-driven process and a bottom-up consumer-driven process."[14] Resonating with his earlier work on fan culture, Jenkins claims that the altering of the relationships between producer, content, and audience may prove empowering for audiences, while he also points to the dangers inherent in commodification.[15]

In this essay, we would like to further explore how empowerment and commodification are related on video websites like YouTube. Following Matt Hills, we do
not see resistance and complicity as mutually exclusive;[16] instead we will look at
how they are intimately intertwined, and take it as our task to disentangle the
issues at stake. We do this by taking two steps. First, we turn to media archaeology as a methodological tool, and we place YouTube firmly within the history of
the culture industries, emphasizing historical continuity rather than the radical
break. We will thus show that YouTube merely represents the latest step in a
process that has always driven the cultural industries, namely a combination of
cost reduction and audience maximalization. From a political-economic point of
view, then, there is nothing radical or empowering about YouTube. Second, we
look at what is actually being broadcast on YouTube and similar websites, which
will offer a more nuanced perspective, which we will substantiate with our case
study of Tudou, which resonates with the examples of Patrick Jered and the Arctic
Monkeys.

YouTube: Broadcast Yourself

To understand the political economy of YouTube, it is worth returning to Elsaesser's essay on FANTASY ISLAND, the quirky 1970s show in which two guests would
have their fantasy fulfilled every week.[17] Elsaesser links the emergence of textual
properties to the economic context out of which they emerge. His analysis of
FANTASY ISLAND shows how the peculiar, dreamlike, even uncanny logic of the
show is actually the result of two interlocking interests – the studios owning studio space and accumulated props, and the stars having to pitch their latest re-
leases. Fantasy Island (the production) thus maximizes investments that had already been made:

> The guest-celebrity is allowed to live any fantasy whatsoever – so long as it coincides
> with a "property" the studio owns, that is to say, so long as it can be "made real" with
> the various prepainted sets, props and costumes that the studio has on the lot. ...
> Fantasy Island ... use[s] property personnel and time when such an expensively main-
> tained, well-organized production site with costly overheads would otherwise stand
> idle.[18]

That media corporations are profit-oriented is hardly an outrageous statement.
The strength of the essay, however, lies in that it shows that media companies go
to remarkable lengths when devising strategies for maximizing return-on-invest-
ments, and the peculiar textual forms that are a result of this (dream-like surrealist collages in FANTASY ISLAND, or grainy images in the case of Reality TV). The

economic principle behind it, however, is straightforward: to create surplus value by reducing costs. One strategy for doing so is by making the audience bear part of the production and distribution costs. The introduction of television, for example, not only represented a change in technology (from film to electromagnetic waves), it also implied a change in *distribution* relations because, unlike cinema, the new technology required that the "consumer" make an initial investment, namely the cost of the TV set (at the time substantial). In other words, whereas the cinematic mode of distribution required the media companies to fully bear the costs of the distribution infrastructure, television (and the business model that was put forward) made the audience bear at least part of the expenses of the reproductive infrastructure. With the arrival of the personal computer in the 1980s, the user had to bear an additional part of the costs: not only one's purchase of the hardware (a computer), but also the cost of the content or software (often in the form of licenses). The advent of the internet, finally, added to the users' costs the monthly subscription fee, making cable TV rather than the major networks the business model for the new millennium.

This short overview of the twentieth century shows that, from their earliest beginnings, media corporations have tried to make the audience bear as much of the costs for production and distribution as they could possibly get away with. With each successive "innovation" consumers were made to bear an increasing part of the distribution and reproduction costs. And it is at exactly this point that the connection with YouTube becomes apparent, since it represents the next step in the industry's century-old aspiration: the minimalization of production and distribution costs.

Until the arrival of YouTube, media production companies had two ways to earn their money: either by selling media content directly to the consumers (cinema, cable TV, CDs, iTunes), or by making the audience watch ads and receiving money from advertisers in return (commercial TV and radio, most websites). What is crucial in both of these approaches is that one way or another the media company had to "yield" some content to be watched or listened to; and this content had to be created (and thus paid for) by the media companies. YouTube breaks with this economic model, in that it is no longer the media company that provides the content that is collectively watched and commented upon. YouTube (the company) does not produce a single second of the millions of hours of video on its website, but relies on its collective user base to generate its content. As a result, YouTube has managed to reduce its production costs to zero, only bearing a portion of the distribution costs, which is – roughly – comprised of server costs and software development. And the main party doing the creative work, supplying artistic content, as well as executing technical chores, is the audience.

The Audience and Immaterial Labor

Instead of a radical and emancipatory break that challenges existing power relations between producers and consumers, then, YouTube represents a gradual
perfection of its business model. Like Reality TV, it reduces above-the-line costs
to a strict minimum.[19] The role played by the audience in this new ecosystem is
no longer the limited role of "the consumer"; rather, the new system joins producer and consumer into a single role – the role of *prosumer* so often heralded by
futurists and business gurus alike. But this also means that the audience is no
longer *passively* laboring away, as Dallas Smythe already famously argued in
1977.[20] In this new system, the audience labors in a very real way, by providing
the creative labor that YouTube transforms into exchange value.

Following the French-Italian Marxist tradition of the journal *Multitudes*, the
concept that best describes this type of labor is "immaterial labor." This is the
term they use for characterizing the changes that capitalist production has under-
gone in the core countries during the last forty years. According to Maurizio Lazzarato, in order for labor to be categorized as immaterial it needs to fulfill two
conditions.[21] First, it needs to have an informational or communicational component. In this sense, almost all work in industrial societies has become increasingly "immaterial," in that most jobs require their workers to manipulate symbols, mostly by means of a computer.[22] Second, immaterial labor is usually not
recognized as "work" as such, because it concerns activities that are not associated with the traditional sphere of production. Here we should think of those
aspects of life that we associate with leisure: cultural and artistic activities, lifestyle choices, (sub)cultural activities and tastes, social relationships and network-
ing – in short, every type of activity that we usually do when we are actually *not*
working. In other words, Lazzarato argues that capitalism has managed to absorb
more and more aspects of social life into its processes of value creation. But this
process is not visible as such to immaterial laborers, since the latter do not feel
like they are actually "working" but are merely "having fun," "expressing identities," or "socializing." That is also why André Gorz claims that contemporary
companies produce "*fausses marchandises*": they market products that they did
not produce themselves, effectively selling us back the products we have made
ourselves.[23]

It is clear that immaterial labor is an accurate description of what YouTube
users do: not only are they in the business of manipulating symbols via a computer, they also do not experience it as work, thus providing the company with the
free labor it subsequently valorizes on the advertising market. Or, as Tiziana Terranova puts it, YouTube users provide labor that is simultaneously "voluntarily
given and unwaged, enjoyed and exploited."[24] YouTube videos are the very embo-

diment of Gorz's *"fausses marchandises,"* as we are being sold our own collective audiovisual products. But there is more to YouTube than the fact that users produce the content they watch; just as important is the fact that it exploits the creative capacities of the crowd. For example, written in the software is the promotion of controversy and conflict. The video response feature incites us to immediately respond to a statement or video, leading to entire generations of arguments stacked upon each other – each of them just a click away. We are also encouraged to add extra layers of meaning to existing videos, by rating them, or adding comments, or putting them into our favorites. Even the purely "passive" use of the YouTube website – the mere watching of a video – will increase its play count, and thus adds information – and thus value – to the website.

Thus, YouTube's slogan "Broadcast Yourself" not only has to be taken literally – we have indeed become broadcasters – it also has to be truncated and pluralized to read "Broadcast Your Selves." When we are watching and posting videos, recording video responses, adding comments, looking into each others' favorites and so on, we are in a very real sense broadcasting our selves: we add something of our personalities and idiosyncrasies to the website – for free, of course. Moreover, the collective "self cloud" that results is a fascinating and ever-changing dynamic system that perfectly manages to capture our attention time and time again.

Censoring, Copying, and Mimicry

The media business is doing well not just in "the West" – itself a problematic homogenizing label – but also in that equally problematic construct "China." On the wave of transnational capitalism currently sweeping over Mainland China, two entrepreneurs, Dutch investor Marc van der Chijs and his Chinese counterpart Gary Wang, founded the video-sharing site Tudou. At a conference in Amsterdam in September 2007, Gary Wang claimed that Tudou streams 15 billion minutes of footage a month, compared to 3.5 billion minutes a month for YouTube.[25] Unreliable figures are used to prove success, producing yet another story that feeds into global fantasies that are saturated with hyperboles, depicting China in terms of amazing growth, a massive consumer market, global power and the like.[26] Van der Chijs is referred to on the Internet as a Dutch hero, able to conquer the Chinese market.[27] Van der Chijs himself proudly claims Tudou to be the biggest video-sharing site in China.[28] Quantitative "facts" such as unique hits and minutes of use are invoked as the new authenticators of the World Wide Web, seemingly making the impact of a site tangible. In line with our previous analysis of YouTube, the operations of Tudou are driven by a marketing logic, meant to attract advertisers and investors, just like the online performances of the Chinese audiences can be interpreted as cheap, immaterial labor. However, to avoid the danger of economic reductionism, we will now explore the cultural and political implications. Tudou provides an important case in point, as do personal weblogs in China.

While the archaeological approach generally inspires a temporal analysis, we would like to place more emphasis on its spatial dimension. When moving to China to explore the working of new technologies, we run the danger of positioning China in a different time zone, belonging either to the past (the primitive Other) or the future (symbolizing a techno-utopia or dystopia). This would be quite wrong, as China is, like us, simply here (rather than there) and now (rather than then). While insisting on China's coevalness, to use Johannes Fabian's term,[29] we would like to see how new technologies may have both similar and different implications in another location, China. When discussing the importance and impact of new technologies like Tudou and blogging in the context of China, three interrelated issues come to mind: state censorship, piracy, and web karaoke. All of these issues urge us to take an approach in which public, text, producer, and authorities are mutually constitutive of each another, propelling an endless circulation of capital, regulations, images, and sounds.

First, state censorship. The Chinese state generally keeps a close eye on media content. This does not render the domain of media completely unfree; differences between, for example, the *People's Daily* and the *Southern Weekly* are vast, the latter taking a far more critical approach towards the government. However, as different journalists explained to us in November 2007, under Hu Jintao, the successor of Jiang Zemin, media control has indeed increased. The picture that China is on a one-way road to more openness seems hasty and perhaps inaccurate. However, new technologies have made it increasingly difficult for the Chinese state to control media content. On Douban 9, a popular blogsite in China, bloggers revealed the case of slavery labor in Shanxi in 2007, which caused a national and international scandal. Bloggers like Zhai Minglai, Gua Daxia, Beifeng, Michael Anti and Wang Xiaofeng – to name but a few – frequently publish critical pieces, challenging the state.[30] For example, in a humorous blog, Wang Xiaofeng ridiculed the attempts of local authorities in Beijing to civilize the people in the wake of the Olympic Games. He poked fun at the authorities' attempts to make Beijingers speak *Putonghua*, rather than their own dialect. Blogging gives more linguistic freedom, allows one to explore the boundaries of the permissible and to circumvent the censors. He explains this in an interview:

> There is a principle in my blog in that my posts must be different from what is published in the printed media. I wanted to write those words that the editors were not used to, or else I would lose interest in writing altogether. But I discovered that

this space is very huge. I am not limited by the printed media and I can let myself go.[31]

In the same interview, he warns us not to exaggerate the impact of new technologies, and urges us to question the alleged "new" in new technologies, when he writes:

> a blog is just a recording tool for recording in the digital era for those who wish to express themselves. In ancient times, literary folks would write words like "Number One Mountain Under the Means" on the face of stone cliffs; other people may write "I was here" on a brick wall. No matter what, this is just about how people are changing their ways of making historical records, no matter if it is on blogs or on bamboo slips.[32]

At the same time, Wang Xiaofeng also gained global fame under his blogname Massage Milk when his blog was removed in March 2006 by the Chinese government, his blog simply stating that "Due to unavoidable reasons with which everyone is familiar, this blog is temporarily closed." As he had expected, it was only a matter of hours before this case of censorship became known worldwide "news" via the global news channels. Later, he revealed it was a hoax, to put up a mirror to the Western media that is so obsessively searching for cases of censorship.

A brief detour to the piracy and copyright issue enables us to further explain the workings of new technologies in China, in particular in relation to the issue of censorship. New media in China allow for a form of digital citizenship that is quite unprecedented. Digitization has sped up the already "rampant" practices of piracy in China. Rampant is a word used by the media industry and the Chinese government, the latter being increasingly insistent on fighting piracy after its entry into the WTO in 2001. The endless duplication of media products in China – on the streets one can immediately find the latest TV series such as *24*, Hollywood blockbusters, and the like – produces a never ending flow of global images, sounds, and texts. Blockbusters as well as art-house movies are on the Chinese market before the censored versions of the movies appear in the theaters, if they are ever released at all, or before we can even see them on TV. With current downloading programs such as bit torrent, TV series and movies have become even more easily available, for both the pirating industry and the computer-savvy consumer. This potentially undermines the global media sector, resisting the enforcement of copyright regimes that seem to protect the industry more than the artist. At the same time, it opens up a media world that was previously inaccessible to Chinese audiences due to import restrictions and censorship policies. Thus, whereas new technologies allow bloggers in China to voice their opinions, and present a partly censored window to the world for Internet users in China (currently roughly 13% of the total population), they also bring in the outside world through peer-to-peer downloading technology, further propelling piracy practices in China, and circumventing the logics of global capitalism and state censorship policies.

The constant influx of global imagery, which produces an increasingly media-saturated world, in combination with the possibilities to produce user-generated content, have resulted in the emergence of not only a politicized, critical blogosphere, but also – in a more entertaining, hilarious sphere –media karaoke. Karaoke can be read as a specific type of sonic and visual mimicry that is believed to have originated in Japan, and that has never traveled well to the West, apart from its gay, camp adaptation.[33] It is hard to underestimate the cultural significance of karaoke in China; it serves as the lubricant for business deals, and as the moment of excess, when one can transcend one's everyday inhibitions. Karaoke enables the audience to slip for a few minutes into a star persona, and thus to leave behind one's everyday self.

In the past, karaoke was pretty much confined to the private space of the karaoke bar or the public town square with its mobile karaoke stand, but the Internet has enabled the emergence of an online karaoke culture. When the Backdormitory Boys released their first playback clip on Tudou in 2005, they mimicked the Backstreet Boy's "I Want It That Way." They became an instant hit on the mainland. These college boys from Guangzhou had a facial expression that turned the original into an absurd love song, the clip is a cultural translation that pokes fun at the original while not taking itself all too seriously.[34] Soon people all over China were watching the Backdormitory Boys on the Internet, just as they had eagerly read the sex diaries of female blogger Mu Zimei from the same city. Whereas the latter became famous for publishing her private life online, the Backdormitory Boys became famous through their ironic appropriations of "Western" (and later also "Chinese") cultural products. The boys are "typical" Chinese in that we see them in their dorm room, a place known for its lack of privacy. Even the third student, sitting in the back of the room, in front of the computer, became well known in China.

During the World Soccer Cup in Germany in 2006, the Backdormitory Boys adopted the German language song "Dadada" from the band Trio, a big hit in Germany in the early 1980s. We see them in "China" soccer T-shirts mimicking "Dadada" by lip-syncing to *"Ich lieb dich nicht, Du liebst mich nicht, aha aha aha."* The clip provokes questions about cultural difference and authenticity: it is simultaneously very "Chinese" (karaoke, the dorm) as well as "Western" (the song, soccer). More importantly, it pokes fun at both, not taking culture very seriously; the clip is an act of cheerful copying, masking and fakery. And when one fakes the real, the fake becomes the new authenticity. When others tried to mimic the Backdormitory Boys, comments on YouTube were generally devastating, for example:

> wannab's, chineseboys didnt ask for imitaters you know.
> this is wannabe the 2 chinese boys!! you're suck!!!!! chinese boys are much bether!!! don't keep try like them because they 2 are the best![35]

The new fake, the outcome of cheerful mimicry of the Other, resulting in practices of web karaoke, have quickly made the Backdormitory Boys famous. In the clip, they laugh ironically while they sing they don't love us (*Ich lieb dich nicht*). They rejuvenate Oscar Wilde's nearly worn-out assertion that we "should treat all the trivial things of life seriously, and all the serious things of life with sincere and studied triviality."[36] Football, politics, Germany, China, dormitories, studying, censors, copyright, why should we care? What remains is joy – the emotion so often ignored in academia, but an emotion that travels so well digitally.

The Backdormitory Boys attest to the possibility of the Internet as a place where one can create one's own stardom and negotiate a new sensibility of authenticity, one that resides in the humorous and the banal, rather than the tragic and the serious. The tragic, being more sacred than the humorous and the ironic, is more visible in cinematic and other cultural representations, for example in the cinema of Tsai Ming-Liang and Zhang Yimou. In other words, digitization feeds the comic aspect more than the tragic, propelling a media culture that thrives on an ironic structure of feeling.

The Industry Strikes Back?

This brief sketch of the Backdormitory Boys hints at important questions of cultural translation, authenticity, and humor. They are also an example of the potential power of the Internet to turn consumers into producers. In the context of China, this can be considered a potentially provocative practice: they circumvent the censors, create themselves as stars and poke fun at the media industry. However, the industry soon struck back with a vengeance. Their immaterial labor quickly materialized into financial rewards. The Backdormitory Boys quickly began performing live and became spokespersons for Motorola and Pepsi. This also signaled the moment that it seemed to lose its subversive powers of both the media industry and the state system (the Chinese state does not like these kinds of performances; it recently moved to ban the popular TV show *Idols*). Not only their subversiveness, but also their fame soon began to fade, as part of the attraction was their virtual mimicry, which authenticated them. They transgressed the newly defined limits of authenticity, moving back from the fake towards the real, from the copy towards the original.

Potentially subversive acts are thus immediately incorporated and implicated in global capitalism. One further example that underlines the power of global capital is blogger Michael Anti's story. The two Chinese characters he chose for his name mean "peace" (an) and "replacement" (ti), respectively. The synthesis "anti" means "peaceful alternative."[37] He himself already notes that "In this political system, everyone has to compromise ... It's not black and white. Many of the people who delete my essays are also my friends."[38] And those who delete them out of political concerns are not necessarily Chinese. In the final days of December 2006, Anti wrote on his blog about the sacking of various discontented and outspoken journalists at *Xin Jing Bao* (*Beijing News*) by the more conservative editors, and called for a boycott. Microsoft soon thereafter deleted his blog. Michael Connolly, the team manager of MSN Spaces, justifies this choice:

> We are an international service, and we work hard to comply with the local laws (for illegal content) and local cultural norms (for inappropriate content) in all the markets we operate in. ... In China, there is a unique issue for our entire industry: there are certain aspects of speech in China that are regulated by the government. We've made a choice to run a service in China, and to do that, we need to adhere to local regulations and laws.[39]

Thus, "Western" or global companies like Microsoft are deeply implicated in the aiding and abetting of state censorship in China. Global capitalism works hand in hand with the communist nation-state to help the nation-state control its citizens and its media output.[40] And this happens in a time of digitization, when new media are increasingly being credited with empowering its users rather than the producers. In 1998, Elsaesser had already pointed to the forces that need to be taken into account when we try to gauge the impact of digitization: processes of economic concentration on a global scale (Microsoft); geo-political realignments (global media companies with the communist nation-state), and legal and institutional changes (increased censorship of the Internet in China, the construction of a national firewall).[41] These elements are of pivotal importance if we are to understand the digital mediascape of China, but they need to be understood in conjunction with the micropolitics of the everyday, in which bloggers use the Web to articulate a voice that would otherwise remain unheard and that may further challenge trust in the current regime of representation in China.[42]

It may be more accurate to read the Backdormitory Boys and the bloggers as part of a subversive culture that is simultaneously being commodified as well as incorporated into the business models of the media conglomerates. Whereas manipulation by the industry is often perceived to be the flipside of cultural appropriation, in practice they feed on one another. The vicious circle of commodification and appropriation propels both creativity and the flow of capital. It is possible to point to moments of subversion, but it is equally possible to trace moments of compliance.

Conclusion: A Brave New World?

Our analysis has shown that new technologies constitute both a continuation and a rupture in the media ecology: they can be read as a further extension of the use of immaterial labor from the audience, as well as enabling audiences to cheerfully appropriate cultural forms, poke fun at cultural differences, undermine copyright regimes, and engage in a pleasurable game that renders the political at most a laughable domain. It would be too easy to ascribe the different analytical take on similar technologies – YouTube and Tudou – as caused by spatial and cultural differences, one coming from the neoliberal West, the other from the authoritarian East, since this would merely substitute a technological determinism with a societal determinism. Instead, we have used the two case studies to show the myriad ways in which convergence and digitization have both empowering as well as exploitative effects, often operating simultaneously. Both case studies also illustrate the fundamental anti-essentialism of media archaeology (the introduction of a new technology never has exactly the same consequences), while also pointing to its very real effects (without digitization the industry would not be able to exploit the audience's immaterial labor, or the Backdormitory Boys would not be able to appropriate German pop songs). By doing so, media archaeology reveals the radical undecidability of technological introductions, allowing us to end on a hopeful note: by studying the past, we open up the future.

Notes

1.   Thomas Elsaesser and Kay Hoffmann, eds., *Cinema Futures: Cain, Abel or Cable? The Screen Arts in the Digital Age* (Amsterdam: Amsterdam University Press, 1998).
2.   Raymond Williams, *Television: Technology and Cultural Form* (London: Routledge, 2003).
3.   Bruno Latour, "On Recalling ANT," *Actor Network Theory and After*, ed. John Law and John Hassard (Oxford: Blackwell, 1999) 15-25.
4.   Thomas Elsaesser, "Cinema Futures: Convergence, Divergence, Difference," *Cinema Futures: Cain, Abel or Cable?* 14.
5.   Howard Reingold, *Smart Mobs: The Next Social Revolution* (Cambridge: Basic Books, 2002).

6.   Rein de Wilde, *De voorspellers: Een kritiek op de toekomstindustrie* (Amsterdam: De Balie, 2000).

7.   Nielsen Netratings, "YouTube U.S. Web Traffic Grows 75 Percent Week over Week, according to Nielsen/Netratings", press release, <http://www.nielsen-netratings.com/pr/pr_060721_2.pdf>. Last visited 28 Oct. 2007.

8.   See <http://www.youtube.com/watch?v=BsQqiWNTPPM>.

9.   See <http://www.elephantsearmusic.com/>.

10.   Interview 29 Jan. 2008.

11.   Interview 29 Jan. 2008.

12.   Laura Barton, "The Question: Have the Arctic Monkeys Changed the Music Business?," *The Guardian* (25 Oct. 2005).

13.   Henry Jenkins, *Convergence Culture: Where Old and New Media Collide* (New York: New York University Press, 2006) 3.

14.   Jenkins, *Convergence Culture* 18.

15.   Henry Jenkins, *Textual Poachers: Television Fans and Participatory Culture* (London: Routledge, 1992).

16.   Matt Hills, *Fan Cultures* (London: Routledge, 2002) 44.

17.   Thomas Elsaesser, "Fantasy Island: Dream Logic as Production Logic," *Cinema Futures: Cain, Abel or Cable?* 143-157.

18.   Elsaesser, "Fantasy Island" 151.

19.   See Ted Magder, "The End of TV 101: Reality Programs, Formats, and the New Business of Television," *Reality TV: Remaking Television Culture*, ed. Susan Murray and Laurie Ouellette (New York: New York University Press, 2004) 137-156.

20.   Dallas Smythe, "Communications: Blindspot of Western Marxism," *Canadian Journal of Political and Social Theory* 1.3 (1977): 1-27.

21.   Maurizio Lazzarato, "Immaterial Labor," *Radical Thought in Italy: A Potential Politics*, ed. Paolo Virno and Michael Hardt (Minneapolis: University of Minnesota Press, 1996) 133-147.

22.   This does not mean that all jobs have become "interesting," or that assembly-line jobs no longer exist. Monotonous jobs like data entry, or call center jobs, entirely fit the above description.

23.   André Gorz, "Économie de la connaissance, exploitation des savoirs, entretien avec Yann Moulier Boutang & Carlo Vercellone," *Politiques des multitudes. Démocratie, intelligence collective & puissance de la vie à l'heure du capitalisme cognitif*, ed. Yann Moulier Boutang (Paris: Éditions Amsterdam, 2007) 541.

24.   Tiziana Terranova, "Free Labor: Producing Culture for the Digital Economy," *Social Text* 18.2 (2000): 34.

25.   See <http://shanghaiist.com/2007/10/11/tudou_now_bigge.php>. Last visited 22 Oct. 2007.

26.   These hyperbolic fantasies are produced in conjunction with inverted, equally one-sided, narratives on massive human rights abuses, environmental disasters, and an assumed alarming lack of democracy and freedom.

27.   See <http://www.zoomz.nl/archief/kent-u-wwwtudouccom-5x-zo-groot-als-youtube/>. Last visited 22 Oct. 2007.

28. See   <http://www.marketingfacts.nl/berichten/20070911_chinese_video_site_tu-dou_streamt_360_miljoen_films_per_week/>. Last visited 22 Oct. 2007.

29. Johannes Fabian, *Time and the Other: How Anthropology Makes its Objects* (New York: Columbia University Press, 1983).

30. See   <http://rconversation.blogs.com/rconversation/2007/11/chinese-blogger.html> for a report on the third blogger conference of China in November 2007. Last visited 15 Nov. 2007.

31. See <http://zonaeuropa.com/20051122_2.htm>. Last visited 15 Nov. 2007. For an on-line interview with Wang Xiaofeng, see <http://www.youtube.com/watch?v=Nt5oy4-V9UWY>.

32. The Phrase "Number One Mountain Under the Means" mockingly refers to the lan-guage generally used by the old Chinese poets and scholars, full of references to the beauty of nature.

33. See Akiko Otake and Shuhei Hosokawa, "Karaoke in East Asia: Modernization, Japa-nization, or Asianization?," *Internationalizing Cultural Studies: An Anthology*, ed. Ack-bar Abbas and John Nguyet Erni (Oxford: Blackwell, 2005) 51-60.

34. For an overview of their work, see <www.backdormitoryboys.com>.

35. Taken from <http://www.youtube.com/watch?v=2y1Vty1hjZU&feature=related>. Last visited 15 Nov. 2007.

36. Oscar Wilde, *The Importance of Being Earnest* (London: Penguin Books, 1994).

37. This description draws on Wei Liu, "Censorship in China's Blogosphere: A Casestu-dy of Anti's Blog and MSN Spaces," unpublished the MA thesis (Queens University, 2007).

38. Philip P. Pan, "Bloggers Who Pursue Change Confront Fear and Mistrust," *Washing-ton Post* (21 Feb. 2006). Available at <http://www.washingtonpost.com/wp-dyn/con-tent/article/2006/02/20/AR2006022001304.html>.

39. Liu 40.

40. Google provides another interesting case in point. When one Googles "Tiananmen Square" outside China, the top hits all depict images of the June 4th massacre in 1989. However, when one does the same in China, what we get to see are holiday pictures, references to the June 4th massacre have been filtered out.

41. Thomas Elsaesser, "Digital Cinema: Delivery, Event, Time," *Cinema Futures: Cain, Abel or Cable?* 201.

42. See Elsaesser, "Digital Cinema: Delivery, Event, Time" 208.

Notes on Contributors

Mieke Bal is Royal Netherlands Academy of Arts and Sciences Professor (KNAW). She is based at the Amsterdam School for Cultural Analysis (ASCA), which she co-founded with Thomas Elsaesser. Her areas of interest range from biblical and classical antiquity to 17th-century and contemporary art and modern literature, feminism and migratory culture. Her books include *A Mieke Bal Reader* (2006), *Travelling Concepts in the Humanities* (2002), and *Narratology* (1985; third edition in press). Her experimental documentaries on migration include A Thousand and One Days, Colony, and the installation *Nothing is Missing*. Occasionally she acts as an independent curator.

Melis Behlil is Lecturer at Kadir Has University in Istanbul. She was part of the "Cinema Europe" research program, directed by Thomas Elsaesser at the Amsterdam School for Cultural Analysis, where she also defended her dissertation entitled *Home Away from Home: Global Directors in New Hollywood* in 2007.

Warren Buckland is Senior Lecturer in Film Studies at Oxford Brookes University. He spent much of the 1990s at the University of Amsterdam teaching film theory with Thomas Elsaesser. Together they wrote *Studying Contemporary American Film* (2002). During that time, Buckland also edited *The Film Spectator* (1995) and wrote *Teach Yourself Film Studies* (1998; third edition 2008) and *The Cognitive Semiotics of Film* (2000). More recently, he authored *Directed by Steven Spielberg* (2006), and has just finished editing *Puzzle Films: Complex Storytelling in Contemporary Cinema* (2008).

Sudeep Dasgupta is Associate Professor of Media and Culture at the University of Amsterdam. He is the editor of *Constellations of the Transnational: Modernity, Culture, Critique* (2007) and has published essays in the fields of media studies, film and philosophy, aesthetics, visual culture, postcolonial theory, and queer theory. He taught in the Media Archaeology course initiated by Thomas Elsaesser in the Film Studies program. Currently, he co-teaches the PhD Theory Seminar at the Amsterdam School of Cultural Analysis.

José van Dijck is Professor of Media and Culture and currently Dean of the Faculty of Humanities at the University of Amsterdam. She is the author of several books, including *Manufacturing Babies and Public Consent: Debating the New Reproductive Technologies* (1995), *ImagEnation: Popular Images of Genetics* (1998), *The Transparent Body: A Cultural Analysis of Medical Imaging* (2005), and *Mediated Memories in the Digital Age* (2007). She chaired the Department of Media Studies from 2001 to 2005.

Charles Forceville is Associate Professor of Media & Culture at the University of Amsterdam, where he coordinates the Research Master Media Studies. In his cognitivist-oriented work he applies insights from narratology, rhetoric, linguistics, and communication and cognition studies to multimodal discourses, including documentary, animation, advertising, comics, and cartoons. He has published in *Metaphor and Symbol, Journal of Pragmatics, New Review of Film and Television Studies, Language and Literature, Humor,* and elsewhere. He is currently co-editing the volume *Multimodal Metaphor.* He shares a critical fascination with Thomas Elsaesser of how advertising threatens to cannibalize programming, thus reducing television viewers to consumers.

Bruce Gray is retired from the University of Amsterdam, where he taught for thirty-five years. He started his career at the Department of Theater Studies. During that time he was head of the University Theater and initiator of the Theatrical Media Studies, which later evolved into the current Media and Culture program. After Thomas Elsaesser's arrival, Gray concentrated on developing the practical side of the film and television program. During his years at the university, he was also involved in various theater, film, and television productions as director, actor, and writer.

Malte Hagener is Associate Professor of Media Studies at Leuphana-Universität Lüneburg. His research interests include the intersection of film and media art, interface culture, European avant-garde cinema, popular cinema of the 1930s, and German film history. He co-authored *Filmtheorie zur Einführung* (2007) with Thomas Elsaesser. He is also the author of *Moving Forward, Looking Back: The European Avantgarde and the Invention of Film Culture, 1919-1939* (2007) and co-editor of *Die Spur durch den Spiegel: Der Film in der Kultur der Moderne* (2004) and *Cinephilia: Movies, Love and Memory* (2005).

Pepita Hesselberth is currently writing her dissertation entitled *Chronoscopy: Performative Sense-Making in Contemporary Mainstream Film and Time-Based Media,* under the supervision of Thomas Elsaesser and Ulrik Ekman. She received a fellowship for this project in "Philosophy, Cinema, and Cultural Theory," which is co-hosted by the Copenhagen Doctoral School in Cultural Studies, Literature, and the Arts (CDS) and the Amsterdam School for Cultural Analysis (ASCA). With Thomas Elsaesser, she co-edited *Hollywood op straat: Film en televisie in de hedendaagse mediacultuur* (2000).

Jeroen de Kloet is Assistant Professor of Media Studies at the University of Amsterdam and works on the cultural implications of globalization in China. He recently co-edited *Cosmopatriots: On Distant Belonging and Close Encounters* (2007), and has published on popular music, cinema, and new technologies in China. His current research project focuses on the Beijing Olympiad and is titled "Celebrations and Contestations of Chineseness: The Beijing 2008 Olympics and 21st Century Imaginations of Place, Culture and Identity."

Jaap Kooijman is Associate Professor of Media and Culture at the University of Amsterdam. His essays on American politics, popular culture, and art have been published in *The Velvet Light Trap*, *Post Script*, *The European Journal of Cultural Studies*, and *GLQ: A Journal of Lesbian and Gay Studies*. He is the author of *Fabricating the Absolute Fake: America in Contemporary Pop Culture* (2008) and the ASCA coordinator of the European Summer School in Cultural Studies (ESSCS), which was co-founded by Thomas Elsaesser.

Tarja Laine is Assistant Professor of Film Studies at the University of Amsterdam. In 2004, she received her PhD in the "Cinema Europe" research program, which is directed by Thomas Elsaesser. She is the author of *Shame and Desire: Emotion, Intersubjectivity, Cinema* (2007), and her essays on emotions and sensations in cinema have been published in journals such as *Discourse: Journal for Theoretical Studies in Media and Culture*, *Studies of European Cinema*, *New Review of Film and Television Studies*, *Post Script*, and *Film and Philosophy*.

Catherine M. Lord lectures in Film and Literature in the Department of Media Studies at the University of Amsterdam. She is a dramatist and filmmaker. She premiered her short film SHE'S BACK AGAIN in New York (2006), and was an assistant director on RAAK / CONTACT, a short that won the Golden Bear at the Berlin Film Festial (2007). She is currently working on a play, *Ghostlight*, the opening act will premiere at the Birmingham Hippodrome in June 2008. She is also co-editor of *Essays in Migratory Aesthetics* (2007).

Julia Noordegraaf is Assistant Professor of Media and Culture at the University of Amsterdam and Program Director of the international MA Preservation and Presentation of the Moving Image, which was founded by Thomas Elsaesser. Her most recent book is *Strategies of Display: Museum Presentation in Nineteenth- and*

Twentieth-Century Visual Culture (2004). She co-directs the research project "Photography, Film and Displacement" at the Amsterdam School for Cultural Analysis. Her current research focuses on the access to and use of audiovisual collections.

Floris Paalman is a PhD candidate in the Department of Media Studies of the University of Amsterdam in the "Cinema Europe" research program, directed by Thomas Elsaesser. He has a background in cultural anthropology and filmmaking, and is currently finishing his dissertation on film, architecture, and urbanism in Rotterdam from the 1920s to the 1970s. He has published on this topic in *Filmische Mittel, industrielle Zwecke* (2007) and *Kinematografie a M sto* (2006). He is also the curator of the film program "Rotterdam Classics" (Gemeentearchief Rotterdam, Lantaren/Venster, 2007-2008).

Dominic Pettman is Associate Professor of Culture and Media at Eugene Lang College, New School for Liberal Arts, New York. He is the author of *Love and Other Technologies: Retrofitting Eros for the Information Age* (2006), *Avoiding the Subject: Media, Culture and the Object* (with Justin Clemens, 2004), and *After the Orgy: Toward a Politics of Exhaustion* (2002). He was a member of ASCA and taught in the University of Amsterdam's Department of Media Studies from 2002 till 2004.

Patricia Pisters is Professor of Film Studies at the University of Amsterdam. She is the author of *Lessen van Hitchcock: een introductie in mediatheorie* (2002; third edition 2007), *The Matrix of Visual Culture: Working with Deleuze in Film Studies* (2003) and co-editor of *Shooting the Family: Transnational Media and Intercultural Values* (2005). She started working at the Department of Media Studies in 1993 as a PhD student and guest lecturer in the international MA film program initiated by Thomas Elsaesser and is currently chairing the Media and Culture program.

Michael Punt is Professor of Art and Technology and Director of Trans-technology Research at the University of Plymouth. He has made fifteen films and published over eighty articles on cinema and digital media. Under Thomas Elsaesser's supervision, he gained his PhD at the University of Amsterdam in 2000. He is the co-author, with Robert Pepperell, of *The Post-Digital Membrane: Imagination Technology and Desire* (2000) and co-editor of *Screening Consciousness: Cinema Mind World* (2006). He is also Editor-in-Chief of *Leonardo Reviews*.

Drehli Robnik teaches film theory at the University of Vienna and Masarykova Univerzita, Brno. He is key researcher at the Ludwig Boltzmann Institute for History and Society in Vienna, in a project on the historicity of cinema with regard to Hollywood (re)visions of World War II. He has written on film theory and aesthetics, on cinema and war, on National Socialism in film, and on horror film. His PhD thesis was supervised by Thomas Elsaesser, and he was part of the "Cinema Europe" research group at the Amsterdam School for Cultural Analysis. An occasional film critic, disk-jockey, and edutainer, he "lives" in Vienna-Erdberg.

Richard Rogers is Associate Professor of Media and Culture at the University of Amsterdam and Director of the Govcom.org Foundation, the group responsible for the Issue Crawler and other info-political tools for the Web. He is author of *Information Politics on the Web* (2004), editor of *Preferred Placement: Knowledge Politics on the Web* (2000), and author of *Technological Landscapes* (1999). He is currently directing the New Media program at the Department of Media Studies.

Laura Schuster is a PhD student in the Department of Media Studies at the University of Amsterdam. She is involved in the "Imagined Futures" project of the Amsterdam School for Cultural Analysis. Her research, under Thomas Elsaesser's supervision, positions developments in contemporary narrative cinema within a larger context of transformations in media technologies and media practices, and changing notions of film spectatorship.

Senta Siewert is a PhD candidate in Film Studies at the Amsterdam School for Cultural Analysis. Her dissertation, entitled *Displacement in Contemporary European Film: A Pragmatic Poetic with Special Focus on the Music*, is supervised by Thomas Elsaesser and will be completed in 2008. She is a member of the "Cinema Europe" and "Imagined Futures" research projects. She has worked on twelve full-length documentary film projects on popular culture and popular music for the German-French TV channel arte, 3SAT and ZDF. These films include FANTASTIC VOYAGES, POP ODYSSEE, LOST IN MUSIC, and YOUTHQUAKE'65.

Jan Simons is Associate Professor of New Media Studies at the University of Amsterdam. He is the author of *Playing The Waves: Lars von Trier's Game Cinema* (2007), *Interface en Cyberspace: Inleiding in de Nieuwe Media* (2002), and *Zwevende Kiezers en Zappende Kijkers: Politiek in Beeld* (1998). Since 1991, he has collaborated with Thomas Elsaesser in education, teaching at both undergraduate and graduate levels, and publishing, including *Writing For the Medium* (1994) and *Double Trouble: Writing and Filming* (1994).

Wim Staat is Assistant Professor of Film and Visual Culture at the University of Amsterdam. In his teaching and research, he has developed an interest in the political representation of cultural identity in film and in the specific ways in which film can be considered as performatively displaying ethical concerns. In the latter perspective, he has written on Terrence Malick's THE THIN RED LINE, Lars von Trier's DOGVILLE in relation to John Ford's version of THE GRAPES OF WRATH, and Claire Denis's L'INTRUS / THE INTRUDER. He is also the co-editor of *Shooting the Family: Transnational Media and Intercultural Values* (2005).

Jennifer Steetskamp is a PhD candidate in the Department of Media Studies at the University of Amsterdam. Her research is on the spatial and temporal politics of contemporary installation art in relation to recent developments inside and outside the realm of visual art. She is a member of the "Imagined Futures" research project and has held an ASCA Fellowship since September 2007. Previously, she worked as a collection manager at the Netherlands Media Art Institute, after having studied Modern Art History, Philosophy, and Cultural Studies in Amsterdam and London.

Wanda Strauven is Associate Professor of Film Studies at the University of Amsterdam. She is the author of *Marinetti e il cinema: tra attrazione e sperimentazione* (2006) and editor of *The Cinema of Attractions Reloaded* (2006). With Thomas Elsaesser, she co-directs the ASCA research project "Imagined Futures," which aims to develop new models of historiography, to rethink the possible futures of film and film studies, and to investigate the cinema as a new public sphere in today's media art.

Jan Teurlings is Assistant Professor of Media and Culture at the University of Amsterdam, where he teaches and researches television production and the culture industries.

Eleftheria Thanouli is Lecturer in Film History at the Film Department at Aristotle University of Thessaloniki. She completed her PhD under the supervision of Thomas Elsaesser at the University of Amsterdam in 2005. Her book *Post-Classical Narration: A New Paradigm in Contemporary World Cinema* is forthcoming.

Marijke de Valck is Assistant Professor of Media and Culture at the University of Amsterdam. She is the author of *Film Festivals: From European Geopolitics to Global Cinephilia* (2007) and co-editor of *Sonic Interventions* (2007) and *Cinephilia: Movies, Love and Memory* (2005). As a PhD student, she was a member of the "Cinema Europe" research project and with Thomas Elsaesser co-organized the international conferences "Cinephilia Take Two: Re-mastering, Re-purposing, Re-framing" (2003) and "Cinema Europe: Networks in Progress" (2005).

Frank van Vree is a historian and Professor of Journalism and Culture at the University of Amsterdam. He works mainly in the fields of history and memory, cultural and intellectual history as well as media and journalism. His publications include *In de schaduw van Auschwitz: Herinneringen, beelden, geschiedenis* (1995), *Journalistieke Cultuur in Nederland* (co-editor, 2002), and *History of Concepts: Comparative Perspectives* (co-editor, 1998). He was one of the founders of the journal *Feit & fictie*. As a member of the Board of the Department of Media Studies he works closely with Thomas Elsaesser.

Michael Wedel is Assistant Professor of Film Studies at the University of Amsterdam and the author of *Der deutsche Musikfilm: Archäologie eines Genres 1914-1945* (2007). A former graduate and PhD student of Thomas Elsaesser, their collaborative projects include a number of jointly written essays, the edited collections *A Second Life: German Cinema's First Decades* (1996), *The BFI Companion to German Cinema* (1999), and *Kino der Kaiserzeit: Zwischen Tradition und Moderne* (2002), as well as the German edition of *Weimar Cinema and After: Germany's Historical Imaginary* (1999).

Key Publications by Thomas Elsaesser

This selected bibliography is organized according to the three acts of the present volume and chronologically ascending within each act. We have included most of the references cited by the different contributors (but not necessarily in the respective acts) as well as other key texts on the topics in question. Thomas Elsaesser's writings, however, are not limited to the topics covered in this volume. For a complete overview of his publications, we refer to his personal website: <http://home.hum.uva.nl/oz/elsaesser/>.

ACT I: Melodrama, Memory, Mind Game

"Tales of Sound and Fury: [Observations on] The Family Melodrama." *Monogram* 4 (1972): 2-15. Rpt. in *Movies and Methods II*. Ed. Bill Nichols. Berkeley / Los Angeles: California University Press, 1985. 166-189. *Film Genre Reader*. Ed. Barry Keith Grant. Austin: University of Texas Press, 1986. 278-308. *Home is Where the Heart is: Studies in Melodrama and the Woman's Film*. Ed. Christine Gledhill. London: BFI, 1987. 43-69. *Imitations of Life: A Reader on Film & Television Melodrama*. Ed. Marcia Landis. Detroit: Wayne State University Press, 1991. 68-91. *Film Theory and Criticism*. Ed. Gerald Mast, Marshall Cohen, and Leo Braudy. New York: Oxford University Press, 1992. 244-258. German trans. "Tales of Sound and Fury: Anmerkungen zum Familienmelodram." *Und immer wieder geht die Sonne auf*. Ed. Christian Cargnelli and Michael Palm. Vienna: PVS, 1994. 93-130.

"From Sign to Mind: The Second Film Semiology?" *The Film Spectator: From Sign to Mind*. Ed. Warren Buckland. Amsterdam: Amsterdam University Press, 1995. 3-7.

"One Train May Be Hiding Another: History, Memory, Identity." *The Lowlands: Yearbook of Flemish Studies*. Rekkem: Ons Erfdeel, 1996. 121-129. Rpt. "History, Memory, Identity and the Moving Image: One Train May Be Hiding Another." *Topologies of Trauma: Essays on the Limit of Knowledge and Memory*. Ed. Linda Belau and Petar Ramadanovic. New York: Other Press, 2002. 61-72. German trans. "'Un train peut en cacher un autre.' Geschichte, Gedächtnis und Medienöffentlichkeit." *Montage / AV* 11.1 (2002): 11-25.

"Subject Positions, Speaking Positions: From *Holocaust, Our Hitler*, and *Heimat* to *Shoah* and *Schindler's List*." *The Persistence of History: Cinema, Television, and the Modern Event*. Ed. Vivian Sobchack. New York: Routledge, 1996. 145-186.

"Time Travel, Trauma and Thresholds." *Kolnoa: Studies in Cinema & Television* 1 (1998): 1-18.

"Truth or Dare: Reality Checks on Indexicality, or the Future of Illusionism." *Cinema Studies into Visual Theory?* Ed. Anu Koivunnen and Astrid Soderbergh Widding. Turku: D-Vision, 1998. 31-50.

"Über den Nutzen der Enttäuschung: Filmkritik zwischen Cinephilie und Nekrophilie." *Filmkritik Bestandsaufnahme und Perpektiven.* Ed. Irmbert Schenk. Marburg: Schüren, 1998. 91-114.

"Antigone Agonistes: Urban Guerilla or Guerilla Urbanism? The RAF, *Germany in Autumn* and *Deathgame.*" *Giving Ground: The Politics of Propinquity.* Ed. Joan Copjec and Michael Sorkin. London: Verso, 1999. 267-302. Online: <http://www.rouge.com.au/4/antigone.html>. French trans. (revised ed.) *Terrorisme, mythes et représentations. La RAF de Fassbinder aux T-shirts Prada-Meinhof.* Lille: Tausend Augen, 2005. Serbo-croatian trans. "Antigone agonistes: Urbana gerila ili gerilski urbanizam? Frakcija Crvene Armije, Nema ka jesen i igra smtri." *Prelom* 6-7 (2006): 153-186.

"Trauma: Postmodernism as Mourning Work." *Screen* 42.2 (Summer 2001): 193-201.

"Was wäre, wenn du schon tot bist? Vom 'postmodernen' zum 'post-mortem'-Kino am Beispiel von Christopher Nolans *Memento.*" *Zeitsprünge. Wie Filme Geschichte(n) erzählen.* Ed. Christine Rüffert, Irmbert Schenk, Karl-Heinz Schmid, and Alfred Tews. Berlin: Bertz, 2004. 115-125.

"Cinephilia or the Uses of Disenchantment." *Cinephilia: Movies, Love and Memory.* Ed. Marijke de Valck and Malte Hagener. Amsterdam: Amsterdam University Press, 2005. 27-44.

"Melodrama Revisited." *AS Mediatijdschrift* 174 (June 2005): 28-45.

"Geschichte(n) und Gedächtnis: Zur Poetik der Fehlleistung im Mainstreamkino am Beispiel von *Forrest Gump.*" *Experiment Mainstream? Differenz und Uniformierung im populären Kino.* Ed. Irmbert Schenk, Christine Rüffert, Karl-Heinz Schmid, and Alfred Tews. Berlin: Bertz + Fischer, 2006. 31-42.

(with Malte Hagener) *Filmtheorie zur Einführung.* Hamburg: Junius, 2007.

Terror und Trauma. Zur Gewalt des Vergangenen in der BRD. Berlin: Kadmos, 2007.

Melodrama and Trauma: Modes of Cultural Memory in the American Cinema. London: Routledge, forthcoming.

"The Mind-Game Film." *Puzzle Films: Complex Storytelling in Contemporary Cinema.* Ed. Warren Buckland. Oxford: Blackwell, forthcoming.

ACT II: Europe-Hollywood-Europe

"Why Hollywood?" *Monogram* 1 (1971): 4-10.

"The Pathos of Failure: The Unmotivated Hero." *Monogram* 6 (1975): 13-19. Rpt. in *The Last Great American Picture Show.* Ed. Thomas Elsaesser, Alexander Horwath, and Noel King. Amsterdam: Amsterdam University Press, 2004. 279-292.

"Primary Identification and the Historical Subject: Fassbinder and Germany." *Ciné-Tracts* 11 (Fall 1980): 43-52. Rpt. in *Narrative, Apparatus, Ideology.* Ed. Philip Rosen. New York: Columbia University Press, 1986. 535-549. *Explorations in Film Theory.* Ed. Ron Burnett. Bloomington: Indiana University Press, 1991. 86-99.

"Il 'Dandy' di Hitchcock." *Per Alfred Hitchcock*. Ed. Eduardo Bruno. Montepulciano: Editori del Grifo, 1981. 93-105. English version. "The Dandy in Hitchcock." *The MacGuffin* (1994): 15-21. Rpt. in *Alfred Hitchcock: Centenary Essays*. Ed. Richard Allen and Sam Ishii-Gonzales. London: BFI, 1999. 3-14. German trans. "Der Dandy Hitchcock." *Alfred Hitchcock*. Ed. Lars-Olav Beier and Georg Seesslen. Berlin: Bertz, 1999. 21-38.

New German Cinema: A History. London: Macmillan, 1989. New Brunswick: Rutgers University Press, 1989. German trans. *Der Neue Deutsche Film. Von den Anfängen bis zu den Neunziger Jahren*. Munich: Heyne, 1994.

"Hyper-, Retro-, or Counter-: European Cinema and Third Cinema Between Hollywood and Art Cinema." *Mediating Two Worlds: The Americas and Europe 1492-1992*. Ed. John King, Ana M. Lopez, and Manuel Alvarado. London: BFI, 1992. 119-135. Rpt. in Thomas Elsaesser. *European Cinema: Face to Face with Hollywood*. Amsterdam: Amsterdam University Press, 2005. 464-481.

"The New German Cinema's Historical Imaginary." *Framing the Past: The Historiography of German Cinema and Television*. Ed. Bruce Murray and Christopher Wickham. Carbondale / Edvardsville: Southern Illinois University Press, 1992. 280-307.

"The German Post-War Cinema and Hollywood." *Hollywood in Europe: Experiences of a Cultural Hegemony*. Ed. David W. Ellwood and Rob Kroes. Amsterdam: VU Press, 1994. 283-302.

"Ingmar Bergman: The Art Cinema." *Sight and Sound* (April 1994): 22-27.

Fassbinder's Germany: History Identity Subject. Amsterdam: Amsterdam University Press, 1996. German trans. *Rainer Werner Fassbinder*. Berlin: Bertz, 2001. French trans. *Rainer Werner Fassbinder: Un cinéaste d'Allemagne*. Paris: Centre Pompidou, 2005.

Ed. *A Second Life: German Cinema's First Decades*. Amsterdam: Amsterdam University Press, 1996.

"American Friends: Hollywood echoes in the New German Cinema." *Hollywood and Europe: Economics, Culture, National Identity 1945-95*. Ed. Geoffrey Nowell-Smith and Steve Ricci. London: BFI, 1998. 142-155.

"Ethnicity, Authenticity and Exile: A Counterfeit Trade?" *Exile, Home and Homeland*. Ed. Hamid Naficy. New York: Routledge, 1998. 97-124.

Ed. *The BFI Companion to German Cinema*. London: BFI, 1999.

Ed. *Hollywood op straat: Film en televisie in de hedendaagse mediacultuur*. Amsterdam: Vossiuspers AUP, 2000.

Metropolis. London: BFI, 2000. German trans. *Metropolis. Der Filmklassiker von Fritz Lang*. Hamburg: Europa, 2001.

"The New New Hollywood: Cinema beyond Distance and Proximity." *Moving Images, Culture and the Mind*. Ed. Ib Bjondebjerg. Luton: University of Luton Press, 2000. 187-204.

Weimar Cinema and After: Germany's Historical Imaginary London: Routledge, 2000.

"The Blockbuster: Everything Connects, But Not Everything Goes." *The End of Cinema As We Know It: American Film in the Nineties*. Ed. Jon Lewis. New York: New York University Press, 2001. 11-22.

(with Warren Buckland) *Studying Contemporary American Film: A Guide to Movie Analysis*. London: Arnold, 2002.

"Too Big and Too Close: Alfred Hitchcock and Fritz Lang." *Hitchcock Annual* 12 (2004): 1-41. German trans. "Zu gross und zu nah: Alfred Hitchcock und Fritz Lang." *Bildtheorie und Film*. Ed. Fabienne Liptay, Thomas Koebner, and Thomas Meder. Berlin: edition text + kritik, 2006. 454-475.

"American Auteur Cinema: The Last or First Great Picture Show." *The Last Great American Picture Show*. Ed. Thomas Elsaesser, Alexander Horwath, and Noel King. Amsterdam: Amsterdam University Press, 2004. 37-69.

"Germany Face to Face with Hollywood: Looking into a Two Way Mirror." *Americanization and Anti-Americanism: The German Encounter with American Culture after 1945*. Ed. Alexander Stephan. New York: Berghahn, 2004. 166-185. Rpt. in Thomas Elsaesser. *European Cinema: Face to Face with Hollywood*. Amsterdam: Amsterdam University Press, 2005. 299-318.

(with Alexander Horwath and Noel King) Ed. *The Last Great American Picture Show*. Amsterdam: Amsterdam University Press, 2004.

European Cinema: Face to Face with Hollywood. Amsterdam: Amsterdam University Press, 2005.

ACT III: Archaeology, Avant-Garde, Archive

"Working on the Margins: Harun Farocki." *Monthly Film Bulletin* (October 1983): 267-270. Rpt. "Working at the Margins: Film as a Form of Intelligence." *Harun Farocki: Working on the Sight Lines*. Ed. Thomas Elsaesser. Amsterdam: Amsterdam University Press, 2004. 95-108.

"American Graffiti: Neuer Deutscher Film zwischen Avantgarde und Postmoderne." *Postmoderne-Zeichen eines kulturellen Wandels*. Ed. Andreas Huyssen and Klaus Scherpe. Reinbek: Rowohlt, 1986. 302-328. Rpt. in *Die Postmoderne im Kino: Ein Reader*. Ed. Jürgen Felix. Marburg: Schüren, 2002. 38-64.

"The 'New' Film History." *Sight and Sound* 55.4 (Fall 1986): 246-251.

"Dada / Cinema?" *Dada and Surrealist Film*. Ed. Rudolf E. Kuenzli. New York: Willis Locker & Owens, 1987. 13-27.

"Early Cinema: From Linear History to Mass Media Archaeology." *Early Cinema: Space Frame Narrative*. Ed. Thomas Elsaesser. London: BFI, 1990. 1-10.

Ed. *Early Cinema: Space Frame Narrative*. London: BFI, 1990.

"Emile Cohl and The Origins of Cinema." *Word and Image* 8.3 (July-Sept. 1992): 284-287.

"What Might We Mean by Media History?" *Geschiedenis, Beeld en Geluid* 28 (Spring 1994): 19-25. Rpt. in *Der Film in der Geschichte*. Ed. Knut Hickethier, Eggo Müller, and Rainer Rother. Berlin: Sigma, 1997. 98-105.

"Back to the Future with Early Cinema?" *Norsk Medietidsskrift* 2 (1995): 35-48.

"Peter Greenaway." *Spellbound: Art and Film*. Ed. Philip Dodd and Ian Christie. London: Hayward Gallery / BFI, 1996. 76-84.

"History and Hyperbole: The Archaeology of Interactive Systems." *Interart Poetics*. Ed. Ulla Britta Lagerroth, Hans Lund, and Erik Hedling. Amsterdam / Atlanta: Rodopi, 1997. 337-340.

(with Kay Hoffmann) Ed. *Cinema Futures: Cain, Abel or Cable? The Screen Arts in the Digital Age*. Amsterdam: Amsterdam University Press, 1998.

"Cinema Futures: Convergence, Divergence, Difference." *Cinema Futures: Cain, Abel or Cable? The Screen Arts in the Digital Age.* Ed. Thomas Elsaesser and Kay Hoffmann. Amsterdam: Amsterdam University Press, 1998. 9-26.

"Digital Cinema: Delivery, Event, Time." *Cinema Futures: Cain, Abel or Cable? The Screen Arts in the Digital Age.* Ed. Thomas Elsaesser and Kay Hoffmann. Amsterdam: Amsterdam University Press, 1998. 201-222.

"Early German Cinema: A Case for 'Case Studies' or for 'Recasting It All'?" *Celebrating 1895: The Centenary of Cinema.* Ed. John Fullerton. London: John Libbey, 1998. 264-277.

"Fantasy Island: Dream Logic as Production Logic." *Cinema Futures: Cain, Abel or Cable? The Screen Arts in the Digital Age.* Ed. Thomas Elsaesser and Kay Hoffmann. Amsterdam: Amsterdam University Press, 1998. 143-158.

"Louis Lumière – the Cinema's First Virtualist?" *Cinema Futures: Cain, Abel or Cable? The Screen Arts in the Digital Age.* Ed. Thomas Elsaesser and Kay Hoffmann. Amsterdam: Amsterdam University Press, 1998. 45-62. Czech trans. "Louis Lumière: prvni virtualista kinematografie?" *Nova Filmova Historie.* Ed. Peter Szczepanik. Prague: Herrmann & Synove, 2004. 246-262.

"Après Lumière: une invention sans avenir, dans l'avenir." *L'Aventure du Cinématographe.* Ed. Philippe Dujardin, André Gardies, Jacques Gerstenkorn, and Jean-Claude Seguin. Lyon: Aléas, 1999. 279-290.

"Wie der frühe Film zum Erzählkino wurde." *Erlebnisort Kino.* Ed. Irmbert Schenk. Marburg: Schüren, 2000. 34-54.

"Realität zeigen: der frühe Film im Zeichen Lumières." *Die Einübung des dokumentarischen Blicks.* Ed. Ursula von Keitz and Kay Hoffmann. Marburg: Schüren, 2001. 27-50.

"Writing and Rewriting Film History: Terms of a Debate." *Cinéma & Cie* 1 (2001): 24-33.

Filmgeschichte und frühes Kino. Archäologie eines Medienwandels. Munich: text + kritik, 2002.

"Harun Farocki: Introduction and Dossier." *Senses of Cinema* (July 2002).

(with Malte Hagener). "Walter Ruttmann: 1929." *1929: Beiträge zur Archäologie der Medien.* Ed. Stefan Andriopoulos and Bernhard J. Dotzler. Frankfurt am Main: Suhrkamp, 2002. 316-349.

Ed. *Harun Farocki: Working on the Sight Lines.* Amsterdam: Amsterdam University Press, 2004.

"An Image from a Film: Johan van der Keuken." *Rouge* 5 (2004).

"Filmmaker, Artist, Media Theorist." *Harun Farocki: Working on the Sight Lines.* Ed. Thomas Elsaesser. Amsterdam: Amsterdam University Press, 2004. 11-40.

"Making the World Superfluous: an Interview." *Harun Farocki: Working on the Sight Lines.* Ed. Thomas Elsaesser. Amsterdam: Amsterdam University Press, 2004. 177-189.

"Political Filmmaking after Brecht." *Harun Farocki: Working on the Sight-Lines.* Ed. Thomas Elsaesser. Amsterdam: Amsterdam University Press, 2004. 133-153.

"Early Film History and Multi-Media: An Archaeology of Possible Futures?" *New Media, Old Media: A History and Theory Reader.* Ed. Wendy Hui Kong Chun and Thomas Keenan. New York: Routledge, 2005. 13-25.

"The New Film History as Media Archaeology." *CiNéMAS* 14.2-3 (Spring 2005): 75-117.

"Discipline through Diegesis: The Rube Film Between Attraction and Integration." *The Cinema of Attractions Reloaded.* Ed. Wanda Strauven. Amsterdam: Amsterdam University Press, 2006. 205-223.

"Casting Around: Hitchcock's Absence." *Johan Grimonprez: Looking for Alfred – The Hitch-cock Castings.* Ed. Steven Bode. Ostfildern: Hatje Cantz, 2007. 136-160.

"Das Digitale und das Kino: Um-Schreibung der Filmgeschichte?" *Zukunft Kino: The End of the Reel World.* Ed. Daniela Kloock. Marburg: Schüren, 2007. 42-59.